Contents

Wisdom in Christian Tradition

Wisdom in Christian Tradition

The Patristic Roots of Modern Russian Sophiology

MARCUS PLESTED

OXFORD
UNIVERSITY PRESS

OXFORD
UNIVERSITY PRESS

Great Clarendon Street, Oxford, OX2 6DP,
United Kingdom

Oxford University Press is a department of the University of Oxford.
It furthers the University's objective of excellence in research, scholarship,
and education by publishing worldwide. Oxford is a registered trade mark of
Oxford University Press in the UK and in certain other countries

First Edition published in 2022

Impression: 1

Published in the United States of America by Oxford University Press
198 Madison Avenue, New York, NY 10016, United States of America

British Library Cataloguing in Publication Data
Data available

Library of Congress Control Number: 2021951945

ISBN 978–0–19–286322–5

DOI: 10.1093/oso/9780192863225.001.0001

Printed and bound in the UK by
Clays Ltd, Elcograf S.p.A.

For two great paradigms of lived wisdom:

Dr Philip Sherrard (1922–95) and Metropolitan Kallistos Ware (1934–)

Preface and Acknowledgments

This book has been over twenty years in the making. It began in earnest in 2001 as a post-doctoral project at Cambridge in the Faculty of Divinity's Centre for Advanced Religious and Theological Studies, sponsored by the Institute for Orthodox Christian Studies with the generous support of the Leventis Foundation. Increasing responsibilities at IOCS and a turn to other research interests contrived, however, to put the project on the back burner for a considerable length of time and it is only in recent years that I have been able to pick it up again. I am grateful to the Department of Theology of Marquette University for a series of course releases and, especially, election to the rotating Henri de Lubac Chair which have enabled me to revive the project and to bring the book, at long last, to completion. Elements of the book have been presented in numerous contexts including the patristics seminars of the Universities of Cambridge and Durham, two Oxford international patristics conferences, the British patristics conference (at the University of Edinburgh), the University of Athens, the Saints Cyril and Methodius Theological Institute of Post-Graduate Studies in Moscow (as part of a series of lectures sponsored by the Templeton Foundation), the Boston College Historical Colloquy, St Vladimir's Theological Seminary, the Fellowship of St Alban and St Sergius, and the Thomistic Institute in the Dominican House of Studies (Washington, DC). Ensuing discussion at these various events has invariably been to the betterment of the book. A number of people have graciously read sections of the *Prolegomena* (Chapter 2) including James Aitken, Michael Cover, John Dillon, and Simon Gathercole. OUP's readers Brandon Gallaher and Paul Gavrilyuk digested the whole manuscript and came up with numerous suggestions and corrections that have been enormously helpful and productive. Irina Paert cast a careful eye over the Russian while Garth and Elizabeth Fowden provided valuable advice on the cover image. All remaining errors are of course my own. Several research assistants have also made tangible contributions, notably Nathaniel Kidd, Joshua Miller, and Daniel Edwards (who also prepared the index). Many thanks to all the above.

Biblical wisdom literature often underlines the familial dimension of wisdom—and with good cause. Between the beginning and end of the project I was fortunate enough to acquire a good wife (cf. Proverbs 31:10 ff) and five fine children (cf. Psalms 126(7):3–5). I am not sure I would have even an inkling about wisdom without the joys and travails of family life. Thus to Mariamni, Konstantin, Raphael, Edmund, Makary, and Beatrix, my sincerest thanks and profoundest love.

Marcus Plested
Milwaukee, Wisconsin

14/27 September 2021
Feast of the Elevation of the Holy Cross

Abbreviations

CCCM	Corpus Christianorum Continuatio Mediaevalis
CCSG	Corpus Christianorum Series Graeca
CCSL	Corpus Christianorum Series Latina
CSCO	Corpus Scriptorum Christianorum Orientalium
CSEL	Corpus Scriptorum Ecclesiasticorum Latinorum
CPG	Clavis patrum graecorum
DS	*Dictionnaire de spiritualité*
DTC	*Dictionnaire de théologie catholique*
ECR	*Eastern Churches Review*
GCS	Die Griechischen christlichen Schriftsteller der ersten Jahrhunderte
GNO	Gregorii Nysseni Opera
JECS	*Journal of Early Christian Studies*
JTS	*Journal of Theological Studies*
LCL	Loeb Classical Library
OCT	Oxford Classical Texts
OECT	Oxford Early Christian Texts
PG	Patrologia Graeca
PL	Patrologia Latina
PO	Patrologia Orientalis
PTS	Patristische Texte und Studien
SC	Sources Chrétiennes
SVTQ	*St Vladimir's Theological Quarterly*
TU	Texte und Untersuchungen zur Geschichte der altchristlichen Literatur

Note on Conventions

English titles are generally used for patristic and other primary sources except where the Greek or Latin is deemed more familiar. Abbreviated forms of titles are given in the bibliography in square brackets under the relevant author. Page references to critical editions are given where available with some exceptions for in-text citations for reasons of economy. I have not generally offered transliteration for Russian titles cited in the footnotes but gloss them in the bibliography. I have maintained the old Russian orthography for pre-Revolutionary and diaspora works.

In a work of this scope, is has proved necessary to consult widely among translations in various languages. Where translations in the text have been drawn or modified from existing English translations this is indicated by the abbreviation 'ET', either in the footnotes or the bibliography. I should like to offer a general thanks to the noble scholars of the Ante- and Post-Nicene Fathers series whom I have made use of more times than I can properly enumerate. I first began reading Bulgakov largely in French back in the 1990s thanks to the stellar labours of Constantin Andronikof. More recently, I have been most grateful for the rising tide of Sophiological works translated by Boris Jakim, Thomas Allan Smith, and many others. Works of the Sophiologists are referenced in accordance with the original Russian version (or other language edition, if earlier) together with the corresponding reference in the English translation, where available (again flagged as 'ET'). These and all other translations have frequently been adapted to a greater or lesser degree according to my own lights.

Modern Russian Sophiology as articulated by Soloviev, Florensky, and Bulgakov is routinely abbreviated as 'Sophiology' with a capital 'S'. The lower-case form 'sophiology' denotes the theology of wisdom more broadly conceived. Lastly, the taxonomy of wisdom developed for this book (S0, S1, S2, and S3) can be found outlined on pp.2–3.

Introduction

Wisdom has seen better days. In the contemporary context we are worlds away from the time when wisdom was a universal and cross-cultural aspiration in all areas of life—from the most mundane to the most sublime. The long-term tensions associated with the Great Church of Holy Wisdom (Agia Sophia) in Constantinople/Istanbul only serve to underline quite how desperately the world needs a generous and all-embracing vision of wisdom rooted in God's own self-giving love and pursued by people of all religions and none. Popular culture retains, of course, some intuitive sense of what it is to be wise but it is hardly a characteristic much prized or evident in our political, economic, or cultural leaders. Nor is wisdom a defining feature of much contemporary discourse about issues of race, gender, or public health. Wisdom is a topic of antiquarian interest, at best, for many contemporary philosophers while even theologians can sometimes be chary of the term, especially in its more metaphysical dimensions. The modern ascendency of the scientific paradigm of knowledge coupled with the Enlightenment's elevation of reason proved tremendously successful in displacing any notion of knowledge which is revealed and lived—let alone knowledge that comes from God and leads to union with him. None of the various footnotes and qualifiers of the modern Western project—whether Kant's sharp delimitation of the claims of reason, or Merleau-Ponty's salutary reminder of the necessarily embodied character of knowledge, or the tremendous assault on the very notions of reason and knowledge within the multiform phenomenon of postmodernism—have managed to supply anything like the paradigm of authentic knowledge afforded by the concept of wisdom.

T. S. Eliot famously lamented the displacement of wisdom by knowledge and knowledge by information.[1] This dismal process is now infinitely compounded by the morass of misinformation, disinformation, partial information, lack of information, and excess of information that defines the contemporary internet. Knowledge, where it remains valued at all, has been parcelled-out, compartmentalized, and broken down into specialisms. The results of this fracturing of knowledge are patently evident in the modern academy and indeed in the educational system more generally. Rather than teaching people how to learn, let alone how to live out their knowledge in a virtuous life ordered to the good, we increasingly

---

[1] T. S. Eliot, *Choruses from 'The Rock'* (Chorus I).

Wisdom in Christian Tradition: The Patristic Roots of Modern Russian Sophiology. Marcus Plested, Oxford University Press.
© Marcus Plested 2022. DOI: 10.1093/oso/9780192863225.003.0001

focus on feeding them information enabling them to perform particular tasks and roles in society, much as one might programme a computer. In a world likely to be ever more challenged by artificial simulacra of human intelligence it seems woefully short-sighted to focus our educational efforts on the mere accumulation of information geared to particular vocations when machines can process data and accumulate information so much more quickly than we can. Instead we should surely focus our efforts on qualities and skills that machines are inherently incapable of: embodied intelligence (thinking with head and heart), craftsmanship, art, creativity, and, especially, the cultivation of wisdom. The post-industrial university will need to pay ever increasing attention to such qualities. Machines will never be wise.

The practice and pursuit of wisdom has, at least until modern times, been a prominent feature of all major religious and philosophical traditions. In theistic systems, wisdom has invariably served to unite in some way the world to its divine source and origin. The question of what lies 'in between' God (or the gods) and the world has long vexed many of the world's great religious and philosophical traditions. Zoroastrianism, Platonism, the Hellenistic mystery religions, Gnosticism, Sufism, classical and Judaeo-Christian wisdom traditions: all instantiate some form or conception of wisdom standing 'in between' the divine and the mundane. Angels and djinns have, similarly, often served as vehicles of wisdom in all three Abrahamic faiths. Polytheistic systems invariably have a deity associated with wisdom or knowledge while Eastern religions (notably Hinduism, Buddhism, and Confucianism) privilege wisdom as a path to perfection and enlightenment. Wisdom is, in other words, a recognizable trait and discernible quality on a global level—and this is important. There is nothing exclusively Christian let alone Eurocentric about the notion of wisdom. While this book deals largely with Christian writers from the Roman, Byzantine, and Latin medieval worlds (so encompassing Asia, North Africa, and Europe), together with several from the modern Russian world (itself a bridge between Europe and Asia), the wisdom teachings explored here contain much that is in principle relevant to any and all human societies.

But what is wisdom as understood in the Christian tradition? Wisdom is a complex and far-ranging topic and it is complex because it is so far-ranging. Emerging out of the encounter between classical and biblical wisdom traditions, Christian reflection on wisdom has operated on several levels. In ascending order, these levels may be roughly schematized as Sophia (S) 0–3:

(S0)   Human wisdom or learning ordered away from God or to the exclusion of God.

(S1)   Wisdom as human craft, skill, knowledge, understanding, experience, and learning/formation (*paideia*), especially as applied to the realities of life. Such human wisdom, when properly lived, embodied, and ordered towards God, predisposes the human being to the reception and experience of the divine gift of wisdom (S2).

(S2)   Wisdom as the divine gift of supernatural knowledge and understanding, guiding and forming humans in a divine *paideia* that brings them into a participatory relationship with God as wisdom and the source of wisdom (S3).

(S3)   Wisdom as a manifestation, attribute, quality, or appellation of God, especially as regarding God's relation to and presence in the creation.

None of these levels of wisdom are exclusive to Christianity—especially if one substitutes 'the divine' or 'the gods' for 'God'. The specifically Christian dimension of wisdom reflection is to be seen largely on level S3, particularly as touching on Trinitarian theology and Christology. Levels S1–S3 are clearly interconnected and often overlap in Christian discourse. For the purposes of this book the term 'sapiential' or 'sapiential theology' is used to denote treatments of wisdom focussing on levels S1–S2, especially where such treatments invoke and engage closely with biblical wisdom literature. The term 'sophiology' is reserved for discourse focussing on level S3. The best sophiology, and the best sapiential theology, is of course that which most effectively spans and unites these three levels.

Christian wisdom, following the three principal stages outlined above (S1–S3), may be seen as the beginning, middle, and end of the human journey: the learning and toil of a good life preparing fertile ground for the reception of the gift and experience of divine knowledge and understanding that is itself an aspect and manifestation of the very nature of God as wisdom. And this journey is inescapably bound up with the world in which we live—not only natural but also social, cultural, economic, and political.

Wisdom's sheer comprehensiveness—covering everything from human life to the divine nature—can easily make it a somewhat baggy and unwieldy concept, one that lends itself all too easily to theological and philosophical confusion. Wisdom's all-embracing quality helps explain why there is such a vast amount to digest when seeking to give an account of *Wisdom in Christian Tradition*: not only the biblical and classical background but also virtually the whole history of Christian theology.

Theological reflection on wisdom has been given a huge boost and stimulus in recent centuries with the emergence of modern Russian Sophiology in the works of, to name the chief figures, Vladimir Soloviev (1853–1900), Fr Pavel Florensky (1882–1937), and Fr Sergius Bulgakov (1871–1944). Modern Russian Sophiology as articulated by these three thinkers—which I shall commonly abbreviate as Sophiology with a capital 'S'—is the most serious and sustained example of reflection on the figure and theme of wisdom to arise since the late Byzantine and high medieval era. Indeed it is arguably also the most creative, constructive, and compelling theological movement, bar none, to have arisen since the Enlightenment and one which stands, not incidentally, in polar contrast to all species of Kantianism and, for that matter, Barthianism.

In Sophiology, wisdom becomes the centre-piece of an arresting and all-encompassing theological vision in which God eternally reveals himself to himself as wisdom, thereby establishing the primal and pre-cosmic union of Creator and creature, absolute and relative—a union denoted by the principle of divine humanity or Godmanhood (*Bogochelovechestvo*). This primal, pre-cosmic, and somehow feminine principle of unity (christened Sophia, using the Greek term for wisdom) is manifest in multiple forms both created and uncreated: in Christ and the Holy Spirit, in Mary and the Church—and indeed in the whole cosmos. She is the 'in-between', the 'and' in 'God *and* the world'—what Platonism calls the $\mu\epsilon\tau\alpha\xi\acute{u}$.[2] The created world is called to realize and return to its divine origin in Sophia, whether in life and art or in economics and the socio-political sphere. It is a heady and powerful, if also often rather mystifying and shifting vision. Sophiology has decisively shaped and continues to shape modern Orthodox theology, albeit very often by way of reaction.[3] It has also had a huge impact on modern Western theology, attracting adherents and detractors across the theological spectrum.[4] In the early twenty-first century Bulgakov, in particular, has begun to enjoy seemingly ever-increasing acclaim and attention, especially outside of the Orthodox Christian tradition.[5] Within Orthodox circles, however, he remains widely viewed with considerable suspicion.

Sophiology thus adds a whole new dimension and problematic to a book attempting to explore *Wisdom in Christian Tradition*. To maintain some hold on this potentially ever-expanding topic, some sort of guiding question is called for and this is flagged up in the book's subtitle: *The Patristic Roots of Modern*

[2] Plato himself does not use the precise term $\mu\epsilon\tau\alpha\xi\acute{u}$ in this sense although the base idea of some sort of intermediary zone or zones between the realm of ideal forms and the world certainly fits with his philosophy. The term does, however, feature in Plotinus, e.g. *Enneads* 5.1.3, where it is used to describe that which lies between the soul and God. This is a concept made much of by Bulgakov; see pp.44–5.

[3] Notwithstanding the strength and success of the anti-Sophiological reaction (on which more below), there are many Orthodox thinkers who have drawn positively on aspects of Sophiology, especially as articulated by Bulgakov. These include Sergei Avernitsev, Alexei Losev, Paul Evdokimov, Nicholas Zernov, Fr Dumitru Stăniloae, Olivier Clément, Philip Sherrard, and, perhaps most notably, St Sophrony (Sakharov) of Essex. Among contemporary Orthodox proponents, Antoine Arjakovsky and David Bentley Hart are among the most ardent and eloquent. Arjakovsky gives an enthusiastic survey of the positive side of the reception of Bulgakov in the Orthodox world in his *Essai sur le père Serge Boulgakov*, 71–81.

[4] Sophiology has been taken up and explored by many Western figures including Hans Urs von Balthasar, Henri Corbin, Donald Mackinnon, Thomas Merton, Rowan Williams, and John Milbank. John Milbank goes so far as to declare that, 'At the dawn of the 21st Century, it increasingly appears that the most significant theology of the two preceding centuries has been that of the Russian sophiological tradition.' 'Sophiology and Theurgy: The New Theological Horizon', 145.

[5] Cf. Cyril O'Regan's comment, 'Arguably, no twentieth-century theologian has quite so much caught fire in contemporary theological conversation as Sergij Bulgakov'. Blurb to Bulgakov's *Tragedy of Philosophy* [ET].

Russian Sophiology. Fleshed out, this question may be posed as follows: *whether and to what extent Sophiology (principally as articulated by Fr Sergius Bulgakov) is grounded in patristic tradition.* Bulgakov is selected for particular focus in that his is by far the most sophisticated and comprehensive instantiation of Sophiology and the most explicitly and extensively rooted in patristic tradition. Soloviev and Florensky receive proportionately less attention corresponding to the degree of their patristic engagements.

Fidelity to patristic tradition is taken exceptionally seriously within Orthodox theology. Any articulation of Orthodox theology that is seen to run counter to or deemed inconsistent with the patristic witness will be widely decried as inadmissible and inauthentic. While the precise nature, meaning, and scope of such fidelity are open to considerable debate, the idea that patristic tradition provides some sort of normative framework or matrix for the articulation of Orthodox theology remains absolutely commonplace with dissenters to this position being in a distinct minority.[6] This is not to say that the patristic tradition is any way superior to or separable from scriptural testimony; on the contrary, patristic tradition is seen as constituting the indispensable context for the correct reading and reception of scripture while scripture itself is viewed as inescapably part of the ecclesial tradition that formed in the first place—a tradition that also expresses itself in Church councils, liturgy, iconography, mystical experience, prayer, canons, music, architecture, and much else. My focus on the specifically patristic dimension of the question is not some sort of patristic fundamentalism but a recognition of the centrality of the patristic witness to the Orthodox conceptualization of tradition and also of the degree to which the various doubts and controversies surrounding Sophiology have revolved around precisely this issue.

In seeking to probe Sophiology's relation to preceding tradition, I have spread the net widely, thus including numerous pre-Nicene texts; controverted figures such as Origen and Evagrius; relatively untapped or lesser-known sources such as Macarius, Silvanus, and pseudo-Clement; and indeed the whole Latin patristic and medieval tradition—a tradition all too often overlooked or indeed positively disparaged within Orthodox theology. Particular emphasis, however, is placed on the authoritative Church Fathers universally accepted within the Orthodox Christian tradition from which (along with very many other ingredients) Sophiology emerged and to whom it appealed for validation. These are the crucial figures, at least as far as Orthodox theology is concerned, for assessing the patristic

---

[6] Here I think of the brilliantly insightful and provocative modern Greek philosopher Stelios Ramphos who has called vocally, including in conversation with me concerning this book project, for Orthodox theology to shake off its shackles to the patristic past. One may also think of the now rather infamous conference hosted in 2010 by the Volos Academy of Theological Studies on the theme 'Neo-Patristic Synthesis or Post-Patristic Theology: Can Orthodox Theology be Contextual?' at which several speakers (including myself) spoke out against the notion of a post-patristic future for Orthodox theology.

grounding of Sophiology. Thus figures such as St Athanasius, the Cappadocian Fathers, Dionysius the Areopagite, St Maximus the Confessor, and St Gregory Palamas loom relatively large in this account.[7] These figures—above all Athanasius and Palamas—are those around whom much of the controversy surrounding the patristic credentials of Sophiology has revolved.

This is not merely a question of the extent to which Sophiology replicates what can be found in authoritative patristic sources in the matter of wisdom—as if one were from some Olympian height grading Sophiology for its strict adherence to a defined panoply of authoritative texts. In such a scenario the answer would have to be an 'up to a point' or a 'beta minus'.[8] But this would be to miss the wood for the trees. The question is much more about the *very nature of tradition*. Tradition, if it is to mean anything, must be a liberating and not a constrictive concept. Tradition, understood as the living continuum of faith, is always much more about the now, about life, and creative affirmation, than about mere conformity to the dead weight of the past. But this is not to commend a species of *aggiornamento* or usher in a brave new post-patristic world for Orthodox theology—this is not how tradition is conceived within the Orthodox Church.

Much more will of course be said about the nature of tradition in the course of this book. For the moment we may find a useful reference point in the practice of iconography. The Orthodox icon works within certain set parameters including defined physical characteristics, colours, architecture, scenery, composition, and so forth. Thus there is no need for Peter, for example, to have a set of keys for us to know it is Peter—Peter is Peter because he looks like Peter (close cropped white beard and hair, etc.). That said, there is room for a tremendous amount of artistic creativity and variety and even, with some caveats, new iconographic forms, within Orthodox iconography.[9] Thus the question here is not much about whether Sophiology formally reproduces earlier teachings but whether it stands in some recognizable continuity with those teachings. St Irenaeus of Lyons accused the Gnostics of taking bits and pieces of the apostolic tradition and reassembling them in an altogether unrecognizable form—much as one might

---

[7] Limitations of space and time have precluded the close study of a number of other figures and traditions including, for example, the Antiochene Fathers (especially St John Chrysostom and Theodoret), St Cyril of Alexandria, St John of Damascus, St Symeon the New Theologian, St Gennadios Scholarios, and the Syriac Fathers. While undoubtedly important sources of wisdom teaching, none of these figures are of decisive importance to the question of the patristic rootedness of Sophiology and are therefore, with great regret, omitted.

[8] Cf. the press magnate Lord Copper's underling, Sanders, in Evelyn Waugh's sublime novel *Scoop* (1938) who could never bring himself to positively disagree with his superior but restricted himself to a diffident 'up to a point, Lord Copper' when wishing to demur. The 'beta minus' reflects a rather modest grade in the Greek alphabetical grading system once widely used in British schools and universities.

[9] Witness, for example, the neo-Coptic image of the 21 Coptic Christians martyred by so-called ISIS in Libya in 2015 painted by the Serbian artist and iconographer Nikola Sarić. Originals at the Collegium Orientale Eichstätt and the Petit Palais (Paris).

disassemble a mosaic of a king and piece it together as an image of a dog or fox.[10] Is this what Sophiology has done—taken bits and pieces of the tradition, along with a great deal of extraneous matter, and put together an image of a quasi-mythical and functionally Gnostic goddess figure? Or have they brought forth from the treasury of the Church, 'from things old and new' (Mt. 13:52), a fresh but also ancient representation of the truth and beauty and knowledge and life so achingly needed and desired by our anguished and riven world?

The book opens with an extended treatment of Sophiology (and its discontents) with particular reference to the theme of patristic fidelity and continuity, and with the emphasis (as ever) on Bulgakov. This emphasis means that I have not attempted a global history of Sophiology in all its manifold dimensions and with all its sources, both religious and philosophical. I do, however, offer (in Chapter 1.1) a brief account of the origins of Sophiology including its main reference points and manifold sources of inspiration, both esoteric and more mainstream. I also attempt to situate it within its immediate philosophical context, notably in respect of German Idealism and (neo-) Kantianism.

Sophiology is, I freely admit, something of a maze or labyrinth in which one can very easily get lost if one tries to master it all at once. The fact that the figure of Sophia tends to shift and change both between and within the works of its main protagonists only adds to its elusiveness. Even Bulgakov seems to have found the whole thing rather perplexing at times. In this labyrinth, my Ariadne's thread has been the guiding question of the patristic rootedness (or otherwise) of Sophiology, and what such rootedness means. This thread is thus the focus of the discussions of Soloviev, Florensky, and Bulgakov that follow (in Chapter 1.2–1.4). In opening up the question of its patristic rootedness, I naturally also draw attention to the importance for the Sophiologists of sources of Orthodox tradition distinct from the patristic writings: especially iconic and liturgical.

A last section of the opening chapter ('Detractors and Defenders') details the controversy sparked by Sophiology in the twentieth century, again with particular reference to themes of patristic fidelity and continuity. It must be said that the power and potential impact of Sophiology have been much diminished by the vigorous and conspicuously successful character of the anti-Sophiological reaction led by figures such as Vladimir Lossky (1903–58) and Fr Georges Florovsky (1893–1979). This reaction, often labelled 'neo-patristic', characterized Sophiology as an alien intrusion rooted in non-o/Orthodox soil and with only very superficial and adventitious connections with authoritative patristic tradition. Bulgakov and his confrères claimed, conversely, to have stumbled across a genuine if under-appreciated lodestone of patristic sophiology. Thus much of the whole problematic of Sophiology revolves around the base question of patristic

---

[10] Irenaeus of Lyons, *Against the Heresies* 1.8.1 (SC 264 114–16).

rootedness (or otherwise). While allowing that there is much of substance in the neo-patristic critique, and that Sophiology itself gives rise to many *quaestiones et dubia*, it is nonetheless the sad case that the stand-off between these two schools of thought has greatly impoverished contemporary Orthodox theology most particularly in terms of its ability to receive and articulate the tradition in a holistic and non-eclectic manner, and in a spirit of humility. Contemporary Orthodox theology has its liberals and conservatives, its *virtuosi* and foot soldiers, its feverish internet users and technological refuseniks, but it has precious few (I think here of the great elders or *startsi*) who dare to shut up and listen in accordance with the divine liturgy's injunction: 'Wisdom! Let us be attentive!'

The middle section of the book (Chapters 2–6) thus serves as something of a listening exercise. Sources, of course, can never quite talk for themselves but it seems to me possible to give a reasonably balanced and comprehensive account of *Wisdom in Christian Tradition* prior to making any very definite judgement on the base question of the patristic rootedness of Sophiology. The reader will find regular but, I hope, relatively unobtrusive references to issues of Sophiological appropriation in these 'listening' chapters. These chapters should be useful to anyone interested in the general theme of wisdom in Christian tradition but who is not necessarily greatly animated by the mysteries and complexities of Sophiology.

Chapter 2 provides a brief account of biblical and classical wisdom traditions by way of *prolegomena*. Within the context of the New Testament, pre-existing wisdom traditions helped make some sense of the encounter with the person of Jesus Christ (for example as teacher and as pre-eternal) while also being soundly exploded by that same encounter. Chapter 3 moves on to sub-apostolic and early Christian reflection on Christ as wisdom, which tended to focus initially on themes of guidance and instruction (*paideia*) while beginning to open out increasingly onto themes of Trinitarian theology (God as wisdom; the Son and/or Holy Spirit as wisdom), Christology (Christ as wisdom—uncreated and/or created), and cosmology (the eternal foundation of the world in the wisdom of God). Such themes are particularly evident in the work of the great Alexandrine theologians, Clement and Origen, ushering in what I have called 'The Golden Age of Patristic Sophiology' (Chapter 4). In the fourth century, issues related to Trinitarian theology and Christology come increasingly to preponderate due to the demands of the multi-facetted and evolving Arian controversy—without, however, quite eclipsing the other dimensions of the wisdom question. Athanasius, the Cappadocian Fathers, and Augustine are, of course, of prime importance in this debate. Chapters 5 and 6 go on to explore the subsequent traditions of the Greek East and Latin West down to Palamas and Aquinas, respectively. These listening chapters thus enable us to explore not only many rich examples of wisdom reflection across levels S1–S3 but also to discern a theological trajectory within the Greek East that opens a 'space' or 'gap' for Sophiology that remains shut in the Latin West.

As Christian theology, with Athanasius, came to clearly articulate the ontological gulf between God and the world, the concept of wisdom helped conceptualize the bridging of the ontological gap between God and the world in terms of the union of uncreated and created wisdom in the person of Christ, by the power of the Holy Spirit. Similar themes are taken up by Augustine albeit with a distinct emphasis on the substantial or essential identity of God with his wisdom. In the Cappadocian Fathers, by contrast, we detect a rather different development whereby it becomes possible to speak of wisdom as divine in a manner consistent with divine simplicity but which does not reduce wisdom to either essence or hypostasis (but as one of the 'glories pertaining to the essence'). This opens the space or gap for Sophiology that can be traced, *mutatis mutandis*, through Dionysius' beneficent processions and Maximus' doctrine of the *logoi* through to Palamas' doctrine of the divine energies. Palamas is of particular import for this study in that he became, for Bulgakov, a source of patristic reference and validation without equal. These figures, along with some indispensable monastic material, are covered in Chapter 5 ('The Greek East').

The post-Augustinian Latin tradition explored in Chapter 6 ('The Latin West') deserves attention not only for its intrinsic interest and importance but because it offers an intriguing counterpoint to developments in Greek patristic theology over roughly the same time period.[11] While the theme of wisdom remained a vitally important locus and reference point within the West, the consistent manner in which divine simplicity was construed from Augustine to Aquinas meant that there is no place for wisdom as divine except in relation to the categories of divine substance (with which it is identical) or person (principally, for exegetical reasons, the person of the Son). Thus the space or gap that opens for Sophiology in the Greek East remains closed in the Latin West. It may also be said, more positively, that the West remained consistently focused on and rooted in wisdom literature and sapiential theology in a way the East often did not. This is a deficiency inherited by Sophiology.

This coverage embraces all the major authoritative figures and texts studied and appealed to by the Sophiologists—and a great deal more. This book thus builds up a considerably fuller picture of Christian reflection on wisdom than that afforded by or reflected in the work of the Sophiologists themselves. Through this detailed survey and discussion of the theme of wisdom in Christian tradition I seek to build

---

[11] Reasons of space preclude the close examination of many other rich sources of western wisdom teaching in the high medieval period—above all Bonaventure. Equally, the subtle cogitations of Duns Scotus on the univocity of the term 'wisdom' as applied to humans and God and the philosophical scepticism of William of Ockham fall outside my purview. Later medieval sources such as Nicholas of Cusa or the Flemish and German mystics will be mentioned as and when they arise in connection with Russian Sophiology.

up a picture of 'sophiology from below'—that is, to get a sense of what sort of theology (or theologies) of wisdom emerge from these sources regardless of the claims and teachings of later Russian Sophiology. These chapters also continue to tease out further the relationship of Sophiology to earlier wisdom teachings and in particular to those figures to whom the Sophiologists themselves appealed—what we might call 'sophiology from above'. It is my hope that this double movement will not only enable some judgement as to the base question of continuity but also to enable greater appreciation of the inherent richness and sheer extent of the wisdom teachings of the Christian tradition.

Chapter 7 is intentionally the most constructive chapter. After a review and attempted resolution of the base question of the book regarding the patristic roots of Sophiology, it sets out to re-envisage and, in a sense, reclaim Sophiology by situating it more firmly and fully within that tradition. Building on certain currents in post-Bulgakovian sophiology (and arguably within Bulgakov's own *oeuvre*), I attempt to flesh out what a re-envisaged sophiology might look like through a process of 'orientation and descent'.[12] Such a sophiology would maintain all of modern Russian Sophiology's most distinctive insights and most pertinent applications while divesting it of some of its more problematic elements, notably its dogmatic ambiguity and mythological remnants. Such an approach involves, in particular, a reconfiguration of Russian Sophiology in line with established theological categories of essence, hypostasis, and energy (this last involving a concerted study of the relationship between Bulgakov's Sophiology and Palamite theology). This process of re-orientation also entails something of a descent or plunge back into the patristic and medieval tradition of both East and West including a reaffirmation of the sapiential theology guarded so jealously by the Latin West and lived out so consistently in the monastic tradition. This plunge is intended precisely to bring and hold together levels S1–S3 of Christian wisdom discourse.[13] The proposal also incorporates certain insights and criticisms of the powerful anti-Sophiological reaction, in particular Fr Georges Florovsky's suggestion regarding the 'Sophia of the Church'.[14] Indeed, it is my hope and contention that Sophiology, duly reconfigured, may yet prove an axis of integration of the so-called 'Russian religious' and 'neo-patristic' schools of thought that have long

---

[12] I borrow the phrase 'orientation and descent' from Philip Sherrard's eponymous collection of poems, *Orientation and Descent*.

[13] Holding these three levels together is no easy task. Much recent Christian theological writing on wisdom has tended to focus on various aspects of the lived human dimension of wisdom (S1) and less so on dimensions S2 and S3. Here I note the invaluable insights of works such as Ellen Charry's *By the Renewing of Your Minds* and David F. Ford's *Christian Wisdom*. Celia Deane-Drummond, in numerous works engaging modern natural science, ranges somewhat more widely. *Creation through Wisdom*, for example, has a pronounced S3 emphasis in express homage to Bulgakov. Other works (for example *Theological Ethics through a Multispecies Lens* and *Shadow Sophia*) focus more on level S1 (or indeed S0). Sophiology itself, along with much of the related scholarship, has tended to focus almost exclusively on level S3 rather at the expense of levels S1–S2.

[14] See further pp.67–8, 240.

dominated modern Orthodox theology. These schools of thought, which in fact have a great deal in common, have been caught in a rather sterile stand-off that has done much to diminish the vigour and witness of modern Orthodox theology and indeed the ability of Orthodox theology to engage constructively in the contemporary theological arena. My constructive proposal will doubtless be too conservative for some and too liberal for others, but it is offered precisely as a way to break through such debilitating dichotomies. The reconfiguration of Sophiology along strictly traditional lines will not please all of Bulgakov's contemporary admirers—especially those for whom continuity with tradition (particularly as touching on Palamas) is of little moment. Similarly, my qualified rehabilitation of Bulgakov will not be popular among those who see the Sophiological question as firmly settled in favour of an unambiguous and unsubtle neo-patristic and neo-Palamite agenda that has consigned Sophiology to the dustbin of history—a dustbin chalked with the pejorative label 'Russian religious philosophy'.

But Sophiology has an enormous amount to offer Orthodox theology, and the world at large, today—both in terms of *chronos* (linear time) and *kairos* (the eternal now of the Kingdom). Much is lost if it is simply dismissed as fanciful or heretical—as it has often been in many Orthodox and other contexts. It is my contention that Sophiology represents a current of thought of immense moment for our time and all times. It is a distinctly Orthodox theological form (for all its non-o/Orthodox constituents) that issues from a tradition that has experienced the travails of the western world—Reformation, scientific revolution, Enlightenment, modernity—extrinsically, not intrinsically. That is not to say that that Orthodoxy does not live in or is not profoundly affected by the modern world, or that it has no answer to the problems of the modern West but, on the contrary, that it offers answers from outside the blind alleys and *aporiae* of modernity, from a tradition that is neither pre-modern, modern, nor postmodern but *unmodern*—and in a good way.

At its best, Sophiology stands for a distinctly unmodern conception of the relationship of God and the world, one that stands in diametric opposition to the prevalent scientific and post-Enlightenment mindset. It is this mindset that has opened the conceptual space for many of the ills of the modern world: the spiritual vacuity and ultimate aimlessness of so much human life; the environmental crisis; the materialism, exploitation, and sheer drudgery endemic within global capitalism; and the erasure of human freedom and personhood within communist and other totalitarian systems. It stands for a conception of knowledge that is lived, embodied, and *received*. It stands for a conception of being that is anchored in the eternal. It stands for meaningful and purposeful construal of human history. It stands for an idea of knowledge entirely unrelated to structures of power. It stands for a reaffirmation and enrichment of the feminine dimension of the Christian understanding of God. It stands for the dignity and integrity of human nature and human work. It stands for the limitless potential of human art and industry. It stands for a vision of the natural world as a vehicle and manifestation of divine power and beauty. It stands for freedom, joy, and hope even in the midst of distress, suffering, and weakness (let us not forget that Bulgakov was a refugee while Florensky died in a Soviet prison camp). It may not be unimpeachable, it may need some tweaking, but it should certainly not be permitted to languish in any sort of dustbin.

1

Modern Russian Sophiology
and Its Discontents

1.1 The Origins of Modern Russian Sophiology

Wisdom lies at the heart of Orthodox Christianity. The Great Church of the Holy
Wisdom (Agia Sophia) in Constantinople (Istanbul) remains its most evocative
architectural symbol and imaginative centre. As the singularly astute travel writer
and historian Robert Byron put it in 1929:

> St. Sophia is the particular visible expression of the first coalescence; it exhales the
> grandeur of Rome, the sanity of Hellas, the mystery of the East, and the
> universality of Christianity. Here, atop the entrant, is no building begun from
> earth, raised stone by stone upon the plans of an engineer; but a form, a dream
> abiding, planted entire from heaven.[1]

Byron's sentiments tally closely with those of Bulgakov who, on entering the
church fresh from his expulsion from Soviet Russia earlier in the same decade,
had found himself similarly captivated:

> Human tongue cannot express the lightness, the clarity, the simplicity, the
> wonderful harmony which dispels all sense of heaviness [...] a sea of light
> pours from above and dominates all this space, enclosed and yet free [...] It is
> the bliss of some final knowledge of the all in all and of all in oneself, of infinite
> fullness in multiplicity, of the world in unity. This is indeed Sophia, the real unity
> of the world in the Logos, the co-inherence of all with all, the world of divine
> ideas. It is Plato baptized by the Hellenic genius of Byzantium.[2]

Both Byron and Bulgakov were overcome by the extraordinary power of this
archetypal liturgical space in which heaven and earth are united under the sign of
wisdom. But the precise nature of the dedication of the Great Church is famously

---

[1] Robert Byron, *The Byzantine Achievement*, 198–9.
[2] Sergius Bulgakov, *Autobiographical Notes*, 94–5 [ET in Pain and Zernov (eds.), *A Bulgakov Anthology*, 13]. Both Byron and Bulgakov knew the church as a mosque, as it was from 1453–1934 (and again, controversially, from 2020).

Wisdom in Christian Tradition: The Patristic Roots of Modern Russian Sophiology. Marcus Plested, Oxford University Press.
© Marcus Plested 2022. DOI: 10.1093/oso/9780192863225.003.0002

elusive: to Christ as wisdom; to wisdom as a divine attribute or principle, to wisdom as the Mother of God, to wisdom as the very nature of the Church herself. All (and more) are possible and indeed each implies and contains the others. Wisdom is an inherently expansive concept.

It was from Agia Sophia that the Slav lands were evangelized and brought into the orbit of Byzantine Christianity. Devotion to wisdom was a distinctive characteristic of the ninth-century missions to the Slavs led by SS Cyril and Methodius. St Cyril's *Life* records youthful dream of mystical marriage to a feminine personification of wisdom.[3] The young man went on to become librarian of Agia Sophia in Constantinople prior to embarking on his missionary career, a career that would lay much of the groundwork for the conversion of the Rus' in the following century.

The emissaries of Grand Prince Vladimir of Kiev were, reportedly, entranced by the Great Church in their embassy to Constantinople, reporting back in glowing terms on the liturgy of the Byzantines:

> We knew not whether we were in heaven or on earth. For on earth there is no such splendour or such beauty, and we are at a loss how to describe it. We know only that God dwells there among men, and their service is fairer than the ceremonies of other nations. For we cannot forget that beauty.[4]

While it took a marriage alliance to seal the deal, there is little doubt that the glories of Agia Sophia (and the Byzantine liturgy more generally) played a decisive rôle in the baptism of Vladmir and his people in 988. The cathedral churches of newly-converted Rus'—in Kiev, Novgorod, and Polotsk—were, like a number of other Churches across Christendom, dedicated to Holy Wisdom in emulation of the Constantinopolitan archetype and as markers of their roots in the missionary endeavours of SS Cyril and Methodius.[5]

From the late thirteenth century a fascinating tradition of iconographic depiction of divine wisdom—usually as a white-clad or burning-red winged angel— developed in Palaiologan Byzantium and across the Slav lands, especially in

---

[3] *Life of Constantine (Cyril)* from Gerhard Podskalsky, *Theologische Literatur des Mittelalters in Bulgarien und Serbien 865–1459*, 274–6. See also Fairy von Lilienfeld, '"Frau Weisheit" in byzantinischen und karolingischen Quellen des 9. Jahrhunderts. Allegorische Personifikation, Hypostase oder Typos?', 113–19, 127–8.

[4] *Russian Primary Chronicle*, §108 (987 AD), 111.

[5] On the dedication of Agia Sophia in Constantinople see Zofia Brzozowska, 'The Church of Divine Wisdom or of Christ – the Incarnate *Logos*? Dedication of *Hagia Sophia* in Constantinople in the Light of Byzantine Sources from 5th to 14th century'. See also Fairy von Lilienfeld, 'Das Patrocinium der "Heiligen Sophia" in Europa und besonders in Rußland'. The dedication of the cathedrals established in ancient Rus' to feasts of the Virgin Mary appears to be a somewhat later development postdating the Tartar invasions. See further Donald Fiene, 'What is the Appearance of Divine Sophia?', 452. The very idea of a patronal feast is itself a later development superseding and in some cases supplanting the earlier annual commemoration of the date of consecration.

Serbia, Novgorod, and newly-emergent Muscovy.[6] For the most part such depictions can readily be identified with Christ who often stands immediately behind the angelic figure but some examples would seem to associate wisdom more closely with the Virgin Mary, the Mother of God. Other instances (usually somewhat later) are a little more mysterious with no obvious Christological or Mariological connection. While it goes beyond the scope of this study to engage in any very developed art historical debate, it can be noted that this iconographic tradition (which has Western corollaries) imagines and personifies wisdom on the basis of the feminine quasi-divine figure of the Old Testament.

Such powerful reference points must be acknowledged when seeking to account for the origins of modern Russian Sophiology. But such reference points, in my reading, are essentially secondary, not primary. Orthodox tradition—whether mystical, ecclesiastical, iconographic, or patristic—is not its *immediate* source and origin. Sophiology was indeed to find considerable and powerful support in that 'unmodern' tradition when it betook itself to look but its *fons et origo* must, rather, be sought within the context of developments in early modern and modern Western European thought and religious culture. Sophiology is a complex phenomenon weaving together many different philosophical, theological, and mystical traditions and trajectories making *Quellenforschung* a particularly hazardous enterprise in this case. While it is hardly feasible to attempt an utterly exhaustive genealogy here, I offer in what follows an outline sketch of its principal sources and motive forces.

Sophiology can perhaps best be understood as part of a long and multi-facetted reaction to certain central and defining features of the emerging modern Western European world. It is, in other words, a species of anti-modernism. This is not to say that it is not itself modern—it is certainly that—but that it stands against some of the key tenets and markers of modernism such as the separation of reason from revelation, overconfidence in the unaided powers of human reason and/or scientific observation, and some form of distancing, separation, or even elimination of God from the world. Modernism in this sense is the net result of many different developments and processes over time. It is first discernible in some aspects of late medieval scholasticism, the Renaissance, and the Reformation but begins in earnest with the rise of the scientific and empiricist world view, the Enlightenment, and the various schools of thought following on from these movements—from Kantianism to Positivism and much else. All of these

---

[6] See further the impressive survey of Peter Balčarek, 'The Image of Sophia in Medieval Russian Iconography and its Sources'; Helga Sciurie, 'Weisheit: Ikonographisch', in *Lexikon für Theologie und Kirche*; Justin Wilson, 'The Allegory of Wisdom in Chrelja's Tower seen through Philotheos Kokkinos'; and the magnificent collection of articles and illustrations in K. C. Felmy and E. Haustein-Bartsch (eds.), *Die Weisheit baute ihr Haus: Untersuchungen zu Hymnischen und Didaktischen Ikonen*. The sumptuous catalogue of the 'Sophia: Wisdom of God' exhibition held at Moscow's Tretiakov gallery in 2000 also has some fine illustrations and excellent accompanying material: *София Премудрость Божия: выставка русской иконописи XIII–XIX веков из собраний музеев России* (no ed.).

developments, while very different and often mutually irreconcilable, are united in militating, in various differing ways and to different degrees, against a participatory account of knowledge and all drive a wedge of one kind or another between God and the world—or even end up pushing God out of the equation altogether. Much of the initial push-back against emerging modernism within the Western European tradition lay in the philosophical traditions of neo-Platonism and in the experience and testimony of the great mystics. We will begin this survey of Sophiology's origins with these more general matrices before moving on to more particular and proximate sources and contexts.

With its intuition of the cosmos as one vast continuum of being and with ample space for wisdom lying somehow 'in between' the divine and the mundane, neo-Platonism constitutes the natural philosophical matrix of Sophiology. A neo-Platonic current had long been part of the philosophical and theological landscape of the Greek East but this current had been somewhat muted in Byzantium by the ascendancy of broadly Aristotelian modes of argumentation from the time of the Christological controversies onwards and, especially, since the condemnation of the Platonic philosopher John Italos in the eleventh century.[7] The Latin West, by contrast, tended to receive neo-Platonism in irregular waves—notably through John Scotus Eriugena's translation of Dionysius the Areopagite in the ninth century and William of Moerbeke's translation of Proclus' *Elements of Theology* in the thirteenth. Such works had a huge impact on figures such as Thomas Aquinas and Bonaventure and became assimilated within the broader scholastic programme.

A further big neo-Platonic wave, but this time of an expressly anti-scholastic bent, came in the fifteenth century as a result of the Byzantine descent on Florence at the time of the reunion council of Ferrara-Florence (1438–9). Here the key figure is George Gemistos Plethon (*c.* 1360–1452), an intellectual colossus who was widely hailed (and saw himself) as Plato *redivivus* or a 'second Plato'.[8] This was a mystical, anti-Aristotelian, and consciously anti-scholastic form of Platonism that was taken up with alacrity by some of the great movers of the Italian Renaissance, notably Cosimo de Medici and the incomparable Marsilio Ficino—respectively founder and first head of the Florentine Academy. This neo-Platonic revival was given further force by the arrival of numerous Greek scholars in Italy as a result of the Turkish conquest of Constantinople and the few other remaining Byzantine enclaves—not all of whom, it must be said, shared Plethon's

[7] On the notion of Byzantine scholasticism see Brian Daley, 'Boethius' Theological Tracts and Early Byzantine Scholasticism' and my *Orthodox Readings of Aquinas*, 44–53.

[8] On Plethon see Philip Sherrard, *The Greek East and the Latin West*, 120–38; C. M. Woodhouse, *George Gemistos Plethon: Last of the Hellenes*; Brigitte Tambrun-Krasker, *Pléthon: Le retour de Platon*; Niketas Siniossoglou, *Radical Platonism in Byzantium: Illumination and Utopia in Gemistos Plethon*; and Vojtech Hladký, *The Philosophy of Gemistos Plethon: Platonism in Late Byzantium, between Hellenism and Orthodoxy*.

anti-Aristotelianism and anti-scholasticism. Later iterations of Platonism, from the Cambridge Platonists to the Russian Sophiologists, stand in direct continuity with the current of anti-scholastic neo-Platonism unleashed by Plethon.

Plethon's form of Platonism also contained within it a decidedly esoteric and theurgic element—indeed he secretly commended the renewed worship of the ancient Greek gods, albeit taking them more as ideal representations than personal deities.[9] Plethon is one of the progenitors of the idea of perennial wisdom (*philosophia perennis*)—a shared tradition and understanding of wisdom at the core of all religious traditions. Plethon put special emphasis on Zoroaster as the first great instantiation of this eternal wisdom also to be contemplated in Pythagoras and Plato. Plethon quite erroneously credited Zoroaster's disciples, the Magi, with the production of the *Chaldean Oracles*—a neo-Platonist mystery poem in which a feminine wisdom figure (Hecate) mediates between the Father (the primal divinity) and the world. The esoteric quality of Plethon's neo-Platonic revival paved the way for the reception in the Renaissance of numerous other esoteric manifestations of Hellenistic thought and religious practice notably the *Corpus Hermeticum* (translated by Ficino), the Kabbalah (translated at the behest of Pico della Mirandola), and Gnosticism.[10] Like the *Chaldean Oracles*, these three complex, mutually interconnected, and not entirely compatible phenomena are united in the prominence they give to the figure and theme of wisdom. The *Corpus Hermeticum* is a disparate group of texts issuing from Roman Egypt dating perhaps to the first century AD and offering a multi-facetted pattern of ascent through wisdom to the God who is wisdom. It purports to convey the teaching of the 'Thrice-Great Hermes', a fusion of the gods Thoth and Hermes in whom the wisdom traditions of Greece and Egypt are ostensibly united.[11] In the Kabbalah, a somewhat later set of texts rooted in Hellenistic Judaism, wisdom is one of the chief forms in which the mysterious deity reveals itself to the creation and draws that creation towards himself. Wisdom (*hokhmah*) is the primal, infinite, and somehow feminine flash of divine self-revelation at the very foundation of the cosmos.[12] In many forms of Gnosticism, a complex set of belief systems that flourished within and, increasingly, alongside Christianity in the second to third centuries AD, wisdom (Sophia) represents an aspect of the divine, again a feminine, that both falls into and ascends out of the realm of flux and change. In all these cases, wisdom serves as a link-piece of the universe offering a path out of the vagaries of the material world and back to the divine source of the universe which is itself to be

---

[9] On some of the details of Plethon's envisaged return to the old gods, see Milton Anastos, 'Pletho's Calendar and Liturgy'.

[10] These and later elements of the Western esoteric tradition are ably documented in Nicholas Goodrick-Clarke's *The Western Esoteric Traditions: A Historical Introduction*.

[11] See Garth Fowden, *The Egyptian Hermes: A Historical Approach to the Late Pagan Mind*.

[12] On the Kabbalah, see the classic accounts of Gershom Scholem in *Origins of the Kabbalah* and *Kabbalah*.

understood, in some sense, as wisdom.[13] This esoteric current of Hellenistic wisdom speculation was to exercise enormous fascination on later philosophers and scientists, from the physician and alchemist Paracelsus (1493–1541) and the visionary Swedenborg (1688–1772) to the more conventionally respectable (but equally esotericist) Sir Isaac Newton (1642–1727). This current also lies behind early modern religious movements such as Rosicrucianism and gave direct inspiration to the Sophiologists, particularly Vladimir Soloviev.

We must also attend to the great mystics of the medieval and early modern West—figures who provided much of the fire and, so to say, *élan vital* of Russian Sophiology. The West had seen something of a parting of the ways between dogmatic theology and mystical theology in the middle ages—a fissure that never opened up, at least not so radically, in the Greek East. A key move here was the distinction of the affective from the intellective or, to put it another way, the head from the heart—a distinction that sets in from the time of Bernard of Clairvaux albeit not without resistance from the likes of Aquinas.[14] Such bifurcations helped promote and encourage mystical endeavour (not least among women) while simultaneously separating or even hiving it off from mainstream academic and ecclesial theological endeavour. Thus the academic and ecclesial theology of later medieval scholasticism, and still more that of the Reformation, has little room for a mystical and experiential account of knowledge or a non-dualist account of the relationship between God and the world. Such accounts, with or without demonstrable connections to neo-Platonism, tended to remain the preserve of the great mystics.

Here we may think of Hildegard of Bingen in the twelfth century with her rich and compelling visions of a personification of wisdom as the 'fiery life of the substance of the divinity' burning within all creation.[15] Equally, we may turn to the lesser-known Beguine Mechthild of Magdeburg in the thirteenth century and her powerful vision of the unity of God and the world: God 'is all things and in all things' and has been so 'eternally'.[16] True wisdom consists in perceiving and hymning this eternal coinherence. Similar intuitions of the mystical unity of God and the creation notwithstanding their essential difference are to be found in the Flemish and Rhineland mystics of the thirteenth to fourteenth centuries: in John of Rusbroec, Meister Eckhart, Johannes Tauler, and Henry Suso. Eckhart is of particular importance here in that he posited a primal superessential godhead beyond all notion of manifestation or revelation or knowledge.[17] This ultimate

---

[13] Gnosticism was known in the Renaissance largely at second hand, through hostile Christian sources. The discovery of the *Pistis Sophia* (a text studied by Soloviev) in the eighteenth century added greatly to first-hand knowledge of Gnostic teachings. For more on the Gnostic Sophia myths see p.116.

[14] See pp.211–12, 215.   [15] See Chapter 6.2.2.

[16] Mechthild of Magdeburg, *The Flowing Light of the Godhead*, II 19, 26 [ET 84, 95].

[17] Eckhart's views on this score are criticized by Bulgakov as excessively neo-Platonic: *Unfading Light*, 137–40 [ET 167–70]. Bulgakov pointedly rejects the Gott/Gottheit framework in which 'Gott' and creation are ontologically continuous.

ground (*Urgrund*) is made known as God and as Trinity, and constitutes the profoundest basis of human thought and being.[18] Henry Suso, Eckhart's staunchest defender from numerous charges of heresy, was a prodigiously popular writer who focussed much of his output on the figure and theme of wisdom. In Suso, wisdom becomes the absolute centre of a remarkable participatory and emphatically non-dualist mystical theology. With two 'best-selling' works (judging by the hundreds of surviving manuscripts): *The Little Book of Eternal Wisdom* (in the vernacular) and the *Horologium Sapientiae* (*Clock of Wisdom*) Suso did much to popularize devotion to wisdom as both uncreated, in reference to the divine nature, and created, in reference to the humanity of Christ.[19]

Moving on now to the more particular and more proximate sources of Sophiology we encounter the strange and beguiling figure of Jakob Boehme (1575–1624).[20] Boehme is perhaps the chief conduit of the transmission of the traditions of German mysticism (especially Eckhart), fused of course with his own peculiar genius and vision, to the Russian world. Boehme had a remarkable vogue in Russia, proving especially popular in the spiritual and mystical revival that marked the late eighteenth and early-nineteenth centuries.[21] Reacting against the rather dry and, to his mind, overly rational official theology and formulaic preaching of his Lutheran background this master-cobbler of Görlitz developed an astonishing and contentious mystical theology in which God, out of the primordial deity (*Urgottheit, Ungrund*), is manifested and revealed both to himself and to the world as Wisdom (*Weisheit*). As he summarizes in a response to criticisms of his early and unfinished magnum opus *Aurora*:

> She [Wisdom] is the highest substantiality (*Wesenheit*) of the deity; without her God would not be revealed, but would be only a will, but through Wisdom he brings himself into being, so that he is revealed to himself.[22]

---

[18] Vladimir Lossky, that great enemy of Sophiology, was a student of Eckhart, writing his *Théologie Negative et Connaissance de Dieu Chez Maitre Eckhart* under the supervision of Étienne Gilson at the Sorbonne. On Eckhart more generally, see Bernard McGinn's *The Mystical Thought of Meister Eckhart: The Man from Whom God Hid Nothing*.

[19] In stark comparison with, say, Hildegard, Suso's vision of wisdom gives little attention to its specifically feminine dimension.

[20] On Boehme, see especially Cyril O'Regan, *Gnostic Apocalypse: Jacob Boehme's Haunted Narrative*.

[21] See Nicholas Lossky, *History of Russian Philosophy*, 10–11 and Georges Florovsky, *Ways of Russian Theology* I, 111n, 152, 171. Nicholas Berdiaev, a great devotee, comments that 'Jacob Boehme must be considered the greatest of the Christian Gnostics. I am using this word not in the sense of the heresies of the first centuries of the Christian era but in the sense of knowledge grounded in revelation and using myths and symbols rather than concepts – contemplative rather than discursive knowledge. This is religious philosophy, or theosophy'. 'Studies Concerning Jacob Boehme: Étude I. The Teaching about the Ungrund and Freedom', 47–8. See also Zdenek David, 'The Influence of Jacob Boehme on Russian Religious Thought'.

[22] *Second Apology to Balthasar Tilken*, 69 (*SS* V.X 119).

Wisdom, for Boehme, is thus the 'expressed being of the divine power'.[23] She provides the inner grammar of the Trinity: the eternal seeing of Wisdom is the Father, the eternal grasping of Wisdom is the Son (who is himself the 'heart' of the Father), and the eternal pouring-forth of Wisdom is the Holy Spirit.[24] Wisdom is also the nexus of the eternal generation of the Son in the Father.[25] She is the eternal virgin of whom the earthly Virgin is a created counterpart.[26] With regard to the creation, she is its eternal source.[27] While herself without being she is the *Ungrund* of all things.[28] The whole creation is founded in her. God and the world are one and they are one in Wisdom.

Boehme was fiercely denounced as a pantheist heretic both in his own time and subsequently—charges not helped by his musings on, for example, magic, the eternity of evil within the divine nature, and the impermanence of gender in the resurrection. But his vision of the total unity of all things in Wisdom came to exercise an enormous hold on many later writers and fellow-mystics. Boehme enjoyed immediate and lasting acclaim in England with admirers such as John Pordage, William Law, William Blake, and Samuel Taylor Coleridge. German devotees included Angelus Silesius, Johann Wolfgang von Goethe (with his devotion to the eternal feminine), and Franz von Baader. Von Baader (1765–1841) is of particular interest in that he promoted a distinctly Platonic version of Sophia corresponding to the empyrean world of ideas and representing eternal humanity or humanity in its divine form (thus corresponding to the Sophiologists' idea of divine humanity). Von Baader also served as a particularly important conduit of Boehmian (and Eckhartian) mysticism into later German philosophy and indeed Sophiology—as Bulgakov recognized.[29] Boehme's arresting and problematic vison thus became a powerful source of inspiration for Sophiology both directly and, through von Baader and German Idealism, indirectly.

With German Idealism we reach the figures of J. G. Fichte (1762–1814), G. W. F. Hegel (1770–1831), and F. W. J. Schelling (1775–1854). All built on and critiqued the monumental work of Immanuel Kant (1724–1804), itself a critique of the Enlightenment's elevation of the claims of reason. Kant had restricted reason's sphere of operation to observable phenomena as collated by the mind while denying authentic knowledge of the extra-phenomenal or noumenal world, such transcendental ideas of things as they are in themselves (including God) being quite beyond human rational cognition. German Idealism after Kant came to radically question his apparent diremption of God

---

[23] *Theosophical Epistles* 47.10 (*SS* IX.XXI 186).

[24] *Six Theosophical Points* 1.1.15–16 (*SS* IV.VI 6).

[25] *Six Theosophical Points* 1.1.22 (*SS* IV.VI 7–8). Note that Boehme does not emphasize the specifically feminine character of wisdom.

[26] *Three Principles*, 18.37 (*SS* II.II 280).   [27] *Three Principles* 14.88 (*SS* II.II 192–3).

[28] *Six Theosophical Points* 1.1.11 (*SS* IV.VI 5).   [29] *Philosophy of Economy*, 120 [ET 130].

and the world and the denial of any sure ground of knowledge beyond the finite and observable world. While Fichte turned to the self-consciousness of the human creature (and indeed the nation) as the way out of the Kantian impasse, Hegel and Schelling developed a functionally pantheistic account of the universe in which the remote and unapproachable Absolute is self-revealed and self-actualized as Trinity and in the created order—in particular in the ideas of the finite human intellect. History is thus the relativization or unfolding of the Absolute in specific human ideas and consequent events. The Absolute (or God prior to his self-realization as God) is the source and sure ground of human knowledge—not the Cartesian *ego*, or Kantian phenomena, or scientific observation. This emphasis on self-revelation (*Selbstoffenbarung*) out of a primal ground of unqualifiable divinity owes much to the vision of Jakob Boehme and his fellow German mystics—albeit here without explicit reference to the figure of wisdom.[30] Hegel called Boehme 'the first German philosopher' while recognizing the inchoate and even 'barbarous' character of his thought.[31] Schelling was, if anything, more deeply indebted to and shaped by this mystical tradition which he was to celebrate in his evocations of the all-unity (*All-Einigkeit*) and all-oneness (*All-Einheit*) of God and the world.[32]

There are, of course, many differences between Hegel and Schelling, for instance in their conception of the Absolute and the relative importance they attach to the Trinity (which both interpret in distinctly heterodox terms). Nonetheless, this German Idealist current with its notion of the self-revelation of the Absolute and the principle of all-unity became a dominant model of philosophy in nineteenth-century Russia, being enthusiastically adopted both in the universities and in (élite) society at large. As one member of the secret Moscow-based 'Lovers of Wisdom' circle (Prince Odoevskii) put it: 'A new sun, rising out of the land of the ancient Teutons, began to illuminate the infinite sphere of knowledge with rays of soaring speculation.'[33] This German Idealist current, this new Teutonic sun, forms the immediate philosophical background to Sophiology providing much of its inspiration and philosophical underpinning.

The foregoing sketch gives us the principal matrices of Sophiology from the more general (neo-Platonism, Hellenistic esoteric traditions, and German mysticism) to the more particular (Boehme, German Idealism). It is no accident that these are all non-Russian sources. In the early modern and modern period alike, much of Russia's intellectual life orbited around non-Russian theological and

---

[30] Cf. Sergius Bulgakov, *The Wisdom of God*, 6: 'Boehme is perhaps the greatest genius among German thinkers. Together with Eckhart, he represents the secret dynamic of the philosophy of Hegel and Schelling [...]'.

[31] *Lectures on the History of Philosophy* III, 189.

[32] See e.g. *Philosophie der Offenbarung* I (Lecture 15), 310–11.

[33] Quoted in Georges Florovsky, *Ways of Russian Theology* II, 11.

philosophical sources. This is not to say the Russian Empire did not produce great thinkers in the eighteenth and nineteenth centuries but rather that such thinkers were decisively shaped by European and especially German religious and philosophical traditions. Thus Grigory Skovoroda (1722–1794) (a relative of Vladimir Soloviev) transposed much of Boehme's vision of wisdom into the Russian-speaking intellectual sphere eloquently hymning the eternal wisdom of God as God's invisible face and living word 'silently thundering within all of us'.[34] Similarly, Piotr Chaadaev (1794–1856) (a friend of Soloviev's father) was instrumental in propagating Schelling's vision of all-unity in the Russian world.

Russia by this time was caught up in a long-running debate between Slavophiles and Westernizers as to whether Russia's future lay in ever-increasing assimilation of Western European culture or in a return to its own native Slav traditions. While Skovorda is sometimes characterized as an early Slavophile and Chaadaev as a Westernizer, neither saw the question in quite so simple terms. Even self-professed Slavophiles such as Ivan Kireevsky (1806–56) and Alexei Khomiakov (1804–60) remained decisively shaped and inspired by German Idealism and Romanticism while consciously seeking out a distinctively Russian and Slavic theological and philosophical path. Notwithstanding their differences, all of these figures exhibit a sense of the coinherence of God and the world and the possibility of authentic and integral knowledge based on participation in a higher reality. And all of these figures, not incidentally, reacted against the broadly scholastic mode of official ecclesiastic and academic theology of the time and began the process of looking back into the patristic tradition of the Orthodox Church for confirmation of their intuitions. Skovoroda was particularly interested in the Alexandrine tradition: in Philo, Clement, and Origen as well as later figures such as Dionysius and Maximus. For Skovoroda, such figures served as a counterblast not only to the scholasticism of the Kiev-Mohyla Academy but also to Enlightenment attacks on the literal sense of scripture.[35] In his controversial *First Philosophical Letter*, Chaadaev juxtaposed the pristine ascetic spirit of patristic Christianity to the asocial and world-denying asceticism of the later Byzantine period lamentably inherited by Russia.[36] The Slavophiles, for their part, encouraged a great revival of patristic and ascetic teaching—including that of the later Byzantine period. Here they were able to tap into the revival of Hesychast monasticism spearheaded by St Paissy Velichkovsky (1722–94) in the late eighteenth century and exemplified in the lives of St Seraphim of Sarov (1754–1833)

---

[34] *Primary Door to Christian Ethics* cited in Vaganova, Софиология протоиерея Сергия Булгакова, 15.

[35] See Petro Bilaniuk, 'An Introduction to the Theological Thought of Hryhorij Skovoroda', in R. Marshall and T. Bird (eds.), *Hryhorij Savyc Skovoroda: An Anthology of Critical Articles*, 251–74. Skovoroda was also an enthusiast of Nilus of Ancyra, under whose name many of Evagrius' more practical and monastic texts circulated.

[36] In R. McNally and R. Tempest (eds.), *Philosophical Works by Peter Chaadaev*, 18–31.

and the Optina Elders. Kireevsky, a sometime member of the 'Lovers of Wisdom' circle, had reportedly been surprised to find in the Church Fathers everything that had captivated him about Schelling.[37] Subsequently, in co-operation with the Optina monastery, he worked assiduously on the publication of numerous patristic and ascetic texts.[38] With additional impetus given by St Philaret Drozdov (1782–1867), Metropolitan of Moscow, a veritable Russian *ressourcement*, was already well underway by the time that Sophiology was unleashed onto the world by the inimitable Vladimir Soloviev.

1.2 Vladimir Soloviev

With Vladimir Soloviev, the story of Sophiology begins in earnest.[39] All this talk of matrices and sources should not be taken to undermine the remarkable and properly original character of his achievement.[40] Soloviev was far more than the sum of his parts, far more than a mere conglomeration of 'influences'.[41] While it is essential to delineate his sources both general and more proximate—as was attempted above—it is important to emphasize that Soloviev received none of them uncritically. Soloviev is a thinker of great significance and one who has exercised and continues to exercise considerable fascination both within and outside the sphere of Orthodox theology.[42]

Soloviev encapsulated in himself much of the religious and intellectual ferment of nineteenth-century Russia. He was well versed and read in an astonishing and eclectic range of sources encompassing Platonic philosophy, German Idealism, writings of mystics and visionaries of all kinds, Hermeticism, Gnosticism (especially the *Pistis Sophia*), the Kabbalah, Indian religion and philosophy, the Church Fathers, and much more. He was something of a mystic himself, experiencing a series of ardent visions of wisdom as an eternal feminine. These visions took place

---

[37] This wry account by a friend is given in Kireevsky, *Complete Works* I, 285–6.

[38] See further Georges Florovsky's *Ways of Russian Theology* II, 21–7.

[39] The bibliography on Soloviev is vast. By way of introduction, see Nicholas Lossky, *History of Russian Philosophy*, 81–133; Georges Florovsky, *Ways of Russian Theology* II, 243–51; Symeon Frank, *A Solovyov Anthology*; Paul Vallière, *Modern Russian Theology: Bukharev, Soloviev, Bulgakov: Orthodox Theology in a New Key*, 109–233; Judith Kornblatt, *Divine Sophia: The Wisdom Writings of Vladimir Solovyov*; Fairy von Lilienfeld, 'Sophia – die Weisheit Gottes: über die Visionedes Wladimir Solowjew als Grundlage seiner "Sophiologie"' and eadem, 'Die Weisheit Gottes: Die Schau der Sophia bei Wladimir Solowjew'; and Oliver Smith, *Vladimir Soloviev and the Spiritualization of Matter*. Among works in Russian, Alexei Losev's contributions are of particular importance: see his Владимир Соловьев and Владимир Соловьев и его время.

[40] To be original in the proper sense of the term is precisely to go back to the sources, the origins, and to make of them something new.

[41] I try to ban my students from using the term 'influence' to avoid a mechanistic and passive model of reception in which no one ever uttered a thought without getting it from someone else.

[42] It is worth noting, for example, quite how much Georges Florovsky's whole career was shaped by Soloviev both positively and (mostly) negatively. Cf. Paul Gavrilyuk (ed.), *On Christian Leadership: The Letters of Alexander Schmemann and Georges Florovsky (1947–1955)*, 26.

in Moscow, the British Library in London (where he had gone to study Gnosticism and the Kabbalah), and the Egyptian Desert.[43] Soloviev launched a great campaign against modern materialism, Kantianism, and Positivism, decrying their spiritual vacuity and lamentable fragmentation of knowledge.[44] He proposed instead an avowedly anti-modernist form of Christian philosophy in which all knowledge is seen as essentially one and inherently participatory.[45]

Sophiology is not, for Soloviev, chiefly or primarily the product of reflection on the biblical figure of wisdom or indeed on the extensive range of patristic treatments of the theme. Nor does it have much to do with wisdom as human learning or divine pedagogy (S1–S2). It is all S3: God as wisdom, especially in relation to the creation. Soloviev's Sophiology is, at root, the product of a philosophical and mystical conviction of the unity of all things in wisdom, a conviction rooted in Schelling and Boehme and corroborated in the many other sources and reference points surveyed above. It was also, crucially, confirmed by his own mystical intuition and experience. Soloviev's central (and distinctly Schellingian) intuition is of the underlying unity of all things. Total or all-unity (*vseedinstvo*) is the essential nature of all that is. This unity is not, however, that of a monad but necessarily entails alterity, otherness. In the footsteps of Boehme and Baader, Soloviev speaks of this eternal alterity as Wisdom (Sophia): God's self-revelation to himself and to the world. God contains the creation from all eternity and the creation contains God from all eternity. This unity of created and uncreated natures is the expression of a primordial divine humanity (*Bogochelovechestvo*)—man in God and God in man. This intuition is perhaps his most decisive intellectual contribution and is foundational to Sophiology. Christ, in this schema, is the supreme instance of divine humanity. But Christ is somehow secondary to Sophia, the underlying principle of all-unity or divine humanity. Sophia longs to manifest herself not only in God and in Christ but in the world, in human history. Soloviev is reluctant to tie down Sophia to the Word of God alone, not least because of his apprehension of the distinctively feminine character of Holy Wisdom. Sophia is neither God nor the world, neither divinity nor humanity, but rather the very unity that unites them. She is the liminal, the 'in-between'.

Soloviev did much to encourage the religious turn that marked the intellectual and cultural achievements of late nineteenth and early twentieth century

---

[43] *Three Encounters* in *Collected Works*, XII, 80–6 [ET in Kornblatt (ed.), *Divine Sophia*, 264–72].

[44] This theme dominates his first major work, *The Crisis of Western Philosophy (Against the Positivists)* (1874) (*Collected Works*, I, 27–170). In a later work he muses on Auguste Comte as a kind of human equivalent of the French Revolutionary Calendar (Comte was born in its Year 7) signalling 'that the human mind had finally and internally broken its former bond with Christianity'.'The Idea of Humanity in Auguste Comte', in *Collected Works*, IX, 173 [ET in Kornblatt (ed.), *Divine Sophia*, 214].

[45] This vision is expressed in another early work, *The Philosophical Principles of Integral Knowledge* (1877) (*Collected Works*, I, 250–407).

Russia—what is often called the 'silver age'.[46] He ranged widely in his work, applying his insights to topics such as art and erotic love. Indeed it has been the glory of Sophiology that it has been prepared to engage so widely with issues of human life and experience. His early and seminal *Lectures on Divine Humanity* (1877–81)[47] electrified audiences and readers with a startling vision of Christianity as the culmination of a cosmic evolutionary process whereby the pre-eternal divine humanity (Sophia) is gradually discerned and manifested in history. In this process the whole creation is called to be gathered up into the primal all-unity. This is a cosmic drama in which the drama of the traditional Eastern Christian notion of *theosis* (deification) is extended to the whole creation.[48]

This is not to say that Soloviev did not take the patristic tradition seriously, nor that his Orthodox upbringing had no impact on his intellectual development. It is, rather, to say that Orthodox tradition was never the prime motor of his philosophical and theological vision, nor the origin of his notion of Sophia. That said, it seems reasonable to claim that he took Orthodox tradition increasingly seriously in his life and work.[49] Soloviev imbibed of the Russian *ressourcement* discussed in the opening section of this chapter, reading widely in the Fathers and making regular reference to them in his published works. The *Crisis of Western Philosophy* (1874), for example, concludes with a call for synthesis of East and West, of Western logical form with the fullness of the spiritual contemplation of the East arguing only such a truly modern philosophy will fulfil the 'covenant of ancient wisdom'.[50] Another early work (his doctoral thesis) the *Critique of Abstract Principles* (1880) affirms that the works of both Eastern and Western Fathers of the Church represent an impressive 'spiritual monument'—albeit one that does not completely suffice to answer all the questions of the age.[51] Overtly theosophical works such as the *Lectures on Divine Humanity* make fairly extensive reference to the Church Fathers as do the more ecumenically-focussed works of the 1880s: *The Great Dispute and Christian Politics* (1883), *The History and Future of Theocracy* (1885–87), *Development of Dogma in the Church in Connection with the Question Concerning Church Union* (1886), and *La Russie et l'Église universelle* (1889). In these works, Soloviev proposes Sophia as the ground and future of Church unity, uniting and exceeding the patristic traditions of East and West and

---

[46] For this context, see further the introduction to the Russian 'Silver Age' in Catherine Evtuhov, *The Cross and the Sickle: Sergei Bulgakov and the Fate of Russian Religious Philosophy*, 1–17.

[47] In *Collected Works*, III, 3–181.

[48] See further Richard Gustafson, 'Soloviev's Doctrine of Salvation'.

[49] Brandon Gallaher makes a strong case for the seriousness with which Soloviev approached the dogmatic inheritance of the Church in 'The Christological Focus of Vladimir Solov'ev's Sophiology'. See further Jeremy Pilch, *'Breathing the Spirit with Both Lungs': Deification in the Work of Vladimir Solov'ev*.

[50] *Crisis of Western Philosophy* (*Collected Works*, I, 151).

[51] *Critique of Abstract Principles* (*Collected Works*, II, 348).

ushering in a new dawn of human civilization in which all conflict and discord are resolved in universal harmony.

But for all his numerous references to patristic sources and his concern for conciliar orthodoxy, it is noteworthy Soloviev does not attempt to ground the notion of Sophia itself in patristic tradition. Soloviev is quite upfront about the origins of Sophiology and saw himself in a long line of philosophers and mystics who had been vouchsafed some inkling of the self-revelation of the Absolute in Sophia. In a piece of automatic writing from 1875 he gives what looks like a fair summary of some of his chief inspirations: 'Kabbalah and Neoplatonism,/Boehme and Swedenborg,/Schelling and me'.[52] In a more conventionally conscious moment in 1877 he singles out Boehme, Paracelsus, and Swedenborg as being of primary importance to him as teachers of wisdom—chiefly because they, like him, combined personal mystical experience with theosophical sophistication.[53]

Sophia, for Soloviev, was a fresh gift to the world, something that had hitherto been, at best, only very dimly apprehended in Church tradition. Soloviev certainly does not wish to contradict the tradition but it is clear to him that the revelation of Sophia is something quite new and ongoing. For Soloviev, such fresh gifts are integral to a dynamic understanding of tradition—tradition itself being reflective of the Church's nature as Sophia in both created and uncreated aspects. In terms of its divine character, the tradition of the Church is static and immovable in its unshakable foundations. But in terms of its human character it is also necessarily dynamic and mobile. Historically, the East has focussed on the former and the West on the latter; the trick, for Soloviev, is to unite these two dimensions of its existence. Thus Church tradition is essentially to be seen as an prerequisite and preliminary step for the full flourishing of the human spirit in total freedom and creativity under the sign of Sophia:

> Holy tradition is the first and most important thing in the Church, but one must not stop at that: strong walls and a free summit are needed. The walls of the Church are a regularly organized and unified ecclesiastical authority, and the summit is free spiritual life.[54]

Only in such circumstances 'will religion and the Church appear in their full significance as the harmonious interaction of the divine and the human, as the

---

[52] *Complete Works and Letters*, II, 354 [ET in Kornblatt (ed.), *Divine Sophia: The Wisdom Writings of Vladimir Solovyov*, 82].

[53] Letter to Sophia Tolstoya, in *Letters* II, 212 (cited in Pavel Florensky's *The Pillar and Ground of Truth* 331 [ET 240]). Soloviev allows that mystics such as Georg Gichtel, Gottfried Arnold, and John Pordage had a genuine experience of Sophia but lacked the wherewithal to articulate that experience with any robustness or precision.

[54] *The Great Dispute and Christian* Politics, in *Collected Works*, IV, 50 [ET in Frank (ed.), *A Solovyov Anthology*, 78].

true sojourn of God in man and in man's free life in God'.[55] In upholding the possibility of exceeding and transcending the tradition in this way, Soloviev appeals to the principle of increasing illumination outlined by St Gregory of Nazianzus in his *Fifth Theological Oration*.[56] But Soloviev's vision of doctrinal development clearly goes far beyond anything envisaged by Gregory. Overall, and notwithstanding such appeals to patristic authority, there is no doubt but that the bold declaration of Sophia that Soloviev made from the high summit of freedom above and beyond the tradition—and on the basis of numerous non-o/Orthodox sources—has been regarded as an impermissible doctrinal *transcensus* by the majority of Orthodox commentators. Soloviev's focus on the Pope of Rome as a source of Church unity together with his own impatience with confessional boundaries have done little to further his reputation among the Orthodox.[57]

Much of the work of his later years was taken up with various other aspects of human flourishing, notably in his work *The Meaning of Love* (1892–94). Work of this period is also marked by an apocalyptic flavour, tinged doubtless by the evident failure of his somewhat utopian dreams for a reunion of the Churches in Sophia and the restoration of a truly just society under the banner of the Tsar. But for all the various stages in his life and thought there is a remarkable continuity in the essential outline of his vision of Sophia. In one of his last works, *The Idea of Humanity in Auguste Comte* (1898) he offers an ode to Sophia in the context of a dissection of the thought of one of his chief foils throughout his career. Here Soloviev reaffirms his heartfelt devotion to:

This great, royal, and feminine being, which is not God, not the eternal Son of God, not an angel, not a saint, but receives homage both from the last represen-tative of the Old Testament and the *progenetrix* of the New, is no other than the true, pure, and perfect humanity, the highest and all-embracing form and the living soul of nature and of the universe, united to God from all eternity and in the temporal process attaining union with him and uniting to him all that is.[58]

---

[55] *La Russie et l'Église universelle*, 78.

[56] *Development of Dogma in the Church in Connection with the Question Concerning Church Union* (*Collected Works*, XI, 33). In the lead-up to the Council of Constantinople (381), Gregory spoke (Oration 31.26: SC 250 326) of the Old Testament revealing the Father and intimating the Son and of the New Testament revealing the Son and intimating the Spirit. Only now, in the era of the Church, is the full and equal divinity of the Spirit revealed. This theory of what Gregory calls 'ascents' (cf. the ascent to Jerusalem or to the Temple alluded to in the Psalms of ascent) is best understood as one of increasing intensity of illumination rather than development of doctrine as such—if such development implies the addition of something previously lacking or hidden.

[57] Soloviev saw in himself a reconciliation of fractured Christendom. As he put it in a letter to Rozanov in 1892: 'The Religion of the Holy Spirit which I profess is wider and of a fuller content than all separate religions: it is neither the sum total nor the extract of its separate organs.' Cited in Nicholas Lossky, *History of Russian Philosophy*, 123.

[58] *Collected Works*, IX, 188 [ET in Frank (ed.), *A Solovyov Anthology*, 58 and also in Kornblatt (ed.), *Divine Sophia*, 225–6].

One sees here in bald terms the enduring problem of modern Russian Sophiology: if Sophia is not God, and not a creature, then what is she? Is this not a fatal ambiguity? Soloviev's successors were to struggle mightily with precisely this question.

This late paean comes, intriguingly, in the context of a discussion of the icon of the Novgorod Sophia in which the figure of wisdom is surmounted by Christ and flanked by John the Baptist and the Mother of God. For Soloviev, this is of course an image of the divine humanity or Sophia, the eternal feminine. He frankly acknowledges that the image owes nothing to patristic or Byzantine exemplars but is rather the product of the peculiar if unconscious genius of the Russian soul. This ancient image of divine humanity is seen to represent and fulfil all the profoundest yearnings of Comte and indeed of modern Western civilization in general. It is, in other words, the unmodern answer to modernism. For Soloviev, the question of the patristic rootedness of Sophiology was never really the point. Sophiology was a splendidly new gift to the Church mediated through numerous often rather esoteric channels, including himself. But in this late treatment of the Novgorod Sophia we can detect in his work a certain turn back to Church tradition (in iconic form) even in the matter of Sophia. This nascent 'unmodern turn', as we shall call it, was to be greatly intensified in the work of Pavel Florensky and, especially, Sergius Bulgakov, both of whom were to give considerably closer attention to the question of specifically *patristic* rootedness.

1.3 Fr Pavel Florensky

Pavel Florensky offers what I consider to be a more essentially ecclesial and considerably less esoteric articulation of Sophiology.[59] Florensky was a remarkable polymath and something of a Renaissance man, with substantial achievements not only in theology but also in science and mathematics.[60] One of the striking features of his Sophiology is the essential connection he draws between asceticism and aesthetics. Beauty, for Florensky, is realized pre-eminently in the great saints—in holiness. The saint reveals the primordial beauty of the creature, no longer separated from the Creator but brought into the life of the Holy Trinity in

[59] Florensky's ecclesiality is very conscious: see *The Pillar and Ground of Truth*, 5–8 [ET 7–9] ('To the Reader'). Ecclesiality itself is a matter of lived experience for Florensky, an experience that is essentially unquantifiable and logically indemonstrable. Orthodoxy must be lived, and lived above all as an experience of beauty and asceticism: 'The Orthodox taste, the Orthodox temper, is felt but is not subject to arithmetical calculation. Orthodoxy is shown, not proved'. Florensky avers that one can become Catholic or Protestant simply 'by reading books in one's study. But to become Orthodox, it is necessary to immerse oneself all at once in the very element of Orthodoxy, to begin living in an Orthodox way.'

[60] See Avril Pyman's excellent introduction, *Pavel Florensky: A Quiet Genius*. See also Ruth Coates on the specific theme of deification, *Deification in Russian Religious Thought: Between the Revolutions, 1905–1917*, 174–207.

and through wisdom. It is above all the ascetics who perceive 'the eternal roots of all creation by which creation is anchored in God'.[61] It is profoundly significant that Florensky begins his principal treatment of wisdom (Letter 10 of his master-work, *The Pillar and Ground of Truth* (1914)) precisely with a mediation on the *staretz* (ascetic elder) Isidor. Sophiology, for Florensky, is essentially an attempt 'to comprehend the beauty of the spiritual life'.[62]

Florensky's theological vision is undeniably attractive and makes extensive use of the Church Fathers. To take one fairly typical example, in defending asceticism against those who would deny or downplay the ultimate significance of the body, Florensky affirms that asceticism is fundamentally orientated on *theosis* or deification and on the holiness of the body: 'patristic theology reveals with ultimate definitiveness the truth that eternal life is the life not of the soul only but also of the body'. He supports this assertion with a remarkable range of patristic and conciliar sources.[63]

In the specific matter of Sophiology, Florensky displays an astonishing degree of biblical, philosophical, and patristic learning while also engaging in extensive and sophisticated art criticism.[64] Like Soloviev, his account is largely on level S3 (God as wisdom, especially in relation to the creation) but with some limited appreciation of levels S1–S2 (wisdom as human skill/learning and as divine gift). Arising out of his perception of the beauty of holiness and the beauty of the world, Florensky avows his belief in Sophia as 'the great root of all creation', that is all-integral creation and not merely *all* creation'. He continues:

> Sophia is the Great Root by which creation goes into the intra-Trinitarian life and through which it receives eternal life from the single source of life. Sophia is the primordial nature of creation, God's creative love, which is 'poured into our hearts by the Holy Spirit which is given unto us' (Rom. 5:5). For this reason, the true I of a deified person, his 'heart', is precisely the love of God, just as the essence of the divinity is intra-Trinitarian love. For everything exists only insofar as it participates in the God of love, the source of being and truth. If the creation is torn away from its root, an inevitable death awaits it.[65]

Wisdom is thus the very link-piece of the universe, grounding the whole creation in the divine essence which is love.

---

[61] *The Pillar and Ground of Truth*, 323 [ET 235].
[62] *The Pillar and Ground of Truth*, 321 [ET 233].
[63] He appeals here to St Gregory of Nyssa, the Macarian writings, St Symeon the New Theologian, St Irenaeus of Lyons, St Methodius of Olympus, St Athanasius the Great, and St John Chrysostom, along with a number of conciliar sources. *The Pillar and Ground of Truth*, 292–3 [ET 213].
[64] His end notes are a treasure trove, many constituting exquisite and impeccably learned mini essays on topics germane to the theme at hand.
[65] *The Pillar and Ground of Truth*, 326 [ET 237].

With regard to the creation, she is its 'guardian angel', the 'ideal person' of the world. She is the shaping reason and the shaped content of the reason of God. She is 'eternally created by the Father through the Son and completed in the Holy Spirit'.[66] She is, furthermore, the 'eternal bride of the Word of God' from whom she receives her creative power.[67] She is one in God and multiple in creation. She is perceived in the creation as the 'ideal person of man', 'as the spark of the eternal dignity of the person and as the image of God in man'. Ultimately, this 'ideal aspect will be revealed in illuminated creation, in transfigured man'.[68] Wisdom is here the divine presence in creation, recalling that creation to its true origin and goal. She is the manifestation of the Kingdom, of hypostatic wisdom, and of the parenthood of God in the world.[69] She is the action of God's triune love in the world.

Permeated with God's love, Sophia seems almost to merge with the Holy Trinity from a religious standpoint while remaining, rationally speaking, 'wholly other' from the three divine persons.[70] He goes on to explain that as a participant in the innermost life of the Holy Trinity she is a fourth but created and therefore obviously non-consubstantial divine 'face' or person (as opposed to hypostasis).[71] As such, she reflects distinctive aspects of the activity of the three divine hypostases. In relation to the Father, she is the ground of creation; in relation to the Son and Word, she is the reason of creation, its meaning and truth; and in relation to the Holy Spirit she is the spirituality of creation, its beauty and holiness.[72] She is, furthermore, the Church in both its heavenly and earthly aspects (as the body of Christ and as the creation turning back to God). Consequently she is also to be identified with the Virgin Mary, the Mother of God, the pinnacle and paragon of creation, humanity, and the Church—the supreme instance of Sophia in the creation.[73]

---

[66] *The Pillar and Ground of Truth*, 326 [ET 237].

[67] While speaking of Sophia as the bride of the Logos, there is nothing in Florensky of Soloviev's frankly Gnostic speculations on the fall of Sophia from communion with the Logos.

[68] *The Pillar and Ground of Truth*, 330 [ET 239].

[69] *The Pillar and Ground of Truth*, 330-1 [ET 240]. These three aspects are associated with, respectively, the Holy Spirit, the Son, and the Father.

[70] *The Pillar and Ground of Truth*, 331 [ET 240] (совсем иное).

[71] *The Pillar and Ground of Truth*, 349 [ET 252]. He uses the Russian term лицо (face, countenance, person) very deliberately not using the term 'hypostasis' which he reserves for the persons of the Trinity. We should understand his references to wisdom as a person in a weak sense, more in line with the import of the terms *persona* and πρόσωπον in the pre-Chalcedonian Church (mask, face, countenance, external presentation of a thing). It is certainly misleading to speak of wisdom as a fourth *hypostasis* in Florensky. Florensky speaks of wisdom as a kind of fourth face or fourth aspect of God's self-revelation to the world and certainly not as any sort of additional divine hypostasis. Cf. ibid., 383 [ET 277]: 'Sophia is not a hypostasis in the strict sense'.

[72] *The Pillar and Ground of Truth*, 349 [ET 252-3]. Cf. 351 [ET 254]: 'Only Sophia is essential beauty in all of creation. Everything else is only frippery and fancy clothes.'

[73] Florensky expresses extraordinary devotion to the Mother of God, remarking that 'the acceptance or non-acceptance of the cry "Most Holy Mother of God, save us!" determines the Orthodoxy or non-Orthodoxy of a mindset'. *Pillar and Ground of Truth*, 366, n.652 [ET 552 n.653].

To attempt a brief summary: Sophia is God's presence in the world and the world's presence in God.[74] She is not herself God but represents the pre-existent divine realm of ideas, the pre-eternal creation, and its manifestation in the world. She is created but eternally so, eternally created by God. Sophia roots the creation in the essential love of God without herself being that essential love. She is the action of the essential love of the Holy Trinity in the world. She is the source of all that is good and true and beautiful and holy in the world. She is the face of God in the world, turning the world to face God.

In her divine and created modes, as God and not God, Sophia is consciously presented as a primal *antinomy*. The idea of antinomy is crucial to an understanding of Florensky's Sophiology and was also a cardinal principle for Bulgakov, especially in his earlier works. Florensky takes the term and some of its conceptualization from Kant but sees the base idea of the 'necessary self-contradictoriness of rationality' as irreproachably ancient, going back at least as far as the pre-Socratics.[75] For Florensky, the dual status of Sophia is no theological farrago but a sign of her very truth. He explains that when the thesis entails the antithesis and the antithesis the thesis then the combination of the two is not false but an antinomy. Kant got nowhere with his antinomies but deserves, Florensky avers, 'eternal glory' for declaiming the concept. In addition to a lengthy logical demonstration of the principle, he gives examples from Trinitarian theology and Christology: the consubstantiality of the Holy Trinity (thesis) is not negated by the threeness of hypostases (antithesis) or the unconfusedness of the natures of Christ (thesis) by their inseparability (antithesis). For Florensky, the dual nature of Sophia operates on the same base principle of antinomy. This is, it has to be said, a somewhat tendentious case in that Sophia lacks the precisely the clear dogmatic and terminological basis that enables God to be confessed as one and three or Christ to be both two and one according to nature and hypostasis, respectively. Florensky does not, sensibly, attempt to ground the principle in patristic works as such, focussing rather on the pre-Socratics, Plato, Nicholas of Cusa (with his notion of the coincidence of opposites), and the later German Idealists.

Antinomy apart, Florensky is convinced that all the central features of his Sophiology are 'scattered in abundance throughout all of scripture and the patristic works'. By central features he means 'the idea of Sophia-Wisdom existing

---

[74] Florensky is acutely conscious of the integral and all-encompassing nature of Sophiology. Indeed, he sees any theology that breaks down and compartmentalizes its subject-matter as inherently problematic and indeed worthy of suspicion: 'Separate aspects of faith disintegrate atomistically only for scholastic theology.' The more grounded in religious experience the theology, the more integral it will be. *The Pillar and Ground of Truth*, 335 [ET 243].

[75] See 'Letter 6: On Contradiction', in *The Pillar and Ground of Truth*. Florensky draws (155–6 [ET 115]) special attention to a one-word fragment of Heraclitus (Fragment 122 in Diels (ed.)) reading simply: ἀγχιβασίην ('contradiction' according to G. F. Tsereteli but also perhaps 'dispute' or even 'approach' – the word is found only in Heraclitus and without any context must remain mysterious).

before the world, of the heavenly Jerusalem, of the Church in its heavenly aspect, or of the Kingdom of God as the ideal person of creation or the guardian angel of creation, or of the hypostatic system of the world-creating thoughts of God, and the true pole and incorruptible aspect of created being.'[76] In 'Letter 10: On Sophia' he avows that he is not going to quote these sources exhaustively in what is, after all, a relatively brief sketch in the form of a letter.[77] But he does delve into scripture and, especially, the patristic tradition at some length in line with his general and apparently sincere commitment to 'remain within the bounds of Church ideas'. It is highly significant that he makes this vow precisely in contradistinction to Soloviev's professed preference for figures such as Boehme, Paracelsus, and Swedenborg as teachers of wisdom.[78] There are certainly elements of Boehme, Schelling, and other such proto-Sophiological sources in Florensky but these are largely mediated through Soloviev and given an ecclesial and ascetic twist in the process. While Florensky displays a properly catholic delight and joy in welcoming and appreciating wisdom wherever it is to be found—in whatever philosophical, scientific, or religious tradition that might be—there is no doubt of the special attention he pays to the 'bounds of Church ideas' demarcated by the Fathers. He does not share Soloviev's positive eagerness to transcend the tradition.

Florensky's approach is, rather, to explore and tease out what the patristic tradition has to say in the matter of the divine wisdom and to use that tradition (in good Orthodox fashion) as the chief guide to the exposition and understanding of scriptural references to wisdom. Florensky quite rightly finds the notion of the pre-existence of creation in terms of the divine ideas widely attested, mentioning St Gregory of Nazianzus and Clement of Alexandria.[79] Intriguingly, he gives little credit to Origen in this respect, notwithstanding his broadly sympathetic but not uncritical comments on the great Alexandrine theologian elsewhere in the book.[80] Florensky points to the various intimations of the pre-existence and eschatological destiny of the Church in writings of the immediate sub-apostolic period: in the *Didache*, the Second Epistle of Clement of Rome (which he knows to be spurious), and, especially, in the *Shepherd of Hermas*.[81] He goes on to find support for his

---

[76] *The Pillar and Ground of Truth*, 332 [ET 241].

[77] He notes (ibid., 332–3 [ET 241–2]) that he has already done much of this background work in an essay on the Church and will do so in a future special work on Sophia. It does not appear that this latter work was ever realized, thus Letter 10 of *The Pillar and Ground of Truth* remains his most extensive treatment of the theme.

[78] *The Pillar and Ground of Truth*, 331 [ET 240–1].

[79] *The Pillar and Ground of Truth*, 328–9 [ET 238–9].

[80] Cf. *The Pillar and Ground of Truth*, 749, n.541 [ET 538, n.542]. Florensky notes that the story of Origen's self-castration is probably no more than the tittle-tattle that invariably accompanies great men but notes that, ironically, the rationalistic structure of his work means that it is deeply imbued with 'the spirit of castration'.

[81] *The Pillar and Ground of Truth*, 333–8 [ET 242–5]. Florensky is very careful to distinguish this ideal pre-existence from the rather more pedestrian and literal Gnostic notions of pre-existence. One

ideas concerning virginity and specifically the Virgin Mary in St Gregory of Nyssa, St Gregory of Nazianzus, St Ambrose of Milan, St Nicholas Kabasilas, and others. But overwhelmingly his most important patristic source is St Athanasius of Alexandria.

Florensky begins his treatment of Athanasius by crediting him, as author of the *Life of Anthony*, as the one who 'defended and ascetically grounded the idea of Spirit-bearing and the deification of creatures more powerfully than anyone else'.[82] Florensky moves on to a compelling and learned discussion of Athanasius' distinction between wisdom as uncreated and wisdom as created, in the latter sense pertaining not only to the incarnation but also to the imprint of divine wisdom on the creation. He finds a striking building metaphor particularly instructive: the imprint of wisdom on the creation being likened by Athanasius to the inscription of the name of a king on the building blocks of a city. All in all, Athanasius emerges as one who clearly affirms created wisdom as pre-existent and as 'a pre-cosmic hypostatic collection of divine prototypes of that which exists'.[83] Athanasius himself would hardly have put it quite like this and indeed Florensky, as we shall see, somewhat overstates the degree to which he can be regarded as a proto-Sophiologist.[84]

Florensky is, nonetheless, very loath to admit that he has in practice gone rather beyond the 'bounds of Church ideas' as far as the patristic tradition is concerned. He is more avowedly deferential to the Church Fathers than either Soloviev or Bulgakov, only occasionally offering a note of mild critique.[85] But there is an admission of the relatively limited nature of patristic sophiology in Florensky's turn to iconographic and architectural considerations in the last sections of Letter 10.[86] These, it must be allowed, certainly form part of the sphere of the 'Church ideas' within whose bounds he wishes to remain. Florensky allows that in the patristic and liturgical tradition of the Church, wisdom invariably centres on the second person of the Trinity whereas the somewhat later Russian iconographic tradition leads us into new dimensions of the idea of wisdom, dimensions more immediately conducive to his own vision of Sophiology. Indeed it is not surprising that he should emphasize works of sacred art given that he sees a special connection between wisdom and creativity,

---

finds the idea of the pre-existence of the Church in contemporary elders such as St Porphyrios of Kavsokalyvia (1906–1991): 'The Church is without beginning, without end and eternal, just as the Triune God, her founder, is without beginning, without end and eternal. She is uncreated just as God is uncreated. She existed before the ages, before the angels, before the foundation of the world [...] She is an expression of the richly varied wisdom of God. She is the mystery of mysteries.' *Wounded by Love: The Life and Wisdom of Elder Porphyrios*, 87.

[82] *The Pillar and Ground of Truth*, 343 [ET 249].

[83] *The Pillar and Ground of Truth*, 348 [ET 251–2].

[84] More on Athanasius and his attempted appropriation by Florensky in Chapter 4.2 and 7.1.3.

[85] For example, his comment on the timidity of Ambrose's meditations on the liturgical veneration of the Virgin Mary. *The Pillar and Ground of Truth*, 367 [ET 265].

[86] *The Pillar and Ground of Truth*, 370–88, 390–1 [ET 267–80, 282].

the creativity of artisans and the artists being one of the chief ways in which wisdom can be manifested in the sphere of human activity.[87]

While it goes beyond the bounds of this study to explore his art criticism in detail, suffice it to say that his meditations on late medieval Russian icons of wisdom in Kiev, Novgorod, Yaroslavl, Moscow, and elsewhere, provide him with ample justification for his presentation of wisdom as distinct from yet intimately related to the persons of the Trinity and indeed to the Virgin Mary, the Mother of God. He also sees in these icons a far more searching and engaging mediation on the specifically feminine character of wisdom than is generally present in the Church Fathers. Florensky is careful to discuss these icons in their proper architectural and liturgical context. His liturgical considerations include a fascinating discussion of the liturgical office of divine wisdom composed by Symeon Shakovsky in the seventeenth century and revised by the Likhoudes brothers in the early eighteenth century. This office celebrates in vivid language the intimate relationship between the Mother of God and wisdom.

Florensky winds up the letter by presenting three sides of Sophia. The Byzantine Greeks focussed on the *speculative-dogmatic* side. The Russians took all of this ready-made but added an appreciation of wisdom as *spiritual perfection* and *inner beauty*, born out of ascetic effort in chastity and virginity. The third side, revealed in Florensky's own time, concerns the *unity* of all creation in God and the idea of the mystical and pre-eternal Church.[88] All this is very revealing of Florensky's intuition of the progressive nature of the revelation of the multi-dimensionality of wisdom. It amounts to an admission that one must indeed go beyond the Fathers or at least recognize the rather limited nature of patristic sophiology. All this puts Florensky on shaky ground against those who find his case insufficiently grounded in the tradition. The second and third sides of wisdom are very much born out of subjective religious sensibility and experience coupled with (in the case of the third side) a substantial dollop of German Idealist philosophy. Even the extensive appeal to the old Russian icons of wisdom relies to a great extent on subjective considerations. Wisdom in this sense is very much in the eye of the beholder.

There is here an interesting disjunct in Florensky between experience (what he calls the religious standpoint) and knowledge (what he calls the rational standpoint)—a disjunct that arguably speaks of an undigested Kantian inheritance. For example, we experience Sophia as God but know her not to be God.[89] Florensky has somehow bracketed off religious experience from rational knowledge and this

---

[87] See his fascinating discussion of the etymology of *Sophia* and cognates in *The Pillar and Ground of Truth*, 752–3, n.571 [ET 541, n.572]. He finds in both the Greek and Sanskrit roots of the term an emphasis on adaptation/making suitable i.e. 'the capability of embodying a certain intention in reality'.

[88] *The Pillar and Ground of Truth*, 389–90 [ET 281–2]. Emphasis in original.

[89] *The Pillar and Ground of Truth*, 331 [ET 240]. Such a glaring contrary cannot readily be resolved simply by an appeal to antinomy.

constitutes something of a fatal flaw in his theology. Can we really bracket off experience from reason in this way—at least if we want to escape the Kantian impasse? If the religious experience of which he speaks cannot be expressed in coherent and consistent (if not of course exhaustive) dogmatic terms, is that experience really quite what he thinks it is?[90] Many of the woes and travails of Sophiology come precisely from the arguably doomed attempt to translate the fleeting vision and powerful poetry of a particular form of religious experience and sensibility into the written prose of dogmatic theology.[91] This tension is evident *a fortiori* in the greatest Sophiologist, and Florensky's dear friend, Fr Sergius Bulgakov, a theologian who was to take the unmodern turn of Sophiology to a whole new level.

1.4 Fr Sergius Bulgakov

Sergius Bulgakov is the most constructive and creative Orthodox theologian of the modern era—indeed one of the greatest theologians of any stamp in the last several centuries.[92] Emerging out of the Russian 'silver age', Bulgakov went on to play a decisive but vigorously contested rôle in the development of the theology of the Russian Diaspora following on from the Bolshevik revolution.[93] The 'silver age' saw religious themes permeate the works of the great artists, thinkers, composers, and poets of the day. This phenomenon was to some extent the legacy of Soloviev and has as one of its most potent expressions the series of St Petersburg

---

[90] Note that his aim is precisely the opposite. He states his overall purpose in the opening line of his masterwork to be: 'Living religious experience as the sole legitimate way to gain knowledge of the dogmas.' *The Pillar and Ground of Truth*, 3 [ET 5].

[91] Florensky appreciates the difficulty, apologizing in advance for the 'crude and hateful pincers and scalpels' with which he is attempting to express truths experienced inwardly by the soul. *The Pillar and Ground of Truth*, 324 [ET 236].

[92] I use this form of his name (Sergius) for several reasons: for familiarity, by analogy with the conventional form of his patron saint, St Sergius of Radonezh (also the patronal saint of the Orthodox-Anglican Fellowship of St Alban and St Sergius with which he was heavily involved), and to reflect the slightly archaic version of his name adopted after ordination (Sergii/Sergij as opposed to Sergei).

[93] For an excellent intellectual biography (albeit only up to 1920), see Catherine Evtuhov's *The Cross and the Sickle*. Rowan Williams' introduction to his *Sergii Bulgakov: Towards a Russian Political Theology* is, as one would expect, well worth reading. There are two good general surveys of Bulgakov's theology in English, both by Catholics: Aidan Nichols, *Wisdom from Above: A Primer in the Theology of Father Sergei Bulgakov* and Robert Slesinski, *The Theology of Sergius Bulgakov*. The former is the more comprehensive while the latter (while excellently written and researched) is composed largely of previously published occasional pieces and lacks overall cohesion. See also the accounts of Paul Vallière, *Modern Russian Theology*, 227–371; Antoine Arjakovsky, *Essai sur le père Serge Boulgakov (1871–1944): Philosophe et théologien chrétien*; and Piero Coda, *Sergej Bulgakov*. In Russian, Lev Zander's Бог и мир (миросозерцание отца Сергия Булгакова) remains the classic study. There has been an uptick in interest in Bulgakov in Russia in the 1990s–2000s; see, for instance, Petr Sapronov's Русская софиология и софийность and Natalia Vaganova's Софиология протоиерея Сергия Булгакова (including a brief section (99–113) on wisdom in patristic and scholastic theology). See also the extensive Bulgakov bibliography compiled by Barbara Hallensleben and Regula Zwahlen: *Sergij Bulgakov, Bibliographie: Werke, Briefwechsel und Übersetzungen.*

Religious-Philosophical Meetings that took place in his memory between 1901 and 1903. Bringing together some of the most prominent Churchmen and intellectuals of the day, the meetings revolved especially around the question of the development of doctrine and the possibility of creative faithfulness to received tradition. While reaching no firm conclusions, the encounter was real and had wide-ranging impact across the cultural firmament. Such contacts encouraged the migration of some prominent thinkers from Marxism—then the philosophy à la mode—through Idealism to Orthodoxy. The fruits of this migration are summed up in the signally prescient volume *Vekhi* (*Signposts*) (1909) which pinpointed tyranny as the necessary outcome of the atheistic and Revolutionary utopianism of the Marxists.[94] Among the contributors was Bulgakov who had himself returned to communion with the Orthodox Church only the previous year.[95]

Bulgakov went on to articulate a wholly remarkable theology oriented on the divine wisdom or Sophia.[96] He goes far beyond both Florensky and Soloviev in the extent and depth of his engagement with patristic treatments of the theme of wisdom. His Sophiology was already well developed in his pre-Revolutionary works but was confirmed, deepened, and somewhat clarified by his experience of exile following on from the Bolshevik Revolution. Bulgakov was expelled as an undesirable intellectual on Lenin's orders and left on one of the famous philosophers' steamers at the end of 1922.[97] As we noted at the beginning of this chapter, he found particular solace in a visit to the Church of Agia Sophia in Constantinople. Indeed he opens the introduction of his Sophiological summary, *The Wisdom of God* precisely with an evocation of this great Church, recalling that first visit:

> This heavenly dome, which portrays heaven bending to earth to embrace it, gives expression in finite form to the infinite, to an all-embracing unity, to the stillness of eternity, in the form of a work of art which, though belonging to this world, is a miracle of harmony itself [...] An ocean of light pours in from above and dominates the whole space below. It enchants, convinces, as it seems to say: 'I am in the world and the world is in me'. Here Plato is baptized into

---

[94] The volume was edited by the intellectual historian and literary critic Mikhail Gershenzon.

[95] 'Heroism and the Spiritual Struggle' in Rowan Williams, *Sergii Bulgakov: Towards a Russian Political Theology*, 69–112.

[96] For Bulgakov, this articulation was something of a mission or calling and certainly no mere academic exercise. In a diary entry for 21 September 1921 he notes: 'God has chosen me, a weak and unworthy man, to be a witness to the Divine Sophia and to Her revelation.' Cited in Klimoff, 'Georges Florovsky and the Sophiological Controversy', 68. Bruce Marshall has suggested (in conversation) that Bulgakov's whole theology may be conceived as the repayment of a debt—a debt incurred through the comfort offered by Sophia in times of acute grief and distress (for instance at the time of the death of his son in 1909). I find this a compelling suggestion.

[97] Lenin had maintained an extensive polemic against Bulgakov from the 1890s regarding him as a defective Marxist even before his turn to Orthodoxy. See Catherine Evtuhov, *The Cross and the Sickle*, 36.

Christianity, for here, surely, we have his lofty realm to which souls ascend for the contemplation of ideas [...][98]

Far more than simply a 'chiselled allegory', the Great Church of the Holy Wisdom is the 'last, silent, revelation of the Greek genius [...] concerning Sophia, the Wisdom of God'.[99] Imperfectly understood at the time and constituting a kind of sacred hieroglyph, further aspects of Sophia were to be intimated in the art and architecture of Russia—very much in line with the intuitions of Soloviev and Florensky. Bulgakov returns to Agia Sophia at the close of the introduction with a rousing call:

> The future of living Christianity rests with the sophianic interpretation of the world and of its destiny. All the dogmatic and practical problems of modern Christian dogmatics and ascetics seem to form a kind of knot, the unravelling of which inevitably leads to sophiology [...] And finally, in contemplating culture which has succumbed to secularization and paganism, which has lost its inspiration and has no answer to give to the tragedy of history, which seems in fact to have lost all meaning—we realize that we can find a spring of living water only by a renewal of our faith in the sophianic, or theandric, meaning of the historical process. As the dome of St. Sophia in Constantinople with prophetic symbolism portrays heaven bending to earth, so the Wisdom of God itself is spread like a canopy over our sinful though still hallowed world.[100]

In Bulgakov's work, wisdom becomes the link-piece of a magnificent theological synthesis connecting Trinitarian theology, Christology, pneumatology, cosmology, ecclesiology, and Mariology.

By way of summary, Wisdom (Sophia) in Bulgakov is understood as denoting the divine life, the unity of the triune deity. She is God's self-revelation both in and outside himself, a single principle capable of existing in both uncreated and created forms: God in the world and the world in God: 'Heaven stoops toward earth; the world is not only a world in itself, it is also the world in God, and God abides not only in heaven but also on earth with man.'[101] She is not a hypostasis but a principle capable of hypostasization: in God, in Christ, in Mary, in the creation. She is that which alone gives meaning to the historical process. She is the principle of the unity of the uncreated and the created, a unity manifested in and founded upon Christ. This mystery of union without confusion, of primordial divine humanity, is poured out upon the whole created order by the Holy Spirit. Thus Sophia is God's self-bestowal both within the Trinity and upon the world.

---

[98] *The Wisdom of God*, 1.   [99] *The Wisdom of God*, 2.   [100] *The Wisdom of God*, 21.
[101] *The Wisdom of God*, 17.

She is the principle of unity and coinherence in God, and between God and the world—the very foundation of all that *is*.

This summary is, of course, only a very potted version of an immensely complex and not entirely consistent theological system. Note that, as in Florensky and Soloviev, the emphasis is squarely on level S3 as opposed to S1–S2: Sophiology remains oddly unsapiential in Bulgakov.[102]

While much of his Sophiology came to him initially from Soloviev, Bulgakov increasingly distanced himself from the esotericism and eclecticism of his some-time master. As he declared in a letter from 1928: 'True life in the Church signifies not just overcoming but becoming free of or outgrowing Soloviev'.[103] Over time (and especially in his works of exile), Bulgakov stresses more and more the profoundly traditional character of Sophiology and seeks to detach it from any 'peculiar exotic Oriental flavour of "gnosis"' which he freely admits can smack of 'rubbish and superstition'.[104] Indeed, Bulgakov became convinced that his Sophiology was essentially the product of a profound meditation upon the scriptural, liturgical, artistic, and patristic inheritance of the Orthodox Church. In *The Wisdom of God* he states plainly that Sophiology is not substantially indebted to the wisdom teachings of Boehme, Pordage, and others: 'modern Russian teaching on Sophia does not derive from these sources, but from holy tradition, which silently pervades the whole history of the Eastern Church'.[105]

Bulgakov thus takes the unmodern turn of Sophiology to a whole new level. Soloviev made only very limited appeal to Church tradition in the specific matter of Sophia while Florensky went much further in claiming Sophiology to be 'scattered in abundance' throughout scripture and the Fathers. Bulgakov goes further still in claiming that the whole thrust of Orthodox Christianity is inherently Sophiological. Sophiology, for Bulgakov, is an example of the kind of creative affirmation that must lie at the heart of any genuinely traditional theology. 'The time has come', writes Bulgakov, 'to sweep away the dust of ages and to decipher the sacred script, to reinstate the tradition of the Church, in this instance all but broken, as a *living* tradition. It is *holy tradition that lays such tasks upon us*.'[106]

It is to the specifically patristic dimension of that tradition that we now turn, beginning with Bulgakov's pre-Revolutionary works. This is not to imply the patristic tradition is commensurate with Church tradition as a whole. Bulgakov quite properly and legitimately draws on liturgy and iconography, and indeed other sources, in his exploration of Sophiology. These sources cannot be dealt with

---

[102] Note also that Bulgakov presents his Sophiology very much as a personal *theologoumenon* and not the teaching of the Church—as witnessed in his complete omission of the theme from his survey book, *The Orthodox Church* (1935).

[103] Cited in Catherine Evtuhov, *The Cross and the Sickle*, 238. The letter also criticizes Soloviev's religious immaturity and dilettantism and doubts he can really be considered a master.

[104] *The Wisdom of God*, 12–13.   [105] *The Wisdom of God*, 7.

[106] *The Wisdom of God*, 5. Emphasis in original.

in any great depth in what follows.[107] While ranging widely through Bulgakov's work the remainder of this section aims principally to discern the nature and contours of Bulgakov's appeal to patristic tradition in the specific matter of Sophiology.

In his *Philosophy of Economy* (1912), Bulgakov challenges Marxism head-on by subverting some of the basic premises of modern economics and proposing Sophia as the transcendental subject of the economy, as of all human activity. Bulgakov decries any economic system based only on material concerns as inherently deathly, iniquitous, and destructive of the human spirit. He also tears apart Kant's theory of practical reason, regarding it as a philosophical dead-end. Acknowledging the impossibility of objective truth based on reason and rightly seeking to escape mere subjectivism, Kant ends up, argues Bulgakov, with a simulacrum or dead image of real knowledge: 'He sought life in death and the sweet smell of the fields in the pent-up air of his study'.[108] In its lack of any sense of truth or resolution outside of the temporal process Kant and neo-Kantianism alike reduce knowledge and history to an 'evil infinity' while remaining trapped in a philosophy of rationalism with no real basis or way-out.[109]

It is worth noting that Kant, and specifically the neo-Kantianism of his own time, remained a foil for Bulgakov throughout his career. This is, as in Florensky, one of the prime motive forces behind his enthusiasm for the notion of anti-nomy.[110] Bulgakov's anti-Kantianism was to be much elaborated and expanded in his *The Tragedy of Philosophy* (1927).[111] The emphasis on reason, which he finds throughout German Idealism, ends up being rather like a spider that spins its thread out of itself rather than relying on 'mystical facts and metaphysical givens'.[112] Philosophy without religion is a chimera. In fact, 'philosophy issues from and returns to religion and, precisely, to religious myth and dogma [...] And religious mystery is guarded by the flaming sword of the cherubim, whose name in the language of philosophy is *antinomy*.'[113]

Coming back to *Philosophy and Economy*, Bulgakov declares (still against Kant and neo-Kantianism) that truth is 'a state of being' united to primordial reality. His vision sees in the economy the striving of the world soul to realize itself in the

---

[107] Bulgakov's arresting liturgical vision can be seen especially in his 'The Eucharistic Dogma' and 'The Holy Grail'. This liturgical dimension in rightly emphasized in Andrew Louth's, 'Sergii Bulgakov and the Task of the Theology'. Bulgakov's iconology is perhaps best summed up in his *Icons and Icon-Veneration*. The liturgical matrix, along with the iconographic tradition embedded within it, forms an inescapable backdrop to Bulgakov's whole theological *oeuvre*. While both are thoroughly congruent with and ultimately inseparable from the patristic tradition, they fall, alas, outside the central area of focus of this study.

[108] *Philosophy of Economy*, 56 [ET 81].   [109] *Philosophy of Economy*, 160 [ET 157].

[110] See further Brandon Gallaher, *Freedom and Necessity in Modern Trinitarian Theology*, 46ff.

[111] Although published (in German) only in 1927, this work was written in the Crimea between 1918 and 1922. It has only relatively recently (1991) been published in Russian.

[112] *The Tragedy of Philosophy*, 20 (all page references are to the English translation).

[113] *The Tragedy of Philosophy*, 88.

natural world. In terms derived from Spinoza via Schelling, Bulgakov declares: '*natura naturans* strives to possess the natural world, *natura naturata*, to make it transparent so that the subject can recognize itself in nature. This is the goal of economy, already beyond history.'[114] Rather than simply a struggle to survive, human work should be creative and joyful. Such activity should enable the human spirit to transcend the merely material as it reveals the properly sophianic character of nature—nature as revelatory of the primordial unity that is Sophia. In this book, his doctoral dissertation, Bulgakov has yet to consciously distance himself from a broadly Solovievian conceptualization of Sophia. Bulgakov relies very heavily on Schelling (and, through him, Spinoza) and credits Soloviev as one of Schelling's greatest epigones.[115] Both, he recognizes, are fundamentally inspired and driven by the mystical natural philosophy of Jakob Boehme and Franz Baader.[116] Biblical wisdom literature is a regular reference point in this work while patristic treatments of wisdom figure only marginally.[117] This is a thoroughly and self-consciously contemporary work that is as yet not especially concerned with maintaining and defending the strictly traditional character of his nascent Sophiology but rather with proposing a new economic and philosophical ideal in a febrile and uncertain world.

Bulgakov was, however, already thoroughly conversant with patristic theology by this time. This is immediately evident in his essay on the *Imiaslavie* (Name-glorifying) controversy, 'The Athos Affair' (1913). Defending a group of Athonite monks persecuted as heretics for holding the holy name of God (specifically the name Jesus Christ) to be itself divine, Bulgakov argues for the consistency of their position with the theology of St Gregory Palamas: if the name of God can be construed as an energy of God, then it can certainly be understood as divine. Bulgakov does not defend all the beliefs and claims of the name-glorifiers but argues with great tenacity that they have raised an important dogmatic issue that should not have been dismissed and condemned by any ecclesiastical authority short of a fully representative general council of the Church.

---

[114] *Philosophy of Economy*, 124–6 [ET 134–6]. *Natura naturans*: nature naturing—the formative principle of creation. *Natura naturata*: nature natured—the natural world formed and shaped by *natura naturans*. This medieval distinction (from the Latin translations of Averroes) is associated especially with Spinoza and was made much of by Schelling.

[115] *Philosophy of Economy*, 73 [ET 93]. Cf. also 119–20, 149 [ET 130, 150].

[116] *Philosophy of Economy*, 59–60 [ET 83–4]. In his appropriation of Schelling's understanding of the world soul, Soloviev is credited with giving 'new philosophical expression to the theories of the classical philosophers, the fathers of the Eastern Church, and Western mystics (in particular Boehme and Baader)'. *Philosophy of Economy*, 60n [ET 84n].

[117] See, for instance, the brief list of Church Fathers and others acknowledging something like a world soul: St Gregory of Nyssa, Dionysius the Areopagite, St Maximus the Confessor, and John Scotus Eriugena. *Philosophy of Economy*, 59 [ET 84]. German mysticism is comparatively more favoured with Angelus Silesius, to give just one example, cropping up more regularly than any patristic witness. On the subject of the world soul he acknowledges elsewhere that St Gregory Palamas clearly refutes the idea, at least in its pagan form (*Unfading Light*, 224n [ET 229n]).

What is most important for our purposes here is that Bulgakov gives vastly more attention to Palamas than Florensky, let alone Soloviev. Indeed, he was increasingly to turn to Palamas as the chief source and reference point of Sophiology within the patristic tradition. This was at a time when the theology of St Gregory Palamas was far from occupying the preponderant place in Orthodox theology that it does today, a development that owes much precisely to those inspired to study Palamas by Bulgakov's trail-blazing but contentious Palamite revival.

Bulgakov greatly expanded the theological and specifically patristic dimension of his work in his last great pre-Revolutionary work, *The Unfading Light: Contemplations and Speculations* (1917).[118] I shall devote a good deal of space to this work since it rather neatly embraces and encapsulates Bulgakov's entire spiritual and intellectual vision, albeit often in somewhat unpolished and under-developed form. Schelling remains an exceptionally important point of reference, as amply evidenced in the copious notes, but Bulgakov also embarks at this time on a sustained discussion of patristic topics with particular reference to the later Greek Fathers, especially Palamas.[119] The book itself is an erudite but distinctly experiential exploration of multiple topics including religious consciousness, apophatic theology, cosmology, and anthropology. There are several appeals to ascetic and mystical fathers in the opening section on religious consciousness[120] but the first sustained discussion of patristic sources comes in the section on apophatic theology.[121] It should be noted that this comes as part of a historical sketch which runs from classical philosophy through to early modern mysticism (Jewish, German, and English). While particular attention is paid to various Church Fathers there is little to suggest that such figures are of greater intrinsic authority than, say, Philo or Nicholas of Cusa. This is not, as yet, an especially

---

[118] The title, which has a long history of Christian usage, is taken from one of Alexei Khomiakov's *Vesper Songs* and refers to Christ, 'God's wisdom, glory, and word', as the unfailing radiance who illumines our way on the rocky and gloomy paths of life. The sub-title is itself very revealing of the tentative and avowedly speculative nature of Bulgakov's theology. Bulgakov calls the book a 'collection of motley chapters' (*Unfading Light*, I [ET xxxvii]) in emulation of Pushkin's characterization of his *Eugene Onegin*. More remotely, it may also allude to Clement of Alexandria's *Stromateis* ('miscellanies') (as per the translator's note in *Unfading Light* [ET], xxxvii).

[119] This is an area pinpointed by Rowan Williams as an especially fertile ground for future Bulgakov research: *Sergii Bulgakov*, 19: 'More needs to be done on Bulgakov's use of the later Greek Fathers'.

[120] Bulgakov singles out Macarius, St Symeon the New Theologian, St John Climacus, St Isaac the Syrian, and St Tikhon of Zadonsk as pre-eminent teachers of prayer, together with later figures and collections such as St Ignatii Brianchaninov, St Theophan the Recluse and the *Dobrotoliubie* (referring to the Russian version compiled by St Theophan). This comes in the context of a spirited discussion of prayer in which Bulgakov asserts that 'Where there is no prayer, there is no religion' and warns against confusing prayer with such theosophical surrogates as 'concentration, meditation, and intuition' (one might add the modern fad of 'mindfulness' here), practices which immerse one in the world and not in God.

[121] The section is headed with a quote from St Augustine (*De ordine* 2.16.44): 'Deus melius scitur nesciendo' ('God is best known through not-knowing'). Such Latin and indeed Augustinian tags were also a recurrent feature in the works of Georges Florovsky.

ecclesial analysis—the figures treated are selected chiefly for their philosophical interest rather than as vehicles of Church tradition. They may also be criticized on philosophical grounds—for instance the Cappadocian Fathers are deemed to have given insufficient thought to their doctrine of divine unknowability regarding it as basically self-evident.[122] That said, Bulgakov's treatments of Maximus and Palamas are undoubtedly significant, not only in terms of his own intellectual development but because of the boost he gave to the study of these figures in Catholic and Orthodox circles alike. Maximus, 'a profound theologian of the Eastern Church who still awaits further evaluation and study', is praised for the delicate and sophisticated balance he achieves between cataphatic and apophatic theology—not that he gets everything quite right.[123] Bulgakov sees a further development in the idea of negative theology in St Gregory Palamas.[124] In his reading of Palamas, Bulgakov relies largely on the rather limited collection of texts in Migne's *Patrologia Graeca*, and thus focusses on the *Theophanes* and the *150 Chapters* (which he generally quotes in the original Greek). Substantial theological texts such as the *Triads* and the extensive rebuttals of Akindynos and Gregoras were not readily available him. He nonetheless displays an impressive command of Palamas' doctrine—something that he was soon to marshal in support of his Sophiological investigations.[125]

Bulgakov goes on in *Unfading Light* to approach the topic of Sophia through a lengthy consideration of creation. The tone of the section on the creation is somewhat more poetic and mystical albeit with many learned discussions of patristic, philosophical (especially Schellingian), and other teachings, some decidedly esoteric and recognizably Solovievian. Bulgakov acknowledges that he is opening up a kind of cryptogram, a hidden and insufficiently appreciated dimension of human life and thought that goes back well beyond any philosophy or theology. His treatment of creation begins with the primordial sense that the world is created, that it has its origin and root outside of itself, in God. God, as the Absolute, has opened up and established the relative in an act of self-bifurcation, a 'creative sacrifice of love': 'Golgotha was not only eternally pre-established at the creation of the world as an event in time, but it also constitutes the metaphysical essence of creation. The divine "it is accomplished" proclaimed from the Cross, embraces all being, refers to all creation'. It is a kind of madness on God's part, establishing the human creation as free and independent, as other, as potential

---

[122] *Unfading Light*, 113 [ET 121].   [123] *Unfading Light*, 121–3 [ET 129–30].

[124] *Unfading Light*, 124–6 [ET 131–4].

[125] This appreciation rather belies Martin Jugie's roughly contemporaneous and perhaps wishful claim that Palamite teaching was 'un dogme à peu près mort' in the Orthodox Church ('Palamite (Controverse)', 1810). The *150 Chapters* and *Theophanes* are the only works published in Migne that deal extensively with the essence-energies distinction. Migne (relying, as ever, on material already available) focusses more on spiritual-ascetic texts. Bulgakov would also have had access to Palamite materials in the *Philokalia* and *Dobrotoliubie* (both the Slavonic and Russian versions) and in Porfirii Uspensky's История Афона.

friend. It is a madness that can only be understood in terms of love: 'for God is mad for man'.[126]

Alongside the human creation and 'the whole tragic process of human history', lies the earth for which Bulgakov expresses the most extraordinary devotion.[127] Bulgakov goes on to emphasize that even in the midst of time and decay and death there is an irrefragable and eternal character to the creation: 'But out of the depths of despondency, in the midst of doleful silence is heard an incessant whisper, timid and faint, but at the same time confident and not to be stifled: you are eternal and were only born for the sake of time; it is in you, you are not in it [. . .] Time is presupposed with eternity, it is nothing other than eternity that stretches into being [. . .]'.[128] This paradoxical correlativity of time and eternity is resolved in Palamite terms: 'God, by remaining through his essence ($o\dot{v}\sigma\acute{\iota}a$) higher than the world, is present in the temporal process by his creative power ($\dot{\epsilon}\nu\acute{\epsilon}\rho\gamma\epsilon\iota a$), is born in it: this correlation of eternity and temporality is held on the edge of the sword of antinomy.'[129] Palamas is, for Bulgakov, an inherently antinomical theologian.[130]

This sophisticated discussion of the interrelatedness of time and eternity leads straight into a discussion of the eternal foundation of the creation in Sophia. Here Bulgakov again reaches intuitively and immediately for Palamite theology, mapping it very precisely onto the language of Schelling. The Absolute, though the process of self-bifurcation already mentioned, becomes a relative Absolute for the creature, an Absolute capable of relation—in other words, God:

By opening himself to the creature God puts off his absolute transcendence and reveals himself in his activity for the creature, in grace or (to use the expression of the dogmatic controversies of the fourteenth century) in his energies. The divinity in its inner-divine life remains transcendent for the creature, but the activities of the divinity, its manifestations, the divine power which pours out into creation, are the same divinity, one, indivisible, and eternal. In this sense the

---

[126] *Unfading Light*, 180 [ET 185]. The arresting phrase 'Dieu est fou de l'homme' is cited in French and attributed to an unnamed French author. It can be found, again attributed only to 'a French author', in Schelling's *Grundlegung der positiven Philosophie*, 320 and *Darstellung des philosophischen Empirismus*, 273. The base idea seems to come ultimately from I Corinthians. Paul Evdokimov, a great perpetuator of Bulgakov's legacy, makes much of the theme in his *L'Amour fou de Dieu*.

[127] Cf. *Unfading Light*, 188 [ET 192]: 'Children of earth, love your mother, kiss her frenziedly, bathe her with your tears, sprinkle her with sweat, drench her with blood, and satiate her with your bones!' Note that the experience of nature as a divine theophany was an integral part of Bulgakov's conversion. See the account of a momentous trip to the Caucasus given in ibid., 7–8 [ET 7–9].

[128] Bulgakov references Maximus as a basis for this intuition regarding time and eternity but gets his citations in a slight muddle, referencing 'Quaest. ad Thalass. Migne t. 90, 1164' while the relevant text is in fact found in *Ambigua* 10 PG 91 1164BC: *Unfading Light*, 200 [ET 204]. As Bulgakov points out, the base idea goes back to Plato's famous description of time as the 'moving image of eternity' (*Timaeus* 37d).

[129] *Unfading Light*, 203–4 [ET 207].

[130] The scope and accuracy of Bulgakov's attempted appropriation of Palamas is discussed more fully below, Chapter 7.1.3.

energy of God in every manifestation, as the activity of God, is inseparable from God, but what appears to the creature is God in creation, the Absolute-Transcendent itself. And the activity of the Holy Spirit in the Christian mysteries likewise is God himself, and so also the Name of God, which is a constantly occurring activity of the power of God, the energy of the divinity, is God.[131]

God's presence and immanence within the creation is thus construed in avowedly Palamite terms. Such language allows Bulgakov to speak of the divine presence in creation as a theophany in the strict sense: God is truly manifest in multiple forms in the creation (according to energy) while remaining single and transcendent (according to essence). Bulgakov explains that this manifestation of God in the creation while not commensurate with the Creator is nonetheless an authentic revelation of God. He uses some well-worn Platonic imagery here likening the dynamic to the way a mirror captures a reflection or the rays of the sun convey the sun. The divine energies 'streaming into the world' disclose the inner-divine life and make the invisible visible: 'on the foundation of the operation of God in the creature, what God is in himself becomes known'.[132]

Bulgakov goes on to the describe the inner life of the Trinity, as reflected 'by mysterious hieroglyphs' in the creation, in a wholly extraordinary and deeply insightful way. As a triunity of 'pre-eternally realized divine love', 'each hypostasis, by giving itself in love, finds itself in the other hypostases, realizes the one divinity'. He speaks of the Father, Son, and Spirit in striking terms—for instance of the Holy Spirit as the 'heart' of God in which the Father loves the Son. Bulgakov is careful to underline that there is no sequence or development in this life of love: 'for the Holy Trinity *is* eternally *beyond* in a single combined act of love and identity'.[133] While full and in need of nothing to complete its perfection, the divinity none-theless freely and without any form of compulsion or necessity 'comes out of itself' and summons to itself the non-divine, the creature. Bulgakov's character-ization of the inner life of the Trinity is compelling and original, offering much rich material for contemporary theology. While scarcely unimpeachable, there is nothing here that positively contradicts the patristic tradition. It can be safely left in the realm of *theologoumena*—points on which a good deal of difference of opinion can be allowed. Where matters become more problematic is in his introduction of Sophia. In going out of himself in the creation through his selfless love, God establishes 'a certain boundary':

And this boundary, which according to the very idea of the thing, is found *between* God and the world, the Creator and the creature, is itself neither the

---

[131] *Unfading Light*, 210 [ET 215].   [132] *Unfading Light*, 210–11 [ET 215–16].
[133] *Unfading Light*, 211 [ET 216].

one nor the other but something completely distinct, simultaneously uniting and separating the one and the other (a certain μεταξύ in the sense of Plato).[134]

Standing in the breach, in this 'in-between', is Holy Sophia, 'the angel of the creature and the beginning of the ways of God. She is the *love of Love*'. She is the exteriorization of the eternal act of divine love and is herself loved eternally by God—God's delight and joy. She is no mere abstract idea but a 'living essence, person, hypostasis'. As loved and loving she is necessarily a subject, a person, a hypostasis. Bulgakov is quite deliberate in his terminology here. Sophia is a 'fourth hypostasis' but of a different order to the hypostases of the Trinity:

> She does not participate in the intra-divine life, *she is not God*, and therefore does not convert the trihypostaseity into a tetrahypostaseity, the trinity into a quaternity. But she is the beginning of a new, created multi-hypostaseity, for after her follow many hypostases (people and angels) who are in a sophianic relation to the divinity. However, she herself is *outside* the divine world, and does not enter its self-contained, absolute fullness. But she is admitted to it according to an ineffable condescension of the love of God, and thanks to this she reveals the mysteries of the divinity and its depths and rejoices, 'plays' with these gifts before the face of God.[135]

As purely receptive and having nothing of herself, she is the 'eternal feminine'. She is the feminine being of the Old Testament, the mysterious figure depicted on ancient Russian icons, the ideal world, in short: everything.

In all this, Bulgakov ventures onto very shaky ground—there is, as we will see, very little in the patristic tradition to support such speculations. On the one hand, he affirms that Sophia is not God. On the other hand, nor is she exactly a creature. She is not created since she has her beginning not in non-being but in God. She borders closely with the world but is foreign to it: 'she is the indeterminable and unattainable bounds between being-creatureliness and super-being, the essence of divinity—neither being nor super-being [...] Occupying the place *between* God and the world, Sophia abides between being and super-being; she is neither the one nor the other, or appears as both at once.'[136] Here we see the same basic problem that we encountered in Florensky. If Sophia is neither creature not Creator, neither one thing nor t'other, then what is she? Bulgakov acknowledges that she does not fit into the usual categories (absolute/relative, eternal/temporal, divine/human). Turned towards God she is his image, idea, and name; turned to the world she is the eternal foundation of the creation—'heavenly Aphrodite as Plato and Plotinus called her in a true presentiment of Sophia. She is the empyrean

---

[134] *Unfading Light*, 212 [ET 217]. On μεταξύ, cf. above, n.2.
[135] *Unfading Light*, 212 [ET 217–18].   [136] *Unfading Light*, 214 [ET 219].

world of intelligible, eternal *ideas* which was revealed to the philosophical and religious contemplation of Plato who confessed it in his truly sophiological teaching.'[137]

Bulgakov is unabashed in his Christian Platonism but it must be allowed that his is certainly a *Christian* Platonism—he shows no hesitation in distancing Christianity from Platonism on questions such as the dialectic of transcendence and immanence, the significance of matter, the rôle of the body, and the nature of evil. But it may well be questioned whether he has sufficiently digested his Platonic inheritance when it comes to his acceptance of a liminal or 'in-between' existence for this empyrean realm of ideas which he identifies with Sophia. Neither divine nor a creature, neither eternal nor temporal, neither spatial nor non-spatial, neither absolute nor relative, the anomalous and 'in-between' character of Sophia causes Bulgakov endless headaches and struggles.[138] He is sure that there simply must be something 'in-between' God and the world in order to hold all things together and this something, or rather someone, he calls Sophia. He might have saved himself a good deal of trouble had he contented himself with Christ, the 'wisdom of God' (I Cor. 1:24), as the one 'in whom all things hold together' (Col. I:17)—an identification that in no way precludes recognition of wisdom as a property of the Trinity. But Bulgakov is convinced that received conciliar and patristic teachings are insufficient to express the truths for which he is groping. He struggles mightily to express the puzzling in-betweenness of Sophia in coherent philosophical and theological terms, not infrequently tying himself in knots as he shuttles between the divine and created 'faces' of Sophia—turned to God and turned to the world.

It is striking that there is little explicit reference to patristic sources in the section on Sophia and what little there is pertains largely to Palamas—from the language of the 'streaming energies' to Palamas as a typical instance of the patristic idea of a world soul.[139] Bulgakov, however, eschews any thorough investigation of patristic roots, contenting himself with a footnote to the work of his friend Pavel Florensky in which one can, he claims, find the theological grounds of Sophiology 'fully and precisely given'.[140] In fact Florensky's treatment of the patristic roots of Sophiology is, as we have seen, by his own account somewhat underdeveloped and provisional, amounting to no more than a 'scattering'.[141] The unmodern turn of Bulgakov's Sophiology was thus only nascent in his last great pre-Revolutionary work—but was already of a distinctly Palamite hue.

Bulgakov would substantially develop and beef-up the patristic and Palamite dimension of his Sophiological vision in his works of exile. Together with some

---

[137] *Unfading Light*, 216 [ET 221].

[138] Even Schelling, Bulgakov writes, had some intuition of this necessary 'in-between' but had as yet no apprehension of Sophia. *Unfading Light*, 215n [ET 220n].

[139] *Unfading Light*, 224n [ET 229n].   [140] *Unfading Light*, 213n [ET 218n].

[141] Cf. above, p.31.

necessary clarifications and corrections he was also, crucially, to expand on the specifically Christological dimension of Sophiology—something noticeably lacking in this early work.[142] This Christological emphasis entailed a concomitant downplaying, but not abandonment, of the notion of antinomy as a validating principle of Sophiology. Such moves certainly strengthen the case Bulgakov makes for his Sophiology without, however, entirely resolving its inherent ambiguities and anomalies—weaknesses that his critics were not slow to exploit.

Bulgakov's principal works of his Parisian exile fall conveniently into two trilogies. The little trilogy (on certain aspects of the creation) consists of *The Burning Bush* (1927), *The Friend of the Bridegroom* (1927), and *Jacob's Ladder* (1929). Dealing with, respectively, the Mother of God, St John the Baptist, and the angels, these works contain a wealth of patristic material. The same may be said of the great trilogy (on divine humanity), comprised of *The Lamb of God* (1933), *The Comforter* (1936), and *The Bride of the Lamb* (1945), dealing, respectively, with Christ, the Holy Spirit, and the Church.[143] Alongside these trilogies there are numerous other important works including 'Hypostasis and Hypostaseity' (1925),[144] *The Tragedy of Philosophy* (1927), 'The Eucharistic Dogma' (1930), *Icons and Icon-Veneration* (1931), *The Orthodox Church* (1935), the summary volume *The Wisdom of God* (1937), and his posthumous publication on the *Apocalypse of John* (1948), a book he regarded as a fitting summation of his life's work.[145]

While Bulgakov's overall vision remains remarkably consistent throughout his years of exile, the works of this period witness to a more consciously ecclesial and patristic sensibility. The shadow of Soloviev begins to loom less large; references to Schelling, German mysticism, the Kabbalah, and other more esoteric sources tend to decrease as the references to scriptural, patristic, and liturgical sources increase. This shift doubtless owes something to his ordination, to the shock of exile, and to the growing need to defend his theology against a rising tide of detractors.[146] It is

---

[142] This is not to say that Bulgakov ignores Christ in this work—far from it—rather that Christology is not as yet a prominent dimension of his Sophiology.

[143] The extent of Bulgakov's engagement with patristic material in the greater trilogy is somewhat obscured by the abridgement or omission of many of Bulgakov's copious footnotes (and some excursuses) in the English translation. This is not the case with the little trilogy or indeed the French translation of both trilogies by the formidable Constantin Andronikof. The French does, however, have issues of its own: for instance the French *Agneau de Dieu* omits the invaluable historical introduction.

[144] This essay, subtitled 'Scholia to *Unfading Light*', clarifies the fourth hypostasis language used in that work, specifying that Sophia is best described not as a hypostasis but as a principle capable of hypostasization. Bulgakov was at this time already coming under attack in the émigré community (notably by Metropolitan Anthony Khrapovitsky) for his views on Sophia.

[145] Dates refer to publication in the original Russian save for the summary *The Wisdom of God* (first published in English translation), *The Orthodox Church* (first published in full in English translation) and *The Tragedy of Philosophy* (first published in German).

[146] Bulgakov was ordained in 1918. He was later to remark that his whole theological vision was 'drunk from the bottom of the chalice'. See Andrew Louth, 'The Eucharist in the Theology of Fr. Sergii Bulgakov', 40, citing the report of Fr Boris Bobrinskoy in, e.g., *La compassion du Père*, 160.

also very much part of the unmodern turn that I have signalled, part of significant shift towards a more traditional and consciously patristic articulation of Sophiology.

The first book of the lesser trilogy, *The Burning Bush*, contains some exceptionally rich material on the patristic foundations of Sophiology. The book began as a presentation of the teaching of the Orthodox Church on the Virgin Mary in contradistinction to the Roman Catholic doctrine of the immaculate conception but expanded to embrace the Mother of God's place as the chief created instantiation of Sophia.[147] Bulgakov devotes considerable space to the defence of his doctrine of *Sophia*, especially in the book's three excurses. Bulgakov returns to the claim that Sophiology is essentially an outworking of the theology of St Gregory Palamas, a position he had outlined in *Unfading Light* and reaffirmed in 'Hypostasis and Hypostaseity'.[148] In an excursus 'On the Glory of God in the Old Testament', Bulgakov insists that the revelations of God's glory (*kavod*) in the Old Testament (e.g. Ex. 16:7, 10; Is. 6:1–7; Ez. 1–2) can only be properly understood within the context of Sophiology. The glory of God is precisely the *wisdom* of God manifest in the world:

> The Divine Glory is Wisdom or, to use the language of St Gregory Palamas, already received within Orthodoxy, the energy of the energies of God, which alone are accessible to the creature, the very essence of God being inaccessible ('transcendent').[149]

Bulgakov emphasizes the Christological and Mariological dimensions of such revelations: revelations of uncreated and created wisdom respectively. He concludes that the Mother of God is to be understood as the supreme creaturely instance of wisdom who by virtue of her perfect deification reveals the triune deity in the world: 'She is the Glory of the world, the Burning Bush, a creature burning in but not consumed by the divine flame of the Holy and Life-giving Trinity.'[150]

A further and more extensive appeal to Palamas is made in the second excursus, 'The Doctrine of the Wisdom of God in the Old Testament'. Bulgakov, it should be noted, places greater emphasis on the Old Testament figure of wisdom than Florensky, let alone Soloviev. In the excursus, Bulgakov discusses the undeniably personal characteristics of the wisdom figure depicted in Proverbs, Wisdom, and Ecclesiasticus along with the patent difficulties in associating that figure with just one of the divine hypostases, whether this be the Son or the Spirit—and here Bulgakov alludes to the interpretations of SS Theophilus of Antioch and Irenaeus

---

[147] St John Maximovitch provides a non-polemical but trenchant critique of Bulgakov's Mariology in his *The Orthodox Veneration of the Mother of God*.

[148] In A. F. Dobbie-Bateman, B. Gallaher, and I. Kukota (tr.), 'Protopresbyter Sergii Bulgakov: Hypostasis and Hypostaticity: Scholia to the *Unfading Light*', 24.

[149] *The Burning Bush*, 212 [ET 117–18].   [150] *The Burning Bush*, 233 [ET 130].

of Lyons, both of whom associate wisdom principally with the Spirit.[151] Bulgakov avers that the patristic tradition is far from clear on the proper interpretation of Old Testament wisdom texts, thus opening the way for what he admits is a personal opinion based on his own engagement with the scriptural witness. Bulgakov finds it impossible to reduce texts such as Wisdom 7 to any one divine hypostasis and points out that references to wisdom as being loved by God, sharing the life of God, and being initiated into the knowledge of God (as in Wisdom 8) make it necessary to somehow distinguish wisdom from God.[152] Bulgakov concludes that wisdom should be understood as the divine self-revelation in the world, a revelation that is proper to all three persons of the Trinity. At this point he refers back again to Palamas, highlighting the description of wisdom as the energy of God in Wisdom 7:26. Bulgakov rightly observes that in St Gregory's theology energy pertains to the Trinity as a whole and not to any one person alone, and that wisdom, *qua* energy, may be designated God—specifically God in the world, not according to essence or hypostasis but according to his life-giving revelation.[153] Bulgakov goes on to opine, in a deeply revealing footnote:

We consider a positive doctrine on this question to be an unresolved task of Orthodox theology. [Orthodox theology] is called upon to elaborate[154] the Orthodox doctrine of the divine energies, distinct from the hypostatic essence of God, and associated with the name of St Gregory Palamas. The author attempted to express this *theologoumenon* in his essay 'Hypostasis and Hypostaseity' [...], to which those interested are referred. We think it appropriate, however, to add that we have in no way advanced some new doctrine. We have simply tried to make sense of the veneration for Divine Sophia that already exists in church tradition, as well as offering some interpretation of this fact. As a result no new dogma is established but only some theological reflection is proposed concerning a dogmatic fact already present in the Church. And anyone who denies the very question denies this fact as well. The *onus probandi* of such a denial of church tradition falls on him.[155]

These are fighting words: anyone who denies the place, prominence, and problematic of wisdom in Church tradition is denying Church tradition itself. While admitting that his articulation of Sophiology is a personal opinion. Bulgakov categorically asserts that it is based on the solid rock of Church tradition—it is a 'theological reflection concerning a dogmatic fact already present in the Church'. Orthodox theology is called to join in this process of outworking in particular

---

[151] *The Burning Bush*, 239 [ET 134]. Cf. Chapter 3.2 and 3.4.
[152] *The Burning Bush*, 239–50 [ET 133–8].   [153] *The Burning Bush*, 249–50 [ET 138].
[154] Развивать: develop, articulate, explicate, elaborate, unfurl.
[155] *The Burning Bush*, 254n [ET 141n].

through further explication and elaboration of the theology of St Gregory Palamas. It is worth noting that while Florensky saw his Sophiology as an outworking of Athanasius, Bulgakov privileges Palamas as his chief patristic support.

Bulgakov does not, of course, ignore Athanasius. Indeed the third excursus of *The Burning Bush* is dedicated precisely to 'The Doctrine of the Wisdom of God in St Athanasius the Great'. Bulgakov had some reservations concerning Athanasius' theology while acknowledging the restrictions entailed by the exigencies of the Arian controversy. Overall, he regards his theology, especially concerning the relationship between God and the world, as 'incomplete, imprecise, unfinished' albeit sufficiently clear in its 'general direction'.[156] Bulgakov does not, for example, see the need to associate wisdom exclusively with the Son (a move that would obviate some of the exegetical difficulties posed by Proverbs 8:22). He also judiciously appealed to the Hebrew text which gives 'possessed' for 'created' and proposes his own interpretation in which the wisdom possessed by God from all eternity represents the eternal world of ideas, as taught (without specific reference to this text) by Dionysius, Maximus, and John of Damascus.[157] Bulgakov was wary of the radical contingency of the world implied in Athanasius' doctrine of creation *ex nihilo*. For his part, he preferred to see the creation as a natural but entirely free consequence of the infinite love of God. Lastly, Bulgakov was also uncomfortable with the ontological discontinuity between uncreated and created wisdom in the Athanasian schema—though was himself obliged in his later work (somewhat against his initial instincts) to accept and embrace precisely such a distinction (albeit within the context of a considerably more developed Chalcedonian Christology). But overall, Bulgakov did see, with some justice, a basic confirmation of elements of his Sophiology in Athanasius: most notably in respect of the double character of wisdom: the created wisdom reflecting and imaging the divine and eternal wisdom—God in the world and the world in God. But for all the attention he lavishes on Athanasius in this excursus, it is interesting that he cannot help but give Palamas the last word. He closes the excursus, and the book, with the observation that:

> The teaching of St Gregory Palamas on the divine energies concerns sophiology according to its inner sense, but to establish the connection would require a special study which would go beyond the confines of the present excursus.[158]

Bulgakov was, alas, never to produce such a study. although he does return to Palamas on occasion in his greater trilogy (*On Divine Humanity*).[159] In the *Lamb*

---

[156] *The Burning Bush*, 266 [ET 146].   [157] *The Burning Bush*, 285–8 [ET 155–6].

[158] *The Burning Bush*, 288 [ET 156]. According to its inner sense: по внутреннему смыслу.

[159] Palamas does not crop up in the remaining two books of the lesser trilogy save for a brief reference to his views on angels—views already discussed in *Unfading Light* (*Jacob's Ladder*, 195 [ET 140]).

of God, arguably his master-work, he references Palamas' teaching on the energies as infinite radiations of the *ousia* and observes, doubtless with an eye to his own detractors, that Palamas was accused of polytheism for this teaching.[160] Shortly after this wry comment, he explicates Palamite teaching in terms of the distinction between God as Absolute and Absolute-Relative:

> In his dogmatic language, St Gregory Palamas expresses this antinomy of the Godhead when he speaks of the being of God, his *ousia*, inaccessible and hidden from the creature and which he distinguishes from his accessible and revealed *energeia*. Leaving aside the question of the appropriateness of these terms, we see that what is at issue here is the relation between God and the world. God *exists* in reality only as energy, while God in himself, *Deus absconditus*, simply does not 'exist'. But in his energy, we know the essence of God, it begins to *exist* only in relation. Thus the fundamental schema of Palamas is the idea of God as Absolute-Relative; he includes relation (but not of course relativity) in the very definition of God.[161]

It must be said that Palamas, apart from this extraordinary paragraph, recedes somewhat into the background in this book—an understandable development given its subject matter. Bulgakov focusses, rather, on the specifically Christological dimension of Sophiology. Indeed, he greatly strengthens his overall case by anchoring his Sophiology much more robustly in Christological dogma. He demonstrates extraordinary expertise in his treatment of the articulation of Christology up to and beyond the Ecumenical Council of Chalcedon (451). He will please many a contemporary sensibility in his willingness to explore and engage constructively with positions and persons designated as heretical. But perhaps the most compelling passages concern the 'dogmatic miracle' of Chalcedon itself, a Christological achievement that is far more than the sum of its Alexandrine and Antiochene parts. Fully recognizing the turmoil unleashed by the Chalcedonian definition, Bulgakov avers that it was theologically ahead of its time, indeed perhaps of any time. Setting the bounds within which infinite possibilities of the dogma of the incarnation might be explored, expounded, and expanded, it serves as a religious symbol whose riches and significance belong to all ages, indeed perhaps particularly to our own time:

> It belongs to no less, and perhaps more, to our own time than to the time of its origin. One would like to think that it is precisely our time, with its yearning for theological synthesis, that is historically the Chalcedonian era, called to a new religious and theological opening-up and appropriation of this gift of the Church.[162]

---

[160] *Lamb of God*, 139–40 [ET 116].   [161] *Lamb of God*, 143n [ET 122n].
[162] *The Lamb of God*, 80 [ET 62].

Bulgakov's own unpacking of the primordial mystery of the unconfused union of divinity and humanity in Christ revolves, as one would expect, around Sophiological considerations. He views the incarnation in terms of the hypostasization of Sophia: Christ 'unites in the unity of his two natures the divine Sophia, as his divinity, and the created Sophia, in his humanity'. He is thus designated 'the wisdom and power of God' in a double capacity: as the hypostasis of the divine and of the created Sophia. So far, so Athanasian. The great strength of *The Lamb of God* is that it grounds Sophiology in classical Trinitarian theology and Christology. It goes some way to eliminating the liminal zone between uncreated and created natures that marked and indeed marred earlier work such as *Unfading Light*. Bulgakov has also rowed back on and clarified the incautious and highly problematic 'fourth hypostasis' language of that work: Sophia is not a hypostasis but a principle capable of hypostasization.[163] But Bulgakov is certainly not prepared to restrict himself to what amounts to a re-stating of patristic positions with some increased emphasis on wisdom themes and terminology. He offers instead a bold and arresting interpretation of the incarnation.

What is perhaps most distinctive about Bulgakov's approach is that he refuses to consider the incarnation solely in terms of the incarnation of the second person of the Trinity. Sophia, he argues, is also hypostatized in the Mother of God (as created wisdom) and Holy Spirit (as divine wisdom). The Mother of God and the Holy Spirit are thus also 'the wisdom of God' existing in created and uncreated forms, respectively. There are, moreover, two hypostases of created wisdom: 'the incarnation of Christ is realized not in one person but in two'. Created wisdom is hypostasized within the divine hypostasis of the Logos and within the female human hypostasis of Mary.[164] Without her nature *and* hypostasis, the incarnation would not have been possible: 'Christ could receive the human nature only through birth. But the human nature does not exist extrahypostatically. Therefore the New Adam could come into the world only through the New Eve.'[165] This is why the icon of the incarnation shows both Christ and Mary—the two hypostases of the incarnation of Sophia.

Anything lacking in the Virgin Mary because of the Fall was made up by the Holy Spirit enabling her to be all that the human creature was intended to be, to be perfectly deified: 'His descent crowned her sophianicity, so that the ontological postulate became a reality.'[166] The birth of the Word of God was the work of created wisdom hypostasized in the Virgin Mary, filled with the Spirit as uncreated wisdom. It was a new birth with no male involvement, mirroring the pattern

---

[163] See further Dobbie-Bateman, Gallaher and Kukota (tr.), 'Protopresbyter Sergii Bulgakov: Hypostasis and Hypostaticity: Scholia to the *Unfading Light*'.

[164] Chalcedon speaks of two natures in one person. Bulgakov bids us in addition to think of one nature (of created wisdom) in two persons (Christ and the Mother of God). *The Lamb of God*, 226–8 [ET 201–2].

[165] *The Lamb of God*, 225 [ET 200].   [166] *The Lamb of God*, 226 [ET 200–1].

of human conception envisaged before the Fall.[167] She is rightly glorified as Queen of Heaven and the personification of the Church—even though the Church has yet to fully grasp the significance of her glorification.[168] As created wisdom, she participates in the incarnation not only in her flesh but also hypostatically, that is, 'spiritually, consciously, in an inspired and sacrificial manner'. The incarnation was her 'personal, spiritual-corporeal work', strengthened by the Spirit.[169]

This is by any estimation a remarkable account of the incarnation. There is, of course, a great deal more to his Christology (particularly in terms of the divine self-emptying or *kenosis*) but what concerns us here it not so much his theological contribution to Christology, which is undeniably vast and rich, but the question of its foundation in Church tradition. Bulgakov characterizes his Christology as an attempt to supply positive content to the largely negative and only broadly prescriptive content of the Chalcedonian Definition. Chalcedon has four 'no's' (without confusion, without separation, without change, without division). Bulgakov proposes a 'yes'—a Sophiological interpretation of the incarnation that gets us to the heart of the unconfused union of divinity and humanity—to its inner meaning and nature.[170] According to Bulgakov, Chalcedon and the three Ecumenical Councils that followed did not go much beyond the outward conjunction of divinity and humanity in Christ. They proclaimed inspired truths, 'but they left them in the form of dogmatic schemata for future theological development'.[171] Bulgakov is quite candid about the fact that he is engaged in just such a process of theological development—one that must go far beyond the kind of summary presentation we find, for example, in St John of Damascus.[172] While he establishes the patristic and conciliar foundations of Christology with great care and expertise, he is very consciously going beyond the Fathers and beyond the councils, venturing into areas they did not and could not. There is no great claim for theological continuity here save in the sense that he is completing a work left unfinished by the Fathers and by the councils. Certainly, he understands his Christological reflections as consistent with patristic and conciliar tradition, indeed as making up what it lacks, but in the final analysis he expressly goes beyond anything that can be readily anchored in that tradition. What is interesting here is the rather different sort of claim he makes about Palamite theology as an express forerunner of Sophiology. While Palamas cuts a relatively low profile in the *Lamb of God* and in the second volume of the trilogy, *The Comforter*, he resurfaces with some éclat in the final volume, *The Bride of the Lamb*.

---

[167] *The Lamb of God*, 227 [ET 201].   [168] *The Lamb of God*, 227 [ET 202].
[169] *The Lamb of God*, 227 [ET 201]. Such statements such as this help explain Bulgakov's cautious and partial sympathy with the notion of the Mother of God as Co-Redemptrix notwithstanding his trenchant rejection of the failed Roman Catholic doctrine of the immaculate conception. Cf. *The Lamb of God*, 232n [ET 206n.].
[170] *The Lamb of God*, 232–3 [ET 206–7].   [171] *The Lamb of God*, 238–9 [ET 210–11].
[172] Ibid. [note that ET excises the reference to the Damascene]. See further the essay on 'Dogma and Dogmatics' and Chapter 7.1.1.

In *The Comforter*, Bulgakov indicates that he is aware of the existence of Palamas' then unpublished work on the vexed question of the procession of the Holy Spirit (the *Apodictic Treatises*). On the basis of excerpts contained in anti-Palamite writers such as Demetrios Kydones, he does not believe it to contain any new arguments in the matter of the *filioque*—a judgement he would surely have changed on actual inspection of the text.[173] Also, in *The Comforter*, when speaking of the gift of the Holy Spirit in the creation, Bulgakov draws a connection to Palamas' teaching. As the energies may be described as God (allowing that God cannot be described as energy: the propositions are not reversible), so the gift of the Holy Spirit in the creation is the Holy Spirit: distinct but not separated from the giver.[174] Having said that, Bulgakov, glossing over the limited nature of his acquaintance with the Palamite corpus, laments: 'Palamas virtually ignores the complex and essential problem of the relation of the energy to the hypostases (if we do not count a number of scattered and imprecise statements).'[175] This is a woeful underestimation of the seriousness with which Palamas approaches this particular question, as we will argue in Chapter 7.1.3. Bulgakov also wonders whether we might not distinguish between the presence of the Holy Spirit and his power along similar lines to those laid out by Palamas in his distinction between divine *ousia* and *energeia*. This would have been an impossible task, however, given that the presence of God in the world is never conceived by Palamas in terms of *ousia*. But in any event, he immediately throws up his hands on the project with the despairing complaint that, 'The theology of Palamas is so undeveloped and incomplete that a special study is still required regarding the true meaning of this doctrine and the actual meaning of its basic concepts.'[176]

In *The Bride of the Lamb*, the third volume of the great trilogy *On Divine Humanity*, we encounter the single most important summary of Bulgakov's mature position on the patristic (and specifically Palamite) foundation of Sophiology. The book is a treatise on ecclesiology, conceived in the light of Sophia. The author of the English translation, Boris Jakim, calls it, 'the crowning glory of Bulgakov's theology (and one of the crowning glories of twentieth-century Christian theology in general), the most mature development of his sophiology'.[177] Within a chapter on the sophianicity of the world, Bulgakov gives an elegant and

---

[173] *The Comforter*, 138 [ET 109]. For Palamas' 'Orthodox *filioque*', cf. my *Orthodox Readings of Aquinas*, 37–9.

[174] Cf. *The Bride of the Lamb*, 70n [ET 61n]: 'God is Sophia as Divinity, but Sophia or Divinity is not the hypostatic God'.

[175] *The Comforter*, 281 [ET 244]. Note that in his earlier work, *The Burning Bush*, 249 [ET 138], Bulgakov had not seen any great problem with the Trinitarian dimension of the essence-energies question in Palamas.

[176] *The Comforter*, 326 [ET 288]. It is of course something of an irony that those who undertook this special study: Georges Florovsky, Vladimir Lossky, and, above all, John Meyendorff did so precisely as a counter to Bulgakov's Sophiology.

[177] *The Bride of the Lamb* [ET], xiii.

revealing précis of patristic sophiology. He opens with the assertion that because the earliest patristic literature is non-systematic (with the exception of St Irenaeus), the problematic of Sophia simply does not arise. It does so only with Origen who, fatally and fatefully, identified Sophia with the Logos. Bulgakov finds that this identification lies at the heart of Origen's and all subsequent Trinitarian subordinationism.[178] The failure to distinguish between the created and divine Sophia skewed the whole of patristic sophiology from the outset. It is the first sin, 'the πρῶτον ψεῦδος, the primordial defect of all patristic sophiology which was forced to fit the entire sophiological problematic into logology and even Christology'.[179] But all was not entirely lost. Bulgakov christens the common patristic understanding of the pre-existence of the divine world of ideas, para-digms, or prototypes an 'applied sophiology'. Here he appeals to St Gregory the Theologian, St John of Damascus, St Maximus the Confessor, Dionysius the Areopagite, and St Augustine.[180] 'This doctrine of the ideal proto-ground of the world', he writes, 'seeps into patristics and occupies a place next to Christology (even a place next to Christological sophiology).' But such Fathers, for Bulgakov, do not sufficiently address the question of the relation of this divine realm of ideas with God the Word and indeed with divine and created Sophia. Are they eternal or created? Do they pertain to God or are they brought forth to provide an ideal ground for the world? Such questions remain unanswered, thus Bulgakov can opine: 'Patristic sophiology remains essentially incomplete on this question, and therefore different interpretations of it are possible.' A full devel-opment of patristic sophiology requires consideration not only of the Logos as wisdom but also of the realm of ideas 'in their mutual correlation and harmon-ization'.[181] Bulgakov goes on to propose his take on the question in terms with which we are by now familiar: these ideas exist in the divine Sophia from all eternity but are implanted in created Sophia in an act of creation to form the ideal foundation of the world. They are thus a self-revelation of the Holy Trinity in both uncreated and created forms. In failing to resolve the question along these lines, patristic theology remains radically underdeveloped, 'like a torso without a head'. In sum, 'patristic sophiology remains in an incomplete and unclear form, a kind of sophiological ambiguity'.[182]

---

[178] The Bride of the Lamb, 20 [ET 15].

[179] The Bride of the Lamb, 20 [ET 16]. Here he references back to his excursus on Athanasius in The Burning Bush: Athanasius was, he claims, forced to distinguish two aspects of Christ (before/outside the incarnation and after it) in order to make sense of his scriptural identification with wisdom.

[180] The Bride of the Lamb, 20–1 [ET 16]. Bulgakov calls Augustine 'Blessed Augustine' in line with common Russian practice. It does not, at least in Bulgakov's case, imply any inferiority of sanctity: the Orthodox Church has no equivalent to the Roman Catholic practice of beatification as a preliminary step towards sainthood.

[181] The Bride of the Lamb, 21 [ET 16–17].

[182] The Bride of the Lamb, 21–2 [ET 17–18]. Незавершенный: incomplete, unfinished.

Bulgakov does not find much improvement in later centuries: 'In Eastern theology, the development of theology after St. John of Damascus is broken off in connection with a general stagnation of thought. Thought is squandered on a fruitless, scholastically schismatic polemic with Rome concerning the procession of the Holy Spirit.'[183] This is, by any measure, a woeful underestimation of the state and scope of Byzantine theology between the eighth and fourteenth centuries, a period dismissed with the blunt comment that, 'The sophiological-cosmological problematic lies dormant for six centuries'.[184] But happily, after six centuries of stagnation, some theological vitality returns:

> Byzantine theology once again approaches this question in St. Gregory Palamas' doctrine of energies, which is essentially an incomplete sophiology. The basic idea of Palamism is that, alongside God's transcendent 'essence', there is his manifold revelation in the world, his radiation in 'energies'. But Palamas' doctrine of essence and energies remains incomplete in relation to the dogma of the Trinity, in particular with the doctrine of the distinctness of the three hypostases and of the unity of the Holy Trinity. The basic idea of Palamism concerning the multiplicity and equal divinity of the energies in God reveals the πολυποίκιλος σοφία τοῦ θεοῦ, 'the manifold wisdom of God' (Eph. 3:10). Palamas considers the energies primarily under the aspect of *grace*, the super-created 'light of Thabor' in the created world. But these energies have, first of all, a world-creating and world-sustaining power which is precisely characteristic of Sophia, the Wisdom of God, in both of her forms: Divine Sophia, the eternal first principle of the world, and created Sophia, the divine force of created life. The sophiological interpretation and application of Palamism lies in the future.[185]

Once again, Bulgakov kicks a full exploration of Palamas' 'incomplete sophiology' into the long grass while bemoaning its insufficient attention to Trinitarian theology.[186] There follows a fascinating excursus on Aquinas whom Bulgakov finds clearly defective in his treatment and understanding of both divine and created Sophia, notwithstanding his admirable apprehension of the pre-existence

---

[183] *The Bride of the Lamb*, 22 [ET 18].

[184] He does, however, allow that St Symeon the New Theologian's doctrine of deification, while not consciously addressing the sophiological problematic, is nonetheless inherently sophiological. *The Bride of the Lamb*, 22n [ET 18n].

[185] *The Bride of the Lamb*, 23 [ET 18–19].

[186] Cf. also *The Bride of the Lamb*, 335 [ET 309]: 'On the one hand, these energies are divine (cf. Palamas' formula: energy is God, *Theos*); on the other hand, they are indeterminately multiple or multiform, since their reception depends on the degree of the recipient's spiritual growth. But according to St. Gregory Palamas these energies remain nonhypostatic and, in general, are not hypostatically qualified. This can be partly explained by the incomplete character of his doctrine, where, in general, the relation between the hypostases in the Holy Trinity and the energies remains unclarified.'

of the divine realm of ideas.[187] The remainder of the book contains only a few further glimmerings of his understanding of Palamas. For instance, the relation between created and uncreated Sophia is explicated in terms of the divine energies. The energies 'radiate from the transcendent incomprehensibility of the divine Ousia-Sophia.[188] And these lightnings illuminate the night of pre-being, of "nothing".' In this way, the uncreated energies of God receive a created, relative, limited, multiple being. Created wisdom is established as an image of uncreated wisdom and, on that basis, the universe is brought forth.[189] But while the actual attention he pays to Palamas is relatively spare, he is sufficiently assured of his overall position as to assert:

> With the adoption of Palamism, the Church has definitively entered onto the path of accepting the sophiological dogma. But the theological realization of this acceptance still requires a long path of understanding. Essential here is he connection with *Imiaslavie* [Name-glorifying] which recognized the divine reality and power of the divine-human name of Jesus and, in general, the power of the name of God in the world. It is not for nothing that *Imiaslavie* is linked with Palamism. However, these particular applications of sophiology do not yet get to the root of the sophiological problem.[190]

This is a bold claim: in accepting Palamism, the Church has set itself on a path towards accepting Sophiology. Bulgakov does not make this claim of any other Church Father or Church teaching. It is no surprise that criticisms of Bulgakov tend to focus not only on more general questions of patristic fidelity but also very much on the specific question of fidelity to the teaching of St Gregory Palamas. Bulgakov makes Palamas the chief field of battle in what was to become a struggle for the heart and soul of Orthodox theology: this is why Palamas is of such central importance in this study. It is no exaggeration to say that Bulgakov set the trajectory and defined the parameters of much of twentieth-century Orthodox theology albeit largely, as it turned out, by way of reaction. Indeed the two most notable features of Orthodox theology in that century—the notion of neo-patristic synthesis and the retrieval and revival of Palamite theology—are both in a real sense the children of Bulgakov, children who rebelled against the father. We shall see how this filial rebellion developed in the following section.

---

[187] *The Bride of the Lamb*, 24–40 [ET 19–33]. Bulgakov finds that Aquinas leaves the realm of ideas ontologically hanging. Cf. pp.216–17.

[188] This is not a term used by Palamas.

[189] *The Bride of the Lamb*, 72 [ET 63]. It is worth noting that Bulgakov sets Palamite theology within the framework of an understanding of God as *actus purus*. This is a connection explicitly rejected by John Meyendorff who regards the notion of God as pure act to be wholly antithetical to the Palamite achievement. 'Theology: East and West', 678.

[190] *The Bride of the Lamb*, 23–4 [ET 19].

1.5 Detractors and Defenders

It is important to recognize that both sides of the Sophia Controversy accepted that the patristic tradition is somehow foundational, that is to say that it provides an indispensable framework and a grounding for the elaboration of Orthodox theology. It was also widely accepted that the appropriation of that tradition could never be simply a question of repetition or reiteration, it had to be a creative retrieval, a creative reaffirmation if Orthodox theology was to meet the challenges and questions posed by the modern world. The crucial question was just how creative that retrieval could be. Could one in some sense correct, complete, or even go *beyond* the Fathers? After years of rumbling, the question of whether Fr Sergius had indeed gone too far beyond the Fathers came to a head in the mid-1930s.

Bulgakov's Sophiology was condemned in 1935 by Metropolitan Sergius (Stragorodsky) of Moscow and, apparently independently, by the ruling synod of the Russian Orthodox Church outside of Russia (ROCOR).[191] Neither of these two authorities (which were not in communion with one another) had any episcopal oversight or canonical jurisdiction over Bulgakov who belonged to the Russian Exarchate of the Patriarchate of Constantinople under Metropolitan Evlogy (Georgievsky) and which was itself not in communion with either Moscow or ROCOR. Nevertheless, the condemnations hit Bulgakov hard, created wide-ranging and intense theological controversy, and poisoned the theological and intellectual life of the Russian diaspora in Paris and beyond for decades. Metropolitan Sergius in his *ukaz* (decree) warned his faithful that Bulgakov's teaching should be shunned as fundamentally foreign to the Orthodox faith. He stops short, however, of characterizing it as strictly heretical. The *ukaz* declares that Bulgakov's teaching gives too much credence to the views of heretics, constitutes a revival of Gnosticism, sees sin and redemption in cosmic rather than personal terms, misunderstands the doctrine of the Holy Trinity, and makes numerous other eccentric and arbitrary assertions.[192] Metropolitan Sergius' information came, by his own account, largely from one Alexei Stavrovsky, a dubious character recently ejected from the St Sergius Theological Institute (of which Bulgakov was Dean) and from the young Vladimir Lossky.[193] Similar accusations were levelled in the ROCOR condemnation, albeit with a greater level of detail and forcefulness including the assertion that Bulgakov's teaching was certainly heretical and required public recantation.

---

[191] On the Sophia affair, see further Alexis Klimoff, 'Georges Florovsky and Sophiological Controversy' and Paul Gavrilyuk, *Georges Florovsky and the Russian Religious Renaissance*, 132–58.

[192] Text with Bulgakov's trenchant reply in О Софіи, Премудрости Божіей. Указь Московской патріархіи и докладные записки проф. прот. С. Булгакова митрополиту Евлогію.

[193] Note that the condemnations were to some extent also assaults on the authority of the Paris Exarchate and on the reputation of the St Sergius Institute.

Bulgakov went to great lengths to defend himself against these condemnations, rightly noting their dubious authority, procedural inadequacy, and misrepresentation of his teaching. He also insisted on the provisional nature of his theological opinions while vigorously asserting his freedom to hold them, grounded as they were in the tradition—scriptural, patristic, liturgical, and iconographic. Metropolitan Evlogy, for his part, appointed a theological commission which acquitted Bulgakov of heresy but raised some theological concerns. A minority report followed which essentially followed the majority view but placed a greater accent on the seriousness of the theological problems in Bulgakov's work.[194] In such a state of ambiguity the official process of investigation ended and Bulgakov went on to complete his greater trilogy with scant concession to his detractors— indeed with an ever greater insistence on the patristic and especially Palamite foundations of his Sophiology.

But while official ecclesiastical processes ended rather inconclusively, the debate about Sophiology rumbled (and rumbles) on. Bulgakov himself set great store by the concept of reception: that is to say conciliar and other teachings must be received over time by the Church if they are to become part of the ecclesiastical firmament.[195] Bulgakov himself (like Origen before him) was quite clear that he was submitting his teaching, his personal theological opinion (*theologoumenon*), to the wider judgement and reception of the Church. In this sense, Bulgakov, it must be admitted, is hoist by his own petard. There is no doubt that the reception of Sophiology in the Orthodox theological world was overwhelmingly negative for much of the twentieth century and this thanks above all to three figures: Vladimir Lossky, Fr Georges Florovsky, and Fr John Meyendorff. While things may be beginning to change as we move further into the twenty-first century, the neo-patristic and neo-Palamite anti-Sophiological reaction retains a powerful hold on Orthodox theology (and not without reason).

Vladimir Lossky (1903–58) was undoubtedly the most vigorous and unabashed critic of Bulgakov. The pamphlet he prepared on *The Sophia Controversy* (1936) denounces Bulgakov in the most strident of terms. In tone it is not unlike some of the more intemperate perorations that pervade contemporary internet platforms. Lossky presents Bulgakov's teaching as a poisonous confection that threatens the very life and identity of the Orthodox Church. It is a revival of Gnosticism, a disavowal of apophatic theology, a species of pantheism, functional Apollinarianism, a triumph of philosophy over theology, a downplaying of the personal dimension of deification, a form of universalism—and all based on delusion. It propagates numerous grave theological errors—above all a confusion of nature and personhood. He regards Bulgakov's interest in Church tradition as merely antiquarian—an archival approach

---

[194] The minority report was prepared by Fr Sergei Chetvernikov and signed, rather reluctantly, by Fr Georges Florovsky.
[195] This viewpoint is adumbrated in the essay 'Dogma and Dogmatics'.

that takes bits and pieces of a functionally dead past and builds them into a monstrous edifice that is comprised largely of esoteric and non-Orthodox elements. Taking his cue from Bulgakov's own work, Lossky pays particular attention to St Gregory Palamas, advising Bulgakov to re-read that Father more thoroughly and so come to appreciate how far removed his thought is from any human philosophy. Lossky claims that, 'Palamas' whole life was a struggle against the philosophical "Thomist" system of the Barlaamites.[196] Gregory did not pursue his own theological or philosophical system but sought rather the Light of impregnable Truth.'[197]

Lossky finds that Bulgakov misunderstands, misrepresents, and misquotes Palamas on multiple occasions—notably in respect of Trinitarian theology and anthropology. Lossky also rightly accuses Bulgakov of misusing a quote regarding multi-hypostaseity[198] and argues that he much overstates what Gregory says of human as opposed to angelic nature. This mis-appropriation is just one part of a broad and profoundly disturbing picture. All in all, Bulgakov's teaching must be strenuously avoided and resisted.

For all that it hits home on numerous points, this pamphlet is not Lossky's best work. In particular, it entirely fails to offer any sort of balance or nuance in its critique. While Lossky never went back on its basic conclusions, he certainly came to regret its tone and the damage it inflicted. Indeed, Lossky's personal esteem for Fr Sergius seems only to have grown in the course of his life. At some risk, he walked miles across German-occupied France to attend Bulgakov's funeral in July 1944.[199] Towards the end of his life he confided to the great Catholic theologian Fr Louis Bouyer that, 'Even if we cannot accept Fr Sergius' conclusions, we must acknowledge that he has posed the right questions.'[200]

None of this gradual mellowing altered Lossky's conviction of the fundamental wrongness of Fr Sergius' system. In his master-work, *The Mystical Theology of the Eastern Church*, Lossky laments the excessive personalism of Bulgakov's Trinitarian theology finding that it witnessed, as had that of Origen, to an endemic propensity within Eastern theology to privilege *hypostasis* over *ousia*.[201] Lossky also bemoans Bulgakov's alleged conflation of ecclesiology with cosmology as giving rise to a confusion that has led to a de-Christianization of the notion of the world.[202] As regards Palamas, Bulgakov's fundamental error, for Lossky, is that he retrojects the divine energies into the divine essence, taking wisdom (an energy of God) to characterize and determine the very principle of the Godhead—the *ousia*.

---

[196] Lossky is on shaky historical ground here: Palamas had no acquaintance with Thomas while Barlaam and his successors (Akindynos and Gregoras) display no sympathy whatsoever with Thomas or Thomism. Cf. my *Orthodox Readings of Aquinas*, 30n.

[197] Lossky, *The Sophia Controversy*, 22.   [198] Lossky, *The Sophia Controversy*, 26n.

[199] See Olivier Clément, *Orient-Occident: Deux passeurs: Vladimir Lossky et Paul Evdokimov*, 91–3.

[200] Louis Bouyer, 'An Introduction to the Theme of Wisdom and Creation in the Tradition', 160.

[201] *Mystical Theology* [ET], 62: Bulgakov privileges person over nature by seeing wisdom-*ousia* as the revelation of the three hypostases.

[202] *Mystical Theology* [ET], 112.

Attributes or energies such as wisdom, argues Lossky, are 'an exterior manifest-ation of the Trinity which cannot be interiorized'.[203] In his lecture courses, he would mention Bulgakov on occasion, for instance, pushing back against Bulgakov's notion of God's self-revelation to himself—a notion Bulgakov had tied to Palamas.[204] But it would be a mistake to restrict the scope of Lossky's disagreement with Bulgakov to specific references such as these. Lossky's whole work stands as a conscious rebuttal of Fr Sergius' teachings, invariably written off as 'Russian religious philosophy' rather than theology proper. With a pronounced accent on mystical experience, apophatic theology, and the Palamite essence-energies distinction, Lossky's distinctive account of Orthodox theology has become paradigmatic.

What has only been appreciated relatively recently are the commonalities between the two writers.[205] Lossky inhabits very much the same cultural, intellec-tual, and theological universe as Bulgakov and shares many of the same basic presuppositions and perspectives—for instance their broadly oppositional accounts of Western and Orthodox theology, the focus they place on the theology of St Gregory Palamas, and their conviction of the need for a creative re-appropriation of patristic tradition.[206] Perhaps the struggles between them were so fierce precisely because they shared so much.

Fr Georges Florovsky (1893–1979) ceded little to Lossky in his antipathy to Sophiology but was most reluctant to engage in any direct public criticism of Bulgakov whom he held in great personal esteem and who had appointed him to the chair of patristics at the newly-founded St Sergius' Institute in Paris. Florovsky did all he could to avoid being sucked into the controversy that convulsed the Russian theological community in Paris during the 1930s. In particular, he largely absented himself from the work of the theological commission established by Metropolitan Evlogy.[207] But Florovsky's attempted self-recusal marked him out as a less than enthusiastic ally of Bulgakov who enjoyed wide support at the Institut Saint-Serge and beyond. Florovsky's standing within the émigré community was much diminished by the Sophia affair and this precipitated his departure to the New World following the conclusion of the Second World War. But even in the United States, where he spent the remainder of his life, Florovsky maintained a

---

[203] *Mystical Theology* [ET], 80.

[204] *Orthodox Theology: An Introduction*, 48. More on Lossky's interpretation of Palamas in Chapter 7.1.3.

[205] Here the pioneering study is that of Rowan Williams: 'The Theology of Vladimir Nikolaievich Lossky: An Exposition and Critique', 32–4 and *passim*. See also Brandon Gallaher, 'The "Sophiological" Origins of Vladimir Lossky's Apophaticism' and my *Orthodox Readings of Aquinas*, 193–7.

[206] Florovsky was considerably more nuanced and less polarized in his account of East–West theological difference than either Bulgakov or Lossky. See my *Orthodox Readings of Aquinas*, 197–204. And while he acknowledged Palamas to represent a kind of apex of the Orthodox theological tradition, in practice he focused more on Athanasius and the Cappadocian Fathers as chief archetypes of the Orthodox theological tradition.

[207] See above, p.59.

strict policy of abstaining as far as possible from overt public criticism of Bulgakov even while making his views abundantly clear in personal conversations and correspondence.[208] While this self-denying ordinance was largely successful, there is no doubt that Florovsky's entire theological vision is thoroughly anti-Sophiological in both conception and execution. In his insistence on strict fidelity to the Fathers, his approach to history, his almost allergic reaction to Origen and indeed heresy in general, and his constant insistence on the deleterious effects of Western theological and philosophical influences on Orthodox thought, Florovsky consciously distances himself from his sometime confessor and mentor.[209] Moreover, Florovsky's accounts of major theological *topoi*—creation, Trinitarian theology, Christology, Mariology, ecclesiology—are all very deliberately designed in silent but obvious contradistinction to those put forward by Bulgakov.[210] Only relatively rarely does the theme and concept of wisdom crop up at all in his work. A short piece on 'The Hagia Sophia Churches' underlines the dedication of the Great Church of Constantinople to Christ as wisdom, an identification that reflected a patristic consensus on this question, notwithstanding Theophilus' and Irenaeus' identification of wisdom with the Spirit. 'There is no reason or hint whatsoever', Florovsky bluntly asserts, 'to suspect that any other dedication of the Sophia-churches was ever known or used in the Byzantine Church.'[211] Florovsky also quite correctly points out the late development of the concept of a patronal feast and the fact that the dedications of the cathedrals of Kiev and Novgorod to the Virgin Mary are, in any case, attested no earlier than the fifteenth century. This is in opposition to the view of 'some scholars who were inclined to see in that [dedication] a special contribution of Russia to the theology of Wisdom'.[212] Florovsky also offers a brief reading of the iconographic tradition of the depiction of wisdom. In terms of Byzantine art, he underscores the relative rarity of

---

[208] As he wrote to Fr Alexander Schmemann in 1949, recalling the situation in Paris 25 years earlier: 'The Church Fathers were ignored and culture began with Solovyov and Dostoevsky [for] Bulgakov, Zenkovsky, and Berd[yaev]. Then I reminded them that the main thing is genuine ecclesiality and, therefore, the patristic foundation, but this was not at all popular'. In Paul Gavrilyuk (ed.), *On Christian Leadership: The Letters of Alexander Schmemann and Georges Florovsky (1947–1955)*, 171.

[209] This distancing, even a form of intellectual parricide, seems to be a regrettably recurrent feature of the modern Orthodox world. One sees it to some degree even in Bulgakov and Soloviev and still more clearly in Florovsky and Bulgakov, Schmemann and Florovsky, and others.

[210] See especially, 'Creation and Creaturehood', 'The Ever-Virgin Mother of God', 'The Lamb of God', 'Saint Gregory Palamas and the Tradition of the Fathers', and 'St. Athanasius' Concept of Creation'. See also Angel Angelov, Pavel Pavlov, and Stoyan Tanev, 'The Sophiological Controversy as a Clash of Different Patristic Interpretations'. In this splendidly documented joint article, the authors compare and contrast the patristic reception and fidelity of Bulgakov and Florovsky to the decided favour of the latter, concluding, 'For Florovsky, this was not just a matter of aligning with the majority of Church Fathers, but rather an ability to think as a member of the Church, rather than as an autonomous religious philosopher'.

[211] 'The Hagia Sophia Churches', 131–3. The piece is a résumé of a conference paper that was never given due the outbreak of the Second World War. The original version has footnotes: 'Christ, the Wisdom of God, in Byzantine Theology'.

[212] 'The Hagia Sophia Churches', 133.

depictions of wisdom and notes that they tend to either depict Christ in some form (especially as an angel) or to depict wisdom as a virgin (drawing here from classical models). The Russian depiction of wisdom, dating back no earlier than the fifteenth century, develops and accentuates these traditional Byzantine motifs without substantially departing from them. The Novgorod icon, for example, is best understood as 'a peculiar sort of Deisis' with Christ as wisdom flanked by the Virgin Mary and St John the Baptist.[213]

In what appears to be a longer but earlier version of essentially the same study, Florovsky also discusses the Old Testament allusions and other symbolism that appear in Russian depictions of wisdom from the sixteenth century onwards.[214] He finds that in such developments, the icon moves from representing faces to representing ideas. Florovsky views this development as part of a broader pattern of Russian appropriation of Western thought and imagery, and so a form of *pseudomorphosis*.[215] A tangible example comes in the appropriation of the *Gnadenstuhl* or Mercy Seat image (the Crucified Christ held by the Father).[216] Along with the wide circulation and emulation of German and Flemish engravings (including various winged depictions of Christ) he draws particular attention to the work of Henry Suso, a mystic and devotee of wisdom whose contribution to devotion to Sophia we have already noted.[217] Florovsky sees in the Novgorod Sophia and related depictions an infiltration of Western forms and models that generated a most unwelcome allegorizing tendency in Russian iconography. In icons of the Kiev Sophia, associating Sophia more obviously with the Mother of God, Florovsky sees even clearer signs of Western influence to the point of celebrating Roman Catholic teachings on the immaculate conception (a doctrine Bulgakov had vigorously opposed). For good measure, he goes on to point out quite how late the various Russian liturgical compositions devoted to wisdom are and thus scarcely immune to *pseudomorphosis*. Florovksy's relatively spare treatment of some of the key iconographic and liturgical witnesses appealed to by the Russian Sophiologists proved remarkably effective in queering that particular

[213] 'The Hagia Sophia Churches', 134–5.

[214] 'О почитании Софии, Премудрости Божией, в Византии и на Руси.'

[215] This is Florovsky's term for the malformation of the Russian Orthodox tradition caused by the influence of Western thought and culture (cf. *Ways of Russian Theology, passim*) Ivan Viskovaty becomes something of a hero for him—a government minister who denounced artistic innovation in C16 Russia, targeting those who painted 'according to their own understanding and not in accordance with sacred tradition'. He was particularly perturbed by images of the Father and of Christ in the form of a winged angel (either white or red), images he plausibly attributed to 'Latin wisdom'. Viskovaty, in accordance with the Council in Trullo, favoured depictions of historical persons rather than allegorizing images or Old Testament prefigurations, 'О почитании Софии', §4.

[216] See further Ágnes Kriza's excellent, 'The Russian Gnadenstuhl'. Kriza's doctoral thesis, 'Depicting Orthodoxy: The Novgorod Sophia icon reconsidered' argues against Florovsky's reading of this icon and seeks more generally to rescue it from the many and various misunderstandings introduced by its involvement in the Sophia controversy. Her own (quite bold) conclusion is that the winged angel Sophia represents the Orthodox Church.

[217] See above, p.19.

pitch—or at least muddying the waters to such an extent that appeals to such sources in support of Sophiology were to lose much of their original force.[218] For all his reluctance to get personally involved in the Sophia affair, Florovsky contributed greatly to the unravelling of some of its key supports.

Between them, Lossky and Florvosky created a neo-patristic paradigm that proved immensely successful in largely side-lining if not entirely quashing modern Russian Sophiology in the latter half of the twentieth century. Claiming to be the true bearers of authentic Orthodox tradition, Lossky and Florovksy were able to push Sophiology into a dark and dubious corner and into a dustbin labelled 'Russian religious philosophy'. But while both did a good deal of leg-work in indicating what a neo-patristic alternative to Sophiology might look like, neither undertook the kind of intensive investigation of St Gregory Palamas that was called for by Bulgakov himself. This was left to a younger contemporary.

Fr John Meyendorff (1926–92) studied at Saint-Serge in the period immediately following Bulgakov's death and at a time when his presence was still very much felt. He went on to play a central rôle in the development of St Vladimir's Orthodox Seminary in New York. But Meyendorff seems to have been less impressed by Bulgakov than his long-standing colleague Fr Alexander Schmemann who admired Fr Sergius greatly, above all as a liturgical theologian and celebrant, while distancing himself from his Sophiology proper.[219] It was Meyendorff who undertook the massive scholarly labour of producing a comprehensive account of Palamas that relied on his whole corpus of works rather than only the painfully limited selection of works previously available in published form.[220] Meyendorff's crowning achievement was his edition in 1959 of the *Triads in Defence of the Holy Hesychasts*, an early but tremendously important dogmatic work in which Palamas fleshes out the doctrine of the essence-energies distinction for the first time. Meyendorff observes in his *Introduction à l'étude de saint Grégoire Palamas*, also published in 1959, that some historians have come to hasty conclusions by using their imagination in the absence of published sources.[221] Whether or not this particular comment is a dig at Bulgakov, it is clear that Meyendorff's presentation of Palamas differs markedly and consciously from that of Bulgakov.[222]

---

[218] Leonid Ouspensky's *Theology of the Icon* follows Florovsky's lead in treating the development of Russian iconography from the sixteenth century onward as a history of gradual decline and *pseudomorphosis* under western influence. He himself favoured and practised a return to Byzantine models and norms.

[219] Cf. Alexander Schmemann, 'Trois images'.

[220] The larger part of Palamas' work (Meyendorff estimates a full three-quarters), including some of his principal dogmatic works, remained unedited and unpublished well into the post-war period. The appendices of his *Introduction à l'étude de saint Grégoire Palamas* (331–415) give an idea of the sheer scale of the manuscript work undertaken by Meyendorff. The appendices are, unfortunately, omitted in the English translation.

[221] *Introduction à l'étude de saint Grégoire Palamas*, 12.

[222] See below, pp.234–5.

Meyendorff also wades into the iconographic discussion very much in line with the broad-brush approach of Florovsky but with far closer attention to art historical detail.[223] He allows that the practice of using Old Testament and angelic forms to depict wisdom has solid roots in late Byzantine and medieval Serbian and Bulgarian art—something Florovsky did not acknowledge. But Meyendorff is clear that such depictions of Sophia pertain very obviously to the second person of the Trinity and sees a continuity of this practice in icons such as Novgorod Sophia which he, like Florovsky, sees as a form of *Deisis*. Meyendorff backs up this assertion with an extensive appeal to the patristic tradition, including a fascinating reference (previously noted by Florensky) to Palamas' disciple Patriarch Philotheos Kokkinos' exegesis of the wisdom figure in Proverbs to refer (1) to the undifferentiated energy of the Trinity; (2) to the Son of God; and (3) to Virgin Mary as the house of wisdom.[224] Like Florovsky, Meyendorff sees a marked decline and confusion from the seventeenth century onwards, a confusion perceptible in the ambiguity of some of the representations of wisdom from this period and in particular in the conflation of wisdom with the person of the Virgin Mary.[225] He sees a similar confusion in the office of holy wisdom produced in the same century by Prince Symeon Shakovsky. Meyendorff concludes his survey with a brief treatment of the attempt by Florensky and Bulgakov to justify their Sophiology by appeal to such images and texts. Meyendorff acknowledges that both figures engaged in a sincere concern to connect the essentially Gnostic mysticism of Soloviev with the tradition of the Church but finds this appeal markedly unsuccessful:

> This concern expressed itself in attempts to interpret the Wisdom iconography – which they knew primarily through its later Russian expressions – and the liturgical creation of Shakhovskoy, to which they tended to attribute too much importance. Of course, the arguments, based on the iconographic and liturgical tradition, were quite peripheral to Florensky's and Bulgakov's basic conception of the Divine Wisdom as the eternal foundation of existence, essence of God himself, but also eternal humanity, by whose power creatures came into being. They used iconographic examples more like proof-texts than real arguments. It is

---

[223] 'L'iconographie de la Sagesse Divine dans la tradition Byzantine' and 'Wisdom-Sophia: Contrasting Approaches to a Complex Theme'. The papers cover much the same ground but the English text, while somewhat briefer on the patristic and iconographic material, has a closing section on post-Byzantine developments, including modern Russian Sophiology.

[224] 'L'iconographie de la Sagesse Divine dans la tradition Byzantine', 262. Cf. Florensky, *Pillar and Ground of Truth*, 557 (n.693). Kokkinos produced five discourses on Proverbs 9:1 ('Wisdom has builded her house'). The reference to energy can be found in Logos 3.15 (Pseftonkas 89–90).

[225] 'Wisdom-Sophia: Contrasting Approaches to a Complex Theme', 400. Meyendorff also draws attention to the objections made in the C15 by the monk Zinovy of Otna to Metropolitan Gennady's establishment of the Dormition of the Virgin as the patronal feast of the cathedral of St Sophia in Novgorod. While Meyendorff finds this development perfectly defensible in that the Mother of God is certainly the house or seat of wisdom, he resists any attempt to identify her with wisdom *per se*.

therefore easy for art historians and historians of Christian thought to approach such questionable references with some irony. And indeed, confusion of methodologies is the worst enemy of authentic knowledge. It remains, however, that the historical rôle and intellectual prestige of the Russian 'sophiologists' are great, and their commitment to religious philosophy – for which some of them paid with their lives – deserves respect on a level different from that of art history. That they were the ones to raise again the issue of Wisdom explains much of the modern interest in the ambivalent and complex theme of the divine *Sophia* in Christian art and in religious thought in general.[226]

Without quite closing down the conversation regarding the depiction of wisdom, and with due respect, Meyendorff is nonetheless quite damning in his dismissal of the iconographic and liturgical appeals of modern Russian Sophiology as threadbare and fanciful. Coupled with his substantive and distinctly anti-Sophiological and anti-Bulgakovian presentation of Palamas, Meyendorff solidified the neo-patristic and neo-Palamite response to Bulgakov in the most uncompromising of terms.[227]

But it would be wrong to suggest that Bulgakov's star was entirely eclipsed by such potent criticisms. The faculty of Saint-Serge remained broadly supportive of Bulgakov for many years after his death.[228] Bulgakov also found a particularly eloquent and powerful defender in Paul Evdokimov. Evdokimov's theology (written largely in French) stands in direct continuity with Bulgakov under whom he studied at Saint-Serge and whom he regarded as 'the greatest theologian of the age'.[229] He called Sophiology 'the glory of modern Orthodox theology' and took pains to preserve and perpetuate its key intuitions—on the relation between God and the world, on primordial divine humanity, and the inescapable duty of Orthodox theology to confront the great issues and problems of our time.[230] And whereas Bulgakov had very deliberately kept Sophia out of his general account of Orthodoxy (*The Orthodox Church*), Evdokimov had no such hesitation in his own book *L'Orthodoxie*. In his account of the creation in this book, Evdokimov speaks of the pre-existent divine realm of ideas as created Sophia (and corresponding to Maximus' doctrine of the *logoi*, 'the created aeonic eternity'), made in the image of the eternal wisdom of God and forming the ideal foundation of the world.[231] The created world is thus a vast icon of the divine wisdom. Each of us is called to conform to our own creation in wisdom, to our

---

[226] 'Wisdom-Sophia: Contrasting Approaches to a Complex Theme', 401.

[227] See also his 'Creation in the History of Orthodox Theology' containing a highly critical account of Sophiology. In this article, Meyendorff finds that in wishing to maintain some sort of continuity between God and creation, Bulgakov effectively denies the doctrine of *creatio ex nihilo* (op. cit., 32).

[228] See, especially, Lev Zander, Бог и мир (миросозерцание отца Сергия Булгакова) and 'Die Weisheit Gottes im russischen Glauben und Denken'.

[229] *L'Orthodoxie*, 36 [ET 45].   [230] *L'Orthodoxie*, 87 [ET 93].

[231] *L'Orthodoxie*, 87 [ET 93].

own *logos*. All true knowledge comes from the contemplation of the underlying wisdom of the created world notwithstanding the perversities and frustrations into which it has fallen on account of human misuse of free will.[232] Perceiving the sophianic character of the cosmos, whether in nature or art or music or human love, enables one to enter into the great cosmic liturgy: the movement of the world towards God and God towards the world.

Evdokimov's work roots all of his teaching in copious patristic testimony but does so in a consciously creative manner deliberately designed to provide a counterpoint to what he saw as the potential neo-scholasticism of the neo-patristic approach.[233] While the difference between the two approaches is more apparent than real (more to do with conclusions reached than method and basic presuppositions), one noticeable difference is the sympathy he displays to figures such as Origen and Evagrius—figures not highly favoured by neo-patristicians and who continue to attract considerable scholarly interest in our own day despite or rather precisely because of the disputed orthodoxy of some of their key positions.[234] Evdokimov also leans heavily on Athanasius, the Cappadocian Fathers (especially Gregory of Nyssa), Maximus (making more of him than does Bulgakov), and Palamas. Like Bulgakov and his neo-patristic epigones, Evdokimov regards Palamas as the apex and summation of Orthodox patristic theology.[235] He follows Bulgakov in emphasizing the theme of wisdom in his exposition of the doctrine of the divine energies, seeing wisdom as the common energy of the three hypostases and remarking that, 'Only Palamism, with its doctrine of the divine energies, allows for a correct sophiology'.[236]

Evdokimov thus provides a useful paradigm for an appropriation of modern Russian Sophiology that maintains its key insights while obviating some of its more problematic tendencies. In particular, Evdokimov avoids positing Sophia in hypostatic terms—whether as distinct hypostasis or principle capable of hypostasization. There is no liminal or antinomical 'in-between' status for Sophia in Evdokimov's thought. He also avoids identifying Sophia with the divine *ousia*, with God's self-revelation to himself. And while he has plenty to say about the feminine dimension in God, he does so largely through his contemplation of the Holy Spirit (*Panagion*) and the Virgin Mary (*Panagia*) and not through means of some sort of eternal feminine within or alongside God. While certainly prepared to expand upon the patristic witness he is far less prone than Bulgakov to correct

---

[232] Cf. *L'Art de l'icône*, 78, 80. Evdokimov has an acute sense of the gravity of the Fall and delves at length into the consequent obscuring of the sophianic character of the cosmos.

[233] *L'Orthodoxie*, 194 [ET 200–1].

[234] Evdokimov also draws deeply from ascetic fathers such as Macarius and SS Diadochus, Ephrem, Isaac of Nineveh, and Symeon the New Theologian.

[235] *L'Orthodoxie*, 25–28, 184–5 [ET 34–35, 191].

[236] *La femme et le salut du monde*, 202 [ET 203n] :'Seule le palamisme, sa doctrine sur les énergies divines, permet une sophiologie correcte.' Cf. *L'Art de l'icône*, 296–7 [ET 348–9]. Evdokimov does not, however, engage in any sort of in-depth study of Palamas.

or chastise the Church Fathers for their various omissions and oversights.[237] He is willing to go beyond the Fathers only in the sense that one seeks to go beyond scripture to encounter the one of whom the scriptures speak.[238] Evdokimov also significantly tones down the specifically Russian dimension of Sophiology, de-emphasizing perplexing Russian icons and marginal liturgical compositions in order to focus on broader and more compelling themes of icon and liturgy. Evdokimov, in short, is rather more successful than Bulgakov in keeping largely within what Florensky called 'the bounds of Church ideas'. Evdokimov's is a relatively spare and dogmatically careful sophiology with Sophia pertaining to the being of God, to the pre-existent realm of divine ideas, and to the world created on that pattern by the divine energy which is wisdom. Pruned in this way of some of its more esoteric, puzzling, and problematic elements, Evdokimov has charted a course towards a new sophiological era—towards the full appropriation of this gift to the Church in a manner perfectly consistent with patristic tradition, towards what he calls a 'correct sophiology'.

But Evdokimov is not our only guide to such a re-envisioning of sophiology. Such a reappropriation will also require the distinctive insights of the neo-patristic approach, in particular those of Fr Georges Florovsky.[239] In a somewhat exasperated letter to Bulgakov in 1926, he gave a hint of what he understood by a properly traditional sophiology:

> I have long insisted that there exist two doctrines of Sophia, one might even say two Sophias, or, more exactly put, two images of Sophia: a true and genuine one on the one hand, and an illusory one on the other. In the name of the former, holy temples were erected in Byzantium and ancient Rus, while the latter served to inspire Soloviev and his Masonic and Western predecessors, all the way back to the Gnostics and Philo. Soloviev simply had no knowledge of Sophia of the Church; he knew the Sophia of Boehme and his followers, the Sophia of Valentinus and the Kabbalah. And this Sophiology is heretical and uncanonical. What you have found in Athanasius belongs to the other Sophia. There is even more about Her in Basil the Great and Gregory of Nyssa — the direct predecessors of Palamas.[240]

For Florovsky, patristic sophiology ('the Sophia of the Church) is to be construed either in terms of Christology or in terms of the divine operation or energy.

---

[237] Antoine Arjakovsky speaks quite rightly of Evdokimov's 'optique neo-patristique' and underlines his insistence that Bulgakov's Sophiology was essentially an outworking of Christology. *Essai sur le père Serge Boulgakov*, 75, 80.

[238] *L'Orthodoxie*, 52 [ET 59].

[239] In deliberately embracing both the neo-patristic and Russian religious 'schools', I am not only affirming their substantial commonalities but also drawing upon the example of theologians such as Paul Evdokimov, Olivier Clément, and Kallistos Ware who very consciously draw on both approaches.

[240] See A. Pentkovskii, 'Письма Г. Флоровского С. Булгакову и С.Тышкевичу', 202–7.

Florovsky argues that the divine energy of wisdom is revealed in creation through history and is articulated by, above all, Athanasius, the Cappadocians, and Palamas. The 'other' Sophia is an ahistorical and substantially non-Christian fiction that has led the Russian Sophiologists into all sorts of delusions and difficulties.

Between them, Evdokimov and Florovsky provide some important pointers as to what a re-appropriated and distinctly patristic, even neo-patristic, sophiology might look like. Like Lossky and Meyendorff, they follow Bulgakov in placing a definite accent on Palamas within their discussions of the patristic rootedness of modern Russian Sophiology. But none of these figures, or indeed anyone else, has ever pursued the question of patristic roots in any great depth. This is the gap this book is intended to fill. A 'correct' and more widely acceptable sophiology (at least as far as Orthodox theology is concerned) will, moreover, stand or fall not only by the general question of patristic fidelity but specifically by the extent it can be shown to be in continuity with the teaching of Palamas. This is no random exigency. As I have repeatedly emphasized in this chapter, Bulgakov himself categorically and consciously ties the banner of Sophiology to Palamite theology. Without Palamas, the whole edifice of Bulgakov's Sophiology collapses—and this by his own estimation. One cannot, in other words, have Bulgakov without also embracing Palamas.

This chapter has explored at some length the question of 'sophiology from above': the nature and contours of the patristic appeal made within modern Russian Sophiology—and the vigorous reaction that appeal provoked. Particular attention has been paid to the unmodern turn within that movement that entailed a concerted shift towards the patristic tradition, most notably and effectively in Bulgakov. But before turning back in earnest (in Chapter 7.1) to the question of patristic (and especially Palamite) roots and the attendant re-envisioning process (Chapter 7.2), the time has come to listen to 'sophiology from below', beginning with scriptural and classical presentations of wisdom.

2

Prolegomena

The following brief account is intended to set the scene for the later Christian reception of the figure and theme of wisdom—hence the modest title 'prolegomena'. While scripture was not the immediate source and inspiration of modern Russian Sophiology, it was absolutely the starting-point of all patristic reflection on the topic. The first section outlines and explores the wisdom literature and wisdom themes of the Old Testament and more specifically of the Greek Old Testament, or Septuagint.[1] The second section tackles the vitally important dimension of the classical wisdom tradition, an important point of reference for the patristic tradition. The third section addresses the treatment of wisdom in the New Testament in which preceding wisdom traditions are both fulfilled and altogether exceeded.

2.1 Wisdom in the Old Testament

We need, at the outset, to be clear what we are talking about and this is by no means a straightforward exercise. Wisdom, in the biblical context, is a multivalent and far-reaching term or, better, nexus of ideas. It brings us to the heart of Israel's complex and multiform self-understanding and self-articulation. The theme of wisdom, in one form or another, is found virtually throughout the Bible albeit in a far from even spread. Those books of the Old Testament especially associated with the theme of wisdom are conventionally classified as 'wisdom literature'. These include Proverbs, Job, Ecclesiastes, the Song of Songs, Ecclesiasticus (The Wisdom of Jesus Ben Sira), and the Wisdom of Solomon. It should, however, be remembered that this classification is simply one of convenience and that the books so delineated are very far from presenting a unified 'theory of wisdom', still less from having a monopoly on the theme.[2]

---

[1] The Septuagint, and not the Hebrew Bible, was the principal text used by the Church Fathers both Greek and (at least until the advent of the Vulgate), Latin. The Septuagint remains the authoritative biblical text of the Orthodox Church.

[2] There is of course a great deal of material on wisdom outside these texts, each of which also addresses many other themes. Conversely, the Song of Songs never mentions wisdom in so many words but is nonetheless routinely treated as a kind of summit of wisdom literature in the Christian exegetical tradition. Will Kynes has recently, with some hyperbole, published *An Obituary for 'Wisdom Literature': The Birth, Death, and Intertextual Reintegration of a Biblical Corpus* in which he reminds us that the classification is a modern one and argues that it only serves to distort our apprehension of

Wisdom in Christian Tradition: The Patristic Roots of Modern Russian Sophiology. Marcus Plested, Oxford University Press.
© Marcus Plested 2022. DOI: 10.1093/oso/9780192863225.003.0003

As for the nature of wisdom itself: this is of course the nub of the question. Scriptural wisdom operates on three main interconnected levels. At its most basic level (S1), wisdom refers to a form of understanding drawn from everyday life and the natural world: knowledge based on experience and observation. More broadly, wisdom emerges as a way of speaking about the divine gift and inculcation of that mode of knowledge, about the educative process of formation (*paideia*) which gives rise to insight and intuitive understanding (S2). At its most developed level (S3), wisdom is presented not only as the object of this process but as an active divine subject or hypostasis calling humans to herself (and she is undoubtedly a 'she').[3] This was, of course, the dimension of the question that most animated the Sophiologists.[4] But while this last presentation of wisdom has an immediate fascination, raising as it does questions regarding the allowability of a complex monotheism (or indeed remnants of polytheism) within the religion of Israel, it should not be divorced from the wider dimensions of wisdom outlined here. An exclusive focus on the wisdom figure or personification runs a severe risk of wholesale distortion and misunderstanding and will certainly not help us in our exploration of wisdom in the later Christian tradition. While wisdom is by no means a univocal theme in the Old Testament, it is nonetheless a broadly coherent one, and one that should be approached as a whole encompassing the three levels or dimensions sketched here: wisdom as human knowledge, as divine gift and formation, and as active divine subject.

I shall in what follows attempt to tease out more fully the nature and character of Old Testament wisdom, working on the basis of what I take to be a representative sample of texts and themes.[5] Let me begin with Deuteronomy:

---

the biblical conception(s) of wisdom. I retain the term with all due caveats as a matter of convenience and note that it remains as yet unburied in the recently published *Wiley Blackwell Companion to Wisdom Literature* (eds. Adams and Goff).

[3] The term 'hypostasis' is of course an anachronism here but is widely encountered in the literature and serves as a useful marker for some kind of distinct divine subject.

[4] Bulgakov gives a potted summary of his reading of Old Testament wisdom references in Excursus II of *The Burning Bush*: 'The Wisdom of God in the Old Testament'. As one might expect, he leans particularly on Proverbs, Wisdom, and Ecclesiasticus (Ben Sira).

[5] Among the vast range of scholarly literature on this topic I should like to single out the following works, all of which have helped form my understanding of Old Testament wisdom: Murphy, *The Tree of Life*; von Rad, *Wisdom in Israel*; Weeks, *Early Israelite Wisdom*; Barton (ed.), *Where Shall Wisdom be Found?* (esp. articles by Moberly, 'Solomon and Job: Divine Wisdom in Human Life' and Hayward, 'Sirach and Wisdom's Dwelling Place'); Crenshaw, *Old Testament Wisdom: An Introduction*; Blenkinsopp, *Wisdom and Law in the Old Testament: The Ordering of Life in Israel and Early Judaism*; Dell and Barker (eds.), *Wisdom: The Collected Articles of Norman Whybray*; Wood, *Wisdom Literature*; Dell, 'Get Wisdom, Get Insight'; Collins, *Jewish Wisdom in the Hellenistic Age*. Of more recent works, Michael Legaspi's *Wisdom in Classical and Biblical Tradition* has emerged as a superbly lucid and suggestive overview of both classical and biblical wisdom traditions while Paul Fiddes, *Seeing the World and Knowing God: Hebrew Wisdom and Christian Doctrine in a Late-Modern Context*, sets up a fascinating dialogue involving Hebrew wisdom and some late- (deliberately not post-) modern thinking. Lastly, Dominque Cerbelaud has attempted a wonderfully comprehensive if somewhat whistle-stop survey in *Sophie: La figure biblique de la Sagesse et ses interpétations*.

Behold, I have taught you statutes and ordinances, as the Lord commanded me, that you should do thus in the land into which you go for an inheritance. Keep them and do them; for this is your wisdom and your understanding before all peoples, who, when they hear all these statutes, will say, 'Behold this great nation is a wise and understanding people.'   (Deut. 4:5–6)[6]

This text brings us straightaway to the heart of an important question within the field of scholarly debate concerning Old Testament wisdom: to what extent is wisdom teaching, literature, and theology compatible with the central tenets and thrust of what is often called Yahwism, the uncompromising and exclusive monotheism revealed only in the Law and only to the chosen people? In some sense this is an artificial question the answer to which is, even leaving aside the intractable question of the character and origins of the underlying source material, often skewed by preconceptions as to the narrowness of Israelite religion in the first place. It is, however, a fact that much (with some notable exceptions) of what we know as wisdom literature has comparatively little to say about the Torah and the special destiny of Israel. But this need not lead us to suppose the existence of two rival and incompatible traditions. Texts such as this make a conscious effort to link Torah and wisdom, claiming that the keeping of the law *is* wisdom. Proverbs and Ben Sira make essentially the same point: 'The fear of the Lord is the beginning of wisdom' (Prov. 9:10); 'The fear of the Lord is all wisdom; and in all wisdom is the performance of the law' (Ecclus. 19:20).

One other issue raised in the quote from Deuteronomy is the international dimension of wisdom. It is undeniable that there are significant commonalities between elements in Israel's wisdom tradition and that of other peoples in the ancient Near East—most famously Proverbs 22:17–24:22, seemingly modelled on the Egyptian *Teaching of Amenemope*. But such commonalities should neither surprise nor overawe us. Knowledge based on experience and observation represents a common storehouse accessible to and transmissible by all peoples. Equally, the communication and inculcation of such knowledge by means of example, admonition, and illustration was bound to produce many and varied patterns of accidental parallelisms and direct influences in the context of the ancient Near East. In other words, Israel's wisdom tradition was neither a wholly autochthonous development, hermetically sealed from outside influences, nor merely a localized instance of an international phenomenon. In the passage cited from Deuteronomy, dialogue with other wisdom traditions is explicitly acknowledged, with the proviso that it is the intimate and organic connection with Torah that is

---

[6] Biblical quotations in this section are from the Septuagint, generally adapted from Brenton, *The Septuagint with Apocrypha: Greek and English*. Books of the Bible are referred to in their usual English forms where these differ from the Septuagint form (e.g. I Kings not III Kingdoms, Isaiah not Esaias).

the distinguishing and superior feature of Israelite wisdom. This dialogue is also acknowledged in the next citation:

> And the Lord gave Solomon wisdom and understanding in great measure, and largeness of heart like the sand on the seashore. And Solomon abounded greatly beyond the understanding of all the ancients, and beyond all the wise men of Egypt. For he was wiser than all other men, wiser than Gaethan the Zarite, and Aenan, and Chalcad and Darala, the sons of Mal. Solomon uttered three thousand proverbs and his songs were five thousand. He spoke of trees, from the cedar that is in Lebanon to the hyssop that grows out of the wall; he spoke also of beasts, and of birds, and of reptiles, and of fish. And all peoples came to hear the wisdom of Solomon, and ambassadors from all the kings of the earth, who had heard of his wisdom.   (I Kings 4:29–34)

Again, the wisdom of Israel, as manifested in Solomon, is favourably contrasted with the wisdom of the nations. The theme of wisdom as gift, as *charism* is also evident: Solomon is endowed with wisdom and understanding in response to his prayer in I Kings 3. Wisdom emerges as no mere human accomplishment but rather as divine gift (S2), something that reminds us once again of the folly of distinguishing too sharply between the Yahwistic and wisdom traditions. As gift, wisdom can, by implication, be lost—but this is no way detracts from the value of the gift, nor from its essentially dynamic character. In the depiction of wisdom summed up in the person of Solomon, wisdom is far more a way of life to which Solomon is called than any sort of static quality. Wisdom certainly gives Solomon insight into the natural world and the human character, but this is an insight given for a very practical purpose. Solomon's exercise of wisdom is what is most at issue here, in particular the use to which he puts his wisdom in the proper and just governance of his kingdom. Such just governance presupposes Solomon's own personal integrity: the future good of the kingdom is explicitly linked to his keeping to God's statutes and ordinances (I Kings 9). Even at the height of his wisdom and prosperity, Solomon still has the capacity to reject his vocation in his uxorious pursuit of false gods (I Kings 10–11).

In such texts, wisdom emerges not so much as the accumulation of information but as the gift of the ability to apply one's knowledge. As gift, wisdom demands and requires faithful commitment to the giver and indeed a distinct sense of humility. This is made crystal clear in Book of Job:

> But where has wisdom been found? And where is the place of knowledge? No mortal knows its way, nor has it been found amongst men. The deep says, 'It is not in me,' and the sea says, 'It is not with me.' It cannot be gotten for gold, and silver cannot be weighed as its price [...] Whence then is wisdom found? And where is the place of intelligence? It is unseen by all men, and hid from the birds

of the air [. . .] God has established its way, and he knows its place. For he looks
over all that is under Heaven, and knows the things of the earth, all the things he
has made. When he set the weight of the winds and the measure of the waters, he
saw and numbered them, and made a way in the roaring of thunder. Then he saw
it and declared it; he prepared it, and traced it out. And he said to man, 'Behold,
the fear of the Lord, that is wisdom; and to depart from evil is knowledge.'

(Job 28:12–28)

In this extraordinary passage we are confronted with the paradoxical dual character of wisdom: at once known and unknown. Wisdom is not accessible to
mortals, bound as they are to the material creation. But at the same time, wisdom
is known to and established by God, and it is God who opens up to man the way of
wisdom. This way of wisdom is connected, once again, with the Torah, with the
keeping of the commandments that is the fear of the Lord. The Book of Job, of
course, also opens up a number of other dimensions of wisdom, most notably the
critique of the conventional wisdom (represented among Job's interlocutors) that
good behaviour necessarily brings material reward and bad behaviour the
opposite.

The close connection between wisdom and the created order is something that
emerges as a leitmotif of Old Testament wisdom. We see it, for example, in the
Psalms: 'O Lord, how great are your works! In wisdom you have made them all;
the earth is filled with your creation (Ps. 103(4):24).[7] This Psalm, like many others,
speaks eloquently of the theophanic character of the material world: the wisdom,
power, and majesty of God are declared by his creation. That creation in turn
echoes and hymns this theophany in its ontological doxology (cf. Ps. 148(9):1–13).

Other texts delve more deeply into the nature of this wisdom-related divine
theophany, notably Proverbs 8. Here we meet the figure of wisdom herself: an
active subject who is unambiguously feminine:

The Lord created me the beginning of his ways for his works. Before time was, in
the beginning before he made the earth, before he made the deeps or the springs
gushed forth, he set me up. Before the mountains were shaped, before the hills, he
begets me. The Lord made fields and wilderness, and the highest inhabited parts
of the world. When he prepared heaven, I was there with him; when he marked
out his throne upon the winds, when he made firm the clouds above, when he set
firm the springs of the earth, when he made strong the foundations of the earth,
then was I beside him ordering all things. I was that in which he rejoiced and
daily was I delighted before him at all times, for he was delighted when he
completed the world and his delight was to be with the children of men. And

---

[7] The numbering is that of the Septuagint with the Hebrew equivalent following in brackets.

now, my son, listen to me: blessed is the man who hearkens unto me, and the one who keeps my ways, keeping vigil daily at my gates and waiting at my entrances. For my goings out are the goings out of life, and in them is prepared favour from the Lord. But they that fall short of me sin against themselves, and they that hate me love death.   (Prov. 8:22–36)

In this very remarkable text, wisdom emerges as intimately connected with God's creation, the ordering principle of the universe, 'the beginning of his ways for his works'.[8] This appears to go even beyond the dialectic of presence and absence in Job 28, making wisdom a partner in the creation. It is worth noting in particular the sense of wisdom as the link-piece between God and his creation, the delight of God that reaches out to the children of men. This outreach is enlarged upon in the passage immediately following:

Wisdom has built her house, she has set up seven pillars. She has slaughtered her beasts, she has mixed her wine in a bowl, she has prepared her table. She has sent out her servants, calling with a high proclamation to the mixing bowl, saying, 'Whoever is foolish, let him turn aside to me!' To those who are without sense she says, 'Come, eat of my bread and drink of the wine I have mixed for you. Leave foolishness, so that you may reign forever. Seek understanding and attain intelligence in knowledge [. . .]. The fear of the Lord is the beginning of wisdom, and the counsel of the saints is intelligence: for to know the Law is [the sign of] a sound mind. For in this way you will live long, and years will be added to your life.   (Prov. 9:1–11)

Wisdom thus is not so much that which we seek but that which seeks us, not the object of enquiry but the active subject and source of all knowledge. The pursuit of wisdom, the answer to her invitation, is seen to demand and require considerable rectitude of life and personal effort. This brings us back to the theme of *paideia*, the training and formation through which we become suitable guests at wisdom's banquet. For all the quasi-mystical overtones of the encounter with Lady Wisdom outlined in the passages just cited, we must not forget that this encounter is very much part and parcel of an eminently practical approach to life, an approach rooted in the experience and contemplation of the realities of life. As Roland Murphy puts it, the real intent of Proverbs is 'to show what life is really like and how best to cope with it'.[9] Wisdom is not only that by which God founded the earth (Prov. 3:19) but also a 'tree of life to all that lay hold upon her and a sure support for those who rely on her, as on the Lord' (Prov. 3:18). To follow the path

---

[8] Note that the semantic range of the Greek ἀρχή encompasses the English words beginning, origin, principle, foundation, rule, power, authority.

[9] Roland Murphy, *The Tree of Life*, 15.

of formation laid down by wisdom is to live rightly in the fear of the Lord. This is a path that brings life in all its fullness: 'Take hold of my instruction (*paideia*) and do not let it go, but guard it for it is your life.' (Prov. 4:13).

This wise way of life is contrasted with the alluring temptations encapsulated in the feminine figure representative of folly in Chapters 5–7. This antithesis of wisdom offers only false love and illicit congress: 'Her house is the way to Hades and her chambers lead down to the chambers of death' (Prov. 7:27). All this is in stark opposition to the love and life offered by wisdom. In this striking version of the widespread two ways tradition, the ways of death and of life, woman emerges as a figure of both redemption and of damnation. As redeemer, wisdom is quite a force to be reckoned with: 'Counsel and surety are mine; prudence (φρόνησις) is mine and strength is mine. By me kings reign, and rulers decree what is just; by me the great are made great and by me princes rule over the earth. I love those who love me, and those who seek me shall find me.' (Prov. 8:14–17).

One final point regarding the treatment of wisdom in Proverbs is the question of reward. It is indeed true that wisdom brings life and love in all their fullness, but this by no means always implies material success: wisdom is a free gift proposed to all, rich and poor alike. Job, of course, goes further in demonstrating the fallacy of a straightforward reward system whereby good conduct automatically brings about material well-being. Such a viewpoint is comprehensively demolished in Ecclesiastes: 'Vanity of vanities, said the preacher, vanity of vanities, all is vanity!' (Eccles. 1:2). Ecclesiastes is a strange book, and one that can be read in very many ways. While it may be interpreted as a kind of 'last gasp' of the exhausted wisdom tradition of Israel, it is probably more accurate to take it rather more as a warning against self-satisfied and simplistic constructs of wisdom, constructs that would have us believe all is rosy when it patently is not. Ecclesiastes presents us with a strange mix of apophaticism and pragmatism. The preacher himself had set out 'to know wisdom, and to perceive the trouble that was upon the earth' but discovered that such perception is beyond human wit and ken (Eccles. 8:16–17). Rather than fretting overmuch as to the ultimate mysteries of life, he counsels us to 'eat your bread with joy and drink your wine with a glad heart' (Eccles. 9:7). There is, ultimately, no way of knowing why there is so much evil under the sun, why 'the race is not to the swift, nor the battle to the strong, nor bread to the wise, nor riches to those of understanding' (Eccles. 9:11). That said, wisdom is recognized as better than power and strength of arms (Eccles. 9:16–18) and a little wisdom as worth more than any amount of glory (Eccles. 10:1). Books, we may note in passing, are not likely to be of any great assistance. As the epilogist tells us: 'of the making of many books there is no end and in much study there is weariness of the flesh' (Eccles. 12:12). The sum of the matter is the familiar refrain: 'Fear God and keep his commandments, for this is the whole man.' (Eccles. 12:13).

The Book of the Wisdom of Solomon shows us very clearly that Ecclesiastes was by no means a last gasp. The theme of wisdom evidently remained an immensely fertile nexus of possibilities within the Jewish Diaspora, particularly as it came into ever closer contact with Greek modes of thought and expression. In this book, wisdom is saluted in the most exalted of terms:

> In her is an understanding spirit, holy, single, manifold, subtle, swiftly-moving, clear, undefiled [...]. For wisdom is more moving than any motion: she pervades and permeates all things because of her purity. For she is a breath ($\dot{a}\tau\mu\acute{\iota}s$) of the power of God, a pure effulgence ($\dot{a}\pi\acute{o}\rho\rho o\iota a$) flowing from the glory of the Almighty: therefore no defiled thing can fall into her. For she is the brightness of the everlasting light, the unspotted mirror of the activity ($\dot{\epsilon}\nu\acute{\epsilon}\rho\gamma\epsilon\iota a$) of God, and the image ($\epsilon\dot{\iota}\kappa\acute{\omega}\nu$) of his goodness. Being one she can do all things, and remaining in herself she makes all things new, entering in all ages into holy souls and making them friends of God, and prophets. (Wisdom 7:25–27)

Here wisdom is seen, once again, as a way of expressing God's self-revelation to and presence in the world, bringing the human creation into union with himself. She is also presented as a particularly existent being or, to use a later term, hypostasis. She is manifestly divine, an exhalation and image of God. She also appears to bear some relation to the Platonic world soul or the Stoic *logos*, the organizing principle of the universe.

The means by which this wisdom brings humanity to union with God is treated in terms of the divine *paideia*, the formation, discipline, or education of man by God in which God gives himself to humans as wisdom so as to make humans what he is. As in Proverbs, this self-offering is splendidly democratic:

> For she goes about seeking such as are worthy of her, and she shows herself to them favourably in the ways, and meets them in every thought. For the beginning of her is the most true desire of *paideia*. And the care of *paideia* is love: and love is the keeping of her laws: and the keeping of her laws is the firm foundation of incorruption; and incorruption brings us near to God. Therefore the desire of wisdom brings us to the kingdom. (Wisdom 6:16–20)

And lest we forget that the eternal life offered by wisdom is in no way separable from the special revelation of God accorded to Israel:

> [Wisdom] preserved the first formed father of the world, that was created alone, and brought him out of his fall, and gave him power to rule all things. But when the unrighteous went away from her in his anger, he perished also in the fury wherewith he murdered his brother. For whose cause the earth being drowned with the flood, wisdom again preserved it, and directed the course of the righteous in a piece of wood of small value. Moreover, the nations in their wicked conspiracy being confounded, she found out the righteous, and preserved him

blameless unto God, and kept him strong against his tender compassion toward his son. [. . .] She delivered the righteous people and blameless seed from the nation that oppressed them. She entered into the soul of the servant of the Lord, and withstood dreadful kings in wonders and signs. She rendered to the righteous a reward of their labours, guided them in a marvellous way, and was unto them for a cover by day, and a light of stars in the night season. She brought them through the Red Sea, and led them through much water: but she drowned their enemies, and cast them up out of the depths of the abyss.   (Wisdom 10:1–19)[10]

This intimate connection between wisdom and salvation history is something Joshua (or Jesus) Ben Sira also makes absolutely clear, again in the context of the Jewish Diaspora. Ben Sira straightforwardly equates the keeping of the commandments with the pursuit of wisdom: 'The fear of the Lord is all wisdom; and in all wisdom is the performance of the law.' (Ecclus. 19:20). Much of the book is concerned, as with all the wisdom texts studied thus far, with eminently practical advice as to how this works in practice both in terms of specific instructions and the process of formation it involves. Ben Sira also explicitly links the cosmological rôle and divine origin of wisdom with the special revelation to Israel:

I came out of the mouth of the most high, and covered the earth as a cloud. I dwelt in high places, and my throne is in a cloudy pillar. I alone compassed the circuit of heaven, and walked in the depths of the abyss. In the waves of the sea and in all the earth, and in every people and nation, I got a possession. With all these I sought rest: and in whose inheritance shall I abide? Then the Creator of all things gave me a commandment, and he that made me caused my tabernacle to rest, and said, Let your dwelling be in Jacob, and your inheritance in Israel. He created me from the beginning before the world, and I shall never fail. In the holy tabernacle I served before him; and so was I established in Sion. Likewise in the beloved city he gave me rest, and in Jerusalem was my power.   (Ecclus. 24:3–11)

This passage asserts very clearly the compatibility of wisdom, understood as universal principle and somehow divine being, with the special dispensation of Israel. It also implicitly claims for the wisdom tradition of Israel a superiority over that of the Hellenic tradition, as Robert Hayward, amongst others, has argued.[11]

While a brief survey such as this can hardly do justice to such complex and multivalent theme as is Old Testament wisdom, it will at least have delineated some of the main ways in which the theme is treated: wisdom as empirical

---

[10] As Bulgakov astutely comments: 'Here human history, more precisely the history of the economy of salvation, and even more precisely, the history of the Church in the history of the human race, is depicted as the work of Sophia, as the making and preserving of the sophianicity of a human being, beginning with its very creation'. *The Burning Bush*, 247 [ET 137].
[11] Hayward, 'Sirach and Wisdom's Dwelling Place'.

knowledge and intuitive understanding bound up with the observance of the Law and superior to that of the nations (S1); wisdom as a divine gift and process of formation (*paideia*) presupposing diligent observance of the commandments (S2); and wisdom as an active feminine divine subject, mediatrix, and cosmological principle somehow both transcending and immanent within the creation (S3). There is no doubt that modern Russian Sophiology does ample justice to the cosmological and theological dimensions of wisdom (S3). Indeed it fully celebrates and delights in all such aspects, very much including wisdom's feminine quality. It must, however, be admitted that it gives considerably less attention to more mundane and lived dimensions expressed in levels S1–S2. The Old Testament's construals of wisdom were, of course, to feed into the New Testament's attempt to make sense of one who claimed both to encompass and to exceed the wisdom tradition of Israel. But before turning to the New Testament, let us look briefly at another tradition that helped shape the early Church's construal of its encounter with wisdom incarnate: that of classical philosophy.

2.2 Wisdom in the Classical Tradition

It is no accident that the distinctive achievement of the ancient Greeks is summed up in the word 'philosophy'—the love and pursuit of wisdom. According to a hoary tradition, Pythagoras was the first of the Greek 'lovers of wisdom' to expressly adopt the title 'philosopher'. As St Augustine puts it:

> Shall we not be alarmed by the example of Pythagoras who dared not profess to be wise, but responded that he was a philosopher, that is a lover of wisdom? From this arose the name, that became thereafter the popular name so that however great one's learning in things pertaining to wisdom, either in one's own opinion or that of others, one is still only called a philosopher.[12]

This 'quest for wisdom' nicely encapsulates the nature of the Greek attempt to come to terms with and penetrate the mysteries and complexities of the cosmos.[13] Aristotle's description of the work of the earliest philosophers has them motivated primarily by their desire to understand the underlying principle or principles of the universe.[14] Various candidates arose: water in Thales, the divine indeterminate

---

[12] *De trinitate* 14.1.2. The same report is found in Diogenes Laertius, *Lives of the Eminent Philosophers* 1.12 (LCL 184).

[13] For some bold and salutary attempts to retrieve, rather against the tide, contemporary philosophy's grounding in the quest for wisdom see Mary Midgely, *Wisdom, Information, and Wonder: What is Knowledge For?* and David Conway, *The Rediscovery of Wisdom: From Here to Antiquity in Quest of Sophia.*

[14] *Metaphysics* 1.3 983b. References to classical works typically use the numbering given in the Oxford Classical Texts series when applicable.

in Anaximander, and air in Anaximanes (all three of Miletus). This quest for understanding was, however, always an endeavour conducted within an explicitly theological context as conveyed in Thales' supposition that 'all things are full of gods' (πάντα πλήρη θεῶν).[15] To marvel at and then seek to understand reality was in no way to detract from the recognition of its divine origin and source. It was also precisely a quest or search that had no illusions as to the provisional nature of any of its conclusions. As the pre-Socratic philosopher Xenophanes of Colophon expresses it in the late sixth or early fifth century BC: 'No man knows, nor will ever know, the clear and certain truth (τὸ σαφές) concerning the gods and all things.'[16] This is not to say that the pursuit of knowledge is useless but rather that it is limited: 'The gods have not revealed all things to mortals from the beginning but in time and by searching they discover better.'[17] Such is the essential paradox at the heart of the Greek philosophical achievement.

It is worth noting that Xenophanes' own work was set down not in prose but in poetry. That notwithstanding, we find in Xenophanes the beginnings of a philosophical critique of poetry, hitherto the unrivalled and unchallenged source of wisdom and truth. Plato, several generations later, was simply restating a truism in describing Homer as the 'educator of Greece', albeit merely as preliminary to a sharp critique.[18] Homer had presented a whole world-view in which the ethical standards expected of man were crystal clear—even if the doom of the gods hung over his every move. Xenophanes, however, pours scorn on the anthropomorphic and often unvirtuous character of the Homeric gods, deities far removed from his own conception of the greatest god, 'all of whom sees, all of whom knows, all of whom hears'.[19] He also goes on to distinguish not bravery or military prowess but wisdom (S1) as the chief human virtue and the most beneficial to the *polis* as a whole: 'for our wisdom (or skill, or talent: σοφίη) is better than the strength of men and horses'.[20]

This debate between poetry and philosophy is also evident in the work of the famous Heraclitus of Ephesus. Homer, he says, may have been the wisest of Greeks, but was not infrequently led astray.[21] Hesiod, similarly, may have had much learning but his mind had not been properly taught.[22] This is, however, more than just a critique of poetry since Heraclitus ranges Xenophanes, Pythagoras, and Hecataeus alongside Hesiod in his list of those whose learning

---

[15] Apud Aristotle, *De anima* 1.5 411a. This is a quote taken up without attribution by Bulgakov, *Unfading Light*, 230 [ET 235].

[16] Fr. 34 (KRS 186). The numbering of fragments follows Diels (ed.), *Die Fragmente der Vorsokratiker* (6th ed.). I have also, for convenience, given the fragment number of the selections given in Kirk, Raven, and Scholfield, *The Presocratic Philosophers* (2nd ed.) (KRS) where this applies. Cf. also Euripedes: 'σοφόν τὸ σαφές (that which is clear/true is also wise)' (*Orestes*, 397).

[17] Fr. 18 (KRS 188).   [18] *Republic* 606e.

[19] Fr. 11, 23, 24 (KRS 166, 170, 172). The quote is from Fr. 24.   [20] Fr. 2.   [21] Fr. 56.

[22] Fr. 40 (KRS 190). Cf. also Fr. 104: Heraclitus mocks those 'who place their trust in the popular bards and take the crowd for their teacher, not realizing that the many are bad, and the good few'.

has produced little of real benefit—an example of what W. B. Yeats would later disparage as 'blear-eyed wisdom [born] out of midnight oil'.[23] In this criticism we can see something of Heraclitus' understanding of the difference between true and false knowledge or wisdom. He takes sense experience as a valuable guide[24] but plainly sees the need to go much further than this, chiefly through his theory of the universal or common reason (λόγος). This inner principle of all things is described in various ways by Heraclitus, most notably, for our purposes, in terms of wisdom.[25] He speaks of the 'one wise thing' (S3) that rules the universe and makes what must be a deliberate parallel in describing the 'one wise thing', so far as we are concerned, as being conformity to that same governing principle (S1–S2).[26] But while aligning ourselves with this principle must be our aim in life (and indeed our responsibility, for 'man's character is his destiny')[27] this in no way demystifies the universe. Even the human soul contains depths that cannot be plumbed.[28] The same is true *a fortiori* of the ruling power of the universe: 'the one truly wise thing does and does not consent to be called by the name Zeus'.[29] Many of Heraclitus' more gnomic remarks attest to this double character of wisdom: both known and unknown—an antinomy also very much in evidence in the Old Testament depiction of wisdom.[30]

Parmenides of Elea stands as a particularly fine example of the power of reason to penetrate beyond surface appearances to the sustaining and underlying reality—again within an explicitly theological, even mystical, context. He uses the epic poetic form to emphasize the oracular character (and hence self-evident truth) of his pronouncements. He also claims direct divine authority, giving us an extraordinarily vivid account of his chariot-born ascent from darkness into light and to an encounter with an unnamed goddess who proceeds to instruct him in the way of truth, as distinct from that of mere opinion or seeming.[31] Parmenides learns from this goddess to place his trust only in that which is uncreated, eternal, and imperishable (but not unlimited), in short, in that which truly *is*. Only on this basis is knowledge possible or indeed desirable.

But it is with Socrates in fifth-century Athens that philosophy really comes into its own. The figure of Socrates emerges, through the lens of Plato, as the archetypal philosopher and one whose account of wisdom squarely encompasses our levels S1–S3. As recounted in the *Apology*, the oracle of Apollo at Delphi, no less, declares that no one is wiser than Socrates. Puzzled by this mark of favour, Socrates measures himself against others with a reputation for wisdom: statesmen

---

[23] 'Among School Children' first published in *The Tower*. [24] Fr. 55 (KRS 197).
[25] He also speaks of this inner principle as fire, war, strife, and justice.
[26] Fr. 32, 41 (KRS 228, 227). The phrase ἐν τὸ σοφόν is used in each fragment.
[27] Fr. 119 (KRS 247). [28] Fr. 45 (KRS 232). Cf. also Fr. 101 (KRS 246): 'I searched out myself'.
[29] Fr. 32 (KRS 228). Cf. also Fr. 93 (KRS 244): 'The lord whose oracle is at Delphi neither declares nor conceals, but gives a sign.'
[30] This antinomical character of classical wisdom was made much of by Florensky, cf. above, p.31.
[31] Fr. 1 (KRS 288).

(overconfident in their own wisdom), poets (inspired but not themselves wise), and craftsmen (wise in the particular but not the general). He concludes that it is his consciousness of his very lack of wisdom that distinguishes him: 'the god is truly wise and in this oracle he tells us that human wisdom has little or no value'.[32]

Socrates nonetheless sets himself on a mission to expose false and elicit true wisdom. Plato's *Theaetetus* is a good example. 'Philosophy', Socrates tells the eponymous young man, 'has no other starting point than a sense of wonder'.[33] While this dialogue—concerned primarily with the nature of knowledge—has few tangible conclusions, it serves above all as a marker of the immense scope of the philosophical pursuit. Other Platonic dialogues have more of substance to say about the goal of this endeavour. In the *Symposium*, the love of wisdom is intimately and organically connected with the love of beauty. As Diotima's famous speech puts it, the culmination of philosophy lies in the vision of true beauty, to which the lover of wisdom/beauty may ascend out of earthly beauty: 'drawing towards and contemplating the vast sea of beauty, he will bring forth many beautiful and noble thoughts and notions in boundless love of wisdom'.[34] The *Phaedrus* elaborates the connection between beauty, love and wisdom. The divine is described as 'beauty, wisdom, goodness, and all such qualities'.[35] The best of souls are those who have seen these qualities most clearly—the lovers of wisdom and beauty.[36] The lover of wisdom is described as the one who seeks to recover the soul's lost 'plumage', the primal heavenly state from which it has fallen. The soul regains its feathers by remembrance of the primordial beatific vision in which it once contemplated all the glories of the heavenly realm—glimpses and shadows of which it catches in the beauties of this world. Socrates calls this winged ascent and illuminative vision the 'most blessed of all mysteries'.[37] He further explains that beauty must be our first guide since the sight of wisdom, if such a thing were possible, would arouse in us a 'terrible desire'.[38]

It is a great mistake to dismiss the more mystical and explicitly theological dimensions of Plato as extraneous flights of fancy that serve only as packaging for the real business of his work: the cool and rational pursuit of knowledge by pure intellectual endeavour. Certainly Plato pushes human reason as far as it will go— but always *sub specie aeternitatis*, always with reference to the divine source of all wisdom. Philosophy was never, for Plato, a process of abstract speculation or the mere accumulation of information. It was, quite literally, a passion that acted upon the whole human being.[39] As the philosopher (and anthroposophist) Owen Barfield put it to C. S. Lewis, who had incautiously referred to philosophy as a subject: 'It wasn't a subject to Plato, it was a way.'[40] It was a way of life requiring

---

[32] Plato, *Apology* 19d–23b. The quote comes from 22e.
[33] *Theaetetus* 155d. This experience is spoken also spoken of as 'dizziness' (155c).
[34] *Symposium* 210d.   [35] *Phaedrus* 246e.   [36] *Phaedrus* 248d.   [37] *Phaedrus* 250bc.
[38] *Phaedrus* 250d.   [39] *Republic* 475b.   [40] C. S. Lewis, *Surprised by Joy*, 212.

intense ascetic effort and the active cultivation of virtue. It required a certain detachment from material anxieties as summed up in Socrates' rhetorical question, 'Is not the love of wisdom a practice of death.'[41] This daily and nightly remembrance of the time of the soul's separation from the body is understood to free the immortal soul from all the fears and concerns of the material and temporal world and to allow access to the underlying reality of things, to the divine world.

This sense of philosophy as a way of life encompassing all aspects of the human condition helps explain the supreme importance Plato gives to human education or *paideia* (S1)—the training, formation, and discipline necessary for the vision and apprehension of the nature of things—in the *Republic* and other works. Plato has no illusion that one can change society without first transforming its members. The educator is the one who through his maieutic method, his pedagogical midwifery, enables individuals to know, so far as is possible, both themselves and the world around them. Without the training and discipline of *paideia* the soul is rather like someone shackled since childhood in a cave, able to see only the shadows cast on the cave wall from a world they cannot see.[42] Naturally enough, such unfortunates take these shadows for reality, for it is the only reality they know. But if one of these prisoners were to be freed he will at first be unable to recognize what he sees in the world outside but will rather be dazzled and blinded by the sun and it will only be after a long process of training and discipline that he will be able to gaze upon that sun, source of light in that truly real world. In this most powerful and poetic of similes the whole Platonic vision of education is encapsulated. The cave simile shows us that the aim of education is the transformative vision and apprehension of the highest good, of reality in all its splendour—a quest for the perfecting wisdom that makes right thinking and right action possible.

Plato's account of wisdom was to prove remarkably enduring within the later neo-Platonist tradition which maintained and expanded its unabashedly metaphysical, mystical, and ascetic character. For Plotinus (205–270 AD), philosophy is, again, necessarily a way of life: 'God on the lips without a good conduct of life is a word.'[43] Plotinus defines wisdom in glowing terms as an immediate and beatifying experience of knowledge: 'That very life is wisdom, not a wisdom built up by reasonings but complete from the beginning, suffering no lack which could set it enquiring, a wisdom primal, unborrowed, not something added to the being, but its very essence'.[44] For Plotinus and his fellow neo-Platonists, wisdom becomes the lynch-pin of the universe, enabling and governing the soul's ascent back to unity with the One. Affirming, against the Gnostics, the

---

[41] Plato, *Phaedo* 81a.
[42] This is, of course, the famous Cave simile of Plato's *Republic* (514a ff.).   [43] *Enneads* 2.9.15.
[44] *Enneads* 5.8.4.

goodness of the material world, Plotinus declares that 'the universe is a life organized, effective, complex, all-comprehensive, displaying an unfathomable wisdom. How, then, can anyone deny that it is a clear image, beautifully formed, of the intellectual divinities? [...] And further, if the order of this universe is such that we are able, within it, to practice wisdom and to live our earthly course by the Supernal, does not that prove it a dependency 'of the divine?'[45] Wisdom is, quite literally, everything for Plotinus: the universe is one vast and glorious continuum of being: the divine wisdom manifested in the world and present within us is one of the chief means by which the soul is to grasp and realize its true identity with God. Such realization enables the soul to ascend out of materiality into the realm of ideas (the 'heavenly Aphrodite') and to find that there is, in truth, precious little 'in between' itself and the One.[46]

The neo-Platonist tradition was itself a reaction to a certain turn or shift to the more practical and applied (and less mystical) dimensions of wisdom (S1) evident in the centuries immediately following Plato. Here the key figure is Aristotle (384–322 BC). Aristotle follows Plato in treating wisdom as the foremost intellectual virtue and in dismissing the equation of wisdom with mere technical skill (τέχνη). His understanding of wisdom is most clearly elaborated in the *Nichomachean Ethics* in which he declares wisdom to be 'the most perfect of the modes of knowledge' and 'the science (ἐπιστήμη) and intellection (νοῦς) of the most exalted things'.[47] Here wisdom represents the consummation of the conjunction between science (deductive reasoning from first principles) and intellection (intuition of first principles).[48] He goes on to make a distinction between this wisdom (σοφία) and its applied counterpart: φρόνησις (prudence or practical understanding). This is not a distinction made by Plato for whom the terms are virtually synonymous. Practical understanding, for Aristotle, pertains necessarily to particular facts and circumstances, whereas wisdom pertains more obviously to the general or theoretical. Practical understanding, thus, has to do with human affairs on both an individual and a socio-political level. It is essentially the application of the general in the particular, right action consequent upon right thinking. And this is the path to happiness: 'The gods [...] rejoice in that which is most excellent and akin to them among men (the intellect, that is) and reward those who most love and honour it, because these have care for the things that are dear to them, and act rightly and well. The fact that all these attributes belong most of all to the wise man is obvious.'[49]

---

[45] *Enneads* 2.9.8. Plotinus here seems to be refuting some species of the Gnostic Sophia myth in which the presence of wisdom in the material world is the result of a fall and not part of the very nature of the good and wondrous cosmos.

[46] Cf. *Enneads* 3.5.2 (the 'heavenly Aphrodite') and 5.1.3 (the 'in between').

[47] For a laudatory attempt to connect Aristotle's understanding of wisdom with contemporary virtue epistemology see Jason Baehr's 'Sophia: Theoretical Wisdom and Contemporary Epistemology'.

[48] Aristotle, *Nichomachean Ethics* 6.6–7 1140b–141b.

[49] Aristotle, *Nichomachean Ethics* 10.8.13 1179a.

Aristotle rejected the claim that wisdom requires the vision of the ideal form of the good. But while his account refuses to situate wisdom outside the individual, the sense of wisdom as the source of the good with regard both to human beings and societies is not, in purely practical terms, so very far removed from that of Plato. The difference lies in their respective suggestions as to the location of wisdom, not so much in the net result. As Aristotle puts it:

> We must not listen to those who advise us 'being human to think human thoughts, and being mortal to think mortal thoughts,' but must put on immortality as much as is possible and strain every nerve to live according to that best part of us, which, being small in bulk, yet much more in its power and honour surpasses all else.[50]

In the move from the Hellenic to the Hellenistic eras, much discourse concerning wisdom becomes increasingly pragmatic and less resolutely metaphysical. Aristotle is in himself symbolic of this transition, a transition all the more evident in the Cynics and the Stoics. These schools share and expand upon Aristotle's hesitation regarding the metaphysical basis and origin of wisdom (S2–S3). In both approaches, discourse concerning wisdom pertains primarily to the moral or ethical plain (S1)—the wise man is effectively synonymous with the virtuous man. None of this, of course, entirely rules out the metaphysical dimension— the shift is rather one of emphasis.

The Cynics, with their often flagrantly illustrated assaults on conventional morality, and their concomitant equation of wisdom with a life lived in accordance with one's own nature, have left us with a vivid portrait of a philosophy that gives no quarter to any other consideration than individual virtue, however peculiarly conceived. The Stoics, for their part, take this same discourse to a somewhat more elevated level, eschewing the more outrageous features of Cynic naturalism and claiming that wisdom consists in living in accordance with the universal reason or *logos* that permeates and governs all existence. In this way they extend the conception of life according to nature from the individual to the cosmic plane. By analogy with Heraclitan fire, the divine and universal *logos* is deemed to be a material of particularly fine quality manifested most especially in the human reason or *logos*. The pursuit of wisdom lies in the effort to act in accordance with this immortal rational principle inherent within the human person. The later Stoics are to be credited with the enduring and frequently quoted definition of wisdom (σοφία) as 'knowledge of things divine and human'.[51] Stoic thinking on

---

[50] Aristotle, *Nichomachean Ethics* 10.7.8 1177b–1178a.

[51] See further, René Brouwer, *The Stoic Sage: The Early Stoics on Wisdom, Sagehood and Socrates*, 7–18. Brouwer traces the definition back to the first century AD and the so-called *Placita*, an abridgement of Aëtius surviving in the works of Plutarch. At around that same time, it also finds its way into the Septuagint, cf. IV Maccabees 1:16.

wisdom is consistently holistic, refusing to separate the metaphysical from the practical business of life—even when the emphasis is very much on practical matters. Much of Stoic thought is dedicated not so much to more abstract principles but to the inculcation of the ability to discern right action or simply good sense (φρόνησις) in a troubled and confusing world.[52] But this is not to imply that σοφία and φρόνησις are somehow separate as theoretical and practical wisdom, respectively—the one necessarily implies and indeed contains the other. As Marcus Aurelius put it with typical succinctness:

> As doctors always keep their knives and instruments at hand to deal with urgent cases, so you too should keep your doctrines at the ready, to enable you to understand things divine and human, and so to perform every action, even the very smallest, as one who is mindful of the bond that unites the two realms; for you will never act well in any of your dealings with the human unless you refer it to the divine, and conversely in your dealings with the divine.[53]

Success in this enterprise, uniting practical and theoretical wisdom through the practice of virtue and the control of passions, constitutes the happy life. As Seneca puts it to his correspondent Lucilius: 'It is clear to you, I know, that no one can lead a happy life, or even one that is tolerable, without the study of wisdom, and that the perfection of wisdom is what constitutes the happy life, although even the beginning of wisdom makes life tolerable.'[54] Seneca sees philosophy as a refuge, as a kind of 'protective badge'. It is 'peaceful and minds its own business' and thus should be pursued with 'calmness and moderation'.[55] In short, philosophy is the way to insulate oneself against the pains and tribulations of this transitory life.

The Sceptics, for their part, lacked even this crumb of comfort. Following on from the Sophists' denial of the possibility of objective knowledge, the Sceptics produced a powerful evocation of the *aporia* of knowledge. This is summed up in Gorgias' three theses: (1) nothing exists; (2) if anything existed, it would be unknowable; (3) if anything existed and were knowable, knowledge of it could

---

[52] Cicero probably exaggerates the gap between σοφία and φρόνησις when he declares, 'The foremost of all the virtues is the wisdom that the Greeks call *sophia*. (Good sense, which they call *phronesis*, we realize is something distinct, that is the knowledge of things that one should pursue and avoid.) But the wisdom that I declared to be the foremost is the knowledge of all things human and divine; and it includes the sociability and fellowship of the gods and men with each other.' *De Officiis* 1.153 [ET 59]. Jerome makes the gap between the two wisdoms even sharper, claiming that, 'The Stoics, too, maintain that wisdom and practical wisdom are different, saying that "wisdom [*sapientia*] is cognition of human and divine matters, and practical wisdom [*prudentia*] is cognition of matters that relate to mortals".' From his *Commentary on the Letter to the Ephesians* 1.9 (cited in Brouwer, *The Stoic Sage*, 11).

[53] *Meditations* 3.1.

[54] 'Liquere hoc tibi, Lucili, scio, neminem posse beate vivere, ne tolerabiliter quidem, sine sapientiae studio, et beatam vitam perfecta sapientia effici, ceterum tolerabile metiam inchoate.' Seneca, *Epistulae morales* 16.1.

[55] *Epistulae morales* 14.11 (LCL 75 90).

not be communicated.[56] The Sceptics held that all philosophical arguments can be countered; all are equally weak and equally strong. In this complete absence of certainty it is best, as Pyrrho of Elis is said to have counselled, to withhold judgement entirely. Only through such a withdrawal from the confusions and contradictions of this world can we attain calm and imperturbability (ἀταραξία). Just as for the Stoics and Cynics, the goal of the Sceptics lies in the equable state of the individual. The Sceptics also attacked many of the Stoic positions, most especially the claim of a divine source of order and right action in the universe. The Epicureans likewise rejected outright the notion of divine providence, seeing it as dangerously fatalistic. They based their ontology squarely on matter and their epistemology (in a deliberate swipe at the Sceptics) on sense experience. They also ranked pleasure (albeit pleasure understood as a rather solemn and unexcited state) as the chief criterion of happiness in this life and spoke of the importance of the friendship of like-minded persons in the pursuit of the good life. As Epicurus expresses this last point: 'Of all the things that wisdom contributes to the blessedness of the complete life, much the most important is the possession of friendship.'[57]

This brief picture of classical wisdom is of course only a very brief dip into a vast sea of inquiry. It should, however, have served to demonstrate the centrality of the notion and pursuit of wisdom within the Greco-Roman world, as also amply attested in material culture with its extensive iconography of wisdom— notably as a personified virtue or associated with a particular goddess.[58] It will also have demonstrated that wisdom was far from being a univocal concept in antiquity: the 'pursuit of wisdom' might sum up the Greek achievement but the wisdom being pursued was certainly not always understood or indeed pursued in the same way. Wisdom, with its cognate terms, emerged as one way of describing the character of the enquiry into the nature and meaning of things—and what to do about it (S1). The limits to this enquiry were rapidly recognized but this sense of the fallibility of human conclusions was to some degree balanced by an appeal to the divine source of such wisdom and knowledge as humans might possess (S2–S3). This explicitly theological approach was also frequently bound up with a mystical dimension, as is evident in the pre-Socratics and, especially, Plato. This dimension was to be renewed and perpetuated within neo-Platonism and indeed in many of the Church Fathers. It is this current which was to be most enthusiastically embraced by the Russian Sophiologists. In the generations after Plato, however, Aristotle's critique of the metaphysical source of wisdom and theory of its twofold nature (abstract and applied) gave way in its turn to a further process of

---

[56] As reported in Sextus Empiricus, *Against the Logicians* 1.65 (LCL 291 34).

[57] *Principal Doctrines* 27 (in Arrighetti (ed.), Epicuro, *Opere*, 149).

[58] See the notes and bibliography in Balčarek, 'The Image of Sophia in Medieval Russian Iconography and its Sources', 594.

reduction whereby wisdom was conceived of—where it was allowed at all—almost exclusively on the applied moral and indeed individual plane—thus on level S1. This pragmatic shift away from the mystical and metaphysical was never to prove congenial territory for the Sophiologists.

By the beginning of the first millennium, Plato's grand vision of a participatory wisdom capable of transforming the *polis* was virtually dead in the water. With Alexander's conquests and, still more, those of Rome, pragmatism not metaphysics, empire not *polis*, was the order of the day. Within the philosophical schools, Stoicism and Scepticism dominated, offering to educated individuals such consolations as they were able to supply—generally through advocating detachment from the vicissitudes of this life. It was into this brave new (and rather unsophiological) world that the uniquely Christian conceptualization of wisdom emerged.

2.3 Wisdom in the New Testament

The New Testament stands as a meeting-point between Old Testament and Greco-Roman wisdom traditions with the emphasis, naturally, on the former. Early Christian reflections on the person of Jesus Christ immediately and intuitively sought to locate this extraordinary figure within the wisdom tradition of Israel both as wisdom teacher and, evidently, something rather more than that.[59]

The Gospel of Matthew offers a clear portrayal of Jesus as the manifestation or embodiment of the Old Testament figure of wisdom. This is perhaps most obvious in the dominical assertion that 'wisdom is justified by her deeds' (Mt. 11:19), where the deeds in question are unambiguously those of Jesus himself (cf. Mt. 11:2).[60] In Jesus' diatribe against the scribes and Pharisees Matthew has 'I' where Luke has 'the wisdom of God' (denoting the one who sends out prophets and apostles) (Mt. 23:34; Lk. 11:49). The lament over Jerusalem which follows (Mt. 23:37; Lk. 13:34) fleshes out still further Jesus' self-identification with the figure of wisdom both in terms of the feminine imagery used (an almost universal *topos* in

---

[59] On wisdom in the New Testament see, amongst a vast bibliography: Aletti, 'Sagesse III. Nouveau Testament'; Ben Witherington III, *Jesus the Sage: The Pilgrimage of Wisdom*; the articles by Dunn, 'Jesus: Teacher of Wisdom or Wisdom Incarnate', Barton, 'Gospel Wisdom', and Hays, 'Wisdom According to Paul', in Stephen Barton (ed.) *Where Shall Wisdom be Found?*; Eckhard Schnabel, *Law and Wisdom from Ben Sira to Paul*; André Feuillet, *Le Christ, sagesse de Dieu, d'après les épîtres pauliniennes*; John Ashton, 'The Transformation of Wisdom. A Study of the Prologue of John's Gospel'; Richard Bauckham, *James. Wisdom of James, Disciple of Jesus the Sage*; the articles by Robinson, 'Jesus as Sophos and Sophia: Wisdom Tradition and the Gospels', Fiorenza, 'Wisdom Mythology and the Christological Hymns of the New Testament', and Pearson, 'Hellenistic-Jewish Wisdom Speculation and Paul', in Robert Wilken (ed.) *Aspects of Wisdom in Judaism and Early Christianity*. New Testament quotations are largely drawn and adapted from existing translations, especially the King James and Revised Standard versions.

[60] The Lucan parallel (Lk. 7:35) and some MSS of Matthew have 'children' for 'deeds'.

Old Testament wisdom literature) and the special care discerned of wisdom for Jerusalem (a feature most evident in Ben Sira and the Wisdom of Solomon). Jesus declares himself 'greater than the Temple' (Mt. 12:6), surpassing even that traditional *locus* of wisdom. He also sets himself firmly above the archetypal wise man, Solomon: 'The queen of the South will rise up at the judgment against this generation and condemn it; for she came from the ends of the earth to hear the wisdom of Solomon, and behold, a greater than Solomon is here.' (Mt. 12:42; Lk. 11:31). The account of the visit of the three wise men of the East similarly represent Jesus as the object and fulfilment of the wisdom of the nations (Mt. 2:1–11). In their worship of him, the mages recognize the child's divine status, a status summed up in the name 'Emmanuel' ('God with us') (Mt. 1:23)—a name that resonates strongly with the Old Testament use of the category of wisdom as a way of articulating the divine immanence and presence.

Thus Jesus, as portrayed by Matthew, is closely identified with the Old Testament figure of wisdom, even if the exact nature of that identification (as with the figure herself) is left open. In the context of this identification, Matthew puts great emphasis on Jesus' rôle as teacher. Here, as in the other Gospels, the most popular form of address for Jesus is 'teacher' or 'rabbi'. The community of the disciples is pre-eminently a learning community guided by Christ the archetypal teacher and master (Mt. 23:8–10), one who speaks directly (and shockingly) on his own authority (Mt. 7:28–9; Mk. 1:27). Acting or not acting upon his divine *paideia* is deemed to have eternal consequences, as is graphically illustrated in the parable of the respective building projects of the wise and foolish man (Mt. 7:24–7; Lk. 6:47–9). The truths he speaks are asserted to be the product not of conventional wisdom but of revelation (Mt. 11:25; Lk. 10:21). Likewise 'flesh and blood' is deemed perfectly inadequate for the apprehension of reality which comes rather by divine revelation (Mt. 16:17). Jesus' *paideia* is a way of life requiring considerable discipline; it is a 'yoke'—albeit an easy one (Mt. 11:29–30; cf. Ecclus. 51:26–7). Those who follow and act upon Jesus' teaching are pictured as scribes 'instructed [or 'discipled': μαθητευθείς] into the kingdom of heaven' (Mt 13:51–2; cf. Wisdom 6:20)—again emphasizing the eternal ramifications of this teaching. This transformational process of discipleship and instruction is seen to give the apostles the capacity to transmit their lived experience of wisdom. They are among those sent out by Christ-Wisdom as 'prophets and wise men and scribes' (Mt. 23:34; Lk. 11:49). The Great Commission, similarly, is framed in terms of teaching and discipleship: 'Go therefore and instruct [or 'make disciples of': μαθητεύσατε] all nations, baptizing them in the name of the Father and of the Son and of the Holy Spirit, teaching them to hold to all that I have commanded you' (Mt. 28:19–20). Thus Matthew ranges across levels S1–S3 with a particular emphasis on the divine *paideia* proffered by wisdom himself.

Many of these themes are developed in the other Gospels though with various different emphases and approaches. In keeping with his raw and almost taciturn style, Mark is relatively reticent on the wider dimensions of the wisdom question as applied to Jesus. He is, however, more than willing to underline the character of Jesus as an entirely exceptional teacher of wisdom (if not explicitly as an incarnation of wisdom). Mark records the consternation of Jesus' fellow-countrymen at witnessing his extraordinary teaching and doings: 'What is this wisdom which is given to him, that such mighty works are wrought by his hands?' (Mk. 6:2). As to the nature of that strange wisdom, Mark emphasizes the deeper meaning of the parables revealed by Jesus to his disciples—he consistently encourages them to dig deeper in their pursuit of meaning (e.g. Mk. 4:11–13, 33–4). We also have in Mark a parallel to Matthew's description of childlikeness as the best guarantee of receptiveness to divine revelation, something his disciples evidently found hard to come to terms with: 'suffer the children to come unto me, do not impede them; for of such is the kingdom of God. Verily, I say unto you, whoever does not receive the kingdom of God as a child shall not enter therein' (Mk. 10:14–15; Mt. 19:14). There is, of course, much in Mark's account which goes far beyond anything that might be said of a traditional wisdom teacher, however eminent, not least the evocation of the second coming in Mark 13 and the declamation that 'Heaven and earth shall pass away, but my words shall not pass away' (Mk. 13:31). Christ's teaching is, again, seen to be of eternal significance and consequence.

Luke develops many of the same wisdom themes evident in his fellow Evangelists, as indicated by the various Lucan parallels already noted. But while Luke underlines the close association between Jesus and wisdom, he is more guarded than is Matthew on Jesus' self-identification with wisdom. Particular to Luke is the way in which wisdom looms large in the account of Jesus' early years: the child 'grew and became strong, filled with wisdom' (Lk. 2:40) and later 'increased in wisdom and stature' (Lk. 2:52). Jesus is also the one who gives wisdom to his disciples: 'I will give you a mouth and wisdom, which none of your adversaries will be able to contradict or resist' (Lk. 21:15). In Acts this powerful wisdom is explicitly connected with the Spirit (Acts 6:3, 10).

The Gospel of John is perhaps the most profoundly sophiological of the four Gospels, the Gospel in which Old Testament wisdom becomes a properly theological category (S3) intricately woven into its faithful witness to Christ. The Gospel of John is permeated with wisdom themes and imagery while, curiously, avoiding the term 'wisdom' itself. The famous 'Word' or 'Logos' of the prologue is undoubtedly firmly rooted in the Old Testament figure of wisdom—the divine and pre-existent associate of God in his work of creation. Just as in the Old Testament, John's wisdom figure bridges the ontological gap between God and the world, manifesting God's immanence and presence in the world. Where John goes beyond any previous localization of wisdom is in his identification of the Logos with the man Jesus Christ The fact that John makes use of the term 'Logos'—already familiar to us on the basis of the discussion of the classical tradition above—emphasizes the extent to which wisdom has been universalized by John, thereby moving away somewhat from the more exclusive association of wisdom with Israel evident in some of the deutero-canonical literature (notably Wisdom and Ben Sira). This is not to say that he in any way neglects the importance of the specifically Jewish context of the incarnation of wisdom. As in Matthew, Jesus is seen to surpass in himself the Temple, with the added clarification that it is his body which is the Temple *par excellence* (Jn. 2:19–21). Chapter 6 reveals the significance of this identification. The most relevant passage (Jn. 6:35–58) begins: 'I am the bread of life; he who comes to me shall not hunger, and he who believes in me shall never thirst.' As with the 'living waters' of John 4 (cf. Ecclus. 15:3), this is an assertion almost certainly intended to recall and surpass wisdom's claim in Ben Sira that, 'They that eat me will yet hunger, and they that drink me will yet thirst' (Ecclus. 24:21). As 'living bread', Jesus gives his body 'for the life of the world' (Jn. 6:51) – life which is eternal by contrast to the more earthly sustenance provided by the manna. In this way, the Mosaic covenant is seen to be at once fulfilled and surpassed in the person of Jesus Christ. The passage continues, 'Verily, verily, I say unto you, unless you eat the flesh of the Son of man and drink his blood, you have no life in you; he who eats my flesh and drinks my blood has eternal life' (Jn. 6:53–4). These words unmistakeably recall wisdom's call in Proverbs 9:5: 'Come, eat of my bread and drink of the wine I have mixed.' Again, we are left with a sense that the Old Testament figure of wisdom has been both manifested and surpassed in Christ.

We need only mention briefly some of the various other dimensions of John's depiction of Christ with wisdom terms and imagery. Early in the Gospel we have Jesus' almost incredulous comment on the limits of traditional Jewish wisdom in his dialogue with Nathanael: 'Are you a teacher of Israel, and you do not know these things?' (Jn. 3:10). His own teaching sets out to redress that deficiency, the dialogue with the Samaritan woman being a particularly beautifully crafted image of the adaptation of divine wisdom to the human level (Jn. 4:7–30). Christ's teaching is represented not as the fruit of book learning but of direct divine revelation (Jn. 7:14–16). He is the fulfilment of the scriptures (Jn. 5:39) and the 'light of the world' (Jn. 1:9, 8:12). Bridging levels S1–S3, he is both the means of approach and the goal of all human enquiry and endeavour: 'the way, the truth, and the life'; to know him is to know and see the Father (Jn. 14:6–7). As locus and vehicle of divine revelation, Jesus both recapitulates and transcends Old Testament wisdom. Such is, in a nutshell, the essence of John's profoundly sophiological depiction of Christ.

In the Pauline epistles we are again unmistakably confronted with a picture of Christ decisively (but certainly not exclusively) influenced by wisdom themes and imagery.[61] Paul is, however, very little interested in Christ as sage or wise man: his

---

[61] Schnabel, *Law and Wisdom* 237–40, gives a very helpful summary of the growing recognition of this dimension of Pauline Christology in C20 scholarship.

vision is above all that of the crucified and risen Christ directly experienced in his own apocalyptic Damascene conversion. It is this experience that lies behind his scorching critique of the Corinthians' faith in merely human wisdom (S0–S1), deeply Hellenic in character and bound up with rhetorical skill and eloquence:

> For Christ sent me not to baptize, but to preach the gospel: not with wisdom of words, lest the cross of Christ be made of no effect. For the preaching of the cross is to them that perish foolishness; but unto us which are saved it is the power of God. For it is written, 'I will destroy the wisdom of the wise, and will bring to nothing the understanding of the prudent.' Where is the wise? Where is the scribe? Where is the disputer of this world? Has not God made foolish the wisdom of this world? For after that in the wisdom of God the world by wisdom knew not God, it pleased God by the foolishness of preaching to save them that believe. For the Jews require a sign, and the Greeks seek after wisdom: But we preach Christ crucified, unto the Jews a stumbling block, and unto the Greeks foolishness. But unto them which are called, both Jews and Greeks, Christ the power of God, and the wisdom of God.   (I Cor. 1:17–24)

But while Paul exposes the futility of the 'wisdom of the world', its vanity and pretension exploded by the unprecedented Ur-event of the Cross, this is no mere obscurantism. Paul gives with one hand what he takes away with the other, offering to the Corinthians a form of wisdom radically different and superior to that in which they previously took comfort: 'Yet among the perfect we speak wisdom, although it is not the wisdom of this age, or of the rulers of this age, who are condemned. But we speak the hidden wisdom of God in a mystery, which God pre-ordained before the ages for our glory.' (I Cor. 2:6–7). This (S2) wisdom is made known in the *paideia* of the Spirit: 'And we speak this [wisdom] not in teachings of human wisdom but in teachings of the Spirit' (I Cor. 2:13).[62] Elsewhere, Paul praises 'the depth of the riches and wisdom and knowledge of God' (Rom. 11:33) and allots to the Church a special rôle in the communication of 'the manifold wisdom of God' (Eph. 3:10).

St Paul is also, on occasion, willing to give some very limited value to the wisdom of the Greeks (S1). According to the account in Acts, he presents the true faith as the fulfilment of all the aspirations of Greek religion and philosophy and goes on to quote the poet Aratus on divine derivation.[63] Such wisdom, however, pales into insignificance when set against the divine gift of wisdom (S2). Revealed through the apparent foolishness of the Cross, divine wisdom transcends,

---

[62] Cf. also the 'spirit of wisdom' of Eph. 1:17 and the 'spiritual wisdom' of Col. 1:9.

[63] Cf. also the quote from Menander in I Cor. 15:32 and, elsewhere in the Pauline corpus, Epimenides (Titus 1:12). In both cases as well-known sayings or proverbs to which a certain credence is attached.

surpasses, and fulfils all earthly wisdom. It becomes ours in the Spirit but remains manifested and embodied in Christ, the supreme principle of all knowledge and intelligibility. All that Paul (or one of his disciples or epigones—the question need not detain us here) writes about the cosmic rôle of Christ reinforces the wisdom dimension of his Christology. Like the Old Testament figure of wisdom, Christ has a mediatory rôle in the creation: 'yet for us there is one God, the Father, from whom are all things and for whom we exist, and one Lord, Jesus Christ, through whom are all things and through whom we exist' (I Cor. 8:6). Similar thinking is evident in the great Christological hymn of Colossians 1:15–20 in which Christ is hymned as the 'image of the invisible God' and the 'first-born of all creation', titles which unmistakably recall passages such as Wisdom 7:26 ('the image of his goodness') and Proverbs 8:22 ('the Lord created me the beginning of his ways for his works'). As the associate of God in the creation and principle of unity in the cosmos Christ fulfils all the functions of the Old Testament figure of wisdom: 'all things were created through him and for him. He is before all things and in him all things hold together' (Col. 1:16–17).[64] The Epistle to the Hebrews witnesses to the same conceptualization of Christ within the broad framework of Old Testament wisdom: he is 'the brightness of his glory and the express image of his substance' (Heb. 1:3).[65]

But for all the evident wisdom themes and imagery in the Pauline depiction of Christ, we must recognize that there is something fundamentally new here. Christ is in himself the embodiment and encapsulation of all that was conveyed in the Old Testament figure of wisdom (and indeed in the notion of Torah). He is the 'wisdom and power of God' *in person* as opposed to wisdom *personified*. As such he encompasses and accomplishes in himself the whole salvation history of Israel and of the universe as a whole. 'In him the fullness of God dwells bodily' (Col. 2:9), reconciling all things to himself and 'making peace by the blood of his Cross' (Col. 1:20). God has made him 'our wisdom, our righteousness and sanctification and redemption' (I Cor. 1:30). To the question 'where shall wisdom be found?', Paul answers categorically: in the historical person of Jesus Christ, 'the wisdom and power of God', 'and him crucified' (I Cor. 1:24, 2:2)—the soteriological and apocalyptic dimension remaining uppermost in his mind.

Moving on from the Pauline corpus, the Epistle of James is a rich source of wisdom teaching. This letter to the diaspora is squarely set within the form of wisdom advice or admonition such as that found in the Books of Proverbs and Ecclesiasticus.[66] One of the first pieces of advice is: 'If any of you lacks wisdom, let him ask God, who gives to all generously and without reproach, and it will be

---

[64] While we may certainly accept some Stoic background here, this is likely to be indirect (i.e. through texts such as the Wisdom of Solomon).

[65] Cf. Wisdom 7:26: 'the radiance of the eternal light and the unspotted mirror of the power of God'.

[66] Here I rely especially on Richard Bauckham, *James. Wisdom of Jesus, Disciple of Jesus the Sage.* The epilogue is particularly brilliant.

given him' (Jas. 1:5). This gift of wisdom (S2) is closely linked with practical endeavour (S1): 'Who is wise and understanding among you? By his good life let him show his works in the meekness of wisdom' (Jas. 3:13). Any pretended wisdom (S0) not born out in such lived experience is 'earthly, unspiritual, devilish'—hence the dangers of being a teacher (cf. Jas. 3:1). Such wisdom to be contrasted with 'the wisdom from above which is first pure, then peaceable, gentle, easy to be entreated, full of mercy and good fruits, without partiality or hypocrisy' (Jas. 3:15–17). Wisdom, for James, is a heavenly gift of knowledge and insight lived out in an upright life. James displays no interest in the personification of Old Testament wisdom (S3) (let alone in connecting that tradition with Christ); nor does he depict Christ as a sage or wise man. Christ remains, for James, much more obviously the apocalyptic 'Lord of glory' (Jas. 2:1).

The apocalyptic dimension of the New Testament is of course consummated in the Book of Revelation. This enigmatic and difficult work contains several explicit, if mysterious, references to wisdom, the first being the exclamation: 'Worthy is the Lamb who was slain to receive power and wealth and wisdom and might and honour and glory and blessing!' (Rev. 5:12). This acclamation would seem to associate Christ with wisdom but not in any very distinctive sense. Wisdom is also one of several qualities found in the hymn of praise in Rev. 7:12: 'Amen! Blessing and glory and wisdom and thanksgiving and honour and power and might be to our God for ever and ever! Amen.' Again, the wisdom evoked here is somehow to be associated with God but not in any very clear or specific sense. There are, in fact, no unambiguous S3 references in Revelation and scarcely anything that might be construed as S1. Wisdom is, however, certainly employed in the sense of revealed understanding (S2) as in the case of the reckoning of the number of the beast in Rev. 13:18: 'Here is wisdom' and the meaning of the vision of Babylon the Great and her unusual beast of burden in Rev. 17:9: 'Here is mind with wisdom'. This latter usage connects with the widespread use of wisdom as an interpretative gift in the Apocalyptic tradition—as, for example, in the Book of Daniel.[67]

To sum up this brief survey, the New Testament clearly presents no univocal sophiology or theology of the divine wisdom. The wisdom tradition of Israel (spanning levels S1–S3) naturally emerged—in terms of genre, themes, and imagery—as a key source and locus for the formation and formulation of the early Christian response to and account of their encounter with that extraordinary individual, Jesus of Nazareth. This response was, however, just as variegated and multiform as the tradition from which it grew. We must consequently be very careful not to read back later Christology or Trinitarian theology into the New Testament writers. Describing Jesus in terms of wisdom can mean a great many

---

[67] Cf. Daniel 2:23 and 9:22 ff. For wisdom in the Apocalyptic tradition, see Rowland, '"Sweet Science Reigns": Divine and Human Wisdom in the Apocalyptic Tradition'. Margaret Barker, in her *The Revelation of Jesus Christ*, has detected a vast hinterland of wisdom themes in the Book of Revelation.

things and does not necessarily imply a proto-orthodox theological position. We must also be clear that wisdom is only part of the picture—themes of Law and prophecy were just as important, if not often more so. We have also had cause to mention the considerably less important dimension of classical philosophy which also has its (admittedly humble) part to play here—even if Hellenic wisdom *per se* is rarely complemented. Moreover, for all that detecting Jewish roots is a laudable and indeed essential enterprise in the study of early Christianity, this account will, for all its brevity, have restated the obvious point that where Christ is considered as the embodiment of all that is embraced by the wisdom tradition of the Old Testament (as in Matthew, John, and Paul) he is also considered as something quite beyond that tradition.

2.4 Sophiological *Epilogomena*

At the close of this preliminary survey of biblical and classical wisdom traditions, it is worth pausing to dwell for a moment on the curiously partial nature of the appropriation of these traditions within Sophiology. There are, simply put, vast swathes of material covered here that are barely touched upon. From the Old Testament, Sophiology gives full credence to the cosmological, quasi-divine, and feminine character of wisdom while neglecting its more mundane and pedagogical aspects. Similarly, classical philosophy is prized more for its mystical intuitions and its sense of wisdom 'in between' God and the world than for what it has to say in the matter of pedagogy or virtuous living. When it comes to the New Testament, the lacunae are even more striking, with a marked reluctance to centre on the historical incarnation as recorded in the Gospels or on the teaching and admonishment of the Epistles. It is highly revealing that the New Testament text most programmatically focussed on within Sophiology should be the Book of Revelation.

Apocalypticism was a prime feature of Soloviev's later work, notably his famous *Tale of the Antichrist* (1900).[68] Bulgakov's work similarly evinces a growing eschatological and apocalyptic character, especially in his last works competed towards the end of the Second World War.[69] Indeed, Bulgakov's last completed work was precisely a commentary on *The Apocalypse of John* which he presented as a fitting conclusion to his life's work, just as the Apocalypse itself concludes the Bible: 'Unexpectedly for me, this book has grown so much in importance as to be, if not the fourth volume of my trilogy, then, at least, its epilogue'.[70] The

---

[68] In *Complete Works*, X, 193–211.

[69] Bulgakov ends each of the books of the major trilogy with the penultimate verse of Revelation: 'Even so, come Lord Jesus!' (Rev. 22:20).

[70] Cited in Lev Zander's unpaginated editor's note prefacing *The Apocalypse of John: An Essay in Dogmatic Interpretation* [ET xviii].

commentary is a stunning text that stands as a permanent testimony to his acute eschatological sensibility and inexhaustible theological creativity. It is noteworthy that Bulgakov should have lavished so much attention on a text that is famously elusive and mystifying—not unlike his own work—and that positively demands theological speculation. Besides a smaller work on the closely connected Gospel of John (published only in the 1980s), Bulgakov does not devote anything like the same attention to the other New Testament material surveyed in the preceding section.[71]

The book stands as something of a Sophiological summary—like *The Wisdom of God* but in a rather different key. Bulgakov finds in Revelation all of orthodox Christology and Trinitarian theology, together with its own distinctive eschatological and apocalyptic twist. I do not think it fanciful to suggest that Bulgakov saw his own work in similar terms: fully embracing doctrinal orthodoxy and the patristic witness (an embrace more often asserted than demonstrated) but adding something quite new and shatteringly revelatory to that tradition. For Bulgakov, the Book of Revelation is philosophy of history in its purest form—an account of the in-gathering of all human purpose and activity into the Kingdom: 'it is a book about the *end* of history, about what will be and how it will be. It is a book about the whole of world history in its content and completion.'[72] Bulgakov reads Revelation as a great paean to Sophia: all its mysterious images gravitate towards the recognition of divine-humanity, of Sophia in both her earthly and heavenly aspects.

The praise of the four living creatures and twenty-four elders in Chapter 4, for example, points to the ontological and pan-temporal doxology of the creation which can only be understood in terms of the mediating principle of Sophia.[73] The relationship between eternity and time, creation and Creator, 'is resolved in the sense that between them ($\mu\epsilon\tau\alpha\xi\dot{\upsilon}$), as uniting and separating them, is set the world of intelligent powers, created eternity and the created heaven, created Sophia, who has her foundation in divine Sophia'.[74] This divine Sophia is the eternal divine humanity—'the Godman before and beyond the incarnation', in whose image human beings are made and which angels too reflect in their 'heavenly humanity'.[75]

Apart from the Apocalypse, it is striking that New Testament themes and imagery play only a modest rôle in Sophiology when it comes to the specific matter of Sophia. Where Sophiology looks to its scriptural foundations (thus in

---

[71] See his 'The Theology of the Gospel of John the Evangelist'. The commentary sets the Gospel firmly within a Sophiological framework, focusing especially on its more cosmic dimensions.

[72] Cited in *The Apocalypse of John* [ET], iii *apud* Zander Бог и Мир II, 305 *apud* Bulgakov's 'Thesen über die Kirche', 133.

[73] By pan-temporal, Bulgakov wishes to invoke a non-linear notion of time that is not strictly eternal and uncreated.

[74] *The Apocalypse of John*, 48 [ET 40].   [75] *The Apocalypse of John*, 49 [ET 40].

Florensky and Bulgakov rather more than in Soloviev), the more ambiguous and indeterminate figure of the Old Testament looms distinctly larger than the historical person of Jesus Christ. Rather than centring itself on Christ, Sophiology remains more in line with the classical philosophical notion of wisdom somehow 'in between' God and the world and associated with the realm of ideas—Plato and Plotinus' 'heavenly Aphrodite'.[76] Somehow, *personification* of Sophia (as Lady Wisdom or the realm of ideas represented by the heavenly Aphrodite) has come to prevail over the *person* of Christ. Much of this relative reticence is doubtless due to a perfectly legitimate refusal to pin down the category of wisdom solely to the second person of the Trinity and thus to avoid the subsuming of sophiology by Christology. But this reticence also speaks of a far more dangerous problem: a docetic tendency within Sophiology as a whole in which the historical incarnation is subordinated to the principle of Sophia or divine-humanity, to what Bulgakov calls 'the Godman before and beyond the incarnation'.

Modern Russian Sophiology, in short, privileges certain select (and almost exclusively S3) aspects of both the Old Testament and the classical philosophical traditions over the historical revelation of Jesus Christ (as the 'wisdom and power of God') in the New Testament. This is bound up with a functional disavowal of the primal significance of the incarnation and a downplaying of the vital peda-gogical dimensions (S1–S2) so prominent in all three sources. In these ways, Sophiology has embraced only a fraction—and arguably not the most important parts—of the classical and biblical wisdom traditions. This pattern of distinctly partial appropriation is also be evident in its reception of patristic tradition, to which we now turn.

---

[76] Plotinus, *Enneads* 5.3.2 (cf. Plato, *Symposium* 180d). For Bulgakov's use of the concept cf. *Philosophy of Economy*, 150–1 [ET 151] and *Unfading Light*, 216 [ET 221]. Bulgakov tended to row back on pagan parallels in his later works while retaining the precise sense of Sophia as the eternal realm of ideas of the creation. Bulgakov's incautious evocation of pagan goddesses gives some justification to Arthur Dobbie-Bateman's note of lament: 'When he named the existential problem Sophia, we behaved like Greeks who thought that Anastasis was a goddess.' (cf. Acts 17:18). 'Footnotes IX in quos fines saeculorum', 6.

3

Wisdom and *Paideia*

Early Christian reflection on wisdom was never especially fertile ground for the Russian Sophiologists. As Bulgakov put it in one of his typically sweeping remarks: 'In the early patristic writings, in the Apostolic Fathers and Apologists, we do not find any theological system (with the exception of St Irenaeus) thus the sophiological problematic is missing.'[1] Appeals to this period are therefore rather thin within Sophiology, even when it comes to Irenaeus. This dismissal shows once again the very partial nature of Sophiology's appropriation of preceding traditions of wisdom reflection and in particular its almost total failure to acknowledge the dimension of human and divine *paideia*.

3.1 The Apostolic Fathers

The writings of the immediate sub-apostolic period offer some remarkable insights into the ways in which the early Church continued its reflection upon the nature and import of the new revelation of wisdom in Jesus the Christ as mediated by scripture and the apostolic tradition.[2] Inseparable from this reflection was the wider question of Christianity's engagement with the Greco-Roman cultural world, most notably in respect of that world's philosophy and *paideia*. In this early period we begin to see the emergence of a distinctively Christian understanding of both wisdom and *paideia*, an understanding which remained fundamentally rooted in scripture while also affirming Christianity's consummation and fulfilment of the classical legacy. It is striking that in these texts the

---

[1] *The Bride of the Lamb*, 20 [ET 15].
[2] On the theme of wisdom in the sub-apostolic period, see the brief remarks in Walther Völker, 'Die Verwertung der Wesiheits-Literatur bei den christlichen Alexandrinen' and Hasso Jaeger, 'The Patristic Conception of Wisdom in the Light of Biblical and Rabbinical Research'. Note that these are among very few works even to touch on the theme, something that comes as part of a wider and curious deficiency in patristic studies. The article 'Sagesse' in the *Dictionnaire de spiritualité*, for example, jumps straight from the New Testament and Philo to Clement of Alexandria. As Robert Wilken justly remarks in an essay on Sextus, wisdom, unlike philosophy, has received very little attention—at most as 'a minor tributary alongside the great river of patristic thought'. He goes on to observe that even where it is treated, wisdom is often studied quite separately from philosophy, a tendency 'doubtless stemming from our modern tendency to think of philosophy as intellectual exercise and wisdom as part of character and lifestyle'. The ancients, of course, knew of no such bifurcation. 'Wisdom and Philosophy in Early Christianity', 143–4.

construal of wisdom is overwhelmingly focussed on levels (S1–S2) and not on the more explicitly theological level (S3).

The epistle of Clement of Rome to the 'Church sojourning in Corinth' (*c.* 90–100 AD) stands as a fine example of an almost seamless integration of classical culture into Christian teaching. Clement makes extensive use of his ample rhetorical skills, building a powerful case by piling example upon example, both scriptural and (to a much lesser extent) secular, in order to demonstrate the ills of internal strife and the blessings of peace. The classical theme of *homonoia* (concord)—so beloved of the ancient *polis*—is repeatedly taken up, while the order of the cosmos is, in the best manner of the Stoics, used as a pattern for the order that ought to prevail in civil society.[3] Similarly Stoic in background is his concept of the complete intermingling or mixture (συγκράσις) of the various ranks in the Church and his appeal to the 'common spirit' that pervades the members of the body (37.4–5).[4] Clement evidently feels sufficiently comfortable in his classical heritage to draw on the myth of the phoenix as an image of the resurrection (25) and on the Roman army as a model of order (37.1–3).

For all these classical trappings, scripture remains Clement's chief frame of reference and his interest is never seriously deflected from the Church and its welfare.[5] His mode of expression—like that of all the Church Fathers—is so perfectly steeped in scriptural language and allusion that it is impossible to exhaust all the references it makes and the resonances it creates.[6] It is also apparent that Christianity, for Clement, represents a superior *paideia* and wisdom (S2) to that attainable within secular culture. He speaks of the '*paideia* which is in Christ', a *paideia* characterized by love and humility (21.8). He characterizes his detractors as, by contrast, 'uninstructed' (ἀπαίδευται) and warns that of such people it is written that the Lord 'breathed on them and they died, because they had no wisdom' (Job 4:21) (39.1, 6). In the quasi-liturgical prayer towards the end of the epistle, Clement gives thanks to God for his child, Jesus Christ, 'through whom you have instructed (ἐπαίδευσας), sanctified, and honoured us' (59.3), and in his final summary he refers to scripture as the 'words of the *paideia* of God' (62.3). While he is more than happy to marshal his classical heritage to underscore his message, that heritage always remains very much in its proper place strictly subordinated to the new Christian *paideia*.

---

[3] On *homonoia* see further Allen Brent, *A Political History of Early Christianity*, 183–6.

[4] See Werner Jaeger, *Early Christianity and Greek Paideia*, 20–3 (and notes). In view of the rhetorical skills on display, Jaeger goes so far as to speak of Clement as being 'like a second Demosthenes': ibid., 13.

[5] See also Frances Young's skilful analysis of Clement's use of scripture as a typical early example of Christian *paraenesis* (or moral admonition) and her observations as to his (again typical) practice of creating a 'collage' or 'mosaic effect' of scriptural texts to make his point: *Biblical Exegesis and the Formation of Christian Culture*, 222–4.

[6] §60 is perhaps a particularly fine example of this 'mosaic effect'.

In keeping with his emphasis on moral admonition and *paideia*, Clement naturally makes very frequent use of biblical wisdom literature. He quotes what looks very like Proverbs 20:27 as a warning that God sees all (21.2–3)[7] and later gives us a substantial extract from the same Book (Proverbs 1:23–33), in which the 'all-virtuous wisdom'[8] details the sorry fate of those who do not humbly take heed to instruction and accept due reproofs: Wisdom herself will laugh at their ruin (57.3–7). The Corinthians' trust in their own human wisdom (S1) appears, moreover, to have changed little from the time of St Paul, hence the citation of Jeremiah: 'Let not the wise man boast in his wisdom' (Jer. 9:23) (13.1) and the reminder that even properly directed wisdom is insufficient for salvation: 'we are not justified by our wisdom, or understanding, or piety, or deeds [...] but by faith [...]' (32.4). But works and faith go hand in hand: properly Christian wisdom is lived out not in mere words but in good deeds (38.2). It leads a direct experience of saving knowledge (39). And the truly wise man will of course use his wisdom for the common good (48.5–6).

The whole thrust of Clement's letter is very much on levels S1–S2—an ordered life based on the *paideia* or instruction of Christ and leading to the saving gift of knowledge. What we do not have in Clement is any developed theology of wisdom (S3)—for example, no explicit reference to Christ *qua* wisdom. The significance of this absence should not, perhaps, be exaggerated. Clement's letter has a very specific purpose—to restore due order and harmony in the Church in Corinth—and anything not obviously serving that purpose simply had no place. Clement nonetheless stands as a key figure in the early development of a distinctively Christian understanding of wisdom that is intimately and organically linked to the notion of *paideia*. In this construal of wisdom, Greco-Roman culture is comprehensively subsumed and transformed within the scriptural matrix.

Less obviously related to the wider pagan world are works such as the *Didache* or *Teaching of the Twelve Apostles* and the *Epistle to Barnabas*, both dating from the late first or early second century. In these texts the wider frame of reference is more obviously that of the Jewish world but in both the emphasis is again very much on levels S1–S2. Wisdom *per se* makes no appearance in the *Didache* but this brief manual of early Christian instruction displays numerous affinities with biblical wisdom literature. We may note, for example, the theme of the 'two ways' including the need to avoid double-mindedness (2.4) and the importance of discipline in the raising of children (4.9). Much of the moral exhortation is framed

---

[7] Discussed in Young, *Biblical Exegesis*, 223.

[8] This is evidently an accepted circumlocution for Proverbs, also used elsewhere for other wisdom books both singly and collectively (in the latter instance as denoting the 'writings' in the classic threefold Jewish subdivision of the scriptures). Cf. Eusebius, *HE* 4.22 (on Hegesippus): 'And not only he but Irenaeus too, and the whole group of early writers used to call Solomon's proverbs the "all-virtuous wisdom".' The Book of Proverbs rapidly became a particularly prominent resource for much early Christian literature—see for example the very substantial chunks of it quoted in the third-century Syriac text the *Didascalia Apostolorum*.

as coming from a parent to a child (3–4), again a traditional wisdom form. The famous anaphora of the *Didache* gives thanks for the 'knowledge and faith and immortality made known though Jesus thy child' (10.2) and goes on to praise God as the one who has 'created all things' (cf. Ecclus. 18:1, 24:8; Wisdom 1:14). The following section affirms authentic teaching will be known in its increase of both righteousness and knowledge, and that the true character of a prophetic teacher will be made known in his behaviour—in short they must practise what they preach (11.2, 8–11). While hardly an overtly sapiential text, the *Didache* is a fine example of early Christian *paideia* built on the foundations of biblical wisdom literature.

The *Epistle of Barnabas* makes more explicit reference to wisdom. It takes 'wisdom, intelligence, understanding, and knowledge' as among the superior virtues gifted to humans (2.3). Similarly, in the context of a long series of admonitions drawn from scripture and a wide range of New Testament material, 'we ought to give thanks that the Lord has given us knowledge of the past and wisdom for the present' (5.3). The wisdom necessary for the proper interpretation of scripture is inherent within us by grace: 'Blessed be our Lord, brethren, who has placed in us wisdom and intellection of his hidden things' (6.10). Such (S2) wisdom is, of course, inseparable from a righteous life, for the 'wisdom of the commandments' (S1) which is one of the means by which the Lord comes to dwell in us, building us into spiritual temples (16.9–10). Finally, following an extended account of the 'two ways' that has much in common with that found in the *Didache* and may come from a shared source (18–20),[9] the author prays that God will give us 'wisdom, intelligence, understanding, and knowledge of his commandments, and patience' (21.5) so that we should be truly 'taught by God' (θεοδίδακτοι) (21.6).

In both the *Didache* and Barnabas we have a similar conception of Christian *paideia* deeply rooted in the Jewish wisdom tradition, for all that both are in little sympathy with the Jews of their own day. But while wisdom is construed in terms of the righteous life and as divine gift (S1–S2), neither text presents any consideration of wisdom as a divine attribute, let alone as manifested in Christ—such explicitly theological (S3) dimensions of the wisdom question do not find a place in these didactic texts.

Also deeply bound up with the Jewish wisdom tradition, although without any trace of anti-Jewish polemic, are the Syriac *Odes of Solomon* (*c.* 100 AD). The *Odes* are, as their title leads us to expect, profoundly impregnated with wisdom themes and imagery.[10] We have frequent allusion to the 'living waters' of wisdom (*Odes*

---

[9] See further Prigent and Kraft (eds.), *Épître de Barnabé* (SC 172), 12–20 and Young, *Biblical Exegesis*, 131–2.

[10] On the *Odes* more generally, see Henry Chadwick, 'Some Reflections on the Character and Theology of the *Odes of Solomon*'.

11.7, 30.1; cf. Ecclus. 15:3),[11] to their intoxicating effect (11.7; cf. Ecclus. 1:16), and their sweetness superior to both honey and the honeycomb (30.1; cf. Ecclus. 24:20). The *Odes* tend, however, to speak of Solomon's gifts not as wisdom *per se* but rather as 'knowledge', 'light', or 'truth', often in close association with love, for which Solomon was also renowned.[12] Only on one occasion is he even called 'wise' (38.13). Wisdom is more often referred to in terms of its being absent: 'lacking in wisdom, / They exalted themselves in their mind' (24.10), or simply inadequate: 'He who created wisdom / Is wiser than his works' (7.7–8). Similarly, 'the thought of the most high cannot be pre-possessed; / And his heart is superior to all wisdom' (28.20). What is perhaps most valuable about the *Odes* is that they offer a unique insight into early Christian hymnography in a form which remains deeply indebted to and rooted in the Jewish wisdom tradition without, however, making any very explicit transference of that tradition to the new Christian revelation. The emphasis is on level S1 with the divine gift of wisdom (S2) construed in terms of knowledge, light, and truth. S3 considerations are, at best, only intimated.

The Epistles of St Ignatius of Antioch (*c.* 107 AD) bring us back more closely to the encounter with pagan society. Like Clement before him, Ignatius makes frequent appeal to the concept of *homonoia*, similarly transferring that concept to the order and harmony that should prevail in the new Christian *polis*, duly gathered around its bishop. Ignatius has relatively little to say about themes of *paideia* but does assert that authentic teaching is necessarily put into practice and that such teaching is supremely instanced in the work of Christ (*Ephesians* 15.1–2). It is, furthermore, Christ-God who grants the gift of wisdom and it is through that gift that Christians are, as it were, nailed to the Cross of Christ, fixed in immovable faith (*Smyrneans* 1.1).[13] Appeals and allusions to Old Testament wisdom literature are common with a frequent use of the paraenetic form and a 'two ways' instruction to shun folly and walk in the way of the wise which leads to Christ, 'who is the knowledge of God' (*Ephesians* 17.2). This last reference is perhaps the closest Ignatius comes to an S3 construal of wisdom. But Ignatius is especially drawn to New Testament wisdom material, notably Paul's excoriation of merely worldly wisdom in I Corinthians 1–2 backed up by his self-designation as a mere 'off-scouring' of the Cross (*Ephesians* 18.1; cf. I Cor. 4.13). But overall, references to biblical material are subordinated to a theology of direct (and very Pauline) apocalyptic experience of the crucified and risen Christ: 'For me my

---

[11] For 'living waters' cf. also Song of Songs 4:15; Jeremiah 2:13, 17:13; Zechariah 14:8.

[12] There are also some intimations of the Jewish *merkabah* tradition (mystical reflection surrounding the fiery chariot of Elijah): 'I went up into the light of truth as into a chariot' (38.1).

[13] I have naturally restricted myself to the most widely accepted 'short recension'. In the longer (and almost certainly inauthentic) recension we have 'wisdom has built herself a house' applied to the incarnation (*Philippians* 3), and Christ described as 'only-begotten God and wisdom and word of God' (*Philadelphians* 6) and as 'full of the Holy Spirit and of divine and sacred wisdom' (*Smyrneans* 13).

archives are Jesus Christ; my inviolable archives are his Cross and his death and his resurrection, and the faith which comes from him.' (*Philadelphians* 8.2). Ignatius' distinctly Christocentric and stavrological focus adds a vitally important dimension to this picture of early Christian construals of wisdom. This is yet another dimension the Sophiologists were never to appropriate fully.

The intriguing *Shepherd of Hermas* (mid second-century) is largely apocalyptic in form, with the various visions vouchsafed to the freed slave Hermas invariably explained, often quite laboriously. This concern for instruction is borne out in the emphasis on the discipline of *paideia*, a discipline of teaching and correction that should be mutual within the Christian community (*Vision* 3.9.10). The *Shepherd* offers a version of the 'two ways' doctrine (*Mandate* 8),[14] frequent censures of 'double-mindedness' (e.g. *Vision* 2.2.7, 3.3.4, 3.7.1, 3.10.9, 3.11.2, 4.2.4; *Mandate* 9.1), and several other uses of scriptural wisdom literature (e.g. *Vision* 4.3.4; *Mandate* 7.1 and 10.1.6). Perhaps most interesting is the *Shepherd*'s connection of the Old Testament figure of wisdom with the Church. The Church was created by God 'by his own wisdom and forethought' (*Vision* 1.3.4). She is, moreover, created 'first of all things' (*Vision* 2.4.1; cf. Ecclus 1:4, Proverbs 8:22)— hence her initial appearance to Hermas in the guise of an old woman. This feminine manifestation of the Church—she also appears later as a young woman—makes the allusion to the biblical figure of wisdom all the stronger.[15] A similar and related allusion is found in Hermas' description of the Son of God: 'Listen and understand, foolish man, the Son of God is older than all his creation so as to be fellow counsellor (σύμβουλον) to the Father in his creation' (*Similitude* 9.12.2; cf. Wisdom 8:9). Connecting the wisdom figure of the Old Testament with the Church and (at least by implication) with the Son of God is an intriguing development.

To conclude this section, it is evident that wisdom themes and imagery are widely found in sub-apostolic sources. Use of the Jewish wisdom tradition is, however, only rarely explicitly theological in character; it is more obviously exploited for its value to Christian *paideia*—especially in terms of its moral and religious dimension (S1). Not that this is any way unimportant: later patristic thinking on wisdom consistently maintains this connection between theory and practice (often in deliberate and invariably unjust contrast to Greek philosophy). Wisdom is also explicitly referred to as a gift (S2) allowing proper interpretation of scripture in Clement and Barnabas and as an aspect of Christ's saving work in Ignatius. It also crops up in a liturgical context in Clement and the *Didache*. Furthermore, we see in the *Shepherd* the beginnings of the interpretation of the Old Testament figure of wisdom in the terms of the Church. Lastly, in Clement and

---

[14] Cf. *Mandate* 6.2 – the two angels that accompany man, one good and one bad.

[15] It is also an image picked up on by the Sophiologists cf. Florensky, *The Pillar and Ground of Truth*, 336–8 [ET 244–45] and Bulgakov, *The Wisdom of God*, 134.

Ignatius we see an explicit encounter with Greco-Roman culture—an encounter in which that culture is very firmly put in its place for all that it is freely put to work, where appropriate, in support of the Christian revelation. There is, in short, a good deal of sapiential theology (S1–S2) in this immediate sub-apostolic period but any very developed sophiology (S3) will remain the work of future generations.

3.2 The Apologists

As we move into the era of the Apologists (second–third centuries), Christian reflection on wisdom becomes more explicitly theological (S3) without losing the (S1–S2) focus on *paideia* witnessed in many of the texts examined in the previous section.[16] At the same time, the engagement with Greco-Roman wisdom becomes increasingly robust in this period. These developments bring with them an increasing sophistication of thought and expression with regard to the theme of wisdom both sacred and profane.[17]

The critique of Greek philosophy (often making use of existing polemical tropes within the classical tradition itself), coupled with an affirmation of authenticity and overwhelming superiority of Christian wisdom, represent a more or less standard framework for Christian apologetic in the second century. The short *Apology of Aristides* (120–130 AD) is no exception, complementing its addressee, Hadrian, as a 'philosopher' but roundly criticizing Greek and other false philosophies. It also speaks of the Christian God in clear S3 terms, 'for he is altogether wisdom and understanding; and in him consists all that consists'.[18] Athenagoras' *Plea for the Christians* (addressed to that most philosophical of emperors, Marcus Aurelius, and to the less impressive Commodus) makes a similar S3 connection between the Son and wisdom while also disparaging the Stoic idea that Athena represents the wisdom pervading all things (22.8).[19] For Athenagoras it is, of course, the Son of God (and not Athena) who is true wisdom as the 'intellect, word, and wisdom' of the Father' (24.2). He makes this point in the context of a

---

[16] Cf. Hasso Jaeger's sage comment, 'In the mind of the Fathers wisdom gravitates to the centre of the Christian faith'. 'The Patristic Conception of Wisdom in the Light of Biblical and Rabbinical Research', 90.

[17] There remain, of course, many difficulties involved with the dating of many of the works and even authors in this period, hence we shall not be attempting any close analysis of the way in which the treatment of wisdom develops within the thought of particular writers or the ways in which they might be regarded as having drawn on or been received by one another.

[18] *Apology of Aristides*, 1 in Robinson (ed.) *The Apology of Aristides*, 36 (translation from page *beth* (p.2) of the Syriac text).

[19] The term used of Athena is φρόνησις, a term that in Stoic usage tends to denote practical wisdom but is also (as here) capable of a more metaphysical interpretation (cf. above, p.86). For the Stoic understanding of Athena as all-pervading wisdom see *Diogenes Laertius, Lives of Eminent Philosophers* 7.88 (LCL 185). The idea is also referenced in the pseudo-Clementine *Homilies* 6.8.

development of the familiar Pauline distinction between (merely) human wisdom (S1) and the gift of divine wisdom (S2), arguing that 'worldly wisdom and divine wisdom differ as much from each other as truth and plausibility: the one is of heaven, and the other of earth' (24.6). The relative nature of worldly wisdom is further illustrated by Athenagoras in connection with the doctrine of the resurrection in which God's wisdom entirely flummoxes even those renowned for their wisdom.[20]

Similar sentiments abound in the *Epistle to Diognetus* (second century), perhaps the most floridly rhetorical of all the apologetic works. This text contrasts the 'empty and ludicrous' and discordant teachings of the pagan philosophers (S0) (8.2) with God's 'wise counsel' disclosed through the Son so that we might truly 'participate, know, and apprehend' his beneficent actions in a manner beyond all expectation (8.10–11). Christian *paideia* (S2) is divine in origin: 'This teaching of theirs has not been found through the thought or study of inquisitive men, nor are they proponents of any human doctrine as some are' (5.3). Their teaching is the product of direct revelation (7.1), mediated by the saviour, the 'teacher' (διδάσκαλον) (9.6).[21]

St Theophilus of Antioch (late C2) gives us a particularly important example of the way in which the theme of wisdom played a crucial rôle in the early Christian attempt to articulate a complex monotheism—a process of articulation that remained firmly set within the language and themes of *paideia*.[22] Theophilus specifies that when he speaks of God as wisdom, he refers to his 'offspring' (γέννημα) (*Ad Autolycum* 1.3). This distinction is made in view of the purposes of creation: 'God by his own word and wisdom made all things; for "for by his word were the heavens established and all their power by the breath of his mouth" (Ps. 32(33):6)' (1.7). This is the most explicit S3 affirmation that we have encountered thus far in this chapter. Active in the creation, God's wisdom has implanted signs of the resurrection in the creation (1.13) and indwelled the prophets (2.9). Wisdom was 'put forth' or 'emitted' (c.f. Ps 44(45):1) and the word begotten 'before all things' (2.10), thereby forming the 'triad' or 'trinity' (τρίας) of 'God, the word, and his wisdom' (2.15).[23]

The cosmological dimension of wisdom in Theophilus is striking and the connection between his trinity and the creation is no mere accident, for he adds, significantly, that it is in the perception and acquisition of God's wisdom that

---

[20] *On the Resurrection* 2 and *passim*.

[21] This comes amidst a string of epithets: Christ is our nourisher, father, teacher, counsellor, physician, mind, light, honour, glory, strength, and life.

[22] See further Daniel Buda, 'Sophia in Theophilus of Antioch'.

[23] In all this he would seem to be suggesting an identification of wisdom with the Holy Spirit. It has to be recognized, however, that there is no very clear distinction between word and wisdom in Theophilus. In practice, the terms appear almost interchangeable. Proverbs 8:22, for example, is taken to refer to the word, the ἀρχή or 'governing principle' of the creation who is the 'spirit of God [. . .] and wisdom, and power of the highest' (2.15).

Christians both see and image God (1.7; 2.15). In other words, God has extrapo-
lated himself as triad in the creation in order to bring humanity to himself in and
through wisdom. There is much here that potentially aligns with Sophiology,
especially the cosmological descent and ascent of wisdom and the distinction of
wisdom from the word—not that Theophilus' triad exactly corresponds to the
more familiar Trinity of Father, Son, and Holy Spirit.[24]

Like the other Apologists, Theophilus elaborates in no uncertain terms the
superiority of the divine wisdom of Christians over the discordant opinions of the
philosophers and poets (2.4).[25] Among Christians, 'the holy word guides, wisdom
teaches, life directs, God reigns' (3.15), whereas the Greeks 'have necessarily lost
the wisdom of God' (3.30). In sum, wisdom, for Theophilus, is not only a matter of
cosmology, or triadology, or indeed classical encounter but also (and perhaps
most importantly) a means of expressing the divine *paideia* (S2) that unites
human beings to God.

This divine wisdom and *paideia* is also a major feature of the work of the
greatest of the Apologists, St Justin Martyr (d. *c.* 165 AD).[26] Justin's sophisticated
treatment of wisdom operates on two main fronts: against the pagans (in his *First*
and *Second Apology*) and against the Jews (in his *Dialogue with Trypho*).[27] Taking
on the polytheists, Justin develops an account of Christianity as the summation of
all the aspirations of philosophy and, by implication, the only truly rational
religion. Much of his argument is centred on an appeal to reason and to the
common love of wisdom (*philosophia*) that should ensure equitable treatment of
the harmless Christians on the part of their rulers. Jesus himself is presented as
superior in wisdom, on account of which he is 'worthy to be called Son of God'
(1 *Apol.* 22.1). Christians have direct access to wisdom by divine revelation (S2),
even if they are 'uneducated and barbarous in speech', since their beliefs and
teachings are 'not the product of human wisdom but are uttered by the power of
God' (1 *Apol.* 60.11). Justin frequently cites pagan philosophy to underline his
points acknowledging that it too has a rôle to play in a properly ordered life. He
does this on the assumption that all that is good and true in the pagan tradition
comes from participation in the universal word or *logos* of God, that ordering
principle of the universe spread throughout the creation and everywhere present
in seminal form: 'whatever either lawgivers or philosophers uttered well, they

---

[24] Bulgakov is nonetheless happy to acknowledge him as one who identified wisdom with the Holy
Spirit: *The Wisdom of God*, 46.

[25] Theophilus is, however, willing to acknowledge the good advice given in the *Sybilline Oracles*: 'Be
wise and treasure wisdom in your breasts' (2.36).

[26] On wisdom in Justin, see especially Joseph Sikora, 'Philosophy and Christian Wisdom according
to Saint Justin Martyr'. See also the chapter on Justin in Henry Chadwick, *Early Christian Thought and
the Classical Tradition* and Eric Osborn, *Justin Martyr*.

[27] The recent editors of the *Apologies* suggest that the *Second Apology* is something like a scrap-
book—'clippings from the cutting-room floor' cobbled together with miscellaneous notes—as against
the more polished and finished *First Apology*: Minns and Parvis, *Justin, Philosopher and Martyr*, 30.

elaborated by finding and contemplating some part of the word' (2 *Apol.* 10.2). Such participation seems to work in two ways: through the direct illumination of the reason and through the widespread and unacknowledged dissemination of scriptural texts and truths among the pagans.[28] It is important not to exaggerate the status Justin gives to Greek philosophy: its share in the truth is never more than partial or shadowy and is attributable in large measure to plagiarism—not that it is in Justin's interests to accentuate this aspect of the question in an apologetic context.

Justin is somewhat freer in the *Dialogue with Trypho*. Philosophy again takes centre stage, but Justin is now also able to appeal to the ample Jewish wisdom tradition. Both interlocutors agree on the importance of philosophy which Justin characterizes as 'the greatest possession and most honourable before God, to whom it leads and with whom it alone associates us' (*Dial.* 2.1). In his famous account of his trawl through the various philosophical schools, Justin neatly conveys the limited but real value of Greek philosophy as a preparatory stage to the 'only sure and useful philosophy' that is Christianity (*Dial.* 8.1). The discussion turns for the most part on the correct interpretation of Scripture, something that absolutely requires the gift of divine illumination (S2): 'But pray that before all else the gates of light may be opened to you; for such things cannot be seen or understood by all but only by those to whom God and his Christ give understanding.' (*Dial.* 7.3). Trypho and his co-religionists should 'learn of us who have been made wise by the grace of Christ' (*Dial.* 32.5). Failure to accept this divine *paideia* and thereby to see the promises concerning Christ in the scriptures comes as the result of God's withholding of the ability 'to perceive the wisdom which is in his words' (*Dial.* 55.3). In the battle for the Old Testament, this interpretative gift of wisdom is Justin's trump card, even if it ultimately fails to convince the enduringly sceptical Trypho.

Although it is the word of God, omnipresent in the creation and incarnate in Jesus Christ, that occupies the central place in Justin's work, he specifies that 'wisdom' is one of the appellations of this 'rational power' created by God in the beginning (S3) (*Dial.* 61.1)—the 'other God' of his rather sketchy trinitarian schema (*Dial.* 56.4).[29] It is this 'word of wisdom' that has spoken through the prophets (for example in Proverbs 8) and 'who is himself this God begotten of the Father of all, and who is the word, and wisdom, and power, and glory of the begetter' (*Dial.* 61.3). This wisdom of which Solomon speaks (in Proverbs 8) was begotten as a beginning before all God's creatures (*Dial.* 62.4, 129.3). This explicit identification of the Old Testament figure of wisdom with the word of God— thereby bolstering the case for Christ's divinity and eternity—was to become

---

[28] See further Mark Edwards, 'Justin's Logos and the Word of God'.

[29] Justin seeks to persuade Trypho that the theophanies of the Old Testament point to 'another God and Lord under the maker of all things' (θεὸς καὶ κύριος ἕτερος ὑπὸ τὸν ποιητὴν τῶν ὅλων).

(through Origen) the most commonly accepted interpretation within the later patristic tradition. Justin's functional disavowal of the feminine character of the Old Testament figure of wisdom was motivated at least in part by fears of pagan infiltration: he is aware of pagan associations between Athena and wisdom and clearly wishes to dissociate the word absolutely from any such feminine divinity (cf. 1 *Apol.* 64.5). Justin's logocentrism also leads him to ascribe the rôle of prophetic inspiration to the word-wisdom of God, not to the Holy Spirit, who in any case comes a rather poor third in his thinking.

In Justin we see a wholescale appropriation and supersession of both Hellenic and Jewish wisdom traditions. Both are taken as preparatory stages to the full revelation of God's word and wisdom in Jesus Christ. Both have value and meaning only in so far as they are understood and lived through the prism of the teaching of this same word and wisdom. These are, of course, bold claims— albeit ones that were central to Christianity's increasingly explicit universalism. Justin was also instrumental in tying the whole content of previous wisdom traditions irrefragably to the person of the Son—a reduction the Sophiologists were, with some justice, to chafe against.

Many of Justin's central precepts are taken to a new pitch by his sometime pupil Tatian (b. *c.* 120 AD), albeit with very little on the S3 level. In his *Oration to the Greeks*, a treatise stuffed full of classical allusions, Tatian pours scorn on the whole cultural edifice of Hellenism, refusing to allow it even the partial truth acknowledged by Justin. Tatian puts the theory of larceny at the centre of his case, using it to expose the utter bankruptcy of Greek thought (S0): 'We have renounced your wisdom', he declares, taking pride rather in the Christian 'barbaric philosophy' (*Oration* 1.3; 35.1).[30] Greek philosophers are lovers of vain noise, not of wisdom (φιλοψόφων καὶ οὐ φιλοσόφων) (*Oration* 3.3).[31] Philosophers are venal and hopelessly at odds with one another (*Oration* 25.1–2). In their discordance they show themselves far from any sort of unitary and authoritative wisdom: 'you who parcel out wisdom are cut off from the wisdom that is according to the truth' (*Oration* 26.2). They fail to practise what they preach and gain no practical profit from their vain speculations: 'while inquiring what God is, you are ignorant of what is in yourselves; and while staring open-mouthed at the sky, you fall down holes' (*Oration* 26.1).[32] Their whole system is, quite simply, useless and unreliable, and of far lesser antiquity than the 'barbarian wisdom' of Christianity (*Oration* 31.40), Moreover, Greek philosophy is available to only a small portion of humanity—

---

[30] Tatian takes delight in pointing out how much of Hellenic culture comes from barbarians in the first place. Cf. Melito of Sardis, Fragment 1.3: 'our philosophy first flourished among the barbarians' (SC 123 220).

[31] Again, note the parallel with the kind of criticisms levelled by the philosophers themselves against the rhetoricians.

[32] The reference here seems to be to the famous cautionary tale concerning Thales of Miletus (recorded in Plato's *Theaetetus* 174a and taken up into *Aesop's Fables*).

specifically the wealthy adult male population. Christianity, by contrast, is open to rich and poor, male and female, young and old (*Oration* 32). In his forthright defence of the unparalleled supremacy of Christian wisdom Tatian shows himself to be decidedly the least apologetic of the Apologists.

Of somewhat similar intractability of temperament is the first great Latin theologian, Tertullian (d. *c.* 220 AD).[33] In his voluminous works, Tertullian has a great deal to say on the subject of wisdom—not that he receives much credit for this within Russian Sophiology.[34] In the *Apology*, he claims that no rulers possessed of even a hint of divine or human wisdom ever persecuted the Christians (*Apology* 5.4–5). He revels in exposing the contradictions of the Hellenic tradition, referring to the famous incident in which the Oracle at Delphi witnessed to the wisdom of Socrates, also known for his sceptical attitude to the pagan pantheon: 'Thoughtless Apollo! testifying to the wisdom of the man who denied the existence of the gods' (*Apology* 46.6). In short, there is no 'likeness between the Christian and the philosopher, between the disciple of Greece and of heaven' (*Apology* 46.18). Philosophy does not start from the fear of God which in itself implies knowledge of God. The 'full and perfect wisdom' of Christians (S2) is thus closed to the philosophers (*To the Nations* 2.2.4) who must content themselves with their empty hankering after conjectures and speculations (S0) (*To the Nations* 2.2.1, 2.4.17). Philosophy is incapable of acquiring sure and certain knowledge—as is evident in Socrates' last hour at which he evinced an 'affected equanimity rather than the firm conviction of ascertained truth' (*Treatise on the Soul* 1.4). True, heavenly wisdom is 'revealed by the Lord' and confounds and confutes earthly philosophy (*On the Soul* 3.2). Indeed, pagan philosophy is the root and parent of Christian heresy and this is the most fundamental reason for us to reject any affinity between Athens and Jerusalem (*On the Prescription of Heretics* 7.9). Wisdom can be a dangerous thing in the wrong hands: the devil was once the wisest and most beautiful of creatures, as is recorded in the account of the fall of the Prince of Tyre in Ezekiel 28 (*Against Marcion* 2.10.2). Wisdom can also be taken away, as it has been from the Jews (*Against Marcion* 3.16.1). Human wisdom (S1) has its rightful place—as indicated by Tertullian's approval of a remark of Lucretius, hailing it as 'worthy of a place in the world's wisdom' (*Against Marcion* 4.8.3). Such wisdom, however, does not bear comparison with the divine wisdom (S2) to which St Paul refers in 1 Corinthians, wisdom which once lay hidden in types and figures and allegories but has now been revealed by Christ (*Against Marcion* 5.6.1).

---

[33] On philosophy in Tertullian, see Carlo Tibiletti, 'Filosofia e cristianesimo in Tertulliano' and Eric Osborn, *Tertullian, First Theologian of the West*, 27–41.

[34] Bulgakov expresses grave reservations over Tertullian's subservience to Stoic materialism and drastically subordinationist account of the Trinity (cf. *The Comforter*, 17–25 [ET 9–15] and *The Bride of the Lamb*, 20 [ET 16]). He does, however, mention him (with some surprise) as a proponent of the doctrine of the divine ideas of creation: *The Burning Bush*, 287 (Excursus III) [ET 156].

Expanding on the nature of the divine wisdom, Tertullian also offers some considerations on level S3. He explains that God created the world not out of pre-existent matter but out of his own wisdom, that is, his own spirit or word. Proverbs 8 thus refers to this created and creative divine wisdom inherent in God from all eternity but put into motion for the purposes of creation.[35] It is this wisdom (*sophia*) which is 'made,'[36] the beginning of God's ways for his works' (*Against Hermogenes* 18.1–4). Wisdom indicates the divine plan for creation, 'this contemplation and ordering being the primal operation of wisdom' (*Against Hermogenes* 20.2). Elsewhere, Tertullian develops this understanding of the word or wisdom of God as the vehicle of God's self-revelation, as the means by which the ideas of the creation are brought into being. For Tertullian, again using the Greek term, wisdom denotes the power and disposition of God and is most aptly applied to the reason or word of God. He continues:

> When at the first God willed, with his wisdom (*sophia*) and reason and word, to put forth in their substances and forms the things which he had planned and ordered within himself, he first brought forth the word himself, having within him his own inseparable reason and wisdom, so that all things might be made through him through whom they had been contemplated and ordered, indeed and already made, in so far as they were in the mind of God. This, however, was still lacking to them, that they should also be made known and maintained in their respective forms and substances. (*Against Praxeas* 6.3)

The construal of wisdom as the divine realm of ideas for the creation is an important development. Tertullian is, however, careful in this passage and what follows to distinguish between God's own 'inseparable wisdom' (with which he associates the divine realm of ideas in eternity) and God's wisdom existing in a distinct *persona*, the persona that speaks in Proverbs 8 and through whom the eternal divine plan is realized in time and space. He adopts an Aristotelian framework to explain that the former is simply an attribute of God, an accident of a particular substance, whereas the latter is of the same substance of God albeit not God *per se* (*Against Praxeas* 26.6). It is this personal wisdom who is rightly called God and, however absurd (but therefore true) it may seem, who was crucified for us (*On the Flesh of Christ* 5.4).[37]

---

[35] Cf. *Against Praxeas* 7.3: 'It is evident that it is one and the same power which is in one place named wisdom (*sophia*), and in another called word, and which was initiated for the works of God.'

[36] Note that Tertullian draws from the Old Latin Bible and so reads made/established (*condidit*) rather than the Vulgate's 'possessed' (*possedit*) at Proverbs 8:22.

[37] The sacrificial dimension of wisdom is underlined in Tertullian's arresting explication of Proverbs 9:2 (which he reads as wisdom having 'slain her own children') in terms of the persecution of the prophets and Christian martyrs (*Scorpiace* 7.1–2).

It is striking that Tertullian gives relatively little attention to the educative function of the divine wisdom. And unlike Justin, he is unwilling to allow to the philosophers anything more than what can be achieved according to the strictly natural light of human reason—including some form of natural theology (*On the Crown* 6.1–2). For Tertullian, the theme of wisdom is almost exclusively a question of cosmology and salvation and not of *paideia*. In this respect he would seem to be equally distanced from both the Jewish and Hellenic wisdom traditions.

Hippolytus (d. *c.* 214 AD), by contrast with Justin and Tertullian, lines up with Theophilus in identifying wisdom (S3) more closely with the Holy Spirit than with the Son. As he puts it: God has engendered his word to create the universe and his wisdom to adorn it (*Against the Heresy of Noetus* 10.3).[38] Hippolytus gives particular attention to wisdom as an interpretative gift (S2), necessary for the proper understanding of the scriptures.[39] In his *Commentary on Proverbs* (taking as his text the phrase 'to know wisdom and instruction (*paideia*)' (Proverbs 1:2)) he adds that, 'He who knows the wisdom of God also receives *paideia* from him, learning through this the mysteries of the word. And those who know the true heavenly wisdom will readily understand the wise words spoken by her' (*Commentary on Proverbs* 1).[40] True to the whole tone and tenor of Proverbs, Hippolytus underlines the very practical and necessarily self-giving dimension of wisdom and *paideia*: 'Observe that the wise man must be useful to many; he that is useful only to himself cannot be wise.' (*Fragments in Proverbs* 16).[41] By contrast with Tertullian, Hippolytus remains steeped in the Jewish wisdom tradition and especially in the dimension of *paideia*.

To sum up this section, the testimony of the Apologists indicates a growing interest in the cosmological, Christological, and Trinitarian aspects of wisdom. The refusal to pin down wisdom exclusively to the Son of God (as in Theophilus and Hippolytus)[42] garnered some interest within modern Russian Sophiology as it fought to broaden the scope of reflection on divine wisdom but such S3 considerations are, however, far from the central thrusts of these texts which remain focussed, for the most part, on themes of divine *paideia* and instruction.

---

[38] In Butterworth (ed.), *Hippolytus of Rome: Contra Noetum*, 69.

[39] See for example *On the Antichrist* 18, 29 (GCS 1.2 14, 19); and *On the Blessing of Isaac and Jacob*, preamble (PO 27 2–3).

[40] In Richard (ed.), 'Les fragments du Commentaire de S. Hippolyte sur les Proverbes de Salomon', 75.

[41] In GCS 1.2 162.

[42] Bulgakov appeals to Theophilus and Irenaeus (but not Hippolytus) in this respect: *The Wisdom of God*, 46.

3.3 Silvanus, Sextus, and the Pseudo-Clementines

We turn now to set of intriguing second- and third-century texts which flesh out further the ubiquity of the notion of divine *paideia* or formation within early Christian wisdom reflection: the *Teachings of Silvanus, Sentences of Sextus*, and the pseudo-Clementine corpus. These are relatively little-known texts that do not figure in the Sophiologists' appeal for patristic support (understandably in the case of Silvanus, which was discovered only at the end of the Second World War). They do, however, offer some important insights into the rich and variegated character of wisdom teaching in the Early Church as it wrestled with its scriptural and classical inheritances. While offering some intriguing suggestions of their own, they also serve to underline further the rather limited nature of Sophiology's appropriation of the early Christian wisdom tradition.

The *Teachings of Silvanus* (the ascription is to the companion of Paul mentioned in Acts) is an outstanding example of Christian wisdom literature and one which draws deeply on both Jewish and Hellenic wisdom traditions. It is a Coptic text dating to the mid second-century and found among the otherwise largely Gnostic Nag Hammadi library (unearthed in 1945) but has no Gnostic characteristics—indeed is arguably anti-Gnostic in its largely positive attitude to the material creation in general and the body in particular. Its presentation of wisdom is, furthermore, wholly removed from the various Gnostic mythologies of wisdom present elsewhere in the corpus. Judging by its similarities with the *Letters of Anthony* it seems that the text had some currency in early monastic Egypt.[43] Silvanus presents a veritable *vade mecum* in the traditional wisdom form of parental admonition to 'my son'. Great stress is put on the cultivation of mind and reason in order to preserve the city of the soul: 'Bring in your guide and your teacher. The mind is the guide, but reason is the teacher' (85). Both mind and reason must be cultivated by acceptance of *paideia* and commitment to an upright life (87). Through such means we ready ourselves to put on the 'high-priestly garment' of wisdom, a gift offered by Christ *qua* wisdom (89). We must flee death and ignorance and return to God, our Father, and wisdom, our mother (91). In becoming self-controlled in soul and body, we will become 'a throne of wisdom' (92). We must be on guard against the counterfeit wisdom of the enemy (95) and seek out rather the redeeming and illuminating divine teacher, Christ (96–8). Christ, the light of the Father, is both comprehensible and incomprehensible (101–2).[44] Christ is the 'tree of life' and 'wisdom' (106). 'For since he is wisdom, he makes the foolish man wise. It [wisdom] is a holy kingdom and a shining robe.

---

[43] Cf. Samuel Rubenson, *Letters of St Anthony*, 49.

[44] Silvanus also teaches that God is everywhere according to his power and nowhere according to his divinity (100–1). The distinction between God's power (cf. energy) and divinity (cf. essence) may legitimately be seen as yet another adumbration of the distinction between God and his attributes or operations that was to become commonplace in the Greek patristic tradition.

For it is much gold which gives you great honour. The wisdom of God became a type of fool for you so that it might take you up, O foolish one, and make you a wise man. And the life died for you when he was powerless, so that through his death he might give life to you who have died.' (107). We must have as a friend this Christ who is 'God and teacher', this Christ who 'broke the iron bars of the underworld and the bronze bolts' (110). Christ has risen from the heart of the Father as first-born and wisdom (112). He is, in words taken from Wisdom 7, 'an emanation of the pure glory of the Almighty. He is the spotless mirror of the working of God, and he is the image of his goodness.' Finally, the closing injunction sums up the treatise as follows: 'Accept the wisdom of Christ [who is] patient and mild, and guard this, O my son, knowing that God's way is always profitable.' (117).

This is on any estimation a remarkable text. What is perhaps most striking is the way on which no disjunction is set up between Christ as redeemer and Christ as teacher: it is a piece of properly Christian *gnosis*. Themes of illumination and remembrance sit harmoniously with themes of salvation and escape from demonic influences. Moral excellence is equated with the keeping of the command-ments while the frame of reference takes in both biblical wisdom literature (on which it is modelled) and Greek philosophy (specifically a Platonic metaphysics and anthropology with a large helping of Stoic and Cynic ethics). We see here, in short, Christian wisdom effortlessly combining Jewish and Hellenic wisdom traditions and offering a paraenetic account of wisdom fully embracing levels S1–S3.

In the *Sentences of Sextus*, an analogous, if less thoroughgoing, attempt is made to combine Greek philosophy and Judeo-Christian wisdom.[45] The *Sentences of Sextus* comprise a substantial set of maxims that became a popular piece of early Christian wisdom literature, being first attested to in Origen. The *Sentences* are steeped in classical, especially Stoic and Pythagorean, wisdom—in fact, they appear to be based partly on a pre-existing set of Pythagorean maxims. As one might expect from this ancestry, the emphasis is very much on wisdom as a moral category, an upright and distinctly ascetic way of life that brings one a certain inner security amidst the vicissitudes of life (S1). There is little in this text on the wider dimensions of the wisdom question (S2–S3). There are also no more than a few distant allusions to biblical wisdom material and minimal reference to the saving work of Christ. By comparison with the *Teachings of Silvanus* it is a thin work when it comes to the theology of the divine wisdom for all that it represents a substantial piece of Christian wisdom literature. We do, however, encounter some

---

[45] On wisdom in Sextus, see especially Wilken, 'Wisdom and Philosophy in Early Christianity' and the splendid materials in Henry Chadwick's edition of the text, *The Sentences of Sextus: A Contribution to the History of Early Christian Ethics*. A partial Coptic version of Sextus is, along with the *Teachings of Silvanus*, preserved in the Nag Hammadi corpus.

intriguing considerations: the wise man is said to be 'like God' (18), one in whom God dwells (144), 'the image of the living God' (190), and one who partakes of the kingdom of God (311). Wisdom is thus a deifying power, an experiential form of knowledge that leads the soul to God (167, 406). As in Theophilus, wisdom is construed as the means by which humans come to image God. While less expansive and less theological than the *Teachings of Silvanus*, the *Sentences of Sextus* stands as a fine example of an early Christian wisdom text in which the emphasis is squarely on the way in which God's divine *paideia* brings humanity ever closer to himself.

I turn now to another rather curious group of texts, the pseudo-Clementine corpus. This corpus, which is not easy to date, appears to be an early fourth-century text in its finished form but with a third-century core. Purporting to be the work of St Clement of Rome but clearly stemming from a later period, it stands as a fascinating if somewhat enigmatic example of wisdom treated within a broadly Jewish-Christian context, albeit one very much enmeshed in the Greek thought-world. The pseudo-Clementine *Homilies* present an account of Christianity as the true philosophy (S1), categorically exploding the vapid and contradictory posturings of the Greek philosophers (S0).[46] In thus attacking the contradictory nature of philosophical conclusions the *Homilies*, interestingly, parallel similar assaults made by the Sceptics against the truth claims of ancient philosophy. They do not, however, end in the same agnostic impasse, expressing confidence in the simple and clear teaching of the apostles, a certain presentation of truth grounded not in feeble reason but in revelation (S2) (1.10–11). St Peter, the principal figure in the corpus, is presented as 'greatest in the wisdom of God' (1.15.6). The philosophers may have sought truth, but they failed to find it, not realizing that conjectures drawn from observation of visible things will never constitute anything more than a relative truth based on their own subjective presuppositions. In a turn of phrase that, ironically, recalls the charges Greek philosophers themselves laid against rhetoricians, the *Homilies* castigate the pretended philosophers as mere 'lovers of words, not of wisdom' (φιλόλογοι οὐ φιλόσοφοι) (2.8.3).[47] Simon Magus' claim to have brought down to earth the archetypal Helen (evidently a variant of the Gnostic Sophia myth) 'who is queen as all-mothering (παμμήτορα) essence and wisdom' is similarly exploded (2.25.1–2).[48]

The pre-eternal counsel of God in Genesis 1:26 is explained (ostensibly by St Peter to Simon Magus) in terms that illustrate the struggle to formulate a complex monotheism, one that preserved God's oneness while allowing for multiple forms

---

[46] The idea of Christianity as the 'true philosophy'—one to which we shall return—is itself a kind of veiled recognition of the fact that philosophy was never simply a discipline of the mind in the ancient world but rather a way of life.

[47] On this theme in the context of later Christian biblical interpretation, see Frances Young, 'The Rhetorical Schools and their Influence on Patristic Exegesis'.

[48] For Gnostic Sophia myths, see below, p.116.

of divine presence and action in the world. God, Peter explains, was speaking to his wisdom (S3) when he said, 'Let us create', the wisdom with whom he is one and who 'is united as soul to God, but is extended by him, as hand, fashioning the universe' (16.12.1).[49] Intriguingly, this account maintains the feminine character of the Old Testament figure of wisdom and explains the creation of the two sexes as a consequence of this dual process of creation. The texts do not explicitly identify Christ, or indeed the Holy Spirit, with wisdom,[50] thereby reminding us that wisdom theology is not necessarily bound up with the nascent doctrine of the Trinity— indeed that this speculation sometimes inhabits something of a 'grey area' between what is later recognized as orthodoxy and heresy.

These three texts, different as they are, offer some intriguing and suggestive takes on wisdom. Silvanus gives us wisdom as heavenly mother, the human being as a 'throne of wisdom', and Christ rising as wisdom from the heart of the Father. Sextus speaks of the acquisition of wisdom as the realization of the *imago Dei* while pseudo-Clement treats wisdom as the divine, feminine and pre-eternal associate of God in the work of creation without obvious reference to the persons of the Son and Spirit. All treat wisdom as the alpha and omega of the Christian life: the divine *paideia* by which humans are brought ever closer to the God who is himself wisdom. While there are certainly some potential connections to be made with Sophiology on the S3 level (wisdom as feminine, wisdom as divine but non-Trinitarian, and a strong Platonic dimension), the consistent connection between wisdom and *paideia* on levels S1 and S2 in these texts is, once again, something that scarcely comes through in the work of the Russian devotees of Sophia.

3.4 St Irenaeus of Lyons

The most substantive treatment of wisdom in this early period is that of St Irenaeus of Lyons (d. *c.* 200 AD), offering a thoroughgoing account of wisdom that does ample justice to all three principal levels of wisdom reflection (S1–S3). Little of this gets through to Bulgakov who, while allowing that his work has some systematic quality, notably fails to make any significant use of Irenaeus beyond some passing mentions, notably the association he makes between wisdom and Holy Spirit.[51]

Irenaeus is the first great theologian of the early Church and one who emphatically had no time for any sort of 'grey area' between orthodoxy and heresy. Irenaeus' forceful *Demonstration of the Apostolic Preaching* begins with a variation

---

[49] The image of wisdom as the 'hand' of God is also found in Irenaeus, cf. below, p.117.

[50] Note, however, the implicit identification of Christ with wisdom in *Homilies* 11.32.1 (including a citation of Mt. 12:42: 'behold, one greater than Solomon is here').

[51] Cf. *The Bride of the Lamb*, 20 [ET 15] and *The Wisdom of God*, 46.

of the familiar 'two ways' wisdom theme (*Demonstration* 1).[52] After this quintes-sentially sapiential opening, he goes on to speak of wisdom under multiple headings. Perhaps most notably, like Theophilus and Hippolytus, he connects the Old Testament figure of wisdom with the Holy Spirit. This wisdom 'arranges and forms' the various powers in the creation and shapes man into the likeness of God, crying within him 'Abba, Father' (*Demonstration* 5).[53] The Holy Spirit inspires the prophets (*Demonstration* 6) and infuses humans with the spirit of wisdom (cf. Is. 11.2–3), the first and highest of Isaiah's seven heavens through which we can ascend to God (*Demonstration* 9).[54] Wrapping up the treatise, he exhorts us to 'ceaselessly give thanks to God who has, through his abundant inscrutable and unfathomable wisdom, saved us and preached the salvation which is from heaven' (*Demonstration* 97).

Even in this short work, we see wisdom functioning on a number of levels, especially as an appellation of the Spirit uniting man to God (S3) and as an illuminating, redeeming, and educative gift (S2). These dimensions, along with much on level S1, are found in more expanded form in Irenaeus' *magnum opus*, *Against the Heresies*. One of his chief concerns in this work is to dismiss the pretended wisdom of the Gnostics, and most especially their multifarious Sophia myths. Gnostic speculations concerning Sophia—usually some form of divine (but fallen) feminine principle—do not inhibit Irenaeus from speaking about the true divine wisdom of which the Gnostic teachers are so obviously destitute (*AH* 1.10.3).[55] He is particularly incensed by the idea that the divine wisdom should ever have fallen into passion or ignorance (*AH* 2.17.8, 18.1). Rather than rejecting the notion of divine wisdom as irredeemably soiled by the Gnostics, Irenaeus is concerned rather to reclaim this cardinally important concept for the mainstream Church tradition while shearing it of all mythological accretions. This stance serves as a useful paradigm for the contemporary appropriation of the theology of the divine wisdom such as is attempted in Chapter 7.

Irenaeus pays especial attention to the anthropological dimension of the wis-dom question. The human form was made 'in no other way than by the wisdom of God' and even our flesh 'participates in the constructive wisdom of God' (*AH*

---

[52] Cf. *Against the Heresies* 5.20.1–2.

[53] See further Sarah Coakley's immensely perceptive comments on the 'incorporative' model of the Trinity in which the Spirit of Romans 8 brings us into the very life of the Trinity: 'Why Three? Some further reflections on the origins of the doctrine of the Trinity' and *God, Sexuality, and the Self: An Essay 'On the Trinity'*, 100–15.

[54] Irenaeus would seem here to be referring to something like the apocryphal *Ascension of Isaiah*.

[55] On the Gnostic Sophia myths, see (amid a large bibliography) the very varying accounts in Christopher Stead, 'The Valentinian Myth of Sophia'; Alastair Logan, *Gnostic Truth and Christian Heresy*; George Macrae 'The Jewish Background of the Gnostic Sophia Myth'; Simone Pétrement, *Le Dieu séparé: les origines du gnosticisme*; Marguerite Techert, 'La notion de la sagesse dans les trois premiers siècles de notre ère'; H. Jaeger, 'The Patristic Conception of Wisdom in the Light of Biblical and Rabbinical Research'; and Robert Grant', *Gnosticism and Early Christianity* and *Irenaeus of Lyons*, introduction.

5.3.2–3). The capacity to receive wisdom is that which chiefly distinguishes the human vocation: 'For the glory of man is God; man is the receptacle of God's operation and of all his wisdom and power' (*AH* 3.20.2). This is a calling beyond even that of the angels (*AH* 5.36.3) and it is through this gift of wisdom that we come to know the Father through his word and wisdom—although the Father always remains beyond our comprehension according to his essence (*AH* 3.24.2).[56] These two, word and wisdom, are the vehicles of his self-revelation (*AH* 4.7.4), his 'hands' in the creation (*AH* 4.20.1, 5.6.1). Wisdom texts (e.g. Prov. 3:19–20, 8:22–5, 27–31) are consistently applied to the Spirit who, with the word, is always with the one God (4.20.1–4).

Wisdom is also used to explicate the incarnate dispensation. The flesh was necessary to display the wisdom that is in Christ (*AH* 3.22.1). Without it, humanity would never have been able to attain any true knowledge of God. Commenting on Moses' vision on Mount Sinai, Irenaeus observes that, 'this signifies two things: that it is impossible for man to see God; but that, through the wisdom of God, man shall see him in the last times, "in the cleft of a rock", that is, in his coming as man' (*AH* 4.20.9).

In all of Irenaeus' treatment of wisdom, frequent appeal is made to biblical wisdom texts. Here we move from S2–S3 considerations to an emphasis on S1— wisdom as a way of life. For example, referring to the very public apostolic preaching (here in explicit contrast to the secret teachings of the Gnostics), Irenaeus tells us that the wisdom by which the Church saves all humankind 'is declared in its going forth and uttering [its voice] faithfully in the streets, is preached on the tops of walls, and speaks continually in the gates of the city. For the Church preaches the truth everywhere and she is the seven-branched candlestick which bears the light of Christ.' (*AH* 5.20.1).[57] In the famous passage on the barbarians (who conform to the ancient apostolic tradition notwithstanding their lack of written texts) Irenaeus specifies that they are 'supremely wise, because of the faith, as to thinking, customs, and way of life, and they please God living in all righteousness, purity, and wisdom' (*AH* 3.4.2). For Irenaeus, wisdom is the defining characteristic of the Christian way of life.

All this amounts to a very rich teaching on wisdom. Refusing to allow wisdom to become the sole property of the Gnostics, Irenaeus places it at the heart of his theological vision. Wisdom is pivotal in his understanding of God's self-revelation to the creation and of the ways in which God draws humanity to himself. Wisdom is used to speak of the mystery of the incarnation but is especially associated with the Holy Spirit. Finally, the divine *paideia* communicated in the apostolic

---

[56] Note (as in Silvanus) the theme of wisdom as revealing the unknowable being or essence of God.
[57] Cf. Proverbs 1:20–1 and Exodus 25:31–7. Note the connection between wisdom and tradition— the living continuum of faith so central to Irenaeus' anti-Gnostic platform.

tradition is defined in terms of wisdom, as is the way of life that that *paideia* necessarily entails.

3.5 *Coda* to Wisdom and *Paideia*

This survey of the place of wisdom in the era of the Apostolic Fathers and Apologists has revealed a very wide spectrum of thought and opinion as to the place and significance of wisdom in the Christian tradition. Without rehearsing again all the many and various instances of the theme, this summary demonstrates something of the sheer depth, breadth, and complexity of wisdom speculation in the period. Wisdom is consistently treated as a way of understanding God's self-revelation to the creation. There is barely an area of Christian reflection in which wisdom does not figure significantly: Trinitarian theology, Christology, cosmology, soteriology, anthropology, pedagogy, epistemology, classical encounter, and the debate over the Jewish inheritance. In this respect we do indeed see the beginnings of patristic sophiology (S3) in this period, albeit always in organic relation to levels S1–S2 and, especially, to the theme of *paideia*. All this makes even more remarkable the extent to which modern Russian Sophiology has almost completely overlooked this period as a resource and reference point with the exception of occasional mentions of the association of wisdom with the Holy Spirit in Theophilus and Irenaeus. But the period as a whole is dismissed as irredeemably unsophiological and thus the huge potential contribution to a theology of wisdom by writers such as Justin, Tertullian, and Irenaeus is effectively nullified. This regrettable short-sightedness not only casts doubt on Sophiology's general claim of patristic rootedness but shows up its very limited apprehension of the nature and scope of patristic tradition.

Much more, of course, remained to be said on the question of wisdom in Christian tradition and it is to the Fathers and teachers of the Alexandrine tradition that we must first turn for this further and more extensive elaboration. The Alexandrines usher in what I have taken the liberty to christen 'The Golden Age of Patristic Sophiology'.

4

The Golden Age of Patristic Sophiology

The 'Golden Age of Patristic Sophiology' encompasses some of the greatest
theologians of the Early Church: Clement, Origen, Athanasius, the Cappadocian
Fathers, and Augustine. In these writers, wisdom emerges as a central theological
locus in S3 terms but always in organic relationship with levels S1–S2. Many of
these figures are regular reference points and significant sources of authority
within modern Russian Sophiology. While offering a rich and sophisticated set
of wisdom teachings, this golden age also witnesses to a divergence in the
construal of divine simplicity in which a space or gap opens up for Sophiology
in the Greek East but not in the Latin West.

4.1 The Early Alexandrines

In the Fathers and teachers of the great city of Alexandria, the multi-dimensional
theme of wisdom becomes a central and indispensable locus of Christian theology,
epistemology, and ethics. This is a tradition that fed directly into modern Russian
Sophiology. This first section deals with Philo, St Clement,[1] and Origen.

4.1.1 Philo of Alexandria

Before venturing to discuss the great Christian writers of Alexandria, a word must
be said about their illustrious Jewish predecessor, Philo of Alexandria (c. 20 BC—
c. 50 AD). Philo, despite the fact that he was largely side-lined in the later Jewish
Rabbinic tradition, had a decisive and formative impact on later Christian
theology—most notably in the cases of SS Clement and Gregory of Nyssa. He

---

[1] There is some dispute within the Orthodox Church as to whether Clement is indeed to be
accounted a saint (in a lecture given at the faculty of theology of the University of Athens I was,
with great courtesy, taken up on this point by the then Dean, Fr George Metallenos). Clement does not
figure in most *synaxaria* (lists and brief lives of recognized saints) currently in use although he does
appear in some earlier *synaxaria* and martyrologies. The fact that he was removed from the Roman
martyrology (founded on both Eastern and Western martyrologies) in the late sixteenth century by
Pope Clement VIII (a deletion confirmed by Benedict XIV in the eighteenth century) does suggest that
he was once accounted a martyr by the universal Church and, given that the Orthodox Church has no
mechanism of demotion or removal, he should therefore be honoured, as a martyr, with the title of
saint. This comes, however, with the recognition that his teaching is not regarded as bearing the
authority of a Church Father *proprement dit* by many Orthodox (and other) scholars.

Wisdom in Christian Tradition: The Patristic Roots of Modern Russian Sophiology. Marcus Plested, Oxford University Press.
© Marcus Plested 2022. DOI: 10.1093/oso/9780192863225.003.0005

became an important source for modern Russian Sophiology in terms of cosmology (including the divine realm of ideas) and, especially, for his non-Trinitarian and somehow feminine construal of wisdom standing 'in between' God and the world.

In Philo we see the emergence of a systematic and profound assimilation of Greek and Jewish wisdom traditions consistently conducted within the context of his searching meditation upon scripture.[2] For Philo, it is wisdom which allows us to see and, more importantly, live out through scrupulous observance of the law the unified meaning of scripture. Wisdom is thus the very basis and principle of the allegorical method of interpretation which he pioneered and which became such a defining feature of the Alexandrine Christian tradition. The allegorical method is, for Philo, not just a hermeneutic tool or a borrowing from the pagan tradition of philosophical commentary but, more significantly, a vocation or way of life.

Wisdom constitutes a far-reaching but essentially unified complex of ideas in Philo. He maintains the practical sense of wisdom (as skill and the learning gained from experience) (S1) found in both Greek and Jewish wisdom traditions, but is most interested in wisdom as a means of speaking about the nature of God's operation in the world and especially in God's gift of knowledge to his rational creation (S2–S3). For Philo, wisdom stands very much 'in between' God and the world, representing the revelation and condescension of the unknowable and unapproachable God who dwells in unfathomable darkness. Wisdom is a quality or attribute of God, one of his 'uncreated powers', that cannot be born by mortals in its unalloyed state except by way of divine condescension (*Deus* 17.77–81).[3] Philo's consideration of the operation and gift of wisdom is, naturally, focused upon the special revelation to Israel as revealed in scripture.[4] In his treatments of Abram/Abraham, Philo allots a certain rôle to human learning (S1), drawing attention to Abram's Chaldean heritage and (through Hagar) contact with the learning of Egypt. Such learning acts as a preliminary stage of preparation that brings one to philosophy which in its turn aids in the acquisition of the illuminating gift of wisdom defined, after the Stoics, as 'the knowledge of all divine and human things and of the causes of them' (S2) (*De congressu* 5.20–4, 14.78–80). Sarah shares in the gift of wisdom principally through her son, Isaac

---

[2] On wisdom in Philo see Jacques Cazeaux, 'Sagesse II: La sagesse selon Philon d'Alexandrie'; Marguerite Techert, 'La notion de la sagesse dans les trois premiers siècles de notre ère' (useful despite her exaggerated case for a lurking goddess figure); Jean Laporte, 'Philo in the Tradition of Biblical Wisdom Literature'; and Roberto Radice, 'Philo's Theology and Theory of Creation'.

[3] On the potential analogy between the Philonic and Palamite conceptions of divine essence and activity, see further Tikhon Pino, 'An Essence-Energy Distinction in Philo as the Basis for the Language of Deification'.

[4] Not, however, in any exclusivist fashion: 'because all the wise are dear to God, and especially those who are wise with the wisdom of the most sacred giving of the law' (*Heres* 5.21).

(*Leg.* II 21.82) while Abraham, Isaac, and Jacob form a kind of wisdom triad representing the various stages of wisdom (*Somn.* I 27.167–71).

It is, however, Moses who emerges as the supreme recipient of divine wisdom—the one who alone has drunk the 'cup of unalloyed wisdom' (*Mos.* II 37.204).[5] In ascending Sinai, Moses 'entered into the darkness where God was; that is to say, into the invisible, and shapeless, and incorporeal world, the essence, which is the model of all existing things'. Seeing the divine prototypes of the creation, he became himself a model or mirror of God, 'a most beautiful and Godlike work' (*Mos.* I 28.158).[6] For Philo (as for Justin and Tatian after him) it is from the incomparable Moses that the Greeks stole such wisdom as they possess (*Heres* 43.214).

Philo, building as always on the biblical narrative, naturally gives wisdom a central rôle in his account of the creation (*Heres* 41.199; *Opif.* 52.148). Wisdom is the 'mother of the world', 'through whom all things came into being' (*De fuga* 20.109). She is, however, also susceptible to masculine designations, for example as 'father' of Rebecca. To explain this, Philo argues that while she is feminine (as daughter) in regard to God, in regard to us she is 'male and father in sowing and begetting in souls learning, *paideia*, science, understanding, and good and worthy deeds' (ibid., 9.51–2).[7] Wisdom permeates creation as light (*De congressu* 9.47–8; *Spec.* III 1.6). Adam is endowed with a certain degree of wisdom at his creation (*Opif.* 52.148) but evidently still has a long way to go. Philo takes the arresting image of the turtledove and the pigeon offered by Abraham to symbolize the unity and distinction between divine and human wisdom—the one ever seeking the heights, the other dwelling amongst men (*Heres* 25–6.126–9, 38.182–3).[8]

Wisdom in Philo is roughly tantamount to the word or *logos* of God. Both wisdom and the word represent a distinct divine agent 'in between' God and the world and may, with allowance for anachronism, be designated as hypostases. Whether these hypostases are strictly eternal is another question.[9] It is certainly feasible to suggest that any apparent divine multiplicity in Philo is merely the result of the divine condescension to the realm of multiplicity, to the created world. In this analysis, Philo's is not in any strictly eternal sense a binitarian or trinitarian schema but more a Platonic *exitus-reditus* schema in which the one God extrapolates and reveals himself in multiple forms (above all as masculine *logos* and feminine *sophia*) in order to return the cosmos to primal oneness. The

---

[5] Cf. *Mos.* I 1.4; *Mos.* II 1.3; *Poster.* 51.174.   [6] Cf. *Deus* 24.110, 32.148).

[7] Behind this lies an assumption, common in antiquity, that the masculine is necessarily superior to the feminine—hence when wisdom is coupled with *logos*, she is invariably secondary.

[8] The feminine image of the dove is also, of course, used of the Holy Spirit in the Gospel narrative—something that can only have encouraged reflection upon his (/her) maternal character in figures such as Macarius-Symeon and the Syriac Christian tradition. Cf. my *The Macarian Legacy*, 43–4.

[9] Radice argues forcefully that they are: 'However, at least in the case of the Logos and even more in that of Wisdom (= *sophia*), these powers seem to be hypostases coeternal with the Creator and collaborators in creation'. 'Philo's Theology and Theory of Creation', 129.

very abundance of deliberately paradoxical images and concepts (of which I have given here but a small fraction) is itself a sign of this descent into the shifting and uncertain world of language and image. Ultimately, wisdom's purpose is to bring the creation out of this endless multiplicity and into divine unity. At that point, her rôle will conceivably cease as she is subsumed back into the utterly simplex deity. But while the precise character of Philo's 'trinity' remains open to further investigation and debate, Philo was certainly an important figure within modern Russian Sophiology with his presentation of wisdom as a divine 'other' in relation to the creation. That said, his usefulness for Sophiology is much problematized by the opaque nature of his estimation of the eternal distinction (or otherwise) of Sophia from God. In the final analysis, Philo's Sophia is patently not, to concur with Florovsky, the 'Sophia of the Church'.[10]

4.1.2 St Clement of Alexandria

Much of Philo's teaching is taken up within a Christian context by St Clement of Alexandria (c. 150–c. 215 AD), albeit with a distinctly more robust understanding of the eternal character of the intra-divine distinction between God and his wisdom. The authority of Clement's teachings remains widely questioned within the Orthodox theological tradition, but he is clearly a thinker of great importance and one whose entire theological vision is shaped and governed by the concept of wisdom (embracing levels S1–S3). Clement was on occasion to be employed as a useful source of support for Sophiology, most notably in respect of the eternity of the divine plan for the creation construed in terms of wisdom.[11] Other aspects of his teaching were, as we shall see, to prove less congenial to the Sophiological project.

Like Philo, Clement achieves a thoroughgoing synthesis between Greek and Jewish wisdom traditions. He cites biblical wisdom literature (especially Proverbs, Ben Sira, and Wisdom) constantly and copiously. Parts of his work are virtual compendia of such material. Clement also makes a conscious appeal to educated pagan culture, expressing the truths of revelation in a manner that appealed to human reason and philosophy while demonstrating revelation's patent surpassing of earthly wisdom. In the background of his life's work we have, as in Irenaeus, an implacable struggle to wrest the concepts of wisdom and knowledge from the hands of Gnostics—then very much a palpable threat to catholic Christianity in the cultural, religious, and philosophical melting pot that was second-century

---

[10] Cf. above, pp.68–9.

[11] Cf. Florensky, The Pillar and Ground of Truth, 329 [ET 239]. Bulgakov does not appeal to Clement for this purpose but does mention him on occasion on other matters, for example on the nature of the soul in Burning Bush, 95n, 97n [ET 166 n.15, n.17].

Alexandria. And as a prominent Christian teacher in that tempestuous city, the pedagogical dimension of wisdom remained uppermost in his mind as he sought to construct a truly Christian *gnosis*.

Clement's three main works, the *Protreptikos*, *Paidagogos*, and *Stromateis* are shot through with references and appeals to wisdom. The *Protreptikos* (or *Exhortation to the Heathen*) begins in earnest with an invocation:

> But let us bring truth from above out of heaven, with all-bright wisdom (φρόνησις) and the holy prophetic choir, down to the holy mountain of God. And may truth, throwing-forth her shining light and illumining all around those that wallow in darkness, and deliver all men from delusion, stretching forth her very strong right hand, which is understanding, for their salvation.
>
> (*Prot.* 1.2.2–3)[12]

Here we see Clement as hierophant, appropriating the initiatory language of the Hellenistic mystery cults and indeed the Gnostics and transposing that language to a resolutely biblical plane. Wisdom (S2) is presented as a saving and illuminating power but, importantly, as a universal gift and not just the preserve of the few (whether Gnostic or educated pagan). Also against the Gnostics, Clement maintains the goodness and eternity of the divine plan for the creation: 'Before the foundation of the world we pre-existed in the mind of God, being destined to be in him, we the rational creatures of the word of God, on whose account we date from the beginning; for "in the beginning was the word".' (*Prot.* 1.6.4; cf. Jn. 1:1).[13] We humans are created 'many-toned instruments of God': 'a beautiful breathing instrument the Lord made man, after his own image'. This image is the 'supra-mundane wisdom (σοφία ὑπερκόσμιος) (S3) of the heavenly word, the all-harmonious, melodious, holy instrument of God' (*Prot.* 1.5.4). The identification of the word with wisdom underlines the fact that, for Clement, wisdom is no nebulous force or errant deity but a hypostatic reality to be identified with the Son of God. This hypostatic wisdom, open to all and not only the initiated élite, is our only refuge, our only means of salvation (*Prot.* 4.63.5), our starting point and our goal (*Prot.* 10.107.2). Clement thus anticipates Origen in tying the notion of wisdom firmly to the second person of the Trinity as part of his anti-Gnostic platform—not an identification the Sophiologists were ever keen to avow.

Much of the *Protrepitkos* is, for all its obvious admiration for much of pagan culture, taken up with a sharp critique not only of the absurdities of pagan religion but also of the discord and excessive specificity of pagan philosophy (S0). We no

---

[12] For φρόνησις as against σοφία, cf. above, p.86.
[13] Clement shares this intuition of the extrapolation and realization of the divine plan for the creation in and through the word or wisdom of God with Tertullian, cf. above, p.110. See further Thomas Torrance, *Divine Meaning: Studies in Patristic Hermeneutics*, 136–8.

longer need to go to Athens for instruction 'for now we have as our teacher him who filled the universe with his holy powers in creation, salvation, beneficence, lawgiving, prophecy, and teaching'. It is this 'only true wisdom, which the best of the philosophers have only guessed at, but which the disciples of Christ have both apprehended and proclaimed' (*Prot.* 11.112.2–3).

The nature of this saving and universally proclaimed pedagogy is, as one would expect from the title, greatly enlarged upon in Clement's *Paidagogos*. The word or wisdom of God is our pedagogue who first exhorts ($\pi\rho\sigma\tau\rho\epsilon\pi\hat{\omega}\nu$), then trains ($\pi\alpha\iota\delta\alpha\gamma\sigma\gamma\hat{\omega}\nu$), then teaches ($\dot{\epsilon}\kappa\delta\iota\delta\dot{\alpha}\sigma\kappa\hat{\omega}\nu$) (*Paid.* 1.1.3.3).[14] This is not a process independent of the sacramental life of the Church. Clement sees baptism as a necessary foundation, cleansing the eye of the spirit, allowing it to perceive and receive the eternal light (*Paid.* 1.6.28.1). Nor is it an abstract enterprise, divorcing us from the world of sense and human relations: the divine pedagogy leads simultaneously to 'the contemplation of God and the performance of holy deeds in everlasting perseverance' (*Paid.* 1.7.53.3).

True to a text so deeply steeped in biblical wisdom literature—books taken here as eminently practical training manuals—the issue of life and how to live it (S1) is central to the *Paidagogos*. The basic principle in this domain is laid out as follows:

> Perfect wisdom, the knowledge of things divine and human, comprehends all things that concern the oversight of the human flock and becomes the craft of life. While we live, wisdom is always accomplishing in us its own proper work, which is the good life.   (*Paid.* 2.2.25.3)

It is perhaps for this reason that Clement is so concerned with issuing advice on a vast range of seemingly rather prosaic subjects, whether this be women's propensity for shoes (*Paid.* 2.11.116.1–2) or men's preoccupation with personal grooming (*Paid.* 3.3.15.1–4). But while his strictures can occasionally seem a trifle bizarre (for example, that men should shave their heads but grow their beards or that women may be permitted white shoes), they do serve to make the point that wisdom, for Clement, is ultimately a supremely practical affair—the devil cannot be allowed to have a monopoly on the details.

Many of the lines laid down in these two works are pursued and developed in Clement's largest work, the *Stromateis*. Greek philosophy emerges here as something of a curate's egg—'good in parts'—or, to use his own simile, like nuts, not all of which (the shell, that is) is edible. Following Philo and Justin, Clement holds that the good parts of philosophy are to a great extent the product of cross-cultural 'borrowing' from Jewish sources, 'the most ancient of all wisdom' (*Strom.* 1.21.101). These good parts are, in fact, stolen, rather like the Promethean fire,

---

[14] It is tempting to see this as a kind of plan for Clement's trilogy of main works, but while it works for the first two of the sequence, the *Stromateis* (or *Miscellanies*) defy any neat categorization.

and it is this spark that imbues them with a 'trace of wisdom' (*Strom*. 1.17.87). Plato, whom Clement holds in great esteem, is described as 'the philosopher who learnt from the Hebrews' (*Strom*. 1.1.10.2) and as having imitated Moses in framing his *Laws* (*Strom*. 1.25.165.1).[15] By divine providence, philosophy has served as 'a kind of preparatory training' (προπαιδεία τις) for the Greeks prior to the advent of the Lord: the way of truth is one 'but into it, as into a perennial river, streams flow from all sides' (*Strom*. 1.5.29.1–2).

This does not amount to mere relativism, an early instance of 'branch theory' or *philosophia perennis*. Drawing and lifting directly from Philo's *De congressu*, Clement uses Hagar and Sarah to represent the ascent from preparatory study to philosophy and to wisdom. Philosophy (S1) is the handmaid to wisdom (S2) which is 'the queen of philosophy, as philosophy is of preparatory culture' (*Strom*. 1.5.29–30). Clement treats philosophy as the supreme product of the natural yearning for understanding that characterizes the human condition. It differs from true wisdom as does desire from its realization (*Strom*. 1.5.32.4), the child from the adult (*Strom*. 1.11.53.2), the stairs from the upper room (*Strom*. 1.20.99.3), or as guessing from certainty: 'The guessing at truth is one thing, the thing itself another; the one results from learning and practice, the other from power and faith.' (*Strom*. 1.7.38.4). We must exercise the discernment of the bee in selecting which parts of philosophy are worthy of our attention (*Strom*. 1.6.33.6), recognizing that none contains more than a glimmer of the truth (*Strom*. 1.13.57–8), and favouring especially those elements which emphasize a life of righteousness—these elements being worthy of the name 'philosophy' (*Strom*. 1.7.37.6). It is more important to act well than to speak well, as Pythagoras himself pointed out, 'exhorting us to consider the waves more pleasant than the sirens, teaching us to cultivate wisdom apart from pleasure' (*Strom*. 1.10.48.6).[16]

But what, exactly, is the use of philosophy? Philosophy, for Clement, has virtue above all as a valuable exercise of the mind, preparing it for the acquisition of divine wisdom: 'Those who are wise in mind have a certain attribute of nature peculiar to themselves; and they that have shown themselves capable receive from the supreme wisdom a spirit of perception in double measure.' (*Strom*. 1.4.26.2). The point here seems to be that the training of the mind, while not itself productive of faith, does nonetheless allow for fuller comprehension of that faith. The corollary to this is expressed as follows: 'But as we say that a man can be a believer without learning, so also we assert that it is impossible for a man without learning to comprehend the things that are declared in the faith' (*Strom*. 1.6.35.2). This might seem to smack of cultural élitism, although it must be noted

---

[15] This comes as part of a general comment on the way in which wisdom governs all that is good in the realm of politics (*Strom*. 1.24–6).

[16] Like the Apologists (his near contemporaries), Clement makes use of arguments employed against the rhetoricians by the philosophers.

from the context that it reads as part of an argument for the need of an ongoing teaching ministry within the Church rather than as any sort of superciliousness towards the *hoi polloi*.

One of the reasons Clement is so keen to approve the intellectual training provided by philosophy—and indeed to extend that training as far as possible to all the baptized—is its value for the defence of the faith: 'I call him truly learned who brings everything to bear on the truth; so that from geometry, and music, and grammar, and philosophy itself, culling what is useful, he guards the faith against assaults' (*Strom.* 1.9.43.4). The Christian sage is one who discerns and reintegrates the (stolen) fragments of truth in barbarian and Hellenic philosophy: 'The one who is experienced in all kinds of wisdom is a gnostic in the fullest sense of the term.' (*Strom.* 1.13.58.2). One can well imagine the usefulness of that sort of gnostic in squaring up to the very real threat posed by the Gnostics in the religio-philosophical bear pit of second-century Alexandria.

Subsequent books of the *Stromateis* revisit and expand upon the material mapped out in the first book. Clement had ended that book with a definition of theology as the vision of God, or *epopteia*—a term familiar from the mystery religions, particularly from the mysteries of Eleusis. Considering this further in the second book, he attempts a resolution of the paradox of divine immanence and transcendence in terms of wisdom. Clement fully recognizes that God is 'a being difficult to grasp and apprehend, ever receding and withdrawing from him who pursues'. At the same time God, while 'in essence remote', is nonetheless 'very near in virtue of that power which holds all things in its embrace' (*Strom.* 2.2.5.3–4). This distinction between unknowable essence and knowable activity, which we have also noted in Philo, Irenaeus, and the *Teachings of Silvanus*, anticipates the later Cappadocian distinction between the divine essence and the divine glories or energies.

Having established that 'the divine alone is naturally wise', Clement goes on to specify that wisdom is 'the power of God and in it the perfection of knowledge is embraced' (*Strom.* 2.9.45.2–3). This powerful wisdom is pre-eminently revealed in the Son: God himself cannot be the object of enquiry, 'but the Son is wisdom and knowledge and truth' (*Strom.* 4.25.156.1). In other words, the Son, as wisdom, is God *revealed*. He is God's agent in the creation, as pre-figured in Proverbs 8 (*Strom.* 7.2.7.4). The Son pervades and communicates wisdom to the creation and it is this all-permeating dynamic which is expressed in Wisdom 7:24 (*Strom.* 5.14.89.4). Clearly there is an element of subordinationism here, a feature of most pre-Nicene theology. As wisdom, the Son is the principal vehicle of God's self-revelation, the intermediary ($\mu\epsilon\sigma\acute{\iota}\tau\eta\varsigma$) between God and the world.[17]

---

[17] Cf. *Paed.* 3.1.2.1.

Considering the nature of the communication of God's wisdom to the creation, Clement places great stress on ethics, on the way of life that enables participation in the divine wisdom. He emphasizes the fear of God that constitutes the beginning of wisdom (*Strom.* 2.7) and takes the Law to be the foundation of all ethics (*Strom.* 2.18). Through a way of life grounded in fear of God and practice of the commandments, wisdom brings us to our final goal of deification, or *theosis* (*Strom.* 18.80.5). Plato, he says, was quite right in seeing the life of wisdom as one of assimilation to God (*Strom.* 2.22). Here Clement is neatly combining typically Jewish themes of *phobos* and *nomos* with the more obviously Greek idea of *theosis*—with the theme of wisdom, common to both traditions, functioning as his axis of integration.

Giving a further definition of the saving gift of wisdom, Clement writes:

And we understand wisdom to be certain knowledge, being a sure and unassailable apprehension of things divine and human, comprehending present, past, and future things, which the Lord has taught us, both through his coming and through the prophets. And it is unassailable by reason, inasmuch as it has been transmitted. And it is wholly true according to [God's] will, being known through the Son. In one aspect it is eternal, in another it becomes useful in time. It is one and the same, and many and different; without any movement of passion, and with passionate desire; perfect, and incomplete. It is this wisdom — uprightness of soul and of reason, and purity of life — that is the desire of philosophy, which is kindly and lovingly disposed towards wisdom, and does everything to attain it.   (*Stromateis* 6.7.54.1–55.2)

This is one of the most extraordinary and comprehensive summaries of wisdom to be found in the whole patristic tradition. As divine, divine gift, and way of life this summary neatly straddles levels S1–S3. As wisdom, God gives himself to his creatures, granting them a clear-sighted and pan-temporal apprehension of the reality and order of things, thereby inculcating in them a pure and rightly ordered way of life.

Clement goes on to discuss the specifically Christian dimension of wisdom:

If, then, we assert that Christ himself is wisdom, and that it was his activity which showed itself in the prophets, by which the gnostic tradition may be learned, as he himself taught the apostles during his earthly ministry; then it follows that the *gnosis*, which is the knowledge and apprehension of things present, future, and past, which is sure and unerring, as being imparted and revealed by the Son of God, is wisdom.   (*Stromateis* 6.7.61.1)

Such wisdom is the source of all good thinking and acting. It operates on many levels, from the non-discursive and unmediated gift of knowledge or intellection

($\nu o \acute{\eta} \sigma \iota s$) of things 'present, future, and past' down to the products of our hand that which we produce as artisans and artists (*Strom.* 6.17.155.3).

Christian wisdom is the only authentic wisdom: 'the only wisdom, therefore, is the God-taught wisdom we possess, on which depend all the sources of wisdom which make conjectures at the truth' (*Strom.* 6.18.166.4–5). This again gives us our three principal levels of wisdom: wisdom as divine personal reality, squarely identified with Christ (S3); wisdom as the gift imparted by Christ, encompassing sure and certain pan-temporal knowledge of things divine and human (S2); and wisdom in the sense of purely human wisdom (S1), which possesses truth in so far as it depends on and participates in the higher categories of wisdom.

How to summarize Clement's teaching on wisdom? One of the clearest points is the emphasis he places on the *paideia* of wisdom, the firm connection he makes between the gift of wisdom and the way of life it brings in its train. Clement never loses sight of his rôle as a Christian catechist, hence the prominence of the pedagogical and ethical dimension throughout his works. He also makes convincing use of wisdom in expressing the paradox of divine transcendence and immanence—for all that his manner of doing so is inescapably subordinationist, practically universal as this was at the time. As for philosophy, notwithstanding his positive estimation of the training of the mind it encourages, Clement keeps it duly subordinated to the truths of divine wisdom.[18] While by no means overestimating the potentialities of the unaided reason, Clement finds a privileged place for it within his world-view. We have here an immensely useful model for the integration of human culture within a schema of revelation, one in which wisdom emerges as the axis around which Hellenic and Jewish traditions are integrated within the new revelation of wisdom in Jesus Christ.

This brings us on to some of the possible weaknesses of Clement's approach, such as the question of the extent to which he has fully appreciated the nature of Christ's saving work. In Clement, wisdom does indeed save but the Cross is far from central. In other words, Christ is the saviour, but is more obviously so as teacher than as redeemer. Equally, for all that Clement does speak of creation *ex nihilo*, the gap between created and uncreated natures is, generally speaking, far from clear in his works (again, in common with most of his contemporaries). But this does not amount to another curate's egg: Clement's is no mean achievement. In his consistent emphasis on the practical and pedagogical dimensions of the question, his telling exploration of the apophatic-cataphatic dialectic in terms of essence and activity, and his construct of an axis of integration of Greek and Jewish traditions, Clement's teaching on wisdom represents, by any estimation, a very significant contribution indeed. So far as Sophiology is concerned, Clement's

---

[18] To put it bluntly, he shows that it is possible for an intellectual to be a Christian without supposing (thankfully) that all Christians need be intellectuals, although all Christians should certainly develop their capacities as far as circumstances allow.

chief potential contribution is in terms of his intuition of the eternity of the divine ideas for the creation. That said, his crystal-clear association of wisdom with the Son and Word of God as the only intermediary between God and man runs counter to the Sophiological attempt to posit an additional mediator in the shape of a non-Trinitarian figure of divine wisdom that in practice bears a closer relationship to that of Philo. We also have in Clement yet another example of the consistent emphasis on the theme of *paideia* within early Christian wisdom reflection.

4.1.3 Origen of Alexandria

In Origen of Alexandria (*c.* 185–*c.* 253), Christian wisdom wholly surpasses and fulfils the old pagan wisdom. More profound and probing than that of Clement (whom he never mentions), Origen's sophiology occupies a central and determining place in his magnificent but problematic theological achievement.[19] While strictly speaking viewed as a condemned heretic within Orthodox theology, his pervasive legacy cannot be ignored.[20] Origen was a figure of enduring fascination for the Russian Sophiologists, most notably Bulgakov. Indeed, for many of Bulgakov's detractors, to attack Origen was to attack Bulgakov—so closely were the two theological *colossi* associated in their minds.[21] There are certainly elements of Origen's legacy that were appealing to the Sophiologists (notably the eternity of the creation grounded in the wisdom that lies 'in between' God and the world and Christ as the union of uncreated and created wisdom).[22] But there is also, as we will see, much in Origen's presentation of wisdom that is quite incompatible with Sophiology—above all the irrefragable connection he makes between wisdom and the Son.

For Origen, wisdom is first and foremost operative on level S3 as one of the distinct aspects (ἐπίνοιαι) of the Son. Indeed it is the *primary* aspect of the Son logically and ontologically prior to any other designation.[23] The Son is 'wisdom in itself' (αὐτοσοφία) (*CC* 6.63) and 'living wisdom' (σοφία ζῶσα) (*CC* 3.81), the one in whom God rejoiced at the creation, 'delighted at her multiform noetic beauty'.[24] While Justin had been worried by the possible pagan connotations of a feminine

---

[19] Perhaps the best account of wisdom in Origen is that of Henri Crouzel, *Origène et la 'connaissance mystique'*, 452–60. Aimé Solignac, 'Sagesse antique et sagesse chrétienne', 101–3, is also useful albeit limited to the *Contra Celsum*. See further Vladan Perišić, 'The Ontological Status of Wisdom in Origen'.

[20] The question of whether and in what manner he was condemned at (or alongside) the Fifth Ecumenical Council is functionally irrelevant given the reception of the condemnation as part of the said council by the subsequent two Ecumenical Councils.

[21] Cf. above, pp.60, 62.

[22] I leave aside the topic of universal salvation as outside the scope of this enquiry into the patristic roots of modern Russian Sophiology. The patristic basis for this teaching is limited and, in any case, the question is independent from the problem of Sophia.

[23] *On John* 1.19.118 (GCS 10 24).   [24] *On John* 1.9.55 (GCS 10 14).

construal of wisdom, Origen's concern is chiefly with the Gnostics. Wary of such interpretations, Origen affirms that wisdom is not to be understood as a feminine: 'We must not, on account of their feminine name and nature, regard wisdom and righteousness as females; for these things are in our view the Son of God' (CC 5.39). Through Origen this becomes absolutely the standard interpretation. Indeed it is Origen who is chiefly responsible for the near obliteration of the feminine dimension in patristic and medieval treatments of wisdom.[25]

Origen thus unhesitatingly applies the various descriptions of wisdom in Wisdom 7 to the Son to assert his incorporeality, omnipotence, eternity, and non-dissimilarity with the Father (DP 2.5–12)—not that this non-dissimilarity excludes his ontological subordination to the Father.[26] On the specific issue of eternal generation, Origen is most explicit and indeed pioneering; no one before him had spoken in such terms:

> The only-begotten Son of God is God's wisdom hypostatically existing [...] And can anyone who has learned to regard God with feelings of reverence suppose or believe that God the Father ever existed, even for a single moment, without begetting this wisdom? [...] Wisdom, therefore, must be believed to have been begotten beyond the limits of any beginning that we can speak of or understand.
>
> (DP 1.2.2)

Even more emphatically than Clement, Origen ties the Old Testament figure of wisdom unambiguously to the person of the Son. Origen continues, also like Clement, by associating this eternal wisdom with the eternal divine plan for the creation:

> And because in this very hypostasis of wisdom there was contained every capacity and form of the creation that was to be, both of those things that exist in a primary sense and those things which happen as a consequence of them, the whole being fashioned and arranged beforehand by the power of foreknowledge, wisdom, speaking through Solomon in regard to these very created things that had been, as it were, outlined and prefigured in herself, says that she was created as the 'beginning of the ways' of God (Proverbs 8:22), which means that she contains within herself both the beginnings and causes and species of the whole creation.   (DP 1.2.2)

---

[25] Such considerations do not exclude the occasional use of feminine imagery, for instance Origen's reference to wisdom as the 'mother of the prophets' (On Jeremiah 14.5) (GCS 6 110). That said, it may be asserted that the enduring neuralgia within patristic and medieval theology regarding feminine depictions of wisdom is essentially a function of an ongoing fear of Gnosticism, a fear that resurfaces in the anti-Sophiological reaction of Lossky and Florovsky.

[26] On John 2.23.151 (GCS 10 80).

The divine ideas for the creation thus exist eternally in the eternally generated wisdom of God. And just as we cannot conceive of God as Father without affirming the eternal generation of the Son, so we cannot conceive of God as almighty and omnipotent without affirming the eternity of the creation within the wisdom of God: 'But if there never was a time when he was not omnipotent, of necessity those things by which he receives that title must also exist; and he must always have had those over whom he exercised power' (DP 1.2.10).

Wisdom is also called the word of God: 'For wisdom opens to all other beings, that is, to the whole creation, the meaning of the mysteries and the symbols that are contained within the wisdom of God' (DP 1.2.3). But it is important to reiterate that it is wisdom, not word, that is the primary designation of the Son. As wisdom the Son is the intelligible structure of God's creation whereas as word he communicates the nature of that intelligible structure to the rational creation; when John says 'in the beginning was the word', this means 'in wisdom was the word'.[27] Similarly, the Son is to be understood as 'beginning' ($\dot{a}\rho\chi\dot{\eta}$) 'only in so far as he is wisdom, not in so far as he is word'.[28]

Wisdom thus constitutes the link-piece between God and the world. Wisdom represents the world in God from all eternity and the means by which God brings that world into being, 'granting her to supply to beings and to matter, from the types within it, shape and form and, I suggest, even being'.[29] Founded and established on the hypostatic wisdom of God, creation has the potential to participate in the divine wisdom: 'Through this wisdom, creation is made possible and all creation subsists, a creation with the capacity to receive the divine wisdom by which it has come to be.'[30]

This leads us on to one of the most interesting parts of Origen's sophiology: its foundation in Christology. Only the soul of Jesus—the single rational being not to fall away from the primal pre-cosmic contemplation of God—was able to receive 'the highest participation in reason itself and wisdom itself and righteousness itself' (CC 5.39). Thus God's wisdom entered the womb of a woman (DP 2.6.2) and, by virtue of this perfect union with the Son, the soul of Christ, with the flesh, 'is rightly called the wisdom of God' (DP 2.6.3). Here Origen unites created wisdom (the soul with the flesh) and uncreated wisdom (the Son), establishing the means by which wisdom is communicated to the rational creation. This Christological focus, with Christ as both created and uncreated wisdom, was to prove of particularly enduring value for much later patristic sophiological reflection.

While S3 considerations gravitate to the fore of Origen's work, it should be emphasized that he never loses sight of levels S1–S2. The communication and living out of wisdom is foundational to Origen's very understanding of the faith:

---

[27] On John 1.19.111 (GCS 10 23).   [28] On John 1.19.118 (GCS 10 24).
[29] On John 1.19.115 (GCS 10 24).   [30] On John 1.34.244 (GCS 10 43).

'There never was a time when God did not wish to make human beings live righteous lives [...] For in every generation, the wisdom of God, passing into souls which it ascertains to be holy, makes them into friends of God and prophets' (*CC* 4.7; cf. Wisdom 7:27). As a counter to Celsus' dismissal of Christianity as a ludicrous set of superstitions suitable only for the grossly uneducated, Origen tells us that Christianity 'invites all to wisdom', that it is a 'practice of wisdom', and that 'the object of Christianity is that we should become wise' (*CC* 3.44, 45).

To become wise, to 'grow in wisdom', is to have Christ grow in us as wisdom and to acquire the 'mind of Christ' (*CC* 5.1).[31] In this divine *paideia*, the Lord is our 'teacher and tutor'.[32] To put it another way, 'each of the sages, in proportion as he embraces wisdom, partakes to that extent of Christ, in that he is wisdom'.[33] Christ has been 'made the way' for us to return to God (*DP* 1.2.4) and his primary operation is to 'instruct and train' (*DP* 1.3.3). Indeed, 'it is possible to say that Christ is a principle of instruction by nature, in so far as he is wisdom and power of God'.[34]

To participate in this wisdom requires an upright life (*CC* 3.60), one modelled on the divine wisdom himself (*DP* 4.4.4). The way of wisdom is a gradual process of training and instruction (*paideia*) that continues even beyond this world (*DP* 3.3.8–9); indeed, it is an unceasing journey (*DP* 4.3.14). This training stamps a clear impression of perfect wisdom within us (*DP* 4.1.7), restoring the *imago dei*, and allowing us to feast at wisdom's banquet (*DP* 2.11.3). This is a banquet which requires us in purity and simplicity of heart to 'place ourselves in the service of the divine wisdom who is Christ Jesus our Lord'.[35] Above all, it is a banquet to which all are called—especially the 'poor in spirit'.[36] A clear template for this ascent in wisdom is provided in the Books of Proverbs, Ecclesiastes, and the Song of Songs which provide, respectively, moral, natural-contemplative, and enoptic training.[37]

In Origen's presentation of the pedagogy of divine wisdom (S2), we encounter a similar problem as in Clement: the conception of redemption seems to be tied up far more closely with themes of education and formation than with the sacrifice of the Cross. It is also unclear how the human soul of Christ's acquisition of wisdom differs fundamentally from that attained, at least potentially, by any other rational intellect. It may justly be asked whether Origen has really grasped the unique and eternal significance of the historical incarnation.

As for human wisdom and learning (S1), it is one of the many great ironies attaching to Origen that someone so explicitly hostile to classical philosophy should be remembered most often as one who allowed philosophy to skew and

---

[31] Cf. *On Jeremiah* 14.10 (GCS 6 114–15): Christ grows in us 'in wisdom and in stature' (cf. Luke 2:52).

[32] *On John* 1.29.201 (GCS 10 36).   [33] *On John* 1.34.246 (GCS 10 43).

[34] *On John* 1.18.107 (GCS 10 23).   [35] *On Genesis* 14.4 (GCS 29 126).

[36] *On Genesis* 16.4 (GCS 29 40–41).

[37] *Commentary on the Song of Songs*, 3.1–7 (SC 375 128–32).

distort his whole theological programme.[38] A consideration of specifically human wisdom may help illumine this apparent contradiction (or at least ambivalence) in his thinking. Origen is at his most dismissive of philosophy in his thundering *Homilies on Exodus*. Drawing I Corinthians into his discussion of Exodus 7, Origen dwells much on the significance of the rod cast down before Pharaoh which becomes a serpent able to consume all the rod-serpents conjured up by the magicians of Egypt. This he takes as a sign of the Cross which is 'a wisdom which devours the wisdom of Egypt, that is to say the wisdom of this world'. Such (S0) wisdom is obliterated by the apparent 'folly' of God. Likewise, the bloodied waters of Egypt are a sign of God's punishment of philosophy for its misleading of children and youths: 'the waters of Egypt are the erroneous and fluctuating ideas of the philosophers'.[39] Elsewhere, these diverse opinions are likened to the fortifications of Jericho, which fall flat before the assault of God's chosen.[40] Merely human wisdom must certainly not be confused with the infallible knowledge of things human and divine gifted by Christ as the wisdom of God (S2).[41]

That said, Origen does, like Clement, acknowledge that Greek philosophy can serve as 'a general education or preparatory introduction to Christianity'.[42] Here, in his famous peroration on the theme of 'despoiling the Egyptians', Origen allows for a discerning use of philosophy under the governing wisdom of God, albeit warning at the same time of its dangers: 'there are some who have used some Greek ingenuity to beget heretical ideas'—by whom he most probably understands the Gnostics.[43] There is even 'a kind of greatness manifest in the words of the world's wisdom', as St Paul himself recognized (*CC* 1.5). What Paul attacked in I Corinthians was not the trained reason or human wisdom *per se* (S1) but 'every false system of philosophy which, according to the scriptures, is brought to nought' (S0) (*CC* 1.13). Paul wished to expose the ephemerality and multiplicity of worldly wisdom, 'which perishes and fades away' and to contrast it with the anagogic and transformative power of the divine wisdom (S2) which 'raises the soul to the blessedness which is with God' (*CC* 3.47).

It is the possession of human wisdom that distinguishes us from the animals (*CC* 4.87). Christians can and must use their reason (*CC* 1.9)—something that applies *a fortiori* to bishops (*CC* 3.48). Even elementary education serves as 'an introduction to all wisdom for those who learn'.[44] Training in human wisdom (S1) acts as 'an exercise for the soul' and a preparation for the gift of divine wisdom

---

[38] But see Mark Edwards, *Origen against Plato* for a defence of Origen's profoundly anti-philosophical tendencies. Cf. also Henri Crouzel, *Origène et la philosophie*.

[39] *On Exodus* 4.6 (SC 321 130-2).   [40] *On Joshua* 7.1 (GCS 30 327–28).

[41] *On Jeremiah* 8.2 (GCS 6 57) (cf. *CC* 3.72). Origen here makes use of the well-established (and originally Stoic) definition of wisdom as 'knowledge of things divine and human' (cf. above, p.85). In *CC* 3.72, he completes the definition with the addition 'and of their causes'—again a commonplace form (cf. Philo, *De congressu* 14.79).

[42] *To Gregory* 1 (SC 148 186–8).   [43] *To Gregory* 1 (SC 148 192).

[44] *On Lamentations* 3 (GCS 6 236).

(S2) which 'comes, through the grace of God who bestows it, to those who have evinced their capacity for receiving it'. Such a gift comes only to the 'more excellent and distinguished' members of the Christian community and is assuredly superior to the lesser gifts of knowledge and of faith (CC 6.13).[45] Indeed, Origen seems very close to suggesting that education in human wisdom is necessary for the reception of divine wisdom (CC 6.14) for all that he frequently protests that the gift is, in principle, open to all.

The distinction between human and divine wisdom is one which, Origen allows, was recognized by the greatest of the Greek philosophers themselves: Socrates, Plato, and Heraclitus (CC 6.12–13). Pondering the Samaritan woman, Origen suggests that human wisdom need not necessarily run counter to the divine wisdom, since it can, Origen suggests, denote 'not false teachings, but the elementary study of truth that concerns those who are still human while the "teachings of the Spirit" are doubtless the "spring of water leaping up unto eternal life"'.[46] Human wisdom (S1), in short, can genuinely be involved in the search for truth (CC 4.30).

Origen completes the work of Clement and Justin in establishing in no uncertain terms the intellectual credentials of Christianity. With greater caution and care than either, he reaches broadly similar conclusions as to the legitimate place of human wisdom and rational enquiry within Christian theology. He does, however, draw back from frankly acknowledging the operation of divine wisdom among the pagan Greeks, preferring to maintain an understanding of human wisdom as an essentially natural faculty, not necessarily opposed to divine wisdom but certainly transcended by it. Origen's high estimation of the value of education has often provoked accusations of cultural élitism although, as with Clement, the essential call is for universal self-improvement and application.

What all this means in practice is borne out most clearly in Origen's approach to the meaning and interpretation of scripture. Human wisdom (S1)—the trained reason—has a place in scriptural exegesis, although the more elevated teachings of the Bible become apparent only through the inculcation of divine wisdom (S2) (cf. DP 4.2.4; On John 13.36). The doctrine of the resurrection, for example, requires 'a high and advanced degree of wisdom to set forth how worthy it is of God' (CC 7.32). Scripture is full of 'enigmas and dark sayings' precisely so as to 'exercise the understanding of those who hear it' (CC 3.45). For instance, no man of sense would take the paradise narrative literally (DP 4.3.1), but to understand what such passages really indicate requires us to read all in consideration of the 'depths of the wisdom of God' (DP 4.3.4) and to listen to all scripture as 'the

---

[45] The exact nature of the difference between wisdom and knowledge here is not easy to pin down, as Crouzel observes (Origène et la connaissance mystique, 459). He suggests that wisdom may be more a habitus and knowledge an act.

[46] On John 13.6.36 (GCS 10 231).

utterances of wisdom' (*DP* 4.3.8). Behind this lies a clear perception that there is not the smallest element of scripture which is void of the divine wisdom.[47] This hidden wisdom—the treasure in the field of which the Gospel speaks—cannot be understood without Christ who is himself wisdom (S3).[48]

What does all this amount to? The most immediately striking affirmation is the insistence on wisdom as the *primary* designation of the Son. This is, of course, in keeping with Origen's engagement with scripture in its totality, and in which references to 'wisdom' vastly preponderate over references to 'word'. Origen's preference for the term is also in keeping with his intuition of the Christian life as one of divine *paideia*. Setting that intuition on the firm basis of the eternal creative wisdom of God, animate and incarnate in Christ, Origen builds up a compelling sophiological vision that remains thoroughly sapiential in character. Like that of Clement, Origen's understanding of wisdom is more in keeping with Florovsky's 'Sophia of the Church' than with the Sophia of Philo.

Origen's vision is not, however, without its problems. The identification of wisdom so firmly with the person or *hypostasis* of Son does lead to scant consideration being given to wisdom as pertaining to the Father or the Spirit—let alone to a shared divine *ousia* (not a concept he entertained). In common with virtually all his contemporaries, Origen's sophiology goes hand in hand with a thoroughgoing subordinationism. In Origen's theology, wisdom operates as a lower level of divinity—transcending the creation but being itself transcended by God the Father. Origen's legacy was such that subsequent theological discussion and commentary found it very difficult to think of wisdom expect as in relation to the Son (and as subordinate to the Father). This was to lead, as we shall soon see, to problems aplenty in the Arian controversy of the fourth century. Origen also consciously rules out wisdom being in any meaningful way feminine. Similarly problematic is (as in Clement) the decentring of the Cross in his overall vision of salvation in terms of *paideia*. While this *paideia* is Christocentric, oriented upon assimilation to Christ and growth in us of the 'mind of Christ', the eternal significance of the Cross and the uniqueness of the historical incarnation is far from evident.

There are certainly important ways in which Origen anticipates modern Russian Sophiology. In Origen, wisdom occupies an ontologically liminal space between God and the creation as a denizen of the 'in-between'. Origen is a significant witness to the apprehension of the eternity of world within the eternally generated divine wisdom: God in the world and the world in God from all eternity. Origen's Christology anticipates Sophiology with his treatment of Christ as both uncreated and created wisdom. While never fully appreciating his emphasis on *paideia*, on Christ as teacher, the Sophiologists also share with

---

[47] *Philocalia* 1.28 (SC 302 202).   [48] *On Matthew* 10.5–6 (GCS 40 5–6).

Origen a certain ambiguity concerning the place of the Cross and the uniqueness of the historical incarnation.

Origen was, however, never received uncritically within Sophiology. Florensky, as we have noted, lamented the rather arid 'spirit of castration' evident in his works while Bulgakov, getting to the heart of the matter, expresses utter dismay at Origen's identification of wisdom with the person of the Son, seeing it as the root of all subsequent subordinationism.[49] The Sophiologists also consciously retrieve the feminine dimension of the Old Testament figure of wisdom, refusing to follow Origen in identifying her exclusively with the person of the Son.

4.2 St Athanasius of Alexandria

Origen's magnificent theological achievement has never been far removed from controversy: great thinkers invariably engender great arguments. By the early fourth century his account of the Holy Trinity had bequeathed a double legacy: eternal generation and thoroughgoing subordinationism finding separate heirs in Athanasius and Arius, respectively. In the fourth century the whole problematic of wisdom (principally on level S3) gravitated to the very centre of theological discussion and debate laying down many of the parameters of subsequent sophiological reflection.

Origen's by now almost universally accepted identification of wisdom with the Son also raised serious exegetical difficulties. Indeed, much of what we may still, with some caution, call the 'Arian controversy', revolved (often seemingly endlessly) around wisdom references such as Proverbs 8:22.[50] Arius stood in a venerable theological tradition which emphasized the Father's uniqueness and transcendence and consequently distinguished him thoroughly from the Son. Arius saw worrying signs of the Sabellian heresy in his bishop, Pope Alexander of Alexandria's use of terms like wisdom to underline the shared nature and unity of the Father and the Son. Arius made hay with this particular text with its seemingly unambiguous reference (in the Septuagint at least) to wisdom (i.e. the Son) as 'created'.[51] This fitted perfectly with his emphasis on a sharp distinction between

---

[49] Florensky, *The Pillar and Ground of Truth*, 749 n.541 [ET 538 n.542]; Bulgakov, *The Bride of the Lamb*, 20 [ET 15].

[50] We must of course be wary of assuming a clearly defined battle between confessed 'Arians' (including semi- and neo- varieties) and Nicenes—such taxonomies are themselves the work of the victors. The real situation was rather more complex than such labels allow: see further Rowan Williams, *Arius: Heresy and Tradition*; Lewis Ayres, *Nicaea and its Legacy*; and Khaled Anatolios, *Retrieving Nicaea*. The bracing revisionism of Maurice Wiles continues to warrant close engagement, notably his *Archetypal Heresy: Arianism through the Centuries*.

[51] Bulgakov makes the sensible point that reference to the Hebrew text ('possessed'), as opposed to the Septuagint ('created'), would have avoided much fruitless wrangling, *The Burning Bush*, 270–1 [ET 148–49]. As Bulgakov notes, this point had also been made in the patristic period by Eusebius of Caeserea and by Jerome.

the Father and the Son, created or begotten (the terms are synonymous for Arius) outside time but *not* eternal—'a perfect creature, but not as one of the creatures'.[52] The Son was established as wisdom by the will of the Father, who alone is wise in essence: 'wisdom existed by the will of a wise God'.[53] He is indeed wisdom, but a created wisdom, an 'in-between' wisdom, worthy of the name only by virtue of his participation in the essential and hypostatic wisdom that is the Father.[54] Wisdom terminology came naturally to Arius, as witnessed also in his description (in the *Thalia*) in terms drawn from Wisdom 7 of the Son as 'effulgence', 'light,' and 'glory of God'. The gospel reference to the Son's 'growth in wisdom' could only serve to confirm the ontological gap between the Father (wise in essence) and the Son (created wisdom). Arius was condemned at the Council of Nicaea in 325, but the problems he raised, with seemingly strong scriptural support, refused to go away.

Arius' eventual nemesis came in the formidable shape of Athanasius (*c.* 297–373), deacon and successor to Alexander of Alexandria. In promoting the anti-Arian cause in the long and tumultuous period of theological conflict following the precarious victory at Nicaea, Athanasius insisted on placing the Son unambiguously on the far side of the ontological gulf between Creator and creation and did so on the basis of an argument from soteriology: only such a Son (as truly God) could save humanity (as truly man). Athanasius' insistence on the impossibility of any sort of middle ground 'in between' uncreated and created natures is intimately bound up with his teaching on the distinction between creation (a function of the divine will) and generation (a function of the divine nature). While a clear-cut ontological distinction between uncreated and created natures (founded on a robust notion of *creatio ex nihilo*) may now seem a self-evident feature of Christian theology, it is important to note quite how much this doctrine owes to the clarification and articulation forced on the Church by the very real and pertinent questions posed by Arius.

Granted Athanasius' insistence on the uncreated-created distinction as the primary distinction within the universe, it is instructive to see how he grapples with wisdom language in reference to the Son. For Athanasius, the Son is the Father's power and wisdom and word 'not by participation, not as if these things came from outside as they do to those who participate in him and are made wise by him [...] but he is the wisdom itself ($a\dot{v}\tau o\sigma o\varphi\acute{\iota}a$), word itself, and power itself of the Father' (*Against the Heathen* 46; cf. *CA* 1.28).[55] Wisdom thus manifests the unity of Father and Son, a unity in which humans may participate by grace.

---

[52] Arius, *Confession* (in Athanasius, *De synodis* 16.2–5).

[53] *Thalia* (in Athanasius, *De synodis* 1.15).

[54] Ibid., cf. Athanasius, *CA* 1.5; Alexander of Alexandria (*vel* Athanasius), *Encyclical Letter to All Bishops* (CPG 2000), 7 (in Athanasius, *De decretis* 35).

[55] Athanasius is careful to point out that this wisdom is neither some created medium (*CA* 2.22) nor the innate wisdom of the Father (*CA* 1.5; 4.2–3). In the former case, creation would be impossible; in the latter, we should either have two wisdoms or make a compound entity of the Father.

When we speak of the Son as wisdom, argues Athanasius, we are speaking of the uncreated wisdom of God himself, eternally begotten of the Father (much as in Origen) (*CA* 1.9). But when we speak of wisdom as created (as texts such as Proverbs 8:22 force us to do), we are speaking either of wisdom *qua* incarnate (*CA* 2.46–7; *De decretis* 3.13–14) or, in another interpretation, more generally of the impress of uncreated wisdom upon the creation:

> For as our word or reason is an image of the Son of God as word, so also the wisdom that arises in us is an image of the same Son as wisdom and it is in wisdom that we, through knowing and acting well, become recipients of the creative wisdom.   (*CA* 2.78)

Athanasius expands this line of thinking by comparing the impress of the divine wisdom on the creation to the son of a king marking his name on each of the buildings of a new city built by his father (*CA* 2.79).[56] Thus, to repeat, Proverbs 8:22 can be seen as speaking either of the divine wisdom or word considered as incarnate or of the created image of divine wisdom implanted in the creation through which humans become participants in uncreated wisdom. Wisdom in Athanasius thus becomes a kind of link-piece between the created and uncreated orders, albeit a link-piece strictly connected with the person of Christ as the one mediator between God and the world.

The Gospel reference to Christ's growth in wisdom is, along similar lines, explained as pertaining to his humanity, not his divinity: 'it was not wisdom, as wisdom, that advanced in respect of itself; but the humanity advanced in wisdom, transcending by degrees human nature, and being deified, and becoming and appearing to all as the organ of wisdom for the operation and the shining forth of the Godhead' (*CA* 3.53). Human deification is thus founded upon the deification of Christ's humanity, a process that is equivalent to growth in wisdom.

Proverbs 8:22 is not, thankfully, the only Old Testament reference to interest Athanasius. He finds Proverbs 8 as a whole a rich source for meditation upon the Son's relation to the Father, for example the mutual 'delight' and 'joy' that point to their shared nature (*CA* 2.82). In the *Festal Letters* he delves into some typically S2 themes, rejoicing in the open and accessible character of the Christian message, as foreshadowed in the egress of wisdom onto the streets (*Ep.* 20.2) and, of course, the famous banquet of wisdom (*Ep.* 7.7). He makes much of Baruch's 'fountain of wisdom' (Baruch 3:12), using it to support the doctrine of the eternal generation of the Son. He also draws on Wisdom 7 to illustrate the all-pervading and richly varying operation of divine wisdom, drawing us all into the life of God (*Ep.* 10.4).

---

[56] Bulgakov rather overinterprets these passages as implying the eternal divine realm of ideas. Cf. *The Wisdom of God*, 64 and *The Burning Bush*, Excursus III.

Athanasius, however, has little time for human wisdom (whether S0 or S1). We have, he claims, gone beyond the age in which God's wisdom was evident only in the images and shadows of created things. Natural theology and, with it, such value as Greek philosophy might once have possessed, have been made obsolete. Wisdom has now taken on flesh and, through his death on the Cross, extended salvation to all who believe and, what is more, spread out upon the whole earth the knowledge of the Father and of the Son (*CA* 2.81–2). This divine wisdom has manifested itself on earth, thereby making foolish and redundant the wisdom of the Greeks (*On the Incarnation* 46–7).[57] Athanasius remains throughout a devotee of the apparent foolishness of God, a foolishness supremely consummated upon the Cross. The crucified Christ is, in reality, the very wisdom of God (*Ep.* 61.1), although it would be absurd to suggest that it was the essential wisdom of God itself that was crucified (*Ep.* 59.2). This is a thoroughly cruciform sophiology quite different in tone and tenor to that of his Alexandrine forebears Clement and Origen.

In sum, it is striking to see just how significant a rôle wisdom themes and terminology (largely on level S3) played in the thought of both Arius and of Athanasius, as in the Arian controversy as a whole. Both Arius and Athanasius take it for granted that wisdom references in scripture refer invariably to the Son and set themselves to their biblical exegeses accordingly. Athanasius, while paying only limited attention to dimensions S1–S2, does, however, go far beyond the bare exigencies of the controversy in developing a theology of wisdom that has considerable value in its own right. He uses wisdom to inform his understanding of creation as the iconic self-revelation of God, a self-revelation that is fulfilled and surpassed in the saving incarnation of the divine wisdom himself. Christology is presented in terms of the union between uncreated and created wisdom, a union which bridges the ontological gap between the universe and its maker. The Crucifixion is presented in terms of the death of the divine wisdom incarnate and deification as growth in wisdom. Through the incarnation, knowledge of the unity of God is manifested and human participation—through faith—in that primal unity made possible. We may legitimately conclude that sophiology stands at the heart of Athanasian theology.

Athanasius was to be marshalled as a key patristic witness for modern Russian Sophiology with Florensky, in particular, seizing on the cosmological dimension of the deifying union of uncreated and created wisdom in the person of Christ.[58] Other aspects of Athanasius' achievement were to sit less easily with the Sophiologists, notably his consistent identification of wisdom with the Son and

---

[57] This is an intuition repeatedly affirmed in *Life of Anthony*. In the *Life*, St Anthony attacks the Arians and proclaims Christ to be 'the eternal word and wisdom of the essence of the Father' (*VA* 69.3: SC 400 316). He also repeatedly demonstrates the superiority of Christian faith over pagan wisdom (e.g. *VA* 78: SC 400 332–4).

[58] Cf. Chapter 1.2, 1.3, and 7.1.3.

his robust understanding of the strict temporality of the creation created *ex nihilo* as an act of the divine will and not as an outpouring of the eternal divine ideas as in Clement or Origen. There is also, in Athanasius, no space for wisdom (on level S3) as anything but uncreated (pertaining to the Son as the eternally begotten and consubstantial wisdom of the Father) or created (pertaining to the humanity of Christ or, more generally, the impress of his uncreated wisdom on the world). In the Cappadocian Fathers, however, just such a space begins to emerge.

4.3 The Cappadocian Fathers

Wisdom remained very much at the forefront of the Arian controversy as it developed and mutated over the fourth century. Indeed, tracing the specific issue of wisdom helps us to discern and make sense of some of the key theological developments of the period from the question of the divinity of the Holy Spirit (much disputed at the time by the Pneumatomachians and others) to the flowering of apophatic theology (against the Eunomians). The principal figures fighting for the orthodox pro-Nicene cause after the death of Athanasius in 373 were the Cappadocian Fathers: SS Basil the Great (*c.* 329–79), Gregory the Theologian (*c.* 330–*c.* 390), and Gregory of Nyssa (*c.* 337–*c.* 394). While the nature of the controversies with which they were involved pushed S3 questions front and centre, all three offer significant contributions on levels S1–S2, very much including the indispensable dimension of *paideia*.

The Cappadocian Fathers are very regular interlocutors within modern Russian Sophiology. Bulgakov, in particular, engages them on many theological topics including Trinitarian theology, Christology, universal salvation, and gender.[59] But they figure surprisingly little in the specific matter of Sophia beyond a rather general appeal to their association of wisdom principally with the Trinitarian being of God and as examples of patristic teaching on the eternal ideas of creation.[60] This is a curious oversight given the extent and richness of their wisdom reflections and the key dogmatic contribution they make in respect of a construal of divine wisdom that is not reducible solely to categories of essence and hypostasis.

---

[59] Bulgakov is a sharp critic of Gregory of Nyssa's apparent suggestion that gender is somehow adventitious and impermanent, seeing here a similarity with Boehme: *The Bride of the Lamb*, 467–8 [ET 441].

[60] Cf. Bulgakov, *The Burning Bush* (Excursus III), 286–7 [ET 155–6] (with reference to Gregory of Nyssa's *In Hexaemeron liber* (PG 44 68D-69A)). Cf. also *The Wisdom of God*, 64–5: another appeal to Gregory of Nyssa (without a supporting reference) and to Gregory the Theologian as a most exact proponent of this doctrine on the basis of a passage in *Carmina Mystica* (PG 37 472). In these passages, both Gregories speak only in rather general terms of the eternal plan for creation without use of the language of ideas or prototypes (or even, in the Theologian's case, wisdom).

The Cappadocians inherited from Athanasius a clear sense of the uncreated-created distinction as the primary distinction of the universe. Indeed Athanasius had succeeded in asserting this distinction so effectively that even radical subordinationists or neo-Arians such as Eunomius and Aetius worked within its parameters. While imperial policy for much of the fourth century shifted away from Nicaea towards a deliberately ambiguous Homean position (the Son is *homoios* or 'like' the Father) and while some traditional subordinationists attempted to maintain an ongoing if nuanced ontological distinction in asserting that the Son is 'like in essence' (*homoiousios*) with the Father, the overall direction of the fourth century was towards Athanasian clarity: either the Son (and, by extension, the Spirit) is God and uncreated (and so *homoousios*—same in essence—with the Father) or not God and thus utterly unlike (*anomoios*) the Father.

Both the Cappadocians and the Eunomians (or Anomeans—'unlikers') accepted this primal distinction coming down, of course, on opposite sides of the equation. In combatting Eunomius, who claimed a degree of certain knowledge of the divine, the Cappadocians were led to emphasize the radical unknowability of the divine essence (*ousia*) while maintaining a sense of the partial knowability of divine attributes or 'glories pertaining to the essence' (wisdom, power, etc.). The essence is to be distinguished from the three hypostases or persons to whom the essence is common and in whom the glories pertaining to the essence are manifest.[61] It is precisely here that a space or gap opens for a construal of wisdom as divine but somehow distinct from categories of *ousia* and *hypostasis*.

4.3.1 St Basil of Caeserea

Basil the Great produced a wholly remarkable sophiology—a feature of his work admirably highlighted in Tomáš Cardinal Špidlík's 1961 book on precisely *La sophiologie de saint Basile*.[62] Along similar lines, Paul Evdokimov lauds the sophianic character of Basil's account of the creation, using it to introduce his own compelling presentation of sophiology.[63] Basil's vision of wisdom is most

---

[61] The Cappadocians were instrumental in defining the difference between the terms *ousia* and *hypostasis* as denoting the general and particular (roughly equating to secondary and primary being in the Aristotelian sense). These terms had been near-synonyms at Nicaea and remained so for Athanasius at least up to the time of the Council of Alexandria in 362. One cannot, of course, reduce the Cappadocian achievement (and, *a fortiori*, the mystery of the Trinity) to such technical refinements.

[62] See further his 'L'idéal du monachisme basilien', 369, 370–2.

[63] *L'Orthodoxie*, 87. Evdokimov introduces his discussion with Basil's sense of the inherent yearning for beauty that is implanted within every human soul (*Longer Rules* 2: PG 31 909 BC). See also, for a decidedly non-Sophiological read of this text, Petr Mikhaylov, 'Sophia, the Wisdom of God, in the *Hexaemeron* of St Basil'.

immediately evident in his various treatments of the created world—most notably his *Homilies on the Hexaemeron* and *Homily on the Beginning of Proverbs*. In the *Homily on the Beginning of Proverbs*, one of his earliest surviving works, Basil approaches Proverbs, naturally enough, as a wisdom text whose function to inculcate wisdom and education (*paideia*). Basil follows Origen in seeing Proverbs as the beginning of a three-stage process of ascent represented by the three Solomonic books: Proverbs providing moral instruction, Ecclesiastes demonstrating the fruitlessness of worldly wisdom and earthly goods, and the Song of Songs conveying something of the heights of mystical union of the soul and God (*Prov.* 388AB).[64] Wisdom is defined by Basil in the familiar Stoic terms employed before him by, among others, Philo, Clement, and Origen of Alexandria: 'wisdom is the knowledge of divine and human things, and of their causes' (*Prov.* 389C). By knowledge of divine things (or theology) Basil understands the kind of wisdom spoken of by St Paul among the perfect (S2) (I Cor. 2:6), which embraces in the first instance the knowledge we can derive of God from the glories and wonders of creation—the sophianic cosmos he would hymn so eloquently in the *Hexaemeron* (*Prov.* 389C–392A). The vexed text of Proverbs 8:22 thus stands, as in Athanasius, for precisely this self-revelation of God in the cosmos (*Prov.* 392AB). Knowledge of human things (S1), by contrast, denotes experiential knowledge of the practical matters of life. This is the kind of wisdom those who are accounted wise in this world have attained through their various vocations and disciplines. Proverbs is largely concerned with this kind of wisdom (*Prov.* 392BC) and is beneficial to all— even those outside the Church (*Prov.* 416C). Such human wisdom may also serve as a kind of preparation for the higher wisdom (S2) which comes from Christ as the fount of wisdom (S3) (*Prov.* 404C, 416C).

Basil's later work, the *Homilies on the Hexaemeron*, gives full vent to the vision of the cosmos as inherently expressive of the divine wisdom that is so evident in the commentary on Proverbs. Basil is at pains to point out that his account of the six days of creation is in no way based on merely worldly wisdom (*Hex.* 1.1) but rather on the revelation of God's goodness and creative power accorded by scripture: 'It is he, blessed nature, bountiful goodness, beloved of all beings endowed with reason, most desirable beauty, the cause of all beings, the source of life, the intellectual light, unapproachable wisdom, it is he who in the beginning created heaven and earth' (*Hex.* 1.2). The whole creation is a manifestation of the impenetrable and ineffable wisdom of God (*Hex.* 5.8). It exists by the command of his 'deep wisdom' (*Hex.* 5.1) and shows in its order and harmony—from the smallest things to the great—the wondrous depths of the inexhaustible wisdom of the Creator (*Hex.* 1.10, 3.6, 3.7, 6.10, 6.11, 7.5, 8.8 and *passim*). God contemplates the creation not with eyes but 'in his ineffable wisdom' (*Hex.* 4.6) and we in turn

---

[64] Cf. Origen, *Commentary on the Song of Songs*, Prologue 3.14–16 (SC 375 136–8).

perceive God's wisdom through self-knowledge: 'One does not come to know God better through contemplation of heaven and earth than through the attentive study of our own constitution; "Knowledge of you", says the Prophet, "is too wonderful for me" (Ps. 138(139):6); that is to say, through the study of myself I have been taught the transcendent nature of the wisdom that is in you'. (Hex. 9.6).

But it is in the context of the polemic surrounding the Son and the Spirit that we see Basil's clearest treatments of wisdom in a Christological and Trinitarian context, most especially the treatises *On the Holy Spirit* and *Against Eunomius*. Basil is firmly in line with the standard interpretation of scriptural wisdom texts as referring in the first instance to the Son (*HS* 6.15, 8.17, 8.19, 8.20). But he by no means confines his understanding of wisdom to the Son. The Son is true wisdom because he has all that he is from the Father (*HS* 8.20). And in so far as the Holy Spirit is accounted the 'Spirit of wisdom' he also is to be understood in terms of uncreated wisdom: 'Thus [such] names are common to the Spirit with the Father and the Son, and he gets these appellations from his natural conformity with them. Where else could they come from?' (*HS* 19.48).

In *Against Eunomius*, wisdom is one of the principal terms used to speak of the unity of Father and Son—something Eunomius is berated for quite failing to understand, being inspired by worldly wisdom alone (*Eun.* 500A; 532A). For Eunomius, as for Arius, the Son is wisdom only in a secondary and derivative sense.[65] For Basil, Paul's designation of the Son as the 'wisdom and power of God' (I Cor. 1:24) clearly demonstrates his equal divinity: 'If Christ is the wisdom and power of God, these things are uncreated and eternal (for God has never been bereft of wisdom and power) and so Christ is uncreated and co-eternal with God.' (*Eun.* 689B).[66] 'Everything you see the Father do, the Son as his wisdom and power does likewise' (*Eun.* 564B). Wisdom is clearly associated with the essence (*ousia*) of God and, as even Eunomius admits, 'everything that comes from essence is essence' in which there is neither greater nor less (*Eun.* 568C). The Son is understood to be the wisdom of God not in by way of habit or convention but as a 'living and active essence'. Echoing Origen, Basil asks how could God ever have existed without his wisdom (*Eun.* 605B). It makes no sense at all to say that Christ became the wisdom and power and God at some point—he is God's wisdom eternally (*Eun.* 705A) as the natural image of the Father (*Eun.* 753B).

The appellation of the Son as wisdom is, then, a key component in Basil's demonstration of the natural and essential unity of Father and Son. Describing the Spirit in terms of wisdom (as he does in *On the Holy Spirit* and elsewhere) completes a Trinitarian interpretation of wisdom. It is fundamental to Basil's

---

[65] Eunomius, *First Apology* 21 (Vaggione (ed.), 60–2).
[66] Basil goes on to specify that that Christ is not the wisdom and power of God in the sense of being an energy or operation of God (καθὸ ἐνέργεια).

anti-Eunomian and anti-Pneumatomachian platform to understand the whole divinity in terms of wisdom. But if wisdom pertains to the essence of God, does that mean it is to be identified with the essence? Not exactly—wisdom is, rather, one of the splendours or glories of God, pertaining to the essence but not itself the essence.[67] As Basil puts it in his Letter 236:

> The Only-Begotten is the image of the invisible God, and image not of bodily form, but of the very divinity and of the glories pertaining to the essence of God (τῶν ἐπινοουμένων τῇ οὐσίᾳ τοῦ Θεοῦ μεγαλείων) an image of power, an image of wisdom, as Christ is called 'the power of God and the wisdom of God'.[68]

Wisdom in this sense is God's nature made known, God's nature revealed to the world. Basil is concerned to maintain that God remains unknown in his essence while making himself known in the 'glories that pertain to the essence'—most notably his power (δύναμις) and his wisdom (σοφία), contemplated chiefly in the Son and the Spirit. This comes in the context of a discussion on the incarnation, specifically Christ's growth 'in wisdom and stature' (Luke 2:52). Basil adopts much the same approach as Athanasius to this passage, taking the reference to 'growth' in divine wisdom to pertain to his humanity.[69]

God makes himself known in various ways and under various names (such as wisdom) for good reason: 'no one name suffices to denote all the glories of God at the same time nor can any name be used without danger' (On Faith, 684AB). A good deal more on this topic is to be gleaned from his Letter 234. Here Basil insists that to know God in his various aspects is in no way to exhaust the divine mystery:

> We say that we know the glory (τὴν μεγαλειότητα) of God, his power, his wisdom, his goodness, his providence over us, and the justness of his judgment; but not his very essence [...] he who denies that he knows the essence does not confess himself to be ignorant of God, because our conception of God is gathered from the many [appellations] which I have enumerated.[70]

God remains unknowable in essence even as he makes himself known as wisdom, goodness, power, and so forth. Basil goes on to affirm that to know God in such attributes does not undermine divine simplicity. The attributes are not to be understood as names of the essence. They are distinct from the essence and the fact that they make known the essence of God in various ways does not make God

---

[67] This whole question is neatly and precisely discussed in Andrew Radde-Gallwitz' *Basil of Caesarea, Gregory of Nyssa, and the Transformation of Divine Simplicity*.

[68] Courtonne III 48; LCL 243 388.   [69] Courtonne III 49; LCL 243 390.

[70] Courtonne III 42; LCL 243 370–2.

in any way multiple. God reveals himself in his operations while remaining perfectly simple. As he continues in *Letter 234*:

> The energies are various, and the essence simple, but we say that we know our God from his energies, but do not undertake to approach near to his essence. His energies come down to us, but his essence remains beyond our reach.[71]

This sense of divine wisdom as a mode of God's Trinitarian self-disclosure that is associated but not identical with the essence, that allows us to know something of God without compromising God's transcendence and unknowability, all points forward in its basic structure and presuppositions to the formulations of St Gregory Palamas and, from there, to modern Russian Sophiology.

To sum up, Basil gives us a rich teaching on wisdom across levels S1–S3. Wisdom is one of the glories pertaining to the essence (but not itself the essence) and contemplated in Father, Son, and Holy Spirit (S3). Through human wisdom, through learning and a good life (S1),[72] the wisdom of God implanted in the creation can be perceived and the soul prepared for the gift of wisdom (S2) that enables participation in the uncreated wisdom of the Holy Trinity. Eunomius is consistently presented as an example of human wisdom that is not so ordered (S0). Basil, in short navigates a careful course whereby divine wisdom is associated but not identified with the nature of God in a manner that avoids the alleged rationalism of Eunomius and his ilk while upholding divine unknowability and simplicity. Basil is also able to affirm the reality of God's self-revelation as wisdom in the Trinity and in the world. It is a powerfully sophiological and deeply sapiential vision which is given further weight by his younger brother, St Gregory of Nyssa. But before turning to the brother, let us turn to the friend: St Gregory of Nazianzus, the Theologian.

4.3.2 St Gregory the Theologian

The figure and theme of wisdom looms somewhat less large in the Theologian than in either Basil or Gregory of Nyssa. By comparison, he gives relatively little attention to Old Testament references to wisdom or even to Christ's designation as the 'wisdom and power of God'. That said, Gregory speaks of God (as Father, Son, and Spirit)[73] as wisdom with some frequency, for instance starkly contrasting

---

[71] Courtonne III 42; LCL 243 372. Cf. also below, n.91.
[72] This is the kind of wisdom commended in his *Address to Young Men* and which is defined as the stuff of human wisdom in the *Homily on the Beginning of Proverbs*.
[73] Cf. *Oration* 38.8: 'When I say God, I mean Father, Son, and Holy Spirit'. This was a radical proposition: before Gregory (and even in Basil) the term 'God' with the definite article (ὁ θεός) invariably meant the Father and not the Trinity.

God's existence as 'the first and true wisdom' in comparison with which our feeble cogitations are as nothing (*Oration* 17.4).[74] Such considerations came in handy in the fight against Eunomius who, along with his followers, are (as in Basil) deemed to be reliant upon earthly wisdom alone (S0)—a 'small instrument' hardly capable of apprehending the natural world let alone the knowledge of God. Even Solomon, the wisest of all men, became ever dizzier the further he plumbed the depths of God and 'declared the discovery of how far wisdom had escaped him to be an achievement in itself' (cf. Eccles. 7:24) (*Oration* 28.20–1). In fine Socratic style, Gregory claims no special gift of wisdom for himself 'unless one allows that my wisdom is knowing that I am not wise and do not come close to the true and first wisdom' (*Oration* 36.1).

Gregory speaks of wisdom not only in relation to Christ (*Oration* 2.98) but also as a property of God, the first nature (S3) (*Oration* 28.13). God's creative work is invariably described in terms of wisdom, most especially the creation of the human being (*Oration* 2.75, 38.11). Wisdom is even referred to as the title God rejoices in above all others (*Oration* 2.50). And it is in the pursuit of wisdom that we preserve the image of God within us: 'This is the nobility that the true wise man and lover of wisdom will embrace' (*Oration* 26.10). As wisdom, God is the source of all wisdom worthy of the name. It is incumbent upon human beings 'to seek wisdom from the true wisdom' (*Oration* 14:30). And this is no mean feat: the wisdom of God is, as Paul affirms in I Cor. 2:7, a deeply hidden mystery (*Oration* 2.99, 40.38).

While acknowledging the familiar definition of wisdom as 'knowledge of things divine and human' (*Oration* 2.50, 28.13), it is clear that Gregory regards true Christian wisdom as far superior to anything envisaged within pagan philosophy. The pursuit of true wisdom (S1–S2), the true philosophy, requires considerable ascetic effort and practical commitment: 'it is impossible to participate in wisdom without behaving wisely'. Only through good practice can we even begin to embark on the path to contemplation (*Oration* 4.113).[75] Wisdom is the chief of all pursuits, embracing all the good (*Oration* 2.50). 'The true and first wisdom', Gregory writes, 'is a praiseworthy life, purified or being purified by God the most pure and most luminous'.[76] It involves a rejection of merely worldly wisdom (S0) ('which consists in words, turns of phrase, and spurious counter-arguments'). This is the true wisdom by which the fishermen have taken the whole world in the net of the Gospel and vanquished the empty wisdom of this world (*Oration* 16.2).[77] Such wisdom, he goes on to say, also implies considerable experience of the practicalities of life (*Oration* 16.20), including the ability to view with

---

[74] A similar point is made in *Oration* 14.20.

[75] Gregory has the Emperor Julian in view here as someone with pretensions to wisdom but who acts far from wisely.

[76] Gregory is presenting his father as an example of such embodied wisdom.

[77] Cf. *Oration* 23.12: we are to theologize 'in the manner of the fishermen, not in that of Aristotle'.

equanimity what a later commentator called the 'slings and arrows of outrageous fortune'.[78]

Growth in such wisdom is, of course, a gradual process—sometimes even a painful process. It is not for nothing that scripture declares fear to be the beginning of wisdom (cf. *Oration* 39.8). But the strenuous path of wisdom is one which leads ultimately to the greatest of all things, to theology understood as the vision of God and incorporation into the divine life: 'For the fear of the Lord is the beginning of wisdom, and, so to say, its first swaddling clothes, but when wisdom has surpassed fear and risen up to love, then it makes us friends of God, and sons instead of servants' (*Oration* 21.6).

In the context of the ongoing Arian controversy, Gregory could hardly avoid dealing with passages like Proverbs 8:22. Indeed his *Fourth Theological Oration (On the Son)*, opens with precisely this question. Gregory sums up his overall approach with wonderful clarity: in reading scripture we proceed by 'ascribing to the divinity the higher and more fitting expressions, and the lower and more human to the one who became the New Adam for us, God made capable of suffering in order to vanquish sin' (*Oration* 30.1). When it comes to Proverbs 8:22 specifically he argues as follows:

> What among beings is uncaused? The Divinity. For no one can speak of the origin of God, or otherwise they would be prior to God. But what is the cause of the humanity, which God assumed for our sake? Obviously to save us. What else could it be? Since, then, we find here clearly both the 'created' (Prov. 8:22) and the 'begets me' (Prov. 8:25), the argument is simple. Whatever we find related to the cause we refer to the humanity, but all that is simple and uncaused we are to apply to his divinity.   (*Oration* 30.2)

Thus Proverbs 8:22 pertains to the humanity of Christ while other statements (such as Proverbs 8:25) refer to his divinity. In both instances we are speaking of wisdom, whether created or uncreated. This is essentially the position of Basil and of Athanasius and one which was to become absolutely normative in the later tradition.

In sum, while the theme of wisdom occupies only a relatively limited place in his theological work, Gregory gives us a valuable and succinct assessment of wisdom in its various guises—from the wisdom that pertains to the nature of God (S3) down to the wisdom born of practical experience (S1). From ascetic practice and wise behaviour we may ascend to contemplation of God's wisdom in

---

[78] In this oration, Gregory is discoursing upon a series of disasters that had afflicted the town of Nazianzus which his father, the bishop, had difficulty in accounting for before his flock. The later commentator is, of course, Shakespeare, *Hamlet*, Act III scene I.

creation and eventually gain the gift of wisdom (S2) that enables human beings to be incorporated into the life of the one who is wisdom.

4.3.3 St Gregory of Nyssa

Basil's younger brother gives perhaps the most sustained theological account of the theme of wisdom of all the Cappadocian Fathers, an account which fully encompasses dimensions S1–S3. Gregory of Nyssa pays close attention to the various scriptural references to wisdom in the Old and New Testaments. One notable feature of his approach is his willingness (like Origen before him) to speak of all scripture as utterances of wisdom—and not only in texts where wisdom is specifically mentioned.[79] For instance, in the treatise *On Virginity* he observes that the soul maintains its inherent beauty even when obscured by the stain of sin: 'This truth is, I think, taught in the Gospel, when our Lord says, to those who can hear what wisdom speaks mystically, that "the Kingdom of God is within you"' (*Virg.* 12; cf. Luke 17:21).[80] In this treatise the pursuit of virginity is routinely presented as the pursuit of philosophy in its fullest possible sense. Invoking Proverbs 4:6 with its injunction to love and embrace wisdom, Gregory argues:

> It is obvious that the saying applies similarly to both men and women, to fill them with zeal for such a marriage. 'There is neither male nor female' (Gal. 3:28), the Apostle says; Christ is all, and in all (Col. 3:11); and so it is perfectly reasonable that the true lover of wisdom should hold fast to the divine object of his or her desire, who is true wisdom; and that the soul which cleaves to the immortal bridegroom should possess love of the true wisdom, which is God.   (*Virg.* 20)[81]

Much of the *Catechetical Oration*, Gregory's elegant statement of the essentials of Christian belief, is structured around the theme of wisdom. In the first instance, belief in God arises out of consideration of the wise and skilful ordering of the cosmos by its Creator (*Or. Cat.*, prologue)—precisely the master theme of Basil's *Hexaemeron*. Belief in the unity of God arises from contemplation of the perfection that must belong to him on account of his 'power, goodness, wisdom, incorruptibility, and other names befitting God' (ibid.).[82] Perception of unity does not, of course, preclude confession of God's existence as Trinity. The divine word or reason (*logos*) shares in all the attributes of the Father: power, goodness, wisdom, and so forth (ibid.). We should not be confused by the homonymy of such words which are of course also used to apply to the human being, since in this case they bear a much-reduced significance—God's word or reason, for

---

[79] Cf. above, pp.134–5.   [80] GNO 8.1 300.   [81] GNO 8.1 328.
[82] Cf. *Or. Cat.* 20–21: All of these qualities manifest in the incarnation.

example, is irrefragable whereas ours is feeble (*Or. Cat.*, 1). God's word and wisdom is, moreover, no mere impersonal quality but a self-subsistent, creative, and willing power (*Or. Cat.* 5). In fashioning the world through this wisdom and word, God equipped his image, the human being, with the capacity to participate in his wisdom, goodness, power, and so forth. This is why the human being was granted the capacity of self-determination in order that he might realize in himself, in so far as is possible for the creature, these perfections (S1–S2) (ibid.). God foresaw all the sorry consequences that this gift of freedom entailed but nonetheless chose to create human beings, allow their fall, and to become himself the instrument of their return to their original vocation. This work of redemption was a task possible for and befitting the author of life, the wisdom and power of God (*Or. Cat.* 8).

But the most extensive of Gregory's treatments of the theme of wisdom comes in his work *Against Eunomius*. Proverbs 8:22 naturally looms large in this text and Gregory for the most part takes his cue from Basil in his own response, pointing out the obscurity of the text and making an appeal to the Hebrew:

> There are some who, in order to subvert the truth, take at face value and without explanation words used cryptically and in the dark form of parable. Thus, in order to support their perverted views, they bring forth the expression 'created' put in the mouth of wisdom by the author of the Proverbs. They say, in fact, that 'the Lord created me' is a confession that the Lord is a creature, as if the only-begotten himself in that saying acknowledged as much. But we need not accept such an argument: they do not give grounds why we must apply that text to our Lord at all; nor can they show that the sense of the word in the Hebrew leads to this and no other meaning, seeing that the other translators have rendered it by 'possessed' or 'constituted'; nor, even if this was the sense in the original text, would its real meaning be so clear and readily apparent, for proverbial teaching does not readily declare its import, but rather conceals it, revealing it only obliquely [...].[83]

This reluctance to attribute Proverbs 8:22 unequivocally to the Son is typical of Gregory's probing and pellucid intellect. Nonetheless, he ends up reaching much the same conclusion as Basil, Gregory of Nazianzus, and Athanasius in applying the text to the incarnate Son. He returns to the theme at greater length in *Against Eunomius* 3.1 in which he insists on the need to ponder this text with careful consideration, paying close attention to its genre and context. He notes that the wisdom who speaks in Proverbs also speaks of herself as 'begotten' and 'set up'— all very different descriptors pointing to the conclusion that, 'no part of this

---

[83] *Against Eunomius* 1.1.298–99 (GNO 1 114–15).

passage is such that its language should be received without examination and reflection'.[84]

But after many such minute considerations, Gregory proceeds to consider the Christological dimension of the saying as revealed to Solomon:

After recounting these and like matters, he goes on to introduce his teaching concerning the human dispensation, why the word became flesh. For seeing that it is obvious to all that God who is over all things has in himself no created or superadded thing whether power or wisdom, or light, or word, or life, or truth, or any of those things which are contemplated in the fullness of the divine bosom [...] For if the wisdom of God is created (and Christ is 'the power of God and the wisdom of God' (I Cor. 1:24), God, it would follow, has his wisdom as a thing superadded, receiving afterwards, as the result of making, something which he did not formerly have [...] Thus the words 'created me' do not apply to the divine and incomposite nature, but from that which was mingled with it in the incarnation from our created nature.[85]

Such affirmations do not exclude a broader consideration of created wisdom. Wisdom himself is begotten eternally from God and in time from the Virgin. But wisdom is also begotten in human beings, when they heed the Gospel:

For if wisdom is begotten in us then God makes in each of us both land and uninhabited land (cf. Prov. 8:26) – land, that which receives the sowing and the ploughing of the word, and uninhabited land, the heart cleared of evil inhabitants.[86]

It is in the Son, in Christ, that human beings are united to the uncreated wisdom that pertains to the divine nature. Paul's assertion that Christ is the wisdom and power of God represents, for Gregory an unambiguous assertion of his divinity and coinherence with the Father: 'For he who has the Father in his entirety in himself, and is himself in his entirety in the Father, as word and wisdom and power and truth, as his express image and brightness, himself is all things in the Father'.[87] Wisdom is certainly to be seen as one of the names of the Son that denote his divinity by expressing divine attributes (unlike names such as vine, shepherd, etc.). He is rightly named wisdom, word, and power 'and all other such relative names, as being named together with the Father in a certain relative conjunction (συζυγία)'.[88]

---

[84] *Against Eunomius* 3.1.41 (GNO 2 18).   [85] *Against Eunomius* 3.1.48–50 (GNO 2 20–1).
[86] *Against Eunomius* 3.1.57–58 in (GNO 2 24).
[87] *Refutation of the Confession of Eunomius* 168 (GNO 2 382–3).
[88] *Against Eunomius* 3.1.133–4 (GNO 2 48).

Moreover, the name wisdom, as Basil had argued, also applies to the Holy Spirit:

Thus we conceive no gap (διάλειμμα) in between [...] [the Son as] wisdom and the Spirit of wisdom, between truth and the Spirit of truth, between power and the Spirit of power, but as there is contemplated from all eternity in the Father the Son, who is wisdom and truth, and counsel, and might, and knowledge, and understanding, so there is also contemplated in him the Holy Spirit, who is the Spirit of wisdom, and of truth, and of counsel, and of understanding, and all else that the Son is and is called.[89]

As a property of the essence of God, the designation of Father, Son, and Spirit as wisdom is a sure marker both of their unity and their distinction (S3): 'One goodness, wisdom, justice, providence, power, incorruptibility – all other attributes of exalted meaning are similarly predicated of each and each has in a certain sense his strength in the other'.[90] It is through contemplations of such divine attributes that we gain a notion of God, but this is a notion of his wisdom, goodness, and so forth and not of his essence which remains hidden to us: 'For God who is by nature invisible is visible in his activities (ἐνεργείαις), being perceived in the attributes that surround him (ἔν τισι τοῖς περὶ αὐτὸν ἰδιώμασι).'[91] He makes the same point in To Ablabius, On Not Three Gods – 'none of the names denote the divine nature itself but make known some aspect of that which pertains to or surrounds it (τι τῶν περὶ αὐτὴν διὰ τῶν λεγομένων γνωρίζεσθαι).'[92]

Gregory of Nyssa's consideration of wisdom represents, in sum, a deepening and widening of Basil's sophiology. Following the lines sketched out by his brother, Gregory gives even closer attention to the various scriptural references to wisdom—including some of the more recondite instances. He also gives greater consideration than Basil to the specifically Trinitarian dimension of wisdom, seeing it as a sign not only of union within God but also of the distinction of persons or hypostases. Like Basil, Gregory specifies that when we name God as wisdom we are naming not the divine nature itself but that which pertains to or surrounds the essence. Gregory also takes up Basil's sense of the wisdom of God implanted within the creation, using that wisdom as a springboard for the human ascent to union with the uncreated wisdom of God—an ascent that necessarily entails considerable ascetic effort.

---

[89] *Refutation of the Confession of Eunomius* 11 (GNO 2 317).
[90] *Against Eunomius* 3.5.47 (GNO 2 177).
[91] *On the Beatitudes* 6 (GNO 7.1 141). While both Gregory and Basil can sometimes use the term 'energies' to denote the created effects of God by which something of God (e.g. his wisdom) can be apprehended it is clear that the 'things around the essence' to which such created effects point are themselves to be understood as divine. Cf above, p.145.
[92] *To Ablabius* (GNO 3.1 43).

4.3.4 Cappadocian *Coda*

While Basil and Gregory of Nyssa are closer to one another in specifics and in the attention they devote to the topic, there is much in common between their sophiology and the admittedly rather sparer treatment of Gregory the Theologian. Where there is a difference is in the apparent absence in the Theologian of the theme of a distinction within God between the essence and the attributes or 'glories pertaining to the essence'. With regard to modern Russian Sophiology, there is much in the Cappadocians of immediate interest, notably the hymning of creation in sophianic terms (especially in Basil) and the consistent construal of Christ in terms of the union of uncreated and created wisdom in all three figures. We have also noted the ongoing dimension of *paideia*, again especially in Basil. What we do not find is any very developed sense of wisdom as representing the divine realm of eternal prototypes for the creation. As in Athanasius, this is a theme present only in comparatively muted form. Conversely, the consistent Cappadocian association of wisdom with the divine nature is a tremendously important development and one which helps detach the notion of wisdom from the near exclusive association with the Son such as had prevailed from the time of Origen onwards. This is certainly a potential boost to Sophiology in its refusal to tie down the notion of wisdom solely to the second person of the Trinity. The notion of wisdom as one of the glories pertaining to the essence (in Basil and Gregory of Nyssa)—that is, as divine but distinct from the essence and irreducible to any particular hypostasis—is, if anything, of even greater potential significance for Sophiology. As further articulated in figures such as Dionysius, Maximus, and Palamas, this intra-divine distinction within the perfectly simple divinity was to open a space or gap for wisdom construed as neither essence nor hypostasis but nonetheless divine. While greater terminological and theological precision would await the work of, in particular, St Gregory Palamas, the Cappadocians set up a trajectory for Greek patristic theology that was not to be mirrored in the Latin West. This divergence is due above all to St Augustine of Hippo.

4.4 St Augustine of Hippo

Wisdom is one of the great master themes of the theology of St Augustine of Hippo (354–430).[93] Augustine offers an immensely rich account of wisdom (spanning levels S1–S3) that makes prolific use of biblical wisdom literature and

---

[93] The potential bibliography here is too vast for a footnote. Some inkling into current scholarship on Augustine (including a good deal on wisdom) can be gleaned from Rowan Williams, *On Augustine* and Lewis Ayres, *Augustine and the Trinity*. See also, more specifically, Alexei Fokin, 'The Wisdom of God as *Ars Dei* in St Augustine: Between Neo-Platonism and Christianity'.

numerous classical tropes. Augustine's account determined much of the shape and course of subsequent wisdom reflection in the Western theological tradition.

Augustine's thoroughgoing sophiology, as with the Western theological tradition as a whole, receives little credit within modern Russian Sophiology. Soloviev displays no special interest while Florensky mentions Augustine on numerous occasions but not in reference to the question of Sophia. Bulgakov, however, deals frequently and *in extenso* with Augustine recognizing the importance of his identification of wisdom (as in the Cappadocians) with the essence of God rather than with any one of the persons,[94] and praises his embrace of the concept of the eternal divine ideas for the creation.[95] But Bulgakov sees Augustine as woefully deficient and problematic in numerous areas, for example in his Trinitarian theology (impersonal and irredeemably filioquist), Christology (proto-Monophysite), and interpretation of Revelation (inadmissibly spiritualizing).[96] Bulgakov devotes a whole excursus to 'Augustine and Predestination' at the close of *The Bride of the Lamb*, finding Augustine's teaching fatal to any notion of human freedom or indeed of any real connection between God and man.[97] Indeed, Bulgakov finds Augustine's whole approach overly rationalistic and argues that he breaks downs the 'unfathomable wisdom of God' into a monstrous and blasphemous construct wholly devoid of mystery: 'Here we find neither antinomy nor legitimate ignorance but simply a dead-end'.[98] Bulgakov finds the whole problematic of Sophia lacking in the Latin doctor's work (as in the Western tradition as a whole) arguing that he utterly fails to address the Ur-question of how the uncreated relates to the created and the infinite to the finite: he simply leaves this question hanging, offering no sort of 'in-between' whatsoever. And Augustine's deficiencies are replicated in the whole subsequent history of Western theology which never overcame the fundamental disjunct set up by Augustine between God in his complete perfection and man in his complete abjection, his very undivine humanity:

> God and man, in Blessed Augustine, are juxtaposed as two opposing, mutually related, but nonetheless alien and impermeable quantities to one another. This juxtaposition gives rise to a fundamental misunderstanding: God becomes an infinite quantity, and humanity a finite quantity that becomes a zero before the infinite. One wonders in what possible sense these two quantities can be juxtaposed and compared? For in this very juxtaposition there is lacking a *tertium*

---

[94] *Burning Bush* (Excursus III), 284n [ET 182n]; *The Wisdom of God*, 38.
[95] *Burning Bush* (Excursus III), 287 [ET 156]; *The Wisdom of God*, 64.
[96] For more on Augustine in Bulgakov see Myroslaw Tataryn, *Augustine and Russian Orthodoxy*, 66–97.
[97] *The Bride of the Lamb*, 587–621 [Not in Jakim translation. ET in Roberto De La Noval, '"Augustinianism and Predestination" by Sergius Bulgakov'].
[98] *The Bride of the Lamb*, 611 [ET 90]. Тупик: dead-end, impasse.

comparationis, the only foundation for such comparison being the idea of divine humanity, of divine and created Sophia. From this fundamental difficulty arise both the errors and secondary effects as well as the fluctuations of thought we find in Blessed Augustine.[99]

What Bulgakov does not delve into is the degree to which Augustine's doctrine of divine simplicity precludes the recognition of wisdom as divine except as identical with the divine essence (and secondarily, principally for exegetical reasons, with the person of the Son). While Augustine's account of simplicity may be argued to have some affinities with the rather less explicit and less extensive treatments of simplicity in Athanasius and Gregory of Nazianzus, it is patently clear that his approach differs fundamentally from that offered by Basil and Gregory of Nyssa. This divergence was to have huge implications for subsequent theological developments in both Greek East and Latin West.

Given that Augustine's mammoth corpus is shot through with wisdom themes and stands for a Christian *paideia* expressly designed to subsume and supplant the old classical *paideia*, it is scarcely possible to adequately compress his contribution within the parameters of a brief section such as this. My aim in what follows is simply to sketch the contours of his theology of the divine wisdom paying particular attention to level S3 as it impinges on modern Russian Sophiology.

Augustine presents us with a remarkably sophisticated synthesis of biblical and classical wisdom traditions. His record of conversion is structured around the pursuit of wisdom, a pursuit that was to govern the whole pattern of his life. The opening passage of *Confessions* announces the theme in no uncertain terms in glorifying the immeasurable wisdom of God (*Conf.* 1.1.1). Later in the *Confessions* (*Conf.* 3.4.7–88) he records how his youthful reading of Cicero's *Hortensius* enflamed him with a passionate love for wisdom, exhorting him 'to love and seek and pursue and hold fast and strongly embrace wisdom itself, wherever found'. While it took him some time to realize that supreme wisdom was to be found in Christ, the basic pattern of his life as a search for true wisdom was, according to his own account, established. This is philosophy in the proper sense of the term: a love for and pursuit of divine wisdom, a pursuit undertaken in full knowledge that the goal itself will never be a permanent possession in this life. Augustine expressly contrasts the pursuit of this eternal and universal wisdom to the vagaries, uncertainties, and seductions of merely earthly philosophy. The *Soliloquies*, written shortly after his conversion to Christianity, speak in very similar terms: 'I invoke you, O God, the truth, in whom and from whom and through whom all things are true which are true. God, the wisdom in whom and from whom and through whom all things are wise which are wise.'[100]

---

[99] *The Bride of the Lamb*, 603 [ET 83–4].   [100] *Soliloquies* 1.1.3 (CCEL 89 5).

Augustine's whole work is ordered around the inculcation of the way of wisdom. In the *De doctrina Christiana*, a potted work intended for Christian teachers and pastors, Augustine marks out the Christian life as a way of wisdom (S1–S2) oriented on Christ (S3). The pursuit of true blessedness that is with Christ requires a long process of purification. It is 'a kind of journey home to our native land' in which divine wisdom incarnate is our foundation and pattern: 'though wisdom was himself our home, he made himself the way by which we should reach our home'.[101] Wisdom became 'our healer and our medicine' in assuming humanity at its point of most acute need.[102] He goes on to detail at some length the seven steps laid down by wisdom incarnate for humans to follow as they approach the unchangeable Trinity: fear, piety, knowledge, resolution, counsel, purification of heart, and the end, which is wisdom.[103] Wisdom is thus not only the alpha but also the omega of the Christian journey.

Augustine presents his mother, Monica, as a shining instance of the *vera philosophia* that is the Christian life. Her acclamation as a true philosopher comes notwithstanding her lack of formal education in the liberal arts which are presented as potentially useful but, as her example shows, inessential stepping stones on the path to the gift of true wisdom. In the Cassiacum dialogues *De beata vita* and *De ordine* Monica emerges as far more advanced in the journey of wisdom than her son and his educated companions.[104] The pivotal vision at Ostia (*Conf.* 9.10.23–5), a rare example of a shared mystical experience, is also centred on an ascent to divine wisdom (S3). Right at the end of Monica's life, discoursing on the character of eternal life, mother and son determined to follow Paul's injunction to 'stretch forward unto those things that lie ahead' (Phil 3:13) and to seek if possible an encounter with 'the eternal wisdom which abides over all'.[105] Reaching a point at which all material concerns appeared to them as insubstantial and irrelevant:

> We lifted ourselves with a more ardent love toward being itself (*id ipsum*) and we gradually passed through all the levels of bodily objects, and even through the heaven itself, where the sun and moon and stars shine on the earth. Indeed, we soared higher yet by an inner musing, speaking and marvelling at thy works. And we came at last to our own minds and went beyond them, that we might climb as

---

[101] *De doctrina Christiana* 1.10.10–11 (CCSL 32 12).

[102] *De doctrina Christiana* 1.14.13 (CCSL 32 13). See further Rowan Williams, *On Augustine*, 141–53.

[103] *De doctrina Christiana* 2.7.9–11 (CCSL 32 36–8).

[104] See further Marianne Djuth, 'Augustine, Monica, and the Love of Wisdom' and Lenka Karfíková, '*Sapientiae* amor: Die Weisheit in Augustins Gespächenaus Cassiciacum'.

[105] Cf. Plotinus' injunction to 'strain and see' (ἀτενίσας ἴδε) supernal beauty in *Enneads* 1.6.9. Augustine and Monica's vision bears close comparison with Plotinus' tractate *On Beauty* but differs markedly in culminating in an encounter with a personal God in which the subject–object distinction is not erased.

high as that region of unfailing plenty where you feed Israel forever with the food of truth, where life is that wisdom by whom all things are made, both which have been and which are to be. Wisdom is not made, but is as she has been and forever shall be; for 'to have been' and 'to be hereafter' do not apply to her, but only 'to be', because she is eternal and 'to have been' and 'to be hereafter' are not eternal. And while we were thus speaking and straining after her, we just barely touched her with the whole effort of our hearts. Then with a sigh, leaving the first fruits of the Spirit (cf. Romans 8:23) bound to that ecstasy, we returned to the sounds of our own tongue, where the spoken word had both beginning and end. But what is like to your Word, our Lord, who remains in himself without becoming old, and 'makes all things new'?   (cf. Wisdom 7:27)[106]

This is one of the most explicit references in patristic literature to an encounter, however fleeting, with eternal wisdom—the wisdom 'by whom all things are made' and which is in some manner to be identified with the Son and Word of God.

Precisely how that eternal wisdom relates to the persons of the Trinity is further elaborated in the *De trinitate*.[107] Here, Augustine specifies that wisdom pertains to substance or essence in God, not to relation.[108] This is an affirmation that was intended to shore-up Nicene orthodoxy against Homean and other critiques.[109] This affirmation came with a distinctive construal of divine simplicity in which God's wisdom is understood as identical with his substance—what is often called the 'identity thesis' of divine simplicity. For Augustine it is not enough (if one truly wishes to defend Nicaea) to say that the Son is the wisdom of the Father since that wisdom might only be 'like' the primal wisdom. It is not even enough to say that the Father and the Son share one wisdom since that sharing might also admit of degrees of divinity: one must go further and affirm that Father and Son are one wisdom and indeed are identical with that wisdom. The same applies to the other divine attributes which are identical not only with God but also with each other: 'the Trinity is simple, because it is what it has'.[110] Names such as 'Word' and 'Father' are relative terms pertaining to the persons whereas wisdom pertains to the very essence of God:

In such names essence is not expressed, since they are spoken relatively (*realtiue*); but in the other term, 'wisdom', since it is also said in respect to essence (which is

---

[106] *Conf.* 9.10.24 (CCSL 27 147–8) [ET 193–4].

[107] See further Williams, *On Augustine*, 171–90 and idem, '*Sapientia* and the Trinity: Reflections on the *De trinitate*'.

[108] Augustine uses both the established Latin term *substantia* (etymologically equivalent to the Greek *hypostasis*) and the neologism *essentia* as broad equivalents to the Greek *ousia*—i.e. as a means of expressing divine unity. See further *De trinitate* 5.8.9–10.

[109] See further Michel Barnes, '*De Trinitate* VI and VII: Augustine and the Limits of Nicene Orthodoxy'.

[110] *City of God* 11.10 (CCSL 48, 330).

wise in itself), essence also is expressed, and the one whose being it is to be wise. Thus the Father and Son together are one wisdom, because one essence, and singly wisdom of wisdom, as essence of essence. And hence they are not therefore not one essence, because the Father is not the Son, and the Son is not the Father, or because the Father is unbegotten, and the Son is begotten, since those names are spoken relatively. But both together are one wisdom and one essence in which to be is the same as to be wise.   (*De trinitate* 7.2.3)

This principle, that in God 'to be is the same as to be wise', naturally also applies to the Holy Spirit:

And so the Father is wisdom, the Son is wisdom, and the Holy Spirit is wisdom, and together not three wisdoms, but one wisdom: and because [in the Trinity] to be is the same as to be wise, there is one essence of the Father, Son, and Holy Spirit. Nor [in the Trinity] is it one thing to be and another to be God; therefore the Father, Son, and Holy Spirit, are one God.   (*De trinitate* 7.3.6)

Thus each of the divine persons *is* the divine wisdom in all its fulness. This notion of the substantial identity of God with his wisdom is integral to Augustine's understanding of divine simplicity and an essential plank of his pro-Nicene theology. It is on this basis, and only on this basis, that he is able to understand and embrace the Pauline recognition of Christ as the 'wisdom and power of God'. In that he is essential wisdom incarnate, it is legitimate to understand scriptural references to wisdom as referring to the Son and therefore to allow that 'When anything concerning wisdom is declared or narrated in the Scriptures, whether as itself speaking, or where anything is spoken of it, the Son chiefly is intimated to us.' (*De trinitate* 7.3.5).

In the *De trinitate* Augustine also discusses wisdom at the human level (S1–S2), distinguishing between wisdom (*sapientia*) and knowledge (*scientia*).[111] *Sapientia* is defined as 'the intellectual cognizance of eternal things' and thus clearly superior to *scientia* understood as 'the rational cognizance of temporal things' (*De trinitate* 12.15.25). Both, however, have their rôle to play as humans seek out the divine wisdom (S3). Later in the *De trinitate*, in the context of his discussion of the trinity that is the mind remembering, understanding, and loving God, Augustine asserts that it is only when the threefold operation of the mind is focussed on God, when, in other words, the mind has attained (or received) wisdom, that the *imago Dei* is realized—without the gift of wisdom (S2) we are still speaking merely of *vestigia*, not of the image itself (*De trinitate*14.12.15).[112] And it is only by realizing the

---

[111] This represents a deepening and qualification of the familiar classical definition of wisdom as 'knowledge of things divine and human'.

[112] Cf. In his *On the Sermon of the Mount*1.3.10 (CCSL 35, 8–9) he provides a further definition of wisdom as the path to the realization of the *imago Dei*: 'Wisdom is the contemplation of the truth, making the whole man peaceful and bringing about the likeness of God'.

image in wisdom that we can cleave to him whose image it is (*De trinitate* 14.14.20). He goes on to say that one can sum up this threefold process as the worship of God which is, as the Book of Job puts it, wisdom (Job 28.28). 'God himself is the supreme wisdom', he writes, 'but the worship of God is the wisdom of man' (*De trinitate* 14.1.1). In so worshipping God, the mind will be wise, 'not by its own light, but by participation in that supreme light; and where that eternal light is, there shall it reign in blessedness. For this wisdom of man is so called, in that it also is of God' (*De trinitate* 14.12.15). Liturgy and prayer are thus among the surest ways in which human wisdom is brought up into the divine wisdom without ever compromising the ontological distinction between the two. As he puts it very clearly in the *City of God*: 'The soul itself even when always wise (as it will be eternally when it is redeemed) will be so by participating in the unchangeable wisdom, which it is not.'[113]

Going back to the *Confessions*, Augustine makes an intriguing distinction between uncreated wisdom (identical with the substance of God) and created wisdom (representing the divine plan for the creation). Thus we must distinguish between that wisdom which is 'manifestly co-eternal and equal unto you, our God, his Father, and by whom all things were created' and 'created wisdom':

> namely, the intelligible nature which, in its contemplation of light, is light. For this is also called wisdom, even if it is a created wisdom. But the difference between the light that lightens and that which is enlightened is as great as is the difference between the wisdom that creates and that which is created. [...] Therefore, there is a certain created wisdom that was created before all things: the rational and intelligible mind of your chaste city. It is our mother which is above and is free and 'eternal in the heavens' [...] This also is the 'heaven of heavens' which is the Lord's – although we find no time before it, since what has been created before all things also precedes the creation of time. Still, the eternity of the Creator himself is before it, from whom it took its beginning as created, though not in time (since time as yet was not), even though time belongs to its created nature.[114]

Created wisdom is thus the pan-temporal 'heaven of heavens', the pattern and mother of the whole creation.[115]

Such is, in the barest of outlines, Augustine's theology of wisdom. The triune God is to be understood as essential wisdom and as identical with his wisdom. It is by the grace of divine wisdom incarnate, communicated by the Spirit of wisdom,

---

[113] *City of God* 11.10 (CCSL 48, 331).   [114] *Conf.* 12.15.20 [ET 280–1].

[115] By pan-temporal I mean Bulgakov's sense of non-linear but yet non-eternal time. Cf. his *The Apocalypse of John*, 48–9 [ET 40]. Note, however, that feminine designations of wisdom (e.g. as 'mother') are largely grammatical for Augustine (*sapientia* being a feminine noun). Augustine expressly denies any great significance to such appellations (cf. *De trinitate* 12.5.5).

that humans may perceive created wisdom, the heavenly mother or 'heaven of heavens' representing the pan-temporal (but not strictly eternal) archetypes of the creation. This created wisdom, implanted in the human creation, reaches its fullest perfection through a good and properly ordered life, patterned on wisdom incarnate and governed by prayer and liturgy. Such a *via sapientiae* brings with it the realization of the *imago Dei* and participation in the uncreated wisdom of God.

This is, in sum, an extraordinarily rich account of wisdom. Augustine's insistence on wisdom as an essential rather than personal or relational category in God was clearly of some interest to the Sophiologists as they sought to detach wisdom from any sort of exclusive association with the Son. His embrace of the doctrine of the divine ideas for the creation was of even greater potential utility, bringing with it a seemingly promising distinction between uncreated wisdom (God) and created wisdom (the realm of divine ideas)—music, one might have thought, to Sophiological ears. Indeed, there is much in Augustine that might have had him reckoned a Sophiologist *avant la lettre*. But Augustine, in Bulgakov's detailed account, totally fails to bridge the uncreated and created orders whether in cosmology, Christology, or anthropology. Any glimmerings of sophianic apprehension are effectively nullified by this basic failure. The whole of Western theology following Augustine is thus, for Bulgakov, a sophiological dead-end.

Augustine, moreover, construes divine simplicity in terms that are fundamentally inimical to Sophiology. His notion of simplicity is profoundly Plotinian—the more perfect a thing is the more simple it is. There can be no room for anything in God that is not the substance of God—no accidents and no multiplicity of any kind. For Augustine, the Trinitarian distinction in no way impinges on this perfect simplicity because the persons are identical with their substance or essence and thus with the attributes: any other construal of divine simplicity would, for Augustine, imperil the Nicene achievement. This 'identity thesis' represents a very different understanding of divine simplicity to that of Basil and Gregory of Nyssa in whom the 'glories pertaining to the essence' (such as wisdom) are united to but distinct from the unapproachable and unknowable essence of God. Thus the gap for Sophiology that opened in the Greek East with the Cappadocians remains, largely thanks to Augustine, tightly shut in the Latin West. We turn now to the subsequent history of these two trajectories, beginning with the Greek East.

5

The Greek East

The Greek East has long been distinguished by the predominately monastic and ascetic character of its theology. This emphasis is already evident in Athanasius and the Cappadocians and remains determinative within the Orthodox tradition to this day. Monks and ascetics, in their turn, have frequently been acclaimed as the truest seekers after wisdom, the truest philosophers. The figures explored in this chapter all represent a distinctly ascetic and monastic approach to wisdom that is necessarily both theoretical and practical.

The ascetic literature of the patristic era is vast and some selection is inevitable. This means that much will necessarily be left out—from the earthy and pithy wisdom of the *Sayings of the Desert Fathers* (with a few exceptions) to the sober wisdom of Barsanuphius and John, and the vast treasures of the lived wisdom displayed in ascetic hagiography. The chapter begins with the three figures most formative of the later Byzantine spiritual and theological tradition: Macarius, Evagrius of Pontus, and Dionysius the Areopagite.[1] This triple inheritance runs like threads of fire through that tradition. The chapter will then turn to two of the greatest monk-theologians of the Byzantine era, SS Maximus the Confessor and Gregory Palamas—both shining instances of this triple inheritance.

Macarius and Evagrius serve as important examples of the lived wisdom of the ascetic ideal to which the Sophiologists (especially Florensky) were wont to appeal. Macarius, in particular, was a colossal presence within the Russian mystical revival of the late eighteenth and nineteenth centuries which forms one of the essential backdrops to modern Russian Sophiology. Dionysius, Maximus, and Palamas, for their part, are of inestimable importance as we try to trace out further the space that opens up for Sophiology in the Greek East in contrast with the post-Augustinian West.

5.1 Macarius (Macarius-Symeon)

Macarius (also known as Macarius-Symeon or Pseudo-Macarius) is the author of a large corpus of texts that constitute one of the great fountainheads of the Eastern

---

[1] Whereas Macarius and Evagrius wrote principally for monastic audiences, this is not so obviously the case for Dionysius. However, I find it warranted to associate him with such monastic writers not only because of his impact on later monasticism and his consideration of specifically monastic topics (see for example his *Ep.* 8) but also because of his own monastic sources and inheritance (see further Alexander Golitzin, *Mystagogy: A Monastic Reading of Dionysius Areopagita*).

Wisdom in Christian Tradition: The Patristic Roots of Modern Russian Sophiology. Marcus Plested, Oxford University Press.
© Marcus Plested 2022. DOI: 10.1093/oso/9780192863225.003.0006

Christian ascetic and mystical tradition. Long ascribed to St Macarius of Egypt, they have since been shown to be the work of an anonymous monastic (hence 'Pseudo-Macarius') writing in Greek in Syro-Mesopotamia roughly between the 370s and 390s. The designation 'Macarius-Symeon' refers to the two principal names under which his works have circulated. For the sake of convenience, I call him simply Macarius, 'the blessed one'.

Macarius' works soon spread across the Eastern Empire and he was paid the sincere compliment of being heavily 'borrowed' from by St Gregory of Nyssa in his *De instituto christiano*.[2] He bridges in a fascinating and unique way the thought-worlds of the Greek and Syriac patristic traditions and has proved to be an enduringly popular and impactful writer not only in the East but also in the West. Most importantly for our purposes, he fed directly into the Russian Hesychast revival that took off in the late eighteenth century.[3] Macarius was widely read in Russian translation and strongly marked the teachings of St Seraphim of Sarov and the Optina Elders. He also contributed to the Russian religious scene through German Pietism, which enjoyed something of a vogue in eighteenth- and nineteenth-century Russia. Macarius had been enthusiastically promoted by Pietist luminaries such as Johann Arndt, Johann Gerhard, and Gottfried Arnold.[4] Arndt's *Wahres Christentum* (*True Christianity*), in particular, is in large part little more than a paraphrase of Macarius[5] and was in turn further 'borrowed' in several of St Tikhon of Zadonsk's (1724–83) classic devotional writings of the mid eighteenth-century.[6] Arnold, who translated Macarius into German, was recognized (with Pordage and Gichtel) as a worthy but second-tier Sophiologist by Soloviev.[7] Florensky and Bulgakov, for their part, adduce Macarius on several occasions as a prime examplar of the ascetic teaching of the Orthodox Church without, however, delving closely into his work. This is yet another regrettable oversight given the compelling and comprehensive nature of his account of wisdom.

Macarius is crystal-clear on the insufficiencies of merely worldly wisdom. While he displays a developed if somewhat diffused philosophical culture, he is typical of the monastic tradition in seeing secular wisdom as futile in and of itself (S0). In one particularly vivid and uncompromising passage he declares:

> Imagine a great city laid waste with its walls destroyed and taken by enemies – its greatness then of no account. Care is needed to give such cities strong walls in

---

[2] Cf. my *The Macarian Legacy*, 50–4.   [3] Cf. above, pp.22–3.

[4] See Ernst Benz, *Die Protestantische Thebais: zur Nachwirkung Makarios des Ägypters in Protestantismus des 17 und 18. Jahrhunderts in Europa und Amerika.*

[5] This very direct and extensive borrowing has yet to properly explored.

[6] Cf. Andrey Ivanov, 'The Impact of Protestant Spirituality in Catherinian Russia: The Works of St. Tikhon of Zadonsk'. Ivanov does not recognize that Arndt's work is itself heavily dependent on Macarius and thus this is hardly a straightforward case of Protestant influence.

[7] Cf. above, p.26 n.53.

proportion to their greatness so that enemies may not enter in. Similarly, souls adorned with knowledge, intelligence, and sharpness of mind are like great cities. But one must take care that they are fortified with the power of the Spirit, so that the enemy should not enter them and lay them waste. The wise men (σοφοί) of the world, Aristotle, or Plato, or Isocrates, being prudent (φρόνιμοι) in know-ledge, were like great cities, but they were laid waste by enemies, because the Spirit of God was not in them.   (II 42.1)

This is a theme he returns to frequently: earthly wisdom is 'uncertain and insubstantial' (I 18.4.13).[8] And it is quite insufficient for exploring the things that really matter—for instance the nature of the soul (II 48.4). It can also be a temptation, like any earthly affection, pulling us away from God if pursued for its own sake (II 5.5). And while properly directed earthly wisdom (S1) in itself is a good and laudable thing, it needs to be tempered with discretion so as not to lead into some form of deception (II 16.9).

Macarius also has much to say on the topic of wisdom on levels S2–S3. Earthly wisdom is vastly inferior to the heavenly wisdom in which Christians participate (II 9.7). True Christians are distinguished from the rest of the human race by the fact that their intellect and mind are forever fixed in a heavenly frame (II 5.4). True Christians participate in the divine wisdom of the Spirit and that grace of wisdom is combined and compounded with their nature so as to bring them to eternal salvation (II 4.7).[9] Such souls even become 'all wisdom' (I 15.1.5). Christianity is, in short, the only true philosophy:

> The wise, the warriors, the brave, the philosophers of God, are those who are led and shepherded inwardly by the divine power. The philosophers of the Greeks learn to speak well; these others may be poor in words, but they rejoice and exult in the grace of God.   (II 17.10)

This true philosophy is described as an immediate experience of knowledge, as entry into 'vision and wisdom, which the powerful, the wise, and the rhetoricians cannot fathom' (II 15.15). It is the pursuit of that which is beyond all that the world contains or can offer, of that which is above all earthly wisdom, reason, and knowledge: the pursuit of the one and only Good and Beautiful (III 26.1.1–2). This pursuit has as its goal participation in the Spirit and union with Christ (II 26.2.3). The human being is brought 'into his wisdom and his communion and becomes his dwelling place and his precious and pure bride' (II 49.4). True wisdom is, then, a form of participatory, immediate, and unitive knowledge. Wisdom is the

---

[8] Ἡ σοφία τοῦ κόσμου, ἣν μανθάνουσιν οἱ ἄνθρωποι, ἀφανὴς τίς ἐστι καὶ ἀνυπόστατος.
[9] Cf. also III 1.2.2.

deifying gift of the Father communicated in and through the Son and Spirit.[10] As 'all wisdom' (I 55.1.6), God draws the creature to himself in and through the divine grace of wisdom.

While clearly associating wisdom with the Trinitarian being of God, Macarius follows the dominant exegetical tradition of both East and West in recognizing that scriptural references to wisdom point in the first instance to the Son. I cannot, however, detect any usages of wisdom in a specifically Christological context (that is to say, in terms of the divinity *and* humanity of Christ). Nor does Macarius ever expand upon the famously controverted text of Proverbs 8:22. Wisdom 7 and I Corinthians are (as for many other patristic writers) the key texts.[11] The Word is, for example, the 'eternal will of the Father, all-powerful wisdom, God from God' (I 37.3).[12] He is 'the wisdom and power of God' (II 11.10; cf. I Cor. 1:24), the one who was 'made wisdom for us' (II 18.1; cf. I Cor. 1:30).[13]

Macarius frequently uses the theme of wisdom to speak about the divine activity. Like Basil, he sees God's manifold wisdom amply manifest in the wondrous ordering of creation (II 4.10). But perhaps his most distinctive usage is in terms of the pedagogy of grace. Observing that there are many languages on earth, Macarius holds that Christians learn one common language, tutored as they are by one wisdom, the wisdom of God (II 32.1). God's wisdom is manifest in the care and subtlety with which he tends and tutors every soul in a divine *paideia*: 'The infinite and incomprehensible wisdom of God works the dispensations of grace incomprehensibly and inscrutably upon the human race in various ways for the trying of our free will' (II 29.1).[14]

Macarius, it should be noted, is no obscurantist. He will even draw some constructive analogies with secular wisdom, noting, for example, the sheer slog and toil required to advance as a school teacher, scribe, rhetor, sophist, or philosopher. How much more time and skill, he exclaims, must it take to grow in the divine wisdom (I 20.3.6). Similarly, Macarius draws attention to the limits of advance in any profession—there will never be a doctor, for example, who can cure all diseases or a philosopher who knows all there is to know within the discipline. If earthly wisdom is beyond full comprehension, how much more so the heavenly wisdom (I 34.12).

Suffice it to say that there is in Macarius a well-developed and multi-facetted treatment of wisdom. Secular wisdom is valued so long as it is not pursued to the detriment of the infinitely more valuable wisdom of God. Pursuit of the divine

---

[10] Wisdom is variously described as the 'wisdom of the Holy Spirit' (e.g. II 4.7) and the 'wisdom of Christ' (e.g. III 1.2.2). I do not read a great deal into this variable usage; it is a function of the profoundly Trinitarian nature of his approach to the theme of wisdom.

[11] We may note that Macarius makes relatively little use of 'wisdom literature' as such.

[12] Cf. Wisdom 7:23: ἡ παντοδύναμος σοφία.

[13] I Corinthians 1:24 recurs frequently in Macarius' thought: cf. I 2.12.6, 3.3.2, 16.4.1.

[14] Cf. also I 20.3.5, 7; II 9.1, 15.41; III 12.2.3.

wisdom in the ascetic life (S1) makes Christians the truest of philosophers. God is wisdom (S3) and communicates himself as wisdom to the creature. The wisdom of God draws the creature into the divine life through the deifying gift of immediate, intuitive, and unitive knowledge (S2). In this process divine wisdom becomes 'combined and compounded' with the very nature of the creature; Macarius uses such bold 'mixing' language freely and decisively. Indeed, the creature may even be said to become 'all wisdom' in its incorporation into the divine life of the one who is 'all wisdom'. But Macarius does not ever lose sight of the ontological gap between creature and Creator—this remains an utterly fixed boundary for him, bridged only by the love of God.[15] What we do not find in Macarius is any very developed treatment of the relationship of uncreated and created wisdom—any answer, that is, to Bulgakov's Ur-question. Such questions are beyond his eminently practical purview. Macarius serves nonetheless as a fine example of the sheer range and depth of wisdom reflection in early ascetic literature. Given that he was such a huge presence in the world of modern Russian spirituality, his example helps give weight to the Sophiologists' claim to be exploring an underdeveloped aspect of the tradition. It is only to be regretted that they did not make more thorough use of him.

5.2 Evagrius of Pontus

While Macarius was a towering figure in the Russian thought-world, the same cannot be said of Evagrius of Pontus (345–399). Evagrius was caught up in the condemnations of Origenism by Pope Theophilus of Alexandria in 400 and Emperor Justinian in 543. He was also condemned by name in 553 within the context of the Ecumenical Council of that year. After 553, his legacy went underground with his more practical monastic works surviving under various pseudonyms (especially Nilus of Ancyra) and some more speculative works surviving in translated form (especially in Syriac). Only in the course of the twentieth century has his legacy been stitched together and his reputation (somewhat) restored—thus one can hardly expect the Sophiologists to have made much of him.[16] But Evagrius has a vast amount to offer in terms of a developed theology of wisdom and, what is more, a whole body of wisdom literature. He is thus of inestimable importance to our study.

With Evagrius we enter into a somewhat different world than Macarius—less vivid, more systematic, and very much more obviously implanted in the Greek

---

[15] Cf. II 49.4: 'He is God, the soul is not God. He is Lord, it a servant. He is Creator, it a creature. He is maker, it a thing made. There is nothing in common between his nature and that of the soul. But through his infinite, ineffable and inconceivable love and compassion, he has been pleased to dwell in this thing of his making, this intellectual creation, this precious and especial work.'

[16] Note that he is, however, embraced with enthusiasm by Paul Evdokimov (cf. above, p.67).

philosophical tradition. And while the legacy of Origen is certainly present in the background of Macarius, Evagrius' engagement with the Alexandrine doctor is far more direct and thoroughgoing. Evagrius is one of Origen's greatest and most significant epigones—indeed he is responsible for much of what goes by the unhappy name of 'Origenism'. But the distinction between Evagrius and Macarius should not be overplayed, particularly if it involves (as has been attempted by Irénée Hausherr and others) a retrojection of medieval categories of intellective *versus* affective mysticisms.[17] Both Evagrius and Macarius eschew any sort of disjunct between the intellect and heart and ground their theology squarely in mystical experience.

Evagrius was in his earlier years a close associate of the Cappadocians, being ordained reader by Basil and deacon by Gregory the Theologian. A promising career in the highest ecclesiastical circles was nipped in the bud by a brewing scandal in Constantinople at the time of the Second Ecumenical Council. Evagrius was forced to quit the capital in some haste and subsequently retreated into the Egyptian desert where he spent the remainder of his days. Here this cultured and highly philosophically literate individual was forced to confront in all humility the simple and uncompromising wisdom of the Desert Fathers. This encounter proved immensely fertile and gives to his work much of its distinctive character and enduring appeal. Evagrius found himself chastened on occasion for his status and learning:

One day at Kellia, there was an assembly about some matter or other and Abba Evagrius held forth. Then the priest said to him, 'Abba, we know that if you were living in your own country you would probably be a bishop and a great leader; but at present you sit here as a stranger.' He was filled with compunction, but was not at all upset and bending his head he replied, 'I have spoken once, and I will not answer; indeed twice, but I will proceed no further.'[18]   (cf. Job 40:5)

Abba Arsenius was in a similar position, having once tutored the children of the imperial family. He too was forced to learn his place notwithstanding his fine education:

One day Abba Arsenius consulted an old Egyptian monk about his own thoughts. Someone noticed this and said to him, 'Abba Arsenius, how is it that you with such a good Latin and Greek education, ask this peasant about your

---

[17] See Alexander Golitzin, 'Hierarchy versus Anarchy? Dionysius Areopagita, Symeon the New Theologian, Nicetas Stethatos, and their Common Roots in Ascetical Tradition', 153 and my *The Macarian Legacy*, 59–71.

[18] *AP (Alph.)*, Evagrius 7 (PG 65 176A) [ET 64].

thoughts?' He replied, 'I have indeed been taught Latin and Greek, but I do not know even the alphabet of this peasant.'[19]

This peasant's alphabet stands for the chastening and stark wisdom of the desert. Another learned monk, named in some sources as Evagrius, memorably lamented the relative insufficiency of book-learning to the same Arsensius:

> 'How is it that we, with all our education and our wide knowledge get nowhere, while these Egyptian peasants acquire so many virtues?' Abba Arsenius said to him, 'We indeed get nothing from our secular education, but these Egyptian peasants acquire the virtues by hard work'.[20]

The erudite monasticism of figures such as Evagrius proved remarkably successful and enduring in transmitting and translating the wisdom of the peasant alphabet and dogged toil of the monks of Egypt into a somewhat more sophisticated philosophical and theological register. He focusses much of his work on levels S1–S2: the practical effort that leads to the acquisition of wisdom. Here one of Evagrius' main strategies is the use of scriptural wisdom literature—not only in terms of scriptural commentary but also in the composition of his own examples of wisdom literature. Works such as *Ad monachos* and *Ad virgines* consciously imitate biblical wisdom literature—in particular the Book of Proverbs. The opening of the *Ad monachos* will serve to give a flavour:

> Heirs of God, listen to the words of God,
> co-heirs of Christ, receive the sayings of Christ;
> so that you may give them to the hearts of your children,
> and teach them the words of the wise.[21]

Other texts in short chapter form (of which Evagrius was something of a pioneer in the patristic tradition), such as the famous *On Prayer*, similarly imbibe and expand on the form of Proverbs while also drawing on the model of philosophical (especially Stoic) sentences. Evagrius evidently found this pithy, broadly self-contained, and largely non-sequential form especially conducive to monastic meditation and *paideia*.[22] By constructing a whole new genre of ascetic wisdom

---

[19] *AP (Alph.)*, Arsenius 6 (PG 65 89A) [ET 10].

[20] *AP (Alph.)*, Arsenius 5 (PG 65 88D–89A) [ET 10]. In *AP (Syst.)* 10.5 (PL 73 912D–913A) the monk is named as Evagrius.

[21] *Ad monachus* 1 (TU 39.4).

[22] For a compelling contemporary Orthodox paradigm of wisdom literature in the *Centuries* format, see Fr Silouan (Lake): *Wisdom and Wonder; Wisdom Songs; Wisdom, Prophecy and Prayer;* and *Wisdom, Glory and the Name.*

literature, Evagrius made a substantial contribution to the storehouse of patristic wisdom, including some very detailed instruction as to how to grow in wisdom and towards the one who is wisdom. In giving such a central emphasis to the theme of *paideia*, Evagrius was restoring a dimension of the Christian wisdom tradition that was in danger of being lost sight of in the midst of seemingly endless doctrinal controversies.

Evagrius' fascination with biblical wisdom literature is also evident in his own scriptural commentary which is squarely focussed on wisdom literature, composing *scholia* on Psalms, Proverbs, Ecclesiastes, the Song of Songs, and Job.[23] While guided to some extent by the base text, Evagrius feels perfectly free to launch into his own precise and pregnant ruminations inspired by the text at hand. In this sense his scriptural commentaries are also themselves to be seen as instances of ascetic wisdom literature.

The specific theme and topic of wisdom is, furthermore, found throughout Evagrius' *oeuvre*. The pursuit of wisdom, as noted in *On Prayer*, is intimately bound up with prayer: 'The state of prayer is one of freedom from passions, which by virtue of the most intense love transports to the noetic realm the intellect that longs for wisdom.'[24] But it is in the *Scholia on Proverbs* that Evagrius puts forward his most developed treatment of wisdom. Here, wisdom is specifically associated with natural contemplation both primary (of invisible things) and secondary (of visible things). Natural contemplation is the second of the three stages into which he divides the spiritual life: practical life, natural contemplation, and theology/ essential knowledge. Within this taxonomy, which was to become standard within the later monastic tradition, wisdom is principally defined as 'knowledge of corporeal and incorporeal things, as well as the judgements and providence contemplated in them'.[25] Wisdom thus forms a kind of link-piece in Evagrius' three-stage schematization of the spiritual life. Proper application to the practical life (S1) inculcates the wisdom of natural contemplation (S2).[26] And wisdom, when acquired, draws us into the life of God who is essential knowledge or wisdom (S3). In this sense wisdom is also to be identified with the Spirit of adoption of Romans 8:15.[27]

---

[23] While doubtless aware of Origen's taxonomy of this literature (see above, p.132), Evagrius' commentaries do not adhere to this schema.

[24] *OP* 53 (SC 589 267). For the element of joy see also *OP* 62 (SC 589 275).

[25] *Scholia on Proverbs* 3 (SC 340 92); cf. *Praktikos* 89 (SC 171 684): The task of wisdom is the contemplation of the *logoi* of corporeal and incorporeal realities.

[26] Cf. *Scholia on Psalms* 99.1 (PG 12 1557C): The virtues as the gates of wisdom. Similarly, psalmody is an image of the multiform wisdom (i.e. the wisdom in creation) whereas prayer represents immaterial and uniform knowledge (*OP* 85). Humility is the 'pledge of wisdom' or 'true philosophy of God' a philosophy provided by God that brings true friendship with wisdom (*On the Vices* 9 and 9 (alternative ending) (SC 591 432, 436).

[27] *Scholia on Proverbs* 101 (SC 340 200).

One intriguing feature of Evagrius' meditations on Proverbs (which come with a noteworthy refusal to get bogged down in Proverbs 8:22) is the relative enthusiasm with which he expands on the feminine dimensions of the divine wisdom intimated in Proverbs. Such enthusiasm is, as we have noted, markedly unusual within the patristic tradition. Thus wisdom is both mother and sister.[28] She is mother because she has given birth to us in God through natural contemplation.[29] She is sister because 'the Father who has created incorporeal nature has created her also'. But Evagrius is careful to point out that such references apply to wisdom as natural contemplation (S2): 'Here by wisdom it does not speak of the Son of God, but rather of the contemplation of bodies and incorporeal things and the judgments and providence within them.'[30]

When dealing with scriptural references to divine wisdom, Evagrius follows the dominant exegetical tradition in ascribing such references principally to Christ. Christ is routinely described as our wisdom.[31] But in the *Great Letter* Evagrius develops a fascinating exegesis by which various scriptural references to the hand and finger of God are ascribed respectively to his power and wisdom, that is to say to the Son and the Spirit. Power and wisdom, Son and Spirit, are magnificent letters through which Father is known, just as rational creatures are letters by which the power and wisdom of the Father (the Son and Spirit) are made known.[32] This adduced connection between the Spirit and wisdom is a fascinating survival of what was, by the fourth century, a largely forgotten exegetical tradition. The *Great Letter* also instances Evagrius' espousal of the doctrine of the pre-existence of the ideas of rational beings within the eternal wisdom of God.[33]

The *Kephalaia Gnostika* add some further details as to Evagrius' understanding of wisdom. Creation is the mirror of the goodness, power, and wisdom of God (*KG* 2.1). In secondary natural contemplation (of visible things) we see the 'multiform wisdom' of Christ whereas in primary natural contemplation (of invisible things) we are instructed as to Christ himself (*KG* 2.2). All is contained in the wisdom of God and he who in thought separates wisdom from God destroys all (*KG* 2.46).[34] God is everywhere present in his creation in his 'multiform wisdom' (Eph. 3:10) but remains transcendent since he is not one among other beings (*KG* 1.43). This dialectic of immanence and transcendence crops up several

---

[28] She is also described as a woman (cf. Prov. 19:14): *Scholia on Proverbs* 197 (SC 340 292).
[29] *Scholia on Proverbs* 79 (SC 340 178–80).   [30] *Scholia on Proverbs* 88 (SC 340 186–8).
[31] Cf. *Scholia on Proverbs* 105, 202 (SC 340 204, 298). Cf. also *Scholia on Psalms* 32.1 (1304B), 33.5 (1308B), 118.3 (1588CD), 131.6 (1649D); and *Scholia on Ecclesiastes* (SC 379 11).
[32] *Great Letter* (in Frankenberg (ed.) 613.188aα—613.189aα).
[33] *Great Letter* (619.191bα—191bβ).
[34] This is not to deny the distinction between God and his wisdom present in the creation but rather to affirm that we must not think of the creation apart from God (and indeed *vice versa*).

times: all creation proclaims God's multiform wisdom but his nature remains hidden (*KG* 2.21); creation reveals God's wisdom but not God's nature (*KG* 5.51).

Through contemplation of God's wisdom we become dwelling places of God: 'The intelligible temple is the pure intellect, which keeps within it the full multiform wisdom of God; the temple of God is he who is a seer of the blessed unity, and the altar of God is the contemplation of the blessed Trinity (*KG* 5.84). Here we may note that while wisdom pertains chiefly to the stage of natural contemplation (S2), it is also very occasionally used to speak of the third stage (S3): 'The contemplation of all things that come into being is limited. Only the knowledge of the blessed Trinity is unlimited for it is essential wisdom.'[35]

Evagrius is, in sum, one of the most self-consciously wisdom-centred writers of the patristic era. His commentaries on biblical wisdom literature and his composition of an extensive corpus of Christian wisdom literature constitute an invaluable storehouse of monastic *paideia* and a veritable *vade mecum* in Christian wisdom (S1–S2). Through the practice and contemplation of wisdom we are inculcated into the essential wisdom of God (S3). Evagrius thus serves as yet another example of the vital importance of the notion of *paideia* within much early Christian reflection on wisdom.

But while the Sophiologists never fully appreciated the dimension of *paideia* within patristic teachings on wisdom, there is much in Evagrius of great potential interest to their project: he provides an additional witness to the idea of wisdom as pertaining to the essence of God while also offering an intriguing late survival of the notion of wisdom pointing not so much to the Son as to the Holy Spirit. Evagrius is similarly unusual in showing some interest in the feminine dimension of wisdom, albeit only on level S2. Evagrius further serves as yet another example of the doctrine of the pre-existent divine ideas of the creation. He also presents us with a remarkable dialectic of transcendence and immanence between the essential and hidden wisdom of God and the 'multiform wisdom' of God implanted in the creation. What we do not find in Evagrius, however, is anything like the distinction between the divine essence and the 'glories pertaining to the essence' of the Cappadocian brothers. In this respect his position may be closer to that of the Theologian. Nor do we find any very searching investigation of how these wisdoms relate to one another—somewhat like Macarius, Evagrius does not delve deeply into Bulgakov's Ur-question of the precise nature of the relation between the creation and the Creator. Had Bulgakov been in a position to enquire more deeply into Evagrius, there is little doubt that he would have found his project, like the patristic tradition as a whole, incomplete.

---

[35] *Scholia on Psalms* 144.3 (as per Pitra (ed.) III 354). This is a relatively rare usage: Evagrius more often speaks of 'essential knowledge'.

5.3 Dionysius the Areopagite

Dionysius the Areopagite[36] (fl. late fifth-/early sixth-century)[37] is an occasional reference point for Sophiology. Soloviev lists him as a great mystic while Florensky cites him on occasion, for example as a witness to the patristic idea that deification is not only a human but also a cosmic vocation.[38] Bulgakov, as is his wont, goes into much greater depth than either of his predecessors. In his earlier works, Bulgakov mentions him as a proponent of the idea of the world soul and as the father of apophatic theology.[39] Later more properly theological works, such as *Jacob's Ladder*, engage the Areopagite at some length, in this case with regard to the angels. But Dionysius was never a major resource for Sophiology proper. His radical apophaticism militates against the decidedly cataphatic revelation of Sophia—something Vladimir Lossky, in particular, made extensive capital out of in his assault on Sophiology. Furthermore, Dionysius' relative reticence regarding the incarnation and more generally the uncreated-created relation make him only of limited interest to the Sophiologists. There is, nevertheless, a profound account of wisdom in Dionysius that can scarcely be overlooked in this survey.

It is no surprise that a writer who adopted the persona of a converted Athenian philosopher should have a great deal to say on the topic of wisdom. The fact that he was evidently concerned to baptize the vast riches of pagan neo-Platonism makes the focus on wisdom all the more consistent. In Dionysius we meet a theology of the divine wisdom (focusing very squarely on levels S2–S3) that was to prove of immense moment for the later tradition.

The *Divine Names*, as the title would lead us to expect, contains a great deal on the name 'wisdom' as applied to God.[40] The treatise opens with a programmatic reference to I Cor. 2:4. Like Paul, Dionysius will speak 'not in the persuasive words of human wisdom but in demonstration of the power of the Spirit-moved theologians'.[41] All-wise and superlatively trustworthy theology is founded on

---

[36] As with (pseudo-) Macarius, I tend to eschew the 'pseudo' when speaking of Dionysius. It is universally accepted (in scholarly circles at least) that he was not the convert of St Paul on Mars' Hill (Acts 17:34). But the author who carefully and consciously cultivated the persona of that mysterious individual does not deserve to be permanently denoted as 'pseudo' with the whiff of fraudulent intent which that moniker carries.

[37] Dates are tricky with Dionysius: the period 475–518 fits with his referencing of the use of the Nicaeno-Constantinopolitan Creed in the Divine Liturgy (not otherwise attested before 475) and his being cited in Christological debate in 518. His silence on the question of the nature(s) of Christ may also put him in the context of the *Henotikon* of Emperor Zeno (in force from 482–519) which had forbidden such discussion.

[38] See Kornblatt, *Divine Sophia*, 86 and Florensky, *The Pillar and Ground of Truth*, 733 n.478 [ET 525 n.479].

[39] *Philosophy of Economy*, 59 [ET 84] and *Unfading Light*, 117 [ET 125].

[40] See Andrew Louth, *Denys the Areopagite*, 92–3 for wisdom within the structure of the *Divine Names*.

[41] *DN* 1.1 (PTS 33 108). By 'Spirit-moved theologians' Dionysius means in the first instance the writers of scripture. Cf. I Cor. 2:4: the 'demonstration of Spirit and of power'.

scripture alone.[42] Wisdom is thus one of the principal names of the nameless and many-named God explored in this treatise. God is celebrated as wise and as wisdom.[43] Dionysius goes on to explain that terms such as 'the beautiful' and 'the wise', like the term 'Lord', 'pertain to the whole divinity'. The same applies to all the divine attributes.[44] He does not, in other words, privilege the Son or Spirit in his naming of God as wisdom.[45] God is unnameable in his hidden essence but nameable in his beneficent processions or powers. For instance, we name him wise or wisdom by virtue of his wisdom-bestowing activity—just as we name God for his deifying activity, being for his being-bestowing activity, or life for his life-giving activity.[46] Thus there is a sense in which wisdom is indeed rightly ascribed to God according to essence in that he is transcendent and hidden wisdom, but that wisdom lies wholly beyond human expression. The wisdom of which we can speak is the wisdom of the beneficent processions or activities of God. The same applies to his goodness, being, life, and other attributes.[47] This distinction between wisdom as pertaining to the inexpressible essence and wisdom as pertaining to the beneficent processions (wisdom, goodness, etc.) corresponds in outline rather exactly to the Cappadocian essence-glories distinction and points forward *mutatis mutandis* to the Palamite essence-energies distinction.[48]

Section 7 of the *Divine Names* is largely taken up with the name of wisdom. God is praised as 'wise, the principle of wisdom, the subsistence of wisdom, and as transcending all wisdom', not simply in degree but in kind for he is 'established above all reason, all intellect, and all wisdom'. Indeed, his wisdom is so beyond any notion we might have of wisdom that it can properly be described, after Paul, as foolishness (cf. I Cor. 1:25).

> Therefore supremely hymning this foolish wisdom that is without intellect or reason let us declare that it is the cause of all intellect and reason, and of all wisdom and understanding. It is the source of all counsel and from it comes all knowledge and understanding. And in it all the treasures of wisdom and knowledge are hidden. For, in accordance with what has already been said, the

[42] *DN* 1.1 (PTS 33 109).   [43] *DN* 1.6 (PTS 33 118).   [44] *DN* 2.1 (PTS 33 122).

[45] Even when he speaks of the name 'word', which he takes to be somewhat prior to the name 'wisdom', Dionysius does not refer it exclusively to the Son. Cf. *DN* 7.4 (PTS 33 198–9).

[46] *DN* 2.7 (PTS 33 133): οὐδὲν ἕτερον νοοῦμεν ἢ τὰς εἰς ἡμᾶς ἐξ αὐτῆς προαγομένας δυνάμεις ἐκθεωτικὰς ἢ οὐσιοποιοὺς ἢ ζωογόνους ἢ σοφοδώρους. Note that being-in-itself has a certain priority over life-in-itself or wisdom-in-itself (αὐτοσοφία) since being-in-itself is prior to any form of participation: *DN* 5.5 (PTS 33 183–4).

[47] *DN* 5.2 (PTS 33 181).

[48] It is beside the point whether or not the Cappadocian, Dionysian, or indeed Maximian distinctions correspond precisely in all particulars to the rather more developed Palamite distinction: the point here concerns rather a discernable trajectory within the Greek patristic tradition up to Palamas and, beyond him, Bulgakov.

beyond-wise and all-wise cause is indeed the subsistence of wisdom itself and of the universal and the particular instantiations of wisdom.[49]

The angelic powers draw from this divine wisdom their simple and blessed intellections and are assimilated to the divine mind through the workings of the same. Human beings have less direct access to the divine wisdom but are none-theless guided along the same path, albeit from a somewhat lower starting point, that of sense perception. But all intellectual activity and even all sense perception has as its source and its goal the divine wisdom.[50] The whole creation beckons us as a manifestation and revelation of the ordering principle of wisdom:

> According to scripture (cf. Ps. 103(4):24; Proverbs 8:30), [wisdom] has made and ever harmonizes all things. She is the cause of the irrefragable adaptation and order of all things, ever connecting the ends of a first group of things with the beginnings of a second and making of the whole a single harmonious symphony.[51]

Wisdom thus corresponds to the divine ideas for the creation underpinning God's presence in the creation and drawing that creation back into union with him.[52]

God is identical with himself according to his essence but extends himself as multiplicity in his beneficent operation or energy:

> Almighty God is present to all providentially, and becomes 'all in all', for the salvation of all, remaining in himself and identical with himself, imparting himself according to single and ceaseless energy with unbending power for the deification of those turned towards him.[53]

In their approach to God, human beings are called to progress well beyond customary understandings of illumination, knowledge, and wisdom into the darkness, unknowing, and foolishness of God. In true unknowing, they are 'united to the super-luminous rays and illuminated by the unsearchable depth of wis-dom'.[54] This is the 'transcendently wise wisdom' for which all human beings should strive and yearn.[55]

The *Mystical Theology* has little on the topic of wisdom—it is simply one of the names of God that must be both affirmed and denied (and then the denial itself denied) as one ascends into the divine darkness of perfect unknowing. The *Celestial Hierarchy*, on the other hand, employs the theme to characterize the

---

[49] *DN* 7.1 (PTS 33 194–5).   [50] *DN* 7.2 (PTS 33 195).   [51] *DN* 7.3 (PTS 33 198).
[52] Bulgakov notes Dionysius as a proponent of the divine ideas or paradigms in *The Burning Bush* (Excursus III), 286 [ET 155–6].
[53] *DN* 9.5 (PTS 33 210).   [54] *DN* 7.3 (PTS 33 198).   [55] *DN* 8.1 (PTS 33 200).

great sacred chain by which wisdom is communicated. As all created things participate in divine being and all living things in the divine life, so also do all rational and intellectual creatures participate in the divine wisdom, 'the self-perfect and beyond-perfect wisdom above all reason and mind'.[56] But rational creatures do not participate equally in the divine wisdom.[57] The angels closest to God—the seraphim, cherubim, and thrones—are those who stand closest to the perfection of divine wisdom and who communicate their direct and immediate experience and vision of wisdom to those below. Thus those below have only an indirect and mediated exposure to the divine wisdom itself. Dionysius interprets the name 'cherubim' to mean 'full of knowledge or effusion of wisdom'.[58] He goes on to explain that 'filled with the ability to impart wisdom they unstintingly communicate what they have received to those below them in an out-pouring of wisdom'.[59]

The *Ecclesiastical Hierarchy* has only a few specific references to wisdom, but these constitute some of Dionysius' most obvious references to wisdom on level S1. The scriptural readings in the *synaxis* present, inter alia, the example of wise kings, the dogged philosophy of men of old that enabled them to endure all sorts of troubles, and many instances of practical wisdom.[60] The monastic life is, similarly, described in familiar terms as the most perfect form of philosophy.[61] The ecclesiastical hierarchy, like all hierarchy, is geared to the inculcation of wisdom and the approach to the one who is himself truly beautiful, wise, and good.[62] While there is nothing like the degree and intensity of wisdom references that are found in the *Celestial Hierarchy*, it is clear that the sacraments and structures of the Church have their own part to play in human ascent towards primordial wisdom.

The *Letters*, by contrast, have a great deal to say about the theme of wisdom. In *Letter 7* (*To Polycarp*) Dionysius articulates an irenic and constructive approach to pagan philosophy, clearly regarding it as God-given and tending, if rightly ordered, to the apprehension of the one who is the cause not only of all beings but of all knowledge of beings.[63] *Letter 9* is largely taken up with an extended exegesis of elements of Proverbs 9:1–5, in particular the house and the mixing bowl of wisdom.[64] Such enigmatic images are, Dionysius explains, among the many puzzling symbols used by the 'fathers of wisdom', the writers of scripture, to initiate Christians into the ineffable mysteries of God.[65] The mixing bowl of the 'beyond-wise and good wisdom' symbolizes the divine maternal providence from

---

[56] *CH* 4.1 (PTS 36 20).   [57] Cf. *CH* 12.2 (PTS 36 44).
[58] *CH* 7.1 (PTS 36 27): πλῆθος γνώσεως ἢ χύσιν σοφίας.   [59] *CH* 7.1 (PTS 36 28).
[60] *EH* 3.4 (PTS 36 83).   [61] *EH* 6.2 (PTS 36 117).   [62] *EH* 1.2 (PTS 36 65).
[63] *Ep.* 7.1–2 (PTS 36 165–9).
[64] Dionysius claims that he explicates the 'seven pillars' in his lost or more probably never-written *Symbolical Theology*: *Ep.* 9.6 (PTS 36 207).
[65] *Ep.* 9.1 (PTS 36 193).

which comes both solid food—simple, stable knowledge of God—and the liquid food of the outpouring of knowledge of that which is variegated and multiform and which leads to the simple, stable knowledge of God:

> Such indeed are the gifts that the divine wisdom gives to those who draw near to her with openness of heart in an unfailing outpouring and overflowing of joy. And this is true joy, and because of these things she is hymned as life-giving, child-nourishing, renewing, and perfecting.[66]

Dionyisus' treatment of wisdom is, like so much of his work, rather distinctive. Wisdom is primal to his understanding of hierarchy, both ecclesiastical and, especially, celestial. He is alive to the feminine dimension of the divine wisdom in a way that few of his patristic peers were. Unusually, he refuses to associate wisdom with any particular person of the Holy Trinity. Wisdom stands as the pre-eternal divine realm of ideas for the creation and thus the grounding of the world in God. Dionysius hymns God as wisdom (and not-wisdom) according to his unknowable and unnameable essence *and* according to his (partly) knowable and nameable beneficent procession as wisdom. While Dionysius figures in twentieth-century Orthodox theology largely in the anti-Sophiological reaction of Lossky and others, he undoubtedly offers a remarkable sophiology of his own and one which, through Maximus and Palamas, was to help pave the way for modern Russian Sophiology in offering a construal of divine wisdom distinct from categories of essence and hypostasis.

5.4 St Maximus the Confessor

The theme of wisdom in the work of Maximus the Confessor (*c.* 580–662) is not one that has attracted any sustained or systematic scholarly attention despite the striking renaissance of interest in Maximus over the last hundred years or more.[67] The theme of wisdom is, in fact, a major leitmotif of Maximus' remarkable theological achievement and one which opens up fresh perspectives on certain key features of his teaching.[68] Maximus was heir to much of the Greek patristic

---

[66] *Ep.* 9.4 (PTS 36 204).

[67] One of the few efforts is my own brief foray in 'Wisdom in St Maximus the Confessor'. What follows is a much expanded version of that very preliminary sketch.

[68] This is a view that has been confirmed in recent years by Paul Blowers (*Maximus the Confessor*, 108–9). Blowers pinpoints wisdom as a master-theme of what he calls, after von Balthasar, Maximus's Theo-drama: 'the activity of Christ as the Logos and Wisdom of God saturates the drama from beginning to end [...] Maximus thus not only renews a Wisdom Christology, he relates to it a Wisdom cosmology and anthropology'. Similarly, 'Salvation, then, comes as an unceasing work of divine Wisdom [...] Maximus' cosmology as a whole is a sustained demonstration of the embodiments of this Wisdom—a Wisdom that is transcendent, immanent, but most importantly free, active,

tradition of wisdom reflection examined thus far and in particular to Origen, the Cappadocians, Macarius, Evagrius, and Dionysius. As he grappled with these various inheritances in his properly original work of synthesis, the theme of wisdom emerged as a crucial dimension within his thinking.

Bulgakov was instrumental in fostering the twentieth-century revival of interest in Maximus. He delves deeply into his Christology in his *The Lamb of God*, praising his labours but characterizing much of his terminology as scholastic (not by way of praise) and lamenting his failure (with the doctrine of the gnomic will) to truly account for the humanness of Christ's human will in relation to the divine will—a failure he sees as tending towards Apollinarianism.[69] Bulgakov also mentioned Maximus on several occasions as a forerunner of Sophiology, notably in respect of the pre-existence of the divine realm of ideas.[70] This appeal came in reference to Maximus' 'signature' doctrine of the divine *logoi*, the inner principles of things eternally grounded in the wisdom and Word of God. But while claiming that Maximus' 'logology' is 'essentially a sophiology',[71] in the final analysis Maximus' sophiological insights are too underdeveloped (especially in terms of the relationship between creature and Creator)[72] and too closely tied up with the person of the Son to be truly satisfactory for Bulgakov. But Bulgakov's limited reference to and estimation of Maximus in no way does justice to the sheer extent and profundity of the Confessor's treatment of wisdom, to which we may now turn.

Anyone acquainted with Maximus will not expect to find a systematic presentation of the topic in his works. But he does give us what amounts to a remarkably developed and coherent treatment of the topic scattered across his magnificent oeuvre. While much of his treatment bears on levels S1–S2, the way of life that leads to the acquisition of the gift of wisdom, he also has a great deal to say on level S3 (God as wisdom).

Maximus speaks of God as wisdom (*QT* 54 463.348-9; *Amb.* 7 1093B) and indeed as 'wisdom in itself' (*CC* 3.27; *QT* 54 447.84). By virtue of the essential unity, the Son is also hailed as 'wisdom in itself' (*Amb.* 7 1081D) and, more specifically, 'by nature the hypostatic Word and wisdom of the Father' (*QT* 63 147.51-2). But such references are commonplace in patristic tradition and do not in and of themselves constitute a developed theology of the divine wisdom—a

---

resilient, resourceful. The Creator's whole creative and salvific work is like a "sacred tent and everything in it [is] a representation, figure, and imitation of Wisdom" [*CT* 1.88].' Blowers also discusses the appropriation of Maximus by Bulgakov: ibid., 310–13.

[69] *The Lamb of God*, 96–102 [ET 76–81].

[70] *The Burning Bush* (Excursus III), 286 [ET 156]; *The Wisdom of God*, 64.

[71] *The Lamb of God*, 148n [ET 126n].

[72] The most extensive and incisive treatment of the created–uncreated question in Maximus is Antoine Lévy's *Le créé et l'incréé: Maxime le Confesseur et Thomas d'Aquin*. See also the pertinent remarks of Nicholas Loudovikos in 'Being and Essence Revisited: Reciprocal Logoi and Energies in Maximus the Confessor and Thomas Aquinas, and the Genesis of the Self-referring Subject'.

sophiology. Maximus, furthermore, makes little use of the category of wisdom to relate the human and the divine in his Christology, the aspect of his work for which he is most renowned and for which he suffered brutal treatment as a confessor of the faith. We do not, for example, find Christ treated as the union of uncreated and created wisdom or even, curiously, any exegesis of Proverbs 8:22. As for the signature doctrine of the *logoi*, Maximus does not, at least on a first reading, seem to make much use of the idea of wisdom in his elaboration of the doctrine. One might, therefore be forgiven for thinking that wisdom is not, in fact, such an overwhelmingly important category for Maximus—at least so far as level S3 is concerned. But such a supposition would, as I hope to show, be mistaken.[73]

It is, of course, as Word (Logos) that Christ is the foundation of the divine *logoi*. As Maximus puts it in *Ambiguum* 7: 'The Word of God [who is] God always and in all things wills to accomplish the mystery of his embodiment' (*Amb.* 7 1084CD). The *logoi* are to be understood as discrete acts of God, what Dionysius calls eternal 'divine wills' or 'predeterminations' (*Amb.* 7 1085A; cf. *DN* 5.10, 9.4, and 13.1). These *logoi* constitute his self-revelation in and to the world. Some *logoi*, as Maximus explains elsewhere, are eternal acts without beginning in time. These include such participable realties as goodness, immortality, infinity, simplicity and in general 'all that is contemplated around the essence' (*CT* 1.48 1100CD).[74] Such qualities correspond to the 'glories pertaining to the essence' of the Cappadocians—attributes of God distinct from but pertaining to the divine essence. Other acts, while eternally willed, have a beginning in time: these are the *logoi* of the created order. God, in his unknowable and imparticipable essence is 'at an infinitely infinite remove' from all that participates and is participated in including all *logoi* (*CT* 1.49 1101A).[75] But in his *logoi* God truly reveals himself to and embodies himself within the creation—indeed he constitutes the very heart of the creation. We have something here very like Bulgakov's 'God in the world and the world in God' along with a strong version of the Cappadocian/Dionysian distinction between the unknowable essence and the glories/processions/divine wills/predeterminations but, as yet, no mention of wisdom.

[73] Cf. Andrew Louth, 'Sophia, the Wisdom of God, in St Maximos the Confessor'. Louth candidly expresses some difficulty in pinning down the place and import of wisdom within Maximus' thought and thus focuses not so much on cosmological or metaphysical matters (i.e. S3) but on epistemology and virtue (i.e. S1–S2) (with a closing and very suggestive remark on liturgy).

[74] καὶ ὅσα περὶ αὐτὸν οὐσιωδῶς θεωρεῖται.

[75] This striking 'infinitely infinite' formulation (also found in *Amb.* 10.78 1168A) was to be of great moment in the C14 Hesychast Controversy, especially in the dispute between Palamas and Akindynos. Palamas had used and continued to use it (cf. *Triads* 3.2.8; *Epistle to Arsenios* 8 (Chrestou II 320–1); and *Theophanes* 13 (Chrestou II 237)) to emphasize the gap between the uncreated essence and uncreated energies of God. Palamas' most formidable enemy, Gregory Akindynos, uses it repeatedly to support his contention that there can be no human participation in the uncreated sphere and that all that is not essence is infinitely removed from God.

On closer inspection, however, it becomes clear that the notion of wisdom is in fact absolutely central to Maximus' understanding of the *logoi* and of Christ as the hypostatic wisdom in whom the *logoi* cohere. Maximus does not explicitly construe wisdom as one of the *logoi* around the essence or indeed as one of the *logoi* of creation. Wisdom in Maximus is, rather, best understood not so much as a divine *logos* but as that which makes possible (across levels S1–S3) the discernment of and participation in the *logoi* and in their causal principle. In other words, if the *logoi* are the means by which God extrapolates himself in the world of multiplicity then wisdom is the means by which God returns the creation to himself in utter simplicity. What follows is an attempt to flesh out and illustrate Maximus' distinctive construal of wisdom along precisely these lines.

Perhaps the first thing to note is just how much Maximus' understanding of wisdom is founded on his meditation on the many scriptural references to wisdom—a mediation that took place within a squarely ascetic and monastic context.[76] He picks up all the various dimensions of biblical wisdom literature: the rôle of wisdom in the approach of man to God, wisdom as a cosmological theme associated with the work of creation, and wisdom as an aspect of the divine being. Thus the theme of wisdom in Maximus is very much a product not only of his deep knowledge of the patristic and ascetic tradition but also of his own searching engagement with scripture.

Regarding his approach to scripture, it is important to underline that wisdom constitutes the very guiding principle of Maximus' hermeneutics. In his exegetical master-work, the *Questions to Thalassius*, he rounds off a complex discussion of a difficult and fairly unpromising passage of Scripture[77] with the observation that nothing is ever written in vain by the Holy Spirit even if we cannot receive or understand it:

> For everything [comes about] mystically and in due time for man's salvation, the beginning and the end of which is wisdom, wisdom which in the beginning brings fear but, in the end, constitutes the fulfilment of desire.
>
> (*QT* 55 513.526–9)

Maximus perceives wisdom not so much as the object of his biblical study but as that by which the meaning of scripture is revealed and indeed as the very content of that revelation. Wisdom thus informs and governs the proper reception of scripture as both starting-point and goal. It is the condition of the possibility of all meaning. This wisdom-centred and profoundly pneumatological hermeneutic runs through Maximus' entire, profoundly scriptural, corpus.

---

[76] Cf. my 'The Ascetic Dimension'. Maximus produced much of his work in the 'centuries' format favoured by Evagrius, a genre that owes much to biblical wisdom literature.

[77] Nehemiah 7:66–9: numbers of men, servants, musicians, horses, mules, camels, and asses in Israel.

Maximus' whole vision of the monastic life is, furthermore, a prelude to wisdom. Ascetic discipline and the cultivation of virtue (S1) are inextricably bound up with the gift of wisdom (S2). In the opening address to the *Ambigua ad Thomam*, he defines 'the beauty of wisdom' sought in the true philosophy of Christian asceticism as 'knowledge put into action'.[78] *Ambiguum* 10 of the *Ambigua ad Iohannem* develops the point in asserting that the knowledge of the *logoi* requires the discipline and exercise of both body and mind—it is both a practical and intellectual exercise. Philosophy simply is not worthy of the name if it is not supported by ascetic endeavour (1108A). This comes with a distinction between philosophy and wisdom as two modes of the contemplation whereby we come to knowledge of the *logoi*. Wisdom (S2) is the superior, embracing everything bearing on the discernment of the *logoi* whereas philosophy (S1) stands principally for the ascetic mode of life and cultivation of virtue that tends to the acquisition of wisdom (*Amb*. 10 1136 CD). Wisdom is here the gift of knowledge that enables immediate and intuitive knowledge of the *logoi*. Such wisdom gives asceticism its point. Those who stick to bodily observances (S1) without the illumination of the mind brought by the Spirit (S2) do not partake of the 'mixing bowl of divine wisdom' (1145A cf. Prov. 9:1–6). None of this is to say that the acquisition of the divine gift of wisdom is automatic on reaching a certain intensity of ascetic practice—Maximus has too fine a grasp of divine-human synergy to allow any whiff of Pelagianism (semi- or otherwise) to creep into his theology of grace:

> The grace of the Holy Spirit does not work wisdom in the saints without the intellect which receives it [. . .] nor any of the charismata without the receptive disposition and inclination of each [. . .] neither does man possess any of these by natural capacity without divine power.   (*QT* 59 47–9.55–62)[79]

The gift of wisdom enables the mind to achieve conformity with its own eternal inner principle or *logos*—becoming, in other words, precisely what it was created to be. In the liturgical context of the *Mystagogy* he declares: 'the mind is and is called wisdom when it directs its proper movements wholly and fixedly towards God'.[80] This is intriguing: the mind *is* wisdom when it conforms to its foundation in uncreated wisdom. This is reminiscent of, and may be related to Macarius' claim that the soul becomes 'all wisdom' in deification; it also bears comparison with Augustine's suggestion that it is in worship (which is wisdom) that the mind is united with the one who is wisdom.[81]

---

[78] *Ambigua ad Thomam*, prologue (CCSG 48 3).
[79] This delicately balanced sense of divine-human synergy is itself distinctly Macarian, cf. my *The Macarian Legacy*, 234.
[80] *Mystagogy* 5 (PG 91 673A).   [81] Cf. pp.162 and 158.

Wisdom's rôle in the perception and realization of the *logoi* and their cause is a recurrent theme. In the *Questions to Thalassius*, Maximus interprets the spirit of wisdom evoked by the prophet Isaiah (Isaiah 11:2) as the ascent to and reunion with the cause of the *logoi* (*QT* 54 461.326–8). Note the 'ascent to and reunion with'. It is important to recognize that for Maximus wisdom is not only a dimension of contemplation (S2) but also the stage beyond contemplation (S3). In *Ambiguum* 65 (1393A) he speaks of wisdom as that which succeeds contemplation (which itself succeeds practical endeavour: here wisdom would seem to correspond to the stage of *theologia* or encounter with essential wisdom in the Evagrian schema). Wisdom at this stage denotes the point at which perception of the *logoi* of creation becomes participation in the unity that holds these *logoi* together, that is, participation in their cause: the hypostatic Word and wisdom of God.

The celebrated *Ambiguum* 41 (1308AB) similarly treats the gift of wisdom as an 'infinite pouring out' of integral knowledge (S2) which allows the human being to attain to a direct and unmediated understanding of reality in which the division between the noetic and the sensible (the penultimate of the five primal divisions of the universe) is broken down and the unity of the creation experienced. Such an unmediated and angelic experience of knowledge furnishes, so far as is possible, an understanding of God 'beyond understanding or explanation'. The final boundary, that between created and uncreated nature, is crossed by love (specifically the love of Christ): 'showing them to be one and the same through the possession of grace'. Thus through wisdom humans come to experience the breaking-down of the 'last wall of division' by Christ and the revelation of uncreated and created natures as 'one and the same'.

Again, this entails a distinction between Christ as wisdom and Christ as Word: if it is as Word that he embodies himself, 'playing' everywhere in the *logoi* of creation,[82] then it is under the aspect of wisdom that he binds the *logoi* together, bringing all things back to himself in unity. As Word, God extrapolates himself in the divine *logoi* whereas as wisdom he gathers those *logoi* together to union in himself:

For the wisdom (σοφία) and prudence (φρόνησις) of God the Father is the Lord Jesus Christ, who holds together the universals of beings by the power of wisdom, and embraces their complementary parts by the prudence of understanding (τῇ φρονήσει τῆς συνέσεως), since by nature he is the fashioner and provider of all, and through himself he draws into one what is divided, and abolishes war between beings, and binds everything into peaceful friendship and undivided

---

[82] Cf. the *aporia* of Gregory of Nazianzus dealt with in *Ambiguum* 71: 'The high Word plays in every kind of form, mixing, as he wills, with his world here and there' [ET Louth, *Maximus the Confessor*, 164].

harmony both what is in heaven and what is on earth (cf. Col. 1:20), as the divine Apostle says.   (*Amb.* 41 1313B)[83]

This sense of wisdom as the unitive action of God is a distinctive feature of Maximus' sophiology. It is, however, also important to recognize that wisdom in Maximus is not (contrary to Bulgakov's judgement) exclusively tied up with the Son. God also grants and is revealed as wisdom by the Paraclete. Wisdom is an energy or operation (ἐνέργεια) of the Spirit that not only destroys folly but is also itself light (*QT* 63 172.75–82). This light or illumination of wisdom is a deifying operation:

> [The Holy Spirit] accords perfection through luminous, simple, and complete wisdom to those found worthy of *theosis*, bringing them by all means and ways to the Cause of beings [...] It is in her [wisdom] that they come to know themselves through God and God through themselves, with no wall or some such thing being interposed. *For there is nothing interposed between wisdom and God* (σοφίας γὰρ πρὸς θεὸν μέσον οὐδέν).   (*QT* 63 159.219–27)[84]

Wisdom here is the unifying and deifying action or *energeia* of God communicated by the Spirit, the *single* operation of the Trinity in the world bringing the world into the divine life—no longer in potentiality but in actuality, through the free acceptance by the creation of the self-emptying of God in the incarnation and the gift of the Spirit. Here the deifying gift or activity of wisdom (S2) appears to be somehow continuous with God (S3): 'for there is nothing interposed between wisdom and God'.

Thus wisdom is on closer inspection absolutely central to Maximus' understanding of the relationship between creature and Creator, in particular to his understanding of *theosis*. Operating in accordance with its own *logos*, the pure intellect becomes, by grace, a 'place of divine wisdom (τόπος τῆς θείας σοφίας)' (*Amb.* 71 1412A). Embracing, if only in part, the infinite depths of the divine wisdom, man 'is and is called' wisdom, God, and abyss, not by virtue of what he is by nature but by virtue of him who dwells in him.[85] This is the nub of deification: God is humanized in us as we are deified in him.[86]

---

[83] This comes in the context of the reintegration of the cosmos through abolition in Christ of the five divisions of the universe: masculine/feminine, paradise/world, heaven/earth, noetic/sensible, and created/uncreated. Maximus also makes a distinction between wisdom and prudence here: the latter brings together the *logoi* of particulars, the former those of universals.

[84] Emphasis mine.

[85] Maximus is commenting here on the passage from Psalms 41(42):7 'deep calleth unto deep' – a passage much loved by Cardinal Newman.

[86] As he puts it elsewhere: 'They say that God and man are paradigms one of the other' – the one created, the other uncreated (*Ambigua* 10 1113B).

Wisdom thus emerges as a pervasive and multi-valent theme across levels S1–S3 in Maximus. Wisdom is the guiding theme of his exegesis and underpins his conception of the ascetic life (S1) as a quest for wisdom (S2). Maximus understands God as wisdom both according to essence and hypostasis (S3). But the principal rôle of wisdom in Maximus' thought is as the basis of the *return movement* of the divine *logoi* in the freely willed re-incorporation of the world into God. Wisdom is thus both the means and the end of the human vocation. It is through the deifying and illumining operation of wisdom that humans can perceive the *logoi* and realize their own nature as wisdom, thereby attaining likeness to and union with uncreated wisdom. This is what Maximus means by there being 'nothing interposed between wisdom and God'. In short, for Maximus, wisdom is the life of God in man and the life of man in God (and, by extension, the life of God in the world and the world in God). It is the very foundation of deification, a way of expressing the coinherence of the creation and the Creator without losing sight of the distinction between their natures. All instances of the theme of wisdom in Maximus are based on this guiding vision.

Bulgakov was, in short, both wrong and right in his estimation that Maximus' logology is 'essentially a sophiology'. There is indeed a powerful and thorough-going theology of wisdom in Maximus. But what Bulgakov does not seem to have appreciated is the extent to which wisdom is a triune and not merely a logocentric category for Maximus. It is indeed as Logos that Christ embodies himself in the *logoi* of the creation but it is through the operation of wisdom granted by the Spirit that the *logoi* are reintegrated into Christ as wisdom and presented to the heavenly Father. Wisdom is thus a far broader and deeper category in Maximus than Bulgakov realized, pertaining to God not only as Logos but as essence, hypostasis, and deifying operation or energy. This model was to serve as the basis and foundation of the sophiology of St Gregory Palamas, by far the most important patristic witness adduced by Bulgakov.

5.5 St Gregory Palamas

The multi-facetted theme of wisdom is the lodestone of St Gregory Palamas' (*c.* 1296–1357/9) work. It is therefore no surprise that the Byzantine composers of the *kontakion* hymn in his honour hail him first and foremost as a 'Holy and divine instrument of wisdom'.[87] Palamas fought a long and bitter battle at the twilight of the Byzantine Empire to uphold the reality of the possibility of human participation in the divine life and in so doing made extensive use of the category of wisdom. It is a theme to which he returns again and again and one which has a

---

[87] ET in Mother Mary and Archimandrite Kallistos Ware, *The Lenten Triodion*, 324.

bearing on virtually every aspect of his thought. Like Maximus, he drew freely on the preceding patristic tradition regarding wisdom and stands, again like Maximus, as something of a synthesis of that tradition. Palamas is of cardinal importance for this study not only as a summation of patristic sophiology but also because of the startling and unparalleled emphasis placed on him by Bulgakov in his attempt to characterize his Sophiology as a natural outworking of patristic and especially Palamite theology. Given the prominence of Palamas in other sections of this book (especially Chapter 1.4 and Chapter 7.1.3), the account given here need only be relatively brief, offering an outline and preliminary discussion of Palamas' theology of wisdom.

It has to be said that Palamas' is not an especially sapiential theology. He makes relatively little use of biblical wisdom literature (with Wisdom 7 being an obvious exception).[88] This is doubtless to some extent a function of the polemical character of much of his corpus, but this relative paucity is also evident in non-polemical works such as his homilies, ascetic discourses, and hagiography. And while he allows human wisdom a strictly limited place in the spiritual and ascetic life, there is little in Palamas to suggest any very deep continuity between such wisdom and its divine counterpart. Where matters become more interesting is precisely in his understanding of wisdom on level S3. Palamas presents his teaching on God as wisdom, like all his teaching, as being in strict continuity with the patristic tradition. In particular, he situates himself very precisely in the trajectory I have traced in the Cappadocians, Dionysius, and Maximus that allows for divine wisdom to be construed not only in terms of essence and hypostasis but also in terms of uncreated divine activity or energy.

When it comes to philosophy, Palamas can be quite as brutal as Tertullian or Tatian. Many of Palamas' choicest remarks about wisdom in this negative sense orbit around his sharp denigration of the 'outer' wisdom of the Greeks: fallen wisdom, false wisdom, fleshly wisdom (S0). One can find almost innumerable excoriations of such wisdom in his works, especially in the *Triads in Defence of the Holy Hesychasts*. He roots the many errors of his opponent Barlaam the Calabrian (whom he consistently and very deliberately styles 'the philosopher') squarely in pagan philosophy which he goes so far as to describe as an 'abortion of wisdom' (*Triads* 1.1.12). Barlaam had dared to cast doubt on the visionary experience of God as light attested to by the monks of Mount Athos, claiming that the best humans can hope for is the kind of illumination vouchsafed to the philosophers of old. This explains the venom behind Palamas' attacks on philosophy in general and 'the philosopher' in particular in this work. It would, however, be wholly wrong to set Palamas up as teaching a radical separation of faith and reason on

---

[88]   Above all Wisdom 7.26: '[Wisdom] is the brightness of the everlasting light, the unspotted mirror of the *energeia* of God'.

this count. Even in the *Triads*, Palamas is at pains to point out that this wisdom is not wisdom properly so-called. There is, Palamas explains, a natural wisdom (S1) implanted by God in the rational creation (*Triads* 1.1.19, 2.1.25). This is a wisdom which can be cultivated through application and learning, for example through the standard profane curriculum in which Gregory himself was trained (*Triads* 1.1.22, 3.1.37). This natural wisdom is capable of great knowledge of the created world and indeed is able to deduce the existence of a Creator, if properly directed. It also has a rôle to play in the proclamation and defence of spiritual truths manifest in scripture and witnessed to in the lives of the saints. In a rather more barbed vein he argues that we can use Aristotelian logic against the philosophers much as we extract venom from snakes to produce antidote.[89] Gregory is quite frank about his own use of certain methods of Greek philosophical argumentation in this regard (*Triads* 2.1.6). Its rôle must, however, be strictly restricted to that of an ancillary. When properly subordinated in this way, philosophy is transposed and transformed by theology.[90]

But in and of itself natural wisdom and philosophy is weak.[91] Most especially, it is relative. Having only itself to fall back on, it can demonstrate no irrefutable proposition—'to every argument there is a counter-argument' (*Triads* 2.1.9). It is also dangerous, not by nature—for it is a gift of God implanted in us—but by misuse. The woes and deficiencies of Greek or 'outer' philosophy are squarely attributable to such misuse of our God-given reason (*Triads* 1.1.20–1). Greek philosophy has failed (*Triads* 1.1.13). And it is because of this long legacy of failure and misuse that philosophy is so dangerous. It has led to pride, to conceit, to an inability to recognize God in his works. It is this misuse of our natural endowments (S0) that is the target of St Paul's blistering critique of wisdom in I Corinthians 1-2 and not, Gregory is careful to point out—natural human wisdom *per se* (S1).[92]

There is, however, a further dimension of wisdom—what Paul goes on to call the wisdom spoken among the mature (I Cor. 2:6). This, for Gregory, is the divine gift of wisdom (S2) which in practice is God's own self-giving activity (S3). The operation of such wisdom does not result from book learning but from a good life built on the practice of the commandments and ascetic effort (*Triads* 1.1.20). Such wisdom is infinitely superior to merely human wisdom and indeed bears no affinity to it.[93] Only this gift of divine wisdom (what he calls 'our theosophy') truly realizes the image of God within human beings (*Triads* 1.1.22). This divine

---

[89] *First Letter to Barlaam* 37 (Chrestou I 281).

[90] *Triads* 2.1.6: in the truly good, the not truly good becomes good. Cf. *Triads* 1.1.9: profane learning must be joined by love and transformed by grace if it is to be of any real effect.

[91] It is also incapable of discernment: cf. *Triads* 2.1.34.

[92] Only that wisdom which opposes itself to God has been rendered foolish: *Triads* 1.1.12–13. Cf. *To John and Theodore* 4.1 (Chrestou V 231–32).

[93] *Triads* 2.1.4–5, 2.1.21, 3.1.38.

wisdom is to human wisdom what the operation of the eye is to the sun. Properly directed sight may perceive the light of the sun, but it does not thereby become light (*Triads* 2.1.7). The gift of divine wisdom is, as intimated by this image of the eye and the sun, bound up with the deifying vision of God as light—the possibility of which Gregory went to such pains to defend. This uncreated light is, he explains, the very wisdom of God (*Triads* 3.1.36).

Where matters become more distinctive and perhaps most interesting is this question of the vision of God and the concomitant doctrine of the essence and energies of God. Palamas' theology turns on the distinction between the incommunicable divine essence (God hidden) and the communicable divine operations or energies (God revealed). God is one, remaining transcendent and unapproachable in his essence while also communicating himself wholly to the creation through his deifying activity. Wisdom is chiefly to be understood precisely as a divine energy by means of which God reaches across the ontological gulf to unite creatures to himself as 'the wisdom of the wise' (*Triads* 3.2.25).[94] For Gregory, the divine wisdom manifest in the creation is not the essence itself but the energy of God the Holy Trinity: 'the divine wisdom allows herself to be shared by those who show themselves wise [...] I speak now of the wisdom contemplated in the Father, the Son, and the Holy Spirit'.[95] The divine energy or operation of wisdom does not belong to any one of the hypostases alone but is communicated (according to the grammar of the *Apodictic Treatises*) from the Father, through the Son, in the Holy Spirit. The divine energy is also (to repeat) God—and God *revealed*.

Palamas' doctrine of the divine energies comes with frequent and specific appeals to the tradition, particularly to the Cappadocians, Dionysius, and Maximus. These are the chief 'God-bearing Fathers' who have upheld the distinction between the unknowable and imparticipable divine essence and the knowable and participable divine operations or energies 'around the essence' such as goodness, wisdom, and power (*Capita* 81–3). The seemingly interminable dispute with Gregory Akindynos, Palamas' most formidable opponent, revolves again and again around the question of wisdom. If divine wisdom is, as Akindynos claimed, identical with God then God would be knowable and participable—or else one would have to allow God's wisdom to be merely created which would, among other things, make of Christ (as wisdom of God) a creature.[96] For Palamas, only a construal of wisdom as an energy of God allows us to maintain the possibility of human participation in God without compromising either divine transcendence or divine simplicity.[97]

---

[94] For further examples, see *Capita* 78, 82, 83, 87.
[95] *Apology* 40 (Chrestou II 125) (cited Meyendorff, *Introduction à l'étude de Grégoire Palamas*, 304). Cf. *Dialogue with Gregoras* 25 (Chrestou IV 226–7): The 'common wisdom' of Father, Son, and Holy Spirit is made known in the creation.
[96] *Against Akindynos* 6.16.61–4 (Chrestou III 431–4).
[97] See further my 'St Gregory Palamas on the Divine Simplicity'.

This dialectic of essence and energy allows Gregory to maintain both divine transcendence and immanence within an overarching narrative of coinherence between God and the world. The divine energies represent God's self-revelation to and in the world. They are both eternal manifestations (corresponding to the Cappadocian 'glories pertaining to the essence', Dionysius' beneficent processions, and Maximus' eternal *logoi*) and manifestations of God in the creation (corresponding to Cappadocian divine activities, Dionysius' 'predeterminations' or 'divine wills', and Maximus' *logoi* of the creation). While remaining inaccessible and unknowable according to his essence, God reveals and manifests himself in the world. Thus God is truly omnipresent throughout the creation:

> God both is and is said to be the nature of all beings, in so far as all partake of him and subsist by means of this participation: not, however, by participation in his nature—far from it—but by participation in his energy.   (*Capita* 78)

> Yet God is also in all things and all things are in God, the one sustaining, the other being sustained by him. Thus all things participate in God's sustaining energy, but not in his essence. Hence the theologians say that the divine omnipresence also constitutes an energy of God.   (*Capita* 104)

All this looks remarkably like Bulgakov's 'God in the world and the world in God', albeit with a pronounced stress on energy rather than the indeterminate figure of Sophia as the foundation of the coinherence of God and the world. For Palamas, Bulgakov's fundamental question: 'What is the world in God and what is God in the world?' is answerable only in terms of the doctrine of the divine energies.[98]

This non-dualist vision of the relation between God and creation underpins much of what Palamas has to say about salvation history, perhaps most notably with respect to the Virgin Mary. Mary is described in the most elevated of terms, for example as 'the beginning, source, and root of the hope stored up for us in heaven'. For Palamas, Mary becomes the 'boundary' (μεθόριον) between created and uncreated nature—the one in and through whom God was able to unite himself hypostatically to human nature and thus open to all human beings through the Holy Spirit the promise of deification.[99] This sense of Mary's cosmic and pan-temporal significance—again, not unlike some of Bulgakov's thinking—is a direct consequence of Palamas' apprehension of the underlying coinherence of God and the world according to energy.

But while wisdom, for Palamas, is principally to be understood as an energy of God, he also recognizes its importance with reference to categories of essence and

---

[98] *The Bride of the Lamb*, 41 [ET 33–34]. Bulgakov is here pointing out that Aquinas has no answer to this question.

[99] *Homilies* 14.15 (*On the Annunciation*) (Chrestou VI 172).

hypostasis. On occasion, he speaks of God as wisdom according to essence: the supreme mind 'is itself wisdom' (*Capita* 34) (although wisdom is not God—the propositions are not reversible). Similarly, in the *Triads*, closely following Dionysius, Palamas asserts that as the source of being, wisdom, and life: 'the superessential and singular hiddenness is properly conceived and named God and wisdom and life, and not only essence' (*Triads* 3.2.23).[100] Dionysius is also behind the further explanation given in *Capita* 78: God both is and is not wisdom, just as he is and is not nature, or goodness, or being. In his energetic condescension to the created world, he manifests himself as the nature of natures, the wisdom of the wise, the being of beings, the good of the good, and so forth. Yet he remains utterly other in his essential nature, wisdom, being, and goodness: of which we may not say or know anything.[101] In each case, the same terms are predicated both of the imparticipable divine essence and the participable divine *energeia*. This reinforces the point that for Palamas the energies are precisely the *ousia revealed*.

In line with long-established tradition, Palamas also recognizes that the Son is to be recognized and confessed as hypostatic and indeed self-hypostasizing (αὐθυπόστατος) wisdom.[102] Scriptural references to wisdom are therefore routinely associated with the Son.[103] While Christ is undoubtedly at the centre of Palamas' understanding of salvation history, Christology proper is not the centre of the debates in which Palamas took part. Hence it is not surprising that he does not speak of the Son as the union of created and uncreated wisdom nor become vexed with texts such as Proverbs 8:22.[104] The association of the Son with wisdom remains secondary, a function of the Son's essential and energetic character *qua* wisdom. Palamas also, intriguingly, associates some biblical references to wisdom with the Holy Spirit. In *Capita* 36 (in a section that draws extensively on Augustine), Palamas discusses Proverbs 8:30 in which the Logos declares: 'I was she who rejoiced together with (συνέχαιρον) him.'[105] This verse leads Palamas to conclude that, 'This pre-eternal rejoicing of the Father and the Son is the Holy Spirit who is, as has been said, common to both.' This use of the biblical figure of wisdom to explicate the intra-Trinitarian relations within essential wisdom is quite remarkable and only serves to underline the depth and extent of his reflection on God as wisdom.

---

[100] Cf. *DN* 5.2 (PTS 33 181).

[101] Even his most radically apophatic statements (e.g. *Capita* 144, 145) do not preclude the naming of God as wisdom, they rather require a simultaneous un-naming.

[102] *Triads* 2.3.5; *Epistles* 1.1 (Chrestou II 316); *Against Akindynos* 6.25.96 (Chrestou III 458) (αὐθυπόστατος σοφία); *To John and Theodore* 4.1 (Chrestou V 231).Cf. *Homilies* 8.7, 21.1, 35.8, 62.4 (ἐνυπόστατος σοφία) (Chrestou VI 111, 247, 382, 668–9).

[103] E.g. *Triads* 1.1.5, 1.1.17.

[104] Indeed he seems to avoid the text altogether, coming closest to it in a reference to Ecclus. 1:4 ('wisdom was created before all things'). This comes in a Trinitarian context: *Apodictic Treatises* 2.4 (Chrestou I 80).

[105] For more on the connection with Augustine see my *Orthodox Readings of Aquinas*, 29–44.

In sum, while Palamas gives only relatively restrained attention to human wisdom and biblical wisdom literature, he certainly offers a thoroughgoing treatment of the divine wisdom. God is to be understood as wisdom according to essence, hypostasis, and, especially, energy. As wisdom, God reveals and communicates himself in a Trinitarian dynamic of salvation, drawing the creation back to himself. By the virtue of this divine operation God himself constitutes the eternal ground of creation and the principle of its deification. One can easily see why Bulgakov was so enthusiastic about Palamas and why he was absolutely right to latch on to Palamas as a potential forerunner of his own theology of wisdom even as he bemoaned the 'incomplete' character of Palamas' treatment of the topic. We will of course return to Bulgakov's attempted appropriation of Palamas in the final chapter.

5.6 *Coda* to the Greek East

Perhaps the abiding characteristic of the wisdom reflection of the Greek East is its foundation in monastic practice and mystical experience. This foundation helps assure a certain continuity and coherence in its estimation and treatment of the theme of wisdom. Building on the 'triple inheritance' of Macarius, Evagrius, and Dionysius, Maximus and Palamas produce a sophiology that embraces and transforms the notion of the divine ideas for the creation and bridges the divide between Creator and creature. Following a trajectory established by the Cappadocians and transmitted in Dionysius, divine wisdom is construed in Maximus and, most clearly, Palamas not only in terms of essence and hypostasis but also in terms of divine energy or operation. While the terminology of this trajectory differs (glories, processions, predeterminations, divine wills, *logoi*, energies) the basic structure is the same: God is wisdom according to his unknowable essence and wisdom according to hypostasis (above all the Son as incarnate wisdom). He is also actualized as wisdom according to his tri-personal divine activity or energy not only in relation to the world (*ad extra*) but in his eternal self-revelation (*ad intra*). This is the principal axis on which the Greek East understands the paradox of divine immanence and transcendence, knowability and unknowability, participability and imparticipability. This is where a space opens for Sophiology, with wisdom construed as divine but not reducible solely to categories of essence and hypostasis.

None of this is to say that the tradition of the Greek East surveyed in this chapter is a monolith or absolutely consistent with all aspects of preceding patristic reflection. By contrast with, say, Athanasius and Augustine, wisdom is not so obviously a Christological category in this period (i.e. pertaining to Christ not only as uncreated but also as created wisdom). Dionysius, in particular, gives very little attention to wisdom as a hypostatic characteristic. Maximus, for his part, tends to associate wisdom principally with the self-gathering of the *logoi* back to their divine origin in Christ as wisdom. This self-gathering is, in Maximus, a distinctly Spirit-led process—something that dovetails well with Evagrius' striking association of the Spirit with the Old Testament figure of wisdom. The feminine dimension of wisdom is generally rather muted, being perhaps best represented in Evagrius and Dionysius. And while Evagrius and Maximus between them produce a mighty corpus of Christian wisdom literature, the specifically sapiential and *paideia*-centred dimension of wisdom reflection in the Greek East does appear to have waned somewhat by the late Byzantine period. Doubtless this was to some extent the result of circumstances: Palamas, in particular, had rather less time for meditative σχολή (leisure) than many of his Greek predecessors or Latin peers.

But for all the polemical concerns and bitter struggles of his tumultuous career, Palamas stands as the summation of Greek patristic sophiology. Palamas provides a very precise treatment of the relation of essential wisdom and the divine persons, specifying that the single operation of God (pertaining to the single essence) is expressed in multiple ways by the divine persons according to a specific grammar (from the Father, through the Son, in the Spirit). No one else comes close to this level of precision, doubtless because no one else was called to fight like he was in defence of the deifying operation of wisdom—for the possibility of the human being becoming, as both he and Macarius put it, 'all wisdom'.

The Greek East, in short, furnishes us with a veritable treasury of wisdom reflection across levels S1–S3. It never lost its appreciation for secular knowledge so long as properly subordinated to theology and, ideally, conditioned by *ascesis*. Its attention was, however, increasingly focused not so much on the level of human wisdom or even ascetic practice and contemplation (S1) but on wisdom as divine gift (S2) and, especially, as uncreated divine activity distinct (but inseparable from) categories of essence and hypostasis (S3). In Palamas, this activity is very precisely construed as the basis of human deification and of the coinherence of God and the world. While allegedly 'incomplete' (in terms of its Trinitarian dimension and its resolution of the base problematic of the relation between Creator and creation), this is undoubtedly promising territory for Sophiology. We turn now to territory it was to find rather less congenial: the Latin West.

6

The Latin West

6.1 Late Antique and Early Medieval

Perhaps the first and most important thing to note about the later Latin West is
the degree to which it remained consistently shaped by Augustine both in terms of
its intense interest in the theme and figure of wisdom and, crucially, in terms of
the identification of divine wisdom with the essence of God. In adhering so closely
to Augustine in these and other matters, the Latin West remained, for Bulgakov, a
barren and dead-end tradition. As he rather sweepingly puts it: 'The theme of
Sophia never had any place in Western theology, either in the Middle Ages, or at
the period of the Reformation.'[1] It is, however, the burden of this chapter to
suggest that this tradition has been too hastily dismissed within Sophiology,
something that only serves to underline further the paucity of its reception of
preceding Christian reflection on wisdom. The figures discussed in this chapter
offer some extraordinary examples of wisdom teaching that deserve the closest
attention not only for their various theological insights but also for the consistency
of their devotion to biblical wisdom literature.

6.1.1 Boethius

Conspicuous lovers of wisdom are some of the chief illuminators of the period
that followed the collapse of the Roman Empire in the West—the so-called 'Dark
Ages'. Perhaps the most famous luminary of this period is Boethius (480–c. 524),
who turned to a decidedly feminine and classical personification of philosophy for
consolation in his hour of deepest need. Boethius lived as a Roman aristocrat and
statesman in the Ostrogothic kingdom of Italy under Theodoric. For reasons that
remain somewhat obscure he was indicted for treason and sentenced to death. His
Consolation of Philosophy dates from his imprisonment prior to his execution.[2]
Boethius was an accomplished philosopher and theologian who was equally at
home in the Latin and Greek thought-worlds. While consciously resonating with

---

[1] *The Wisdom of God*, 5. This sophiological barrenness is even worse in Protestantism, both liberal
and so-called 'orthodox' (ibid., 5–6). Soloviev and Florensky similarly find little of real sophiological
import in the post-Augustinian West prior to the emergence of the medieval mystics.
[2] See further Heather Erb, 'The Varieties of Wisdom and the Consolation of Philosophy'.

Wisdom in Christian Tradition: The Patristic Roots of Modern Russian Sophiology. Marcus Plested, Oxford University Press.
© Marcus Plested 2022. DOI: 10.1093/oso/9780192863225.003.0007

biblical wisdom literature and themes,[3] Boethius' figure of wisdom is principally that of the pagan philosophical tradition—a tradition that unites intellectual endeavour with the heroic cultivation of virtue. Wisdom is, for Boethius, more an attainment (S1) than a gift (S2).

It is in the pursuit and acquisition of wisdom that human beings become god-like, being configured to the divine source of all things. In his commentary on Porphyry's *Eisagoge* (for many centuries the standard introduction to Aristotle) Boethius defines philosophy as follows:

> Philosophy is the love, study of, and in a way, friendship with wisdom. Not of that wisdom which is involved in the knowledge and know-how of some arts and skills, but of that wisdom which, needing nothing else, is the living mind and primal reason of all things. This love of wisdom on the part of the intelligent soul is an illumination by that pure wisdom and a kind of attraction and calling to it, such that the study of philosophy is seen to be the study of divinity and friendship with that pure mind.[4]

It is through philosophy that human beings acquire intimacy with and are illumined by true wisdom (S3), the 'living mind and primal reason of all things'. This wisdom, very different than merely human knowledge, brings human beings into union with the *summum bonum*, the supreme good.

There is, however, little in all this to distinguish Boethius from the broadly neo-Platonic wisdom tradition in which he stands. By contrast with Augustine he does not, even in his more overtly theological works, identify divine wisdom with Christ. Nor does he employ the term or concept of wisdom in his Trinitarian theology except as a function of his conception of divine simplicity. This can be seen in his discussion of terms such as Father, Son, Spirit, and Trinity, which cannot be substantially but only relatively predicated of God since they pertain to the diversity of persons and not to the simplicity of the divine unity. On the other hand, names such as 'God, truth, justice, goodness, omnipotence, substance, immutability, virtue, wisdom, and all other conceivable predicates of the kind are applicable substantially to the divinity'.[5] By virtue of his broadly philosophical construal of divine simplicity, Boethius has no place for wisdom as hypostatic let alone as (in the Greek tradition) divine but distinct from the substance of God. We

---

[3] Cf. the use of Wisdom 8:1 in *Consolation* 3.12 (CCSL 94 61).

[4] *In Isagoge* 1.3 (CSEL 48 7) [ET McInerny, *Boethius and Aquinas*, 8].

[5] *Whether Father, Son, and Holy Spirit may be Substantially Predicated of the Divinity* (LCL 74 39). Boethius has an uncompromising doctrine of divine simplicity. Cf. *The Trinity is One God Not Three Gods:* 'Now God differs from God in no respect, for there cannot be divine essences distinguished either by accidents or by substantial differences belonging to a substrate' (LCL 74 13). Cf. also *Consolation* 3.12 (CCSL 94 62): God as identical with his goodness.

now turn to a slightly younger contemporary of Boethius, Cassiodorus, who offers a more overtly Christian but less explicitly theological account of wisdom.

6.1.2 Cassiodorus

Cassiodorus Senator (*c.* 485–*c.* 580) was, like Boethius, a statesman in the court of King Theodoric but lived to see out his days in a long period of monastic retirement. In the wake of the tumultuous Roman re-conquest of Italy, Cassiodorus spent a period of perhaps fifteen years in Constantinople, returning to Italy in 557. His sojourn in the capital marked his work with a pronounced sense of the enduring if often febrile unity of Greek East and Latin West. His *Exposition of the Psalms*, replete with references to wisdom, dates from this period.

Cassiodorus' work is deeply steeped in biblical wisdom literature, as is amply evident in his magnum opus, the *Institutes of Divine and Human Learning*. Cassiodorus keeps worldly wisdom at more of a remove than does Boethius, clearly asserting the superiority of the heavenly wisdom contained in the Christian scriptures. This is not to say secular learning is a bad thing; indeed it can be most useful, including in the explication of scripture, serving as the beginning of the path to 'universal and perfect wisdom'.[6] Cassiodorus goes on in the second book of the *Institutes* to outline and commend what became known as the *quadrivium* and *trivium*, characterizing these as the 'seven pillars of wisdom' (cf. Prov. 9:1).[7] This emphasis on human *paideia* was to remain a consistent feature of wisdom reflection in the West. But while secular learning (S1) has its place, universal and perfect wisdom is ultimately a gift from God (S2) for which secular learning is by no means a prerequisite.[8] Secular learning can also be a snare, preventing men and women from receiving the redemptive wisdom which comes down from the 'Father of lights' (Jas. 1:17). Many philosophers, writes Cassiodorus, have become enmeshed in merely secular wisdom and consequently unable to reach the source and true light of wisdom (S3).[9]

6.1.3 St Gregory the Great

Pope Gregory the Great (*c.* 540–604) stands as an important bridge figure between East and West, having spent a chunk of his life as papal *apocrisarius* in Constantinople (579–585/6). Gregory deals frequently with wisdom themes in his extensive corpus, above all in his mammoth *Moralia on Job*. Gregory's account

---

[6] *Institutes* 1.27.1 (Mynors 68).   [7] *Institutes* 2 (Mynors 89–163).
[8] *Institutes* 1.28.2 (Mynors 69–70); cf. *Institutes* 1.28.4 (Mynors 70–1).
[9] *Institutes* 1.28.3 (Mynors 70).

of wisdom is thoroughly sapiential, thoroughly grounded in biblical wisdom literature. While embracing levels S1–S3, the emphasis is very much on levels S1–S2. A figure of incalculable impact on the later Latin tradition, and the Latin author most read in the Christian East, Gregory's treatment of wisdom deserves close attention.[10]

The *Moralia on Job* constitutes a remarkable and thoroughgoing meditation on wisdom themes. Indeed, it is probably the most extensive sustained treatment of wisdom in a single work to be found in the whole patristic tradition. Gregory engages in a reading of Job that is both minute in its detail and gloriously expansive in its range. Gregory reads Job in the light of and alongside other wisdom literature of the Old Testament, using I Corinthians and Revelation as hermeneutical keys to the meaning of those texts.[11] He is generally disdainful of earthly or secular wisdom, emphasizing again and again the superiority of the divine wisdom that is to be identified in the first instance with the Son. Such authentic wisdom as humans possess is a gift from God, communicated most obviously by the Holy Spirit. But the acquisition and retention of wisdom requires great struggle and even, when necessary, experience of affliction, as painfully and acutely seen in the example of Job. Gregory's meditations on Job are infused with monastic compunction and humility. While it is scarcely possible to do full justice to Gregory's very wide-ranging treatment of wisdom in this relatively brief section, the following paragraphs will attempt to sketch its lineaments.

Gregory clearly identifies Christ as the incarnate wisdom of God and explicitly identifies him with the Old Testament figure of wisdom (*Moralia* 1.15).[12] Like much of the patristic tradition, Gregory gives little emphasis to the feminine character of this figure. For Gregory, Christ is wisdom in a way in which humans can never be: 'with whatever brightness and transparency the saints may shine, it is one thing for men to be wise in God, and another thing for a man to be the wisdom of God' (*Moralia* 18.79). When speaking of Christ as wisdom there is a sense, rather like what we find in Athanasius, in which he is to be understood as both created and uncreated wisdom:

---

[10] For Gregory's legacy in the Latin West see Jean Leclercq, *The Love of Learning and the Desire for God*, 26. In the Orthodox East, he is known as Gregory Dialogos as author of the *Dialogues* and credited with the composition of the liturgy of presanctified gifts celebrated on weekdays in Great Lent.

[11] I Corinthians crops up times beyond counting. *Moralia* 29.1 is a good and fairly typical example. Revelation is cited 74 times, showing an intensity of interest not present in the East at this time.

[12] Cf. *Moralia* 2.40: Christ as 'incarnate wisdom'; *Moralia* 4.64: 'And as the wise man [Solomon], in the setting forth of Wisdom, says concerning the same Son: "For she is the brightness of the everlasting light" (Wisdom 7:26) [...]'; *Moralia* 6.3: 'the very presence of eternal wisdom in the flesh'; *Moralia* 18.61: 'So then what wisdom is it, the holy man is contemplating, but that of which Paul the Apostle says, "Christ the Power of God, and the Wisdom of God"? (I Cor. 1:24); concerning which it is written by Solomon, "Wisdom has builded her house" (Prov. 9:1); and of which the Psalmist says; "In wisdom have you made all things" (Ps. 103(4):24).'

This wisdom coeternal with God has a 'way' in one sense, and in another sense a 'place' but only a 'place' if one does not understand it as a local place (cf. Job 28:23). For God is not capable of being held close after the manner of a body. But, as has been said, a non-local place is meant. The 'place' of wisdom is the Father, the 'place' of the Father is wisdom as it is said, wisdom herself bearing witness, 'I am in the Father, and the Father in me' (John 14:10). So then the very same wisdom has a 'way' in one sense, and a 'place' in another; a 'way' by the passing by of the humanity, a 'place' by the settledness of the Godhead. For she does not pass by in so far as she is eternal, but she does pass by in so far as for our sakes he appeared subject to time.   (*Moralia* 19.5)

By extension, wisdom can also refer to the Church, the body of Christ. This is an intriguing and distinctive identification on Gregory's part, one which allows for something of the feminine character of biblical wisdom to seep in. The seven churches of Revelation are identified with the seven pillars of wisdom of Proverbs 9:1 and taken to denote the whole catholic Church spread throughout the world (*Moralia* 1.17, 17.43, 23.6). Founded on the union of divinity and humanity in Christ, the Church is rightly referred to as the house of wisdom. Christ's body is the 'house of wisdom' in that he is both God and man, 'the inhabitor and the inhabited':

But this can be rightly understood in another sense also, if the Church is called the house of wisdom. And she has hewn out for herself seven pillars, because she has severed the minds of preachers from the love of the present world, and has raised them up to bear the fabric of this same Church.   (*Moralia* 33.32)

While wisdom references in scripture are routinely applied to the Son as both created and uncreated wisdom or, in some cases, to the Church, Gregory follows Augustine in treating wisdom as an essential quality in God and as a function of divine simplicity:

to the simple nature of deity it is not one thing to be, and another thing to be wise, nor one thing to be wise, and another to be strong, forasmuch as the strength is identically the same as the wisdom which is the essence of the deity [. . .].   (*Moralia* 17.46)

There is thus an identity between God and his wisdom that can never be attained by human beings who are wise by participation and not by nature:

Now wisdom both is and is wise, nor is it one thing for her to be, and another thing to be wise; but the servants of wisdom are indeed able to be wise, but their being is not the same thing as being wise. For they may be, and not be wise [. . .]

Now wisdom has being, she has life; but that which she has, she is herself. Wherefore she lives unchangeably, because she lives not by contingency, but essentially.   (*Moralia* 18.81)

The Trinitarian dimension of wisdom is evident in Gregory's emphasis on wisdom as a gift of the Holy Spirit, the greatest of the interdependent and mutually reinforcing seven gifts of the Spirit (*Moralia* 1.38ff.).[13] Wisdom is essentially a divine action in the creature welling up from within the human person to whom it is gifted.[14] As divine gift, this created wisdom is far superior to secular wisdom.[15] But there is of course a vast difference between the wisdom vouchsafed to humans (S2) and the source of wisdom (S3), between 'wisdom created and wisdom creating' (*Moralia* 18.61). There is no hint of uncreated divine operations or energies here. But there is sufficient continuity between gift and giver for the same term to be used univocally of both God and human beings: 'What wonder is it, if we call the maker of the wise "wise" whom we know to be wisdom itself?' (*Moralia* 9.4.).

All human wisdom, however, pales into utter insignificance by comparison with the divine wisdom:

All human wisdom, however powerful in acuity, is foolishness, when compared with divine wisdom. For all human deeds which are just and beautiful are, when compared with the justice and beauty of God, neither just nor beautiful, nor have any existence at all. Blessed Job therefore would believe that he had said wisely what he had said, if he did not hear the words of superior wisdom in comparison with which all our wisdom is folly.

Job has to learn his unwisdom the hard way, giving us a powerful lesson in humility:

When holy men, therefore, hear the words of God, the more they advance in contemplation, the more they despise what they are, and know themselves to be either nothing, or next to nothing. Let blessed Job then reply to the words of God, and, as he advances in wisdom, find himself to be a fool, saying, 'I have spoken foolishly, and things that above measure exceeded my knowledge (Job 42:3).'

(*Moralia* 35.3)

---

[13] Cf. *Moralia* 2.71: wisdom as a kind of 'first born offspring by the gift of the Holy Spirit'.

[14] Cf. *Moralia* 3.15: 'the riches of internal wisdom', 'the treasure of wisdom unfailingly springing up within'.

[15] Gregory ascribes only very limited value to secular wisdom: cf. *Moralia* 9.12 on the Bible's use of pagan names of stars and constellations. On Gregory and secular wisdom, see further Robert Markus, *Gregory the Great and his World*, 37–8.

Thinking oneself wise is probably the most dangerous thing of all:

> For they who seem to themselves to be wise, cannot contemplate the wisdom of God [...] If, therefore, we seek to be truly wise, and to contemplate wisdom itself, let us humbly acknowledge ourselves to be fools. Let us give up hurtful wisdom, let us learn praiseworthy folly. (*Moralia* 27.79)

The gift of wisdom is never inalienable, as the chastening example of Solomon shows (*Moralia* 2.2). Gregory reads Job as an extended test of such wisdom as humans possess—a test designed to make possession of wisdom more sure and steadfast (*Moralia* 2.78). The retention of wisdom requires of human beings much ascetic toil and what Gregory calls 'digging of the heart'.[16] The treatise contains a vast amount of advice as to the cultivation of practical wisdom that draws widely on biblical wisdom literature. Anger, to take just one example, is seen as particularly destructive of wisdom.[17] The 'true wisdom of man', the best antidote to pride, is humility (*Moralia* 28.11). The 'fortress of wisdom', similarly, is purity of heart (*Moralia* 8.85).

The possession of wisdom typically, but not always, becomes firmer over time, for 'wisdom is taught by multitude of years. Because, though length of life does not confer intelligence, yet it gives it much exercise by constant practice' (*Moralia* 23.12). And life is not likely to yield much growth in wisdom without some distress and affliction such as that experienced by Job:

> The more the sound of inward wisdom by the grace of its secret inspiration bursts forth upon us, the more does it affect us with distress. For no one would outwardly lament that which he is, if he had not been able to perceive within, that which as yet he is not. (*Moralia* 23.43)

Participation and growth in heavenly wisdom grants to human beings an inner tranquillity and steadfastness of interior wisdom (*Moralia* 18.68). This inner

---

[16] *Moralia* 4.8: 'Wisdom does not lie on the surface of things, for it is deep in the unseen. And we then lay hold on the mortification of ourselves, in attaining wisdom, if, relinquishing visible things, we bury ourselves in the invisible; if we so seek for her in the digging of the heart [...]'. Cf. also *Moralia* 9.105; 29.62; 31.53 (x2) 'the soil of the heart'. This is reminiscent of Macarius' signature theme of 'working the earth of the heart' see my, *The Macarian Legacy*, 154, 239. Taken with the distinctive language of taste and mystical experience noted below, I find it highly probable that Gregory had some acquaintance, direct or indirect, with Macarius—perhaps dating from his spell in Constantinople or even plausibly in connection with the recently discovered C6 Latin translation of Macarius (cf. Clemens Weidmann, 'Vorankündigung: Eine unbekannte lateinische Übersetzung der Predigten des Pseudo-Makarios').

[17] Examples are innumerable. See for example *Moralia* 5.78 on the dangers of losing one's temper: 'By anger wisdom is parted with, so that we are left wholly in ignorance what to do, and in what order to do it; as it is written, anger rests in the bosom of a fool (Eccles. 7:9) [...] By anger life is lost, even though wisdom seem to be retained; as it is written, anger destroys even the wise (Prov. 15:1 (LXX))'.

tranquillity constitutes a kind of freedom that can render its possessor able to manage and regulate earthly affairs with great skill, success, and due disinterestedness. Gregory points to Daniel and Joseph as men who were conspicuously competent in government precisely because of their participation in heavenly wisdom:

> For being full of wisdom from above, they distinguish how they may at once be free to one thing inwardly, and busied with another thing outwardly [...] and when the affairs of business make a din without, within the most peaceful repose is maintained in love; and the turmoils of employments outwardly clamouring, reason as presiding judge disposes of within, and with tranquil governance regulates the things, which all around it are too little tranquil.   (*Moralia* 18.70)

The apostle Paul is often used as a paradigmatic instance of growth in wisdom. Gregory reads Paul rather as the Byzantines did: as a shining instance of mystical experience.[18] Paul's experience of wisdom is described in terms of taste—a taste and experience that left him very aware of how little he could comprehend or express:

> For Paul [...] after he had tasted inward wisdom, after the barrier of paradise had been opened, after the ascent of the third heaven, after the mysteries of heavenly words, still says, 'I count not myself to have apprehended' (Phil. 3:13). Paul, then [...] both reached to heavenly secrets and yet stood sublimely in humility of heart.   (*Moralia* 28.13)

Gregory's accent on taste is particularly striking.[19] Through great humility and progress in virtue humans can sometimes have a brief and fleeting intimation of the unchangeable light of the divinity even through the interposition of our beclouded nature. This partial vision only serves to increase the bonds of love being a 'taste of marvellous sweetness' (*Moralia* 5.53). This contact with the immensity of God's light is utterly transformative but too much for human beings to bear for long: 'And when it tastes that inward sweetness, it is on fire with love, it longs to mount above itself, yet it falls back in broken state to the darkness of its frailty' (*Moralia* 5.58).

For Gregory, there is an organic connection between knowledge and love in true wisdom. Authentic knowledge is experiential and best described in terms of taste: 'It is one thing to know somewhat concerning God, and another to taste with

---

[18] On Paul among the Byzantine see Maximos Constas' superb, 'The Reception of St. Paul and of Pauline Theology in the Byzantine Period'.

[19] Cf. *Moralia* 30.39. On taste and mystical experience in Gregory, see further Leclercq, *The Love of Learning and the Desire for God*, 32.

the mouth of understanding the thing that is known' (*Moralia* 11.9). Those who possess merely outward knowledge are far from being truly wise:

> For if these persons ever seem to acquire wisdom, they feed, as it were, on the husks of things, and not on the marrow of their inmost sweetness; and with their brilliant abilities, they frequently reach only to the outside of things, but know not the savour of their inward taste; for, in truth, though sharp-sighted outwardly, they are blind within. Nor do they form such a notion of God, as tastes secretly within, but such as when thrown outward gives a sound. And though they gain in their understanding a knowledge of some mysteries, they can have no experience of their sweetness: and if they know how they exist, yet they know not, as I said, how they savour. And so it is frequently the case, that though they speak boldly, yet they know not how to live up to what they profess.   (*Moralia* 23.31)[20]

This connection between taste and wisdom, this sense of wisdom as experiential, lived, and tasted knowledge, was to mark much of the later Latin tradition. Indeed, following Gregory, the Latin tradition came to define wisdom precisely and even etymologically in terms of taste.

Overall, Gregory's profoundly sapiential and properly sophiological teaching was to shape much subsequent Latin teaching on wisdom—most notably that of Aquinas, for whom Gregory is an overwhelmingly important authority, the most quoted Church Father in the *Summa theologiae* after Augustine, and a major source for the *Catena aurea*. While certainly deeply inspired by Augustine, Gregory's account of wisdom is distinctly his own. His account is more sober, more scriptural, more acutely aware of the fragile and essentially nugatory character of merely human wisdom, and more obviously monastic, tinged throughout with compunction, repentance, and humility. Gregory has largely shed the broadly neo-Platonic dimension of Augustine's participatory sophiology in respect of his understanding of human partaking of divine wisdom. For Gregory, participation in divine wisdom is a way of speaking about the gift of wisdom granted to wise men and women on a conditional and provisional basis. There is little of the ongoing anagogical dynamic of participation in the divine wisdom that one finds in Augustine. But Gregory does take from Augustine the affirmation that wisdom pertains to the divine essence and is identical with the essence, even if scriptural references to wisdom are to be ascribed principally to the Son. He also shares with Augustine a sense of the unity between knowledge (*scientia*) and wisdom (*sapientia*). And, again like Augustine and indeed many of the Greek Fathers, he sees uncreated and created wisdom united in Christ. But perhaps his most distinctive contributions are his identification of wisdom with

---

[20] For more on taste and mystical experience see, for example *Moralia* 4.66, 5.14, 6.22, 6.48, 7.17, 15.20, 15.53, 15.71, 16.8, 16.33, 18.92, 23.31, 23.41, 23.43, 23, 28–9.

the Church and his understanding of wisdom as lived and tasted knowledge, not a merely affective experience distinct from all intellectual activity. This holistic understanding was to come under acute pressure in the later medieval period.

6.1.4 The Venerable Bede

Pope Gregory was the prime mover behind the missions sent from Rome to convert the Anglo-Saxons and the Anglo-Saxon Church he helped found was to produce a number of great devotees of wisdom, perhaps most notably the Venerable Bede (c. 673–735) and Alcuin of York, both of whom consciously take up Gregory's profoundly Christological and Christocentric reading of wisdom. Bede ends his most famous work, *The Ecclesiastical History of the English People* with a prayer to Jesus that he be brought at length before the 'fount of all wisdom and stand before your face forever'.[21] Within his extensive and profoundly sapiential *oeuvre* are several commentaries on wisdom literature, notably on the Song of Songs and on Proverbs, together with a treatise on the temple of Solomon. Although writing in the far-flung Anglo-Saxon Kingdom of Northumbria, Bede's exegetical work (embracing levels S1–S3) draws widely and deeply on the preceding patristic tradition, both Latin and Greek, and remained of great authority for the later Latin tradition. His commentary on the Song, for example, is the single most important source of the twelfth-century *glossa ordinaria* on that Book while Aquinas' *Catena aurea* treats Bede's Gospel commentaries as of exceptional value, making him the third most cited author after Chrysostom and Augustine. In its emphasis on Christ as wisdom (S3), Bede's Song commentary freely draws on the feminine dimensions of the Old Testament figure of wisdom, depicting Christ as nurturing and mothering wisdom. The sight of the glory of God is the bread of angels, but we humans need material intermediaries through which to rise to apprehension of the divinity—hence the incarnation which took place 'so that in this way the wisdom of God who consoles us as a mother may refresh us from that very same bread and lead us through the sacraments of the incarnation to the knowledge and vision of divine splendour'.[22]

Bede also takes up from Pope Gregory the association of the biblical figure of wisdom with the Church.[23] The Church is, furthermore, the bride of Christ-wisdom intimated in the Song of Songs and herself the house and source of wisdom. She is the 'garden enclosed' from whence flow the 'living waters' of wisdom.[24] With its depiction of Christ-wisdom as mother and the Church as wisdom and the bride of

---

[21] *Ecclesiastical History of the English People* 5.24.3 (SC 491 194).
[22] *In Cantica canticorum* 3 (CCSL 119B 258) [ET 123].
[23] *In Proverbia Salomonis* 1.9.1 (CCSL 119B 62).
[24] *In Cantica canticorum* 3 (CCSL 119B 263).

wisdom, Bede does much to accentuate the often-neglected feminine dimension of divine wisdom.

6.1.5 Alcuin

Alcuin of York (*c.* 740–804) was if anything even more enamoured of and devoted to wisdom themes than was Bede.[25] Together with Eanbald, future Archbishop of York, Alcuin built a church dedicated to *alma Sophia*, holy Wisdom, in York, consecrated on 30 October 780.[26] A near contemporary calendar records the dedication as *Titulus Agiae Sophiae*.[27] This is a unique dedication in England and exceptionally rare in western Europe.[28] It was, by Alcuin's own account, a magnificent building: lofty with strong columns, curving arches, inlaid ceilings and windows, galleries, and no fewer than thirty altars—all in all 'shining with beauty'.[29] The dedication suggests a possible emulation of the Great Church of *Agia Sophia* in Constantinople.[30] Such an emulation need not have been strictly architectural (Alcuin describes the church as a basilica) but certainly fits with Alcuin's consistent and distinctive focus on Christ as wisdom incarnate and the source of all wisdom worthy of the name.

Alcuin was a great liturgical compositor and produced a votive mass of wisdom, the *Missa de Sancta Sapientia*. This mass includes an invocation to *agiae sophiae* (again in the transliterated Greek form).[31] The mass proved both popular and enduring, being included in missals right up to that of Pius V of 1570.[32] It has no Eastern equivalent until the compositions of Shakovsky in the seventeenth century. Alcuin was among the first in the Latin West to appoint wisdom texts for

[25] See further Fairy von Lilienfeld, '"Frau Weisheit" in byzantinischen und karolingischen Quellen des 9. Jahrhunderts. Allegorische Personifikation, Hypostase oder Typos?', 119–22.

[26] Text in Peter Godman, *The Bishops, Kings and Saints of York*, ll. 1507–20. See also Donald Bullough, *Alcuin: Achievement and Reputation*, 320–6; Douglas Dales, *Alcuin: His Life and Legacy*, 25; and Richard Morris, 'Alcuin, York and the *Alma Sophia*'. 'Alma' can also be rendered 'nourishing' or 'bountiful' (so Bullough, op. cit., 321).

[27] Bullough, *Alcuin: Achievement and Reputation*, 323.

[28] One other instance is the Lombard Church of *Santa Sophia* in Benevento, built around 760 and modelled on the Great Church of the Holy Wisdom in Constantinople. The dedication also mirrors the dedication of many central Churches of newly converted Slav peoples to Holy Wisdom.

[29] From Alcuin's description the Church sounds quite capable of inspiring the kind of raptures recorded of the emissaries of Grand Prince Vladimir of Kiev or indeed of Robert Byron or Sergius Bulgakov on visiting its namesake in Constantinople (cf. above, pp.13–14).

[30] No remains of the Church have been found, thus its location and ground plan remain a matter of conjecture. It must be allowed that the dedication could plausibly also relate to the cult of the martyr Sophia recently revived in Rome but there is no other evidence to support this.

[31] 'Deus qui misisti filium tutum et ostendisti creaturae creatorem, respice propitius super nos famulos tuos, et praepara *agiae sophiae* dignam in cordibus nostris habitationem'. In Deshusses (ed.) *Le Sacramentaire grégorien: Ses principales formes d'après les plus anciens manuscrits* II 41 1818 (emphasis mine). Alcuin was not himself very well-versed in Greek and seems to reserve the Greek form for specifically divine wisdom as opposed to the more generally applicable *sapientia*.

[32] See Gerald Ellard, 'Alcuin and Some Favored Votive Masses'.

the scriptural readings on Marian feasts following a practice already established in the Greek East. Alcuin also composed a great deal of biblical exegesis, including commentaries on Proverbs, Ecclesiastes, and the Song of Songs—but with less of an interest in the specifically feminine dimension of wisdom than that of Bede.[33] Wisdom literature was evidently a special interest and love, as also seen in its preponderance in his correspondence.[34] Alcuin follows in the line of Origen in seeing these books as a kind of progress in wisdom.

Alcuin's *Disputatio de vera philosophia* upholds a distinctly Christian and monastic understanding of what constitutes true philosophy while also commending and defending the place of the liberal arts within a Christian educational system.[35] This short but immensely impactful text appears to have been written at the court of the Frankish King Charlemagne at which Alcuin spent much of the 780s and 790s. It formed part and parcel of Alcuin's vision for a renaissance of learning in western Europe, a programme enthusiastically sponsored by King Charles as he looked to build a new and improved Roman empire in the West. Alcuin brought with him to Europe all the riches of Anglo-Saxon scholarship and transmitted them to a wide and illustrious circle of students. While recognizing the inferiority of the liberal arts (S1) to biblical wisdom (S2), Alcuin argues that they are to be seen as divinely instituted, a counterpart to the seven gifts of the spirit and corresponding to the seven pillars of wisdom. The liberal arts are valuable for their utility in the refutation of heresy but also and more importantly serve as precious steps in the mind's ascent to God, wresting it away from materiality and bringing it into wisdom's house (cf. Prov. 9:1).[36] They are not, of course, to be pursued as an end in themselves and are of little use if not properly directed towards wisdom incarnate (S3). Christ is the wisdom in whom all human wisdom coheres and finds its true end and purpose. Plato, for example, 'burned with love of secular wisdom but remained ignorant of the celestial wisdom that leads to eternal life'.[37]

Alcuin's principal theological works make extensive use of the category of wisdom. His *De fide sanctae et individuae Trinitatis* stands in a long line of Latin theologians going back to Augustine who connect God's existence as wisdom with the doctrine of divine simplicity. Many of his other writings, including works on virtues and vices and on rhetoric, similarly structure much of what they have to teach around the theme of wisdom. He was also not above using wisdom themes to flatter, inspire, and educate his formidable royal patron, claiming in one elegant letter-poem that he 'is giving utterance to the highest arts

---

[33] Alcuin too has an honourable place in Aquinas' *Catena aurea* with 148 citations.

[34] Bullough, op. cit., 226–7.

[35] In PL 101 849–54. See further Mary Alberi, 'The "Mystery of the Incarnation" and Wisdom's House (Prov. 9:1) in Alcuin's *Disputatio de vera philosophia*'' and eadem, '"The Better Paths of Wisdom": Alcuin's Monastic "True Philosophy" and the Worldly Court'.

[36] *Disputatio* 853D.   [37] *Disputatio* 852D.

for noble ears' and that he 'leads through patristic meadows, and is duly followed by, him who rules with the glorious crown of lofty wisdom'.[38] In sum, it is fair to say that wisdom constitutes the single most important master-theme of Alcuin's life and work. Thus it should be no surprise to find it included within his epitaph at the monastery of St Martin in Tours:

> My name was Alcuin, and I always loved wisdom (*sophiam mihi semper amanti*).
> Pray, reader, for my soul.[39]

Alcuin was instrumental in leading and fostering what is sometimes called the Carolingian renaissance, a remarkable revival and renewal of patristic and philosophical learning in the Frankish West. He passed on his love of wisdom and wisdom literature to his many well-placed and influential disciples, most notably the great bishop and exegete Hrabanus Maurus, the first Latin commentator on Ben Sira (Ecclesiasticus) and author of a fetching poem on the divine wisdom.[40] This distinctly sapiential mode of theology was to endure down to the close of the middle ages.

6.1.6 John Scotus Eriugena

One of the later beneficiaries and continuators of the wisdom-centred revival of learning sparked by Alcuin was the famed and controversial Irish scholar John Scotus Eriugena (*c.* 810–*c.* 877).[41] Eriugena was quite exceptional in western Europe in his mastery of Greek and delighted in pointing out its superior range and nuance over and against the Latin tongue.[42] Precisely where he learnt Greek remains a mystery. He may have picked up a basic knowledge in Ireland and improved it on the continent.[43] In any event, his extensive use of Greek patristic and philosophical material appears to post-date his arrival in Francia and does not necessarily support the existence of a strong Greek patristic and philosophical culture in his native land. Eriugena is perhaps best known for his translation of Dionysius the Areopagite undertaken at the instigation of King Charles the Bald on the basis of a manuscript gifted to the Franks by the Roman Emperor Michael

---

[38] *Carmen* 59 in MGH 1.1 273 [ET Bullough, op. cit., 391].

[39] See Luitpold Wallach, 'The Epitaph of Alcuin: A Model of Carolingian Epigraphy'.

[40] The poem is given in Theresa Hainthaler et al. (eds.), *Sophia: The Wisdom of God*, 17.

[41] Eriugena has generated considerable scholarly interest of late. I have found the following general studies particularly helpful: John O'Meara, *Eriugena*; Dermot Moran, *The Philosophy of John Scottus Eriugena*; Deidre Carabine, *John Scottus Eriugena*; Bernard McGinn and Willemien Otten (eds.), *Eriugena: East and West*.

[42] Cf. *Periphyseon* V 955A (CCCM 165 132).

[43] See O'Meara, *Eriugena*, 7–9 and Moran, *The Philosophy of John Scottus Eriugena*, 56–7 on this question.

II. This work of translation with accompanying commentary was to be of incalculable impact on the later Latin tradition. By this means, Eriugena became the principal conduit for the entry of the late neo-Platonism of Proclus into the Latin West, an event that was to be of decisive importance for the emergence of modern Russian Sophiology. Eriugena also impacted Sophiology through his inspiration of later Christian Platonist mystics such as Meister Eckhart and Nicholas of Cusa, and indeed the functionally pantheistic Idealism of Schelling and Hegel.

Alongside Dionysius, Eriugena also translated other great luminaries of Christian Platonism, such as Gregory of Nyssa and Maximus the Confessor. While certainly well-grounded in the Latin patristic tradition, above all in Augustine, he came to inhabit the thought-world of the Greek Fathers to a remarkable degree, articulating an intense and coherent mystical vision centred on the participatory relationship between God and the world consummated in the *theosis* or deification of the human creation.[44] Eriugena also stands out for his bold and rigorous use of human reason without necessarily depending on scripture and patristic tradition. In this sense he anticipates some of the more daring and speculative flights of later medieval scholasticism. As mystic and scholastic, as an Irish theologian and philosopher inhabiting a substantially Byzantine thought-world at the Frankish court, Eriugena is a figure who bridges many different cultural, theological, and philosophical traditions. He is undoubtedly of compelling interest for this study.

Eriugena, unlike most Western theologians, receives some credit from Bulgakov. In *Philosophy of Economy*, Eriugena is credited for his embrace of the Platonic world soul (equivalent to Sophia), including the perception of some form of pre-existent divine humanity.[45] But in *Unfading Light*, Eriugena is heavily criticized for allowing his Platonic inheritance to get the better of him in embracing Plotinus 'emanative pantheism' and utterly failing to recognize the enduring ontological gap between creature and Creator.[46] This judgement helps explain why Eriugena tended to drop out of Bulgakov's purview as he sought in his works of exile to put forward a distinctly unmodern and firmly patristic construal of Sophia.

For Eriugena, the wisdom sought through both philosophy and theology is one and the same.[47] This wisdom is to be pursued through action and contemplation, a

---

[44] Moran puts it well: 'it was his reading of Greek theology which provoked him to a new reading of the Latin tradition and ultimately to the first attempt at a mediaeval synthesis of Christian wisdom': *The Philosophy of John Scottus Eriugena*, 46.

[45] *Philosophy of Economy* 59, 120, 223 [ET 84, 130, 205].

[46] *Unfading Light*, 157–60 [ET 165–67]. Bulgakov thus sees Eriugena's ontological monism as paving the way for Eckhart, Boehme, and, ultimately, Spinoza.

[47] When Eriugena says that we are saved only through philosophy he has in mind not only the academic discipline as such but the contemplation and pursuit of the wisdom implanted in us by the divine wisdom himself: 'every human soul is made immortal by the study of wisdom which is innate in itself' (*Annotationes on Martianus* 17.12).This early work is a commentary on Martianus Capella's *De nuptiis Philologiae et Mercurii* (C5), in which Mercury stands for heavenly wisdom and the learned bride for earthly wisdom. This text was notably popular in the C9, as attested by several commentaries of the time.

way of life that certainly includes the liberal arts.[48] It is a form of unitive knowledge that ultimately brings human beings into a deifying union with the God who is wisdom. As a function of divine simplicity as understood by Eriugena, God is to be understood as identical with his wisdom. Here Eriugena stands squarely with his Latin forebears and Greek philosophical interlocutors as against the prevailing tendency of the Greek patristic tradition from the Cappadocians through Dionysius and Maximus to Palamas. This understanding of divine wisdom in the context of divine simplicity was to underpin Eriugena's first entry into theological controversy. Commissioned by Archbishop Hincmar of Rheims to refute Gottschalk of Orbais' teaching on double predestination (of the elect and of the damned), Eriugena's response in the short treatise *On Divine Predestination* (851) was to argue that the thorny problem of predestination can best be solved by recourse to reason. Since he is wisdom, God's knowledge must be single and cannot will two things: election and reprobation. For Eriugena, God wills the salvation of all, but human beings can reject their calling through sin and the misuse of free will. Furthermore, any notions that would involve God in time (such as *pre*-destination) must be ruled inapplicable to the one who is outside and beyond time. This was hardly the response desired by Hincmar, given that it virtually does away with the doctrine of predestination altogether. Unsurprisingly, Eriugena's teaching on this point was condemned as a new species of Pelagianism at the councils of Valence (855) and Langres (859). Jerome's deliciously acerbic comment on the earlier Celtic theologian Pelagius, 'weighed down by Scots porridge (*pultes scottorum*)', was revived for this purpose.[49]

But this rebuke did little to damage Eriugena's immediate prospects, unlike the unfortunate Gottschalk who was to languish for much of life in prison. Eriugena went on after this affair to compose his famous translation of Dionysius and to produce his masterwork the *Periphyseon* or *On the Division of Nature*. This work marks the high point of Eriugena's integration of the Greek and Latin patristic thought-worlds. The *Periphyseon* develops some of the themes of *On Divine Predestination* to remarkable effect. He specifies, for example, that God does not and cannot know evil since his knowledge is simple and formed by the substantial good, himself—and of course evil can have no purchase in God himself.[50] God's ignorance is necessarily 'the highest and true wisdom'.[51] God is also described, in good Dionysian terms, as beyond wisdom: 'the creative cause of the whole universe is beyond nature and beyond being and beyond all life and wisdom

---

[48] 'Just as many waters from diverse sources flow together and run down into the bed of the one river, so the natural and the liberal arts are returned into one and the same meaning of interior contemplation, which the highest source of all wisdom, who is Christ, insinuates from all sides through the diverse speculations of theology.' *Commentary on the Celestial Hierarchy* 1 (CCCM 31 16) [ET Moran, *The Philosophy of John Scottus Eriugena*, 193].

[49] Report (from Jerome's *Commentary on Jeremiah*). See Canon 6 of Valence in Mansi XV 6.

[50] *Periphyseon* II 596AB (CCCM 162 96–7).   [51] *Periphyseon* II 594A (CCCM 162 94).

and power and beyond all things which are said and understood and perceived by all sense'.[52] God's essence is wholly beyond human knowledge and apprehension and is best evoked in terms of darkness, as non-being and no-thing. When we speak of creation *ex nihilo* we are properly speaking of creation out of God's own wisdom in whom lie from all eternity the co-essential ideas of the creation.[53]

The divine abyss is knowable in a strictly limited sense only on the basis of its creative acts or processions, which show 'that it is (quia est) but not what it is (quid est)'.[54] Given the limits to our knowledge of God, it is better to speak of not knowing him than of knowing him. This ignorance is human beings' truest wisdom.[55] There is, however, little in Eriugena to suggest that he has taken up Dionysius' distinction between God's utterly unknowable essence and his eternal processions (such as wisdom)—his broadly Augustinian and neo-Platonic construal of divine simplicity would seem to preclude such a distinction. Where he does speak of processions, these appear to be created effects.[56] That said, this whole question is muddied by the rather hazy nature of the created-uncreated distinction in his thought.

The whole creation, for Eriugena, is certainly to be understood as a revelation and manifestation of divine wisdom. In particular, the human creation is to be understood as 'created wisdom' patterned on God's 'creative wisdom' (the Word) and which, in its pre-lapsarian state, 'knows all things which are made in it before they are made'.[57] In the return to God, Christ as creative wisdom is the pattern and paradigm. Christ as head and exemplar of the whole human race both 'understands all things' and 'is the understanding of all things'.[58] In a passage uniting Maximus and Augustine, Eriugena affirms that it is through descent into human nature by grace that the divine wisdom raises human beings through *theosis*,

---

[52] *Periphyseon* III 622A (CCCM 163 7). Cf. *Periphyseon* I 460B (CCCM 161 188–91): God is aptly called 'ΥΠΕΡΣΟΦΟΣ (that is, more than wise) and ΥΠΕΡΣΟΦΙΑ (that is, more than wisdom)'. Note again Eriugena's fondness for Greek terminology.

[53] 'God did not receive any external matter or cause for the creation of the universe in his wisdom, for external to him there is nothing; nor did he find within himself anything not coessential with himself from which to make in his wisdom the things that he wished to make.' *Periphyseon* III 664D–665A (CCCM 63 66). Note that the ideas are co-essential and eternal but not strictly co-eternal, cf. above, n.62.

[54] *Periphyseon* II 551A (CCCM 62 234–5).

[55] *Periphyseon* II 593CD (CCCM 62 412–13). This radically apophatic conclusion places him worlds away from much of the preceding Latin tradition: cf. Moran, op. cit., 148.

[56] Eriugena explicitly confirms that this is the case with God's procession as wisdom: *Periphyseon* I II 623A (CCCM 163 196–7).

[57] *Periphyseon* IV 779A (CCCM 164 55). In the same context: 'For great and most miserable was that fall in which our nature lost the knowledge and wisdom which had been planted in her, and descended into a profound ignorance concerning herself and her Creator.' *Periphyseon* IV 777CD (CCCM 164, 53).

[58] *Periphyseon* II 545A (CCCM 162 210–11: versions III and IV only). See further *Periphyseon* I 455C (CCCM 161 23): the being, order, and motion of things point to God as Father (essence), Son (wisdom), and Holy Spirit (life). While acknowledging that God is wise by essence and that wisdom is a Trinitarian operation, Eriugena for the most part identifies wisdom with the second person of the Trinity.

forming a 'kind of composite wisdom' as human wisdom is united to the divine archetype.[59]

Eriugena's namesake the apostle John serves as a fine instance of this sophiological construct of deification. John, 'the spiritual eagle', was able to write with such perspicuousness of the wisdom of God precisely because he was united to that wisdom:

> John, therefore, was not just a man but more than a man when he rose above himself and all things that are and, transported by the ineffable power of wisdom and by purest acuity of mind, entered into that which is beyond all things: the secrets, that is, of the one essence in three subsistences and the three subsistences in the one essence. He would not have been able to ascend into God without first becoming God.[60]

United to God, John is able to see and declare that 'all things were made through him'. Eriugena explains the full import of this saying:

> All things were made by the God-Word himself, or by the Word-God himself [...] For his generation from the Father is itself the creation of all causes [...] Hear the divine and ineffable paradox, the unopenable secret, the invisible, unfathomable, and the incomprehensible mystery. Through him, who was not made but generated, all things were made but not generated. The principle, from whom all things are is the Father; the principle, through whom all things exist is the Son. The Father speaks his word, the Father puts forth his wisdom, and all things are made. The prophet says, 'In wisdom hast thou made them all'.[61]

Here Eriugena clearly affirms the eternity (but not co-eternity) of all creation within the wisdom or Word of God.[62] The whole creation is a revelation and

---

[59] *Periphyseon* 449A–D (CCCM 161 143–7). Eriugena is developing Maximus' *Ambiguum* 10 (especially 1113B) and an unidentified text from Augustine. It is noteworthy that Eriugena's account of deification is more wisdom-centered than the base text in which love is the cardinal principle. The wisdom dimension comes in via the appeal to Augustine (including the arresting notion of a 'kind of composite wisdom (quasi composita [...] sapientia').

[60] *Homily on the Prologue of John* 5 285CD (CCCM 166 10) (the term rendered subsistence is *substantia*).

[61] *Homily on the Prologue of John* 7 287AB (CCCM 166 13–14). Note that it is in begetting his wisdom that the Father knows himself: *Periphyseon* II 603B (CCCM 162 107).

[62] Cf. *Periphyseon* III 635BC (CCCM 163 25): 'It was agreed between us concerning the primordial causes of all things that they were made by the Father in his only-begotten word (that is, in his wisdom), at the same time, once and for all, and eternally, so that in the same way that the wisdom of the Father is eternal, and coeternal with the Father, so also all things which are made in it are eternal, except that they are all made in that which is not made but generated and which is their maker; for in the establishing of the universal creature, since the will of the Father and the Son is one and the same, so also is the activity one and the same. Therefore in their primordial causes all things are eternal in the wisdom of the Father but not coeternal.' This careful distinction was not enough to save him from charges of pantheism.

manifestation of the wisdom of God and called to return to union with that wisdom. This double movement of wisdom (God in the world and the world in God) is often spoken of by Eriugena in classically Platonic terms of descent and ascent. Human beings and indeed angels become *loci* of the divine presence according to their degree of sanctity and wisdom and 'as a consequence of the descent of the divine wisdom and of the ascent of the human and angelic understanding'.[63] In the final stages of this ascent into the primordial unity, mind becomes knowledge (knowledge of all things after God), knowledge becomes wisdom (knowledge of the truth), and wisdom collapses into the very darkness of divine ineffability.[64] At this point the subject-object distinction disappears and there is 'nothing but God alone in the same way that in the clearest air there is nothing but light (nisi sola lux)'.[65] Such is the pinnacle moment of Eriugena's sophiology: the apparent end of the creature as a distinct existent.

Eriugena's theology has had considerable impact over the centuries, even if its full complexity and implications have frequently eluded sympathizers and detractors alike. His work was especially popular in the twelfth century. The *Periphyseon* circulated in various anthologized and abridged forms such as the *Clavis physicae* of Honorius of Autun. The *Homily* is attested by a vast number of surviving manuscripts while the *Commentary on the Celestial Hierarchy* appears to have enjoyed only a limited circulation.[66] The further circulation of his ideas was somewhat limited by the condemnation of the *Periphyseon* in the thirteenth century, condemned by association with pantheistic teachings of the time.[67] But his work, especially as a transmitter of Dionysius, remained of profound importance within medieval scholasticism.[68]

Eriugena's work differs somewhat from that of his predecessors in the post-Augustinian West. He is less concerned with preserving the remnants of pagan civilization than Boethius or even Cassiodorus. His use of biblical wisdom literature is far less thoroughgoing than that of Gregory, Bede, or Alcuin. But perhaps what is most distinctive about his teaching is that he perceives a certain continuity of being between uncreated and created wisdom. This is most evident in his construal of creation *ex nihilo* as the procession of the coessential and eternal divine ideas from God into being and his monistic understanding of deification. Eriugena's distinctive account of the relation between creature and Creator is

---

[63] *Periphyseon* I 449D (CCCM 161 146–7).

[64] *Periphyseon* V 1020D–1021A (CCCM 165 856–9). Here Eriugena is developing Maximus the Confessor's treatment of Christ's (and, consequently, our) ascent through the primal divisions of the universe and back to primordial unity (*Ambigua* 41). Cf. above, p.179.

[65] *Periphyseon* V 1021B (CCCM 165 858–9).   [66] O'Meara, *Eriugena*, 217.

[67] The condemnation of the *Periphyseon* was essentially on grounds of its perceived pantheistic tendencies. Pope Honorius III ordered all copies of the work burned in 1225.

[68] Cf. O'Meara, *Eriugena*, vii: 'Eriugena had more influence in western Christendom than is generally recognized, even if the spirit of the times, guilt by association, and finally a flood of Aristotelianism told against him.'

arguably the product of his reception of a neo-Platonism unshorn of its emana-tionism. It is this undigested, or at any rate only partly digested, Platonic dimen-sion to his thought that gives some basis to the charges of pantheism that were to prove so detrimental to his legacy—a judgement in which even Bulgakov (himself no stranger to the same charge) was to concur: 'One may call Eriugena's doctrine a work of genius, but it is not Christian.'[69]

6.2 The High Middle Ages

Building on the earlier Latin tradition, above all Augustine, the figures surveyed in the preceding section bequeathed a powerful legacy of wisdom themes and theology to the High Middle Ages. This legacy is evident in virtually all the great theologians of the period. One immediate thing to notice is the consistency with which the Latin theological tradition continues to treat divine wisdom in terms of divine simplicity as articulated by Augustine. Investment in biblical wisdom literature also remains at a high pitch, as does interest in the lived experience and pedagogy of wisdom.

6.2.1 Anselm of Canterbury

By the time of the greatest Latin theologian of the eleventh century, Anselm of Canterbury (*c.* 1033–1109), Augustine's understanding of divine simplicity was clearly absolutely standard. In his *Proslogion*, composed while still at the Abbey of Bec in Normandy prior to his tumultuous stint as Archbishop of Canterbury, Anselm declares: 'you are the very life by which you live, and the wisdom by which you are wise.'[70] Similarly:

> You are life, wisdom, eternity, and every true good [. . .] You are so much a kind
> of unity and identical to yourself that you are in no way dissimilar to yourself;
> indeed, you are unity itself, conceptually indivisible. Therefore, life and wisdom
> and the other [attributes] are not parts of you but all of them are one, and each of
> them is entirely what you are, and what the other [attributes] are.[71]

Divine simplicity in this Augustinian and neo-Platonic mode entails far more than being non-composite but also total identity between God and his attributes and indeed—and this is problematic—between the attributes themselves. The mutual

---

[69] *Unfading Light*, 160 [ET 167]. Bulgakov is quoting with apparent approval the judgment of Albert Stöckl.
[70] *Proslogion* 12 (Schmitt I 110).   [71] *Proslogion* 18 (Schmitt I 114).

identity of the attributes, while present in Augustine, is much more emphatic in Anselm (and, after him, in Aquinas). One may very well wonder (as Duns Scotus was later to do) how, for example, life is identical with wisdom.[72]

Moreover, Anselm's construal of divine simplicity leaves human beings at a far distant remove from the divine wisdom, a chasm spanned only (and very inadequately) by remote analogy: 'if wisdom in the knowledge of created things is lovely (*amabilis*), how lovely is the wisdom which has created all things from nothing!'[73]

In the *Monologion*, Anselm provides some further indicators of his understanding of divine wisdom. He specifies, for example, that the Trinity is one supreme wisdom as it is one supreme essence:

> Just as the Son is the substance and wisdom and power of the Father in the sense that he has the same essence and wisdom and power as the Father; so likewise the Spirit is the essence or wisdom or power of the Father and the Son and has all identically that they have.[74]

Having said that, Anslem is careful to maintain a certain sense of negative (if not properly apophatic) theology:

> For whatever names may be applied to that nature do not reveal it to me in its proper character but intimate it through some likeness [...] nor is the name wisdom sufficient to reveal to me that through which all things were created from nothing and preserved from nothing.[75]

It is worth noting that Anselm does not make extensive use of the category of wisdom in speaking of the incarnation, even in his masterwork *Cur Deus homo?* He asserts that the incarnation took place 'in accordance with supreme wisdom' and Christ in his humanity is never without 'the power, the might, or the wisdom of God'.[76] But such considerations are at best incidental to a work that focusses more on themes of redemption and atonement—and which Bulgakov found to typify the 'harsh ascetic and legalistic thought of the West'.[77] Florensky similarly treats him as a typical scholastic while admiring and making use of his motto 'Credo ut intelligam'.[78]

All in all, Anselm presents us with only a very limited use of wisdom themes and stands principally as a marker of the dominance of Augustine's model of

---

[72] This is precisely one of the main thrusts of Alvin Plantinga's compelling critique of the (Latin) doctrine of divine simplicity in his *Does God have a Nature?*
[73] *Proslogion* 24 (Schmitt I 118).   [74] *Monologion* 58 (Schmitt I 69).
[75] *Monologion* 65 (Schmitt I 76).   [76] *Cur Deus homo* 2.13 (Schmitt II 112–13).
[77] *The Lamb of God*, 373 [ET 343].
[78] *The Pillar and Ground of Truth*, 62 [ET 47] cf. Anselm, *Proslogion* 1 (Schmitt I 100).

divine simplicity at the dawn of the second millennium. But while his rather jejune treatment might just fit Bulgakov's narrative of a sophiological 'dead-end', some of the richest Western treatments of wisdom were yet to come.

6.2.2 Hildegard of Bingen

The incomparable Hildegard of Bingen (1098–1179) presents us with an extraordinarily dense and vivid treatment of wisdom themes.[79] Indeed there is such a wealth of mystical sophiology (principally on level S3) in Hildegard that she stands as an obvious forerunner to modern Russian Sophiology, to which she undoubtedly contributed indirectly through later German mysticism. The Sophiologists' failure to explicitly acknowledge Hildegard as a forebear is surprising but likely to be a function of her relative obscurity in the scholarly and ecclesial worlds of the nineteenth and early twentieth centuries.

Hildegard received a startling set of visions that she set down in her works the *Scivias*, *Liber vitae meritorum*, and *Liber divinorum operum*. Her *Life* reports her assertion that her visions came from wisdom herself. Expanding on Song of Songs 5:4 ('My lover put his hand through the opening; my heart trembled within me, and I grew faint when he spoke'), she declares: 'Wisdom teaches me in the light of love and orders me to say in what manner I was granted this vision. I do not speak these words concerning myself, but it is true wisdom who speaks [...]'.[80] Hildegard recounts several visions of the Old Testament figure of wisdom in various guises (for instance as knowledge of God, wisdom, and love). Wisdom appears to Hildegard as terrible and gentle, radiant and beautiful, dazzling and mysterious. She is intimately related to God: 'she was in the most high Father before all creatures, giving counsel in the formation of all the creatures in heaven and earth; so that she is the great ornament of God and the broad stairway of all the other virtues that live in him, joined to him in sweet embrace in a dance of ardent love'. She is by no means exclusively associated with the Son of God, rather the various colours with which she is adorned stand for the labours of the prophets and patriarchs of the Old Testament (green), the virginity of Mary (white), the blood of the martyrs (red), and the love of the contemplatives (blue).[81]

Elsewhere, Hildegard expands on wisdom's work in the creation:

But all wisdom comes from God the Lord of all. With his wisdom he predestined all things and composed all things in the world, and with that same wisdom he distinguished each thing. It was this very wisdom who knew and tasted heavenly things and travelled round the circle of the heavens in her royal ministry. She

---

[79] See especially Barbara Newman, *Sister of Wisdom: St. Hildegard's Theology of the Feminine*.
[80] *Life of Hildegard* 2.2 (CCCM 126 22).   [81] *Scivias* 3.9.25 (CCCM 43A 538–9).

crossed the earth in her service, establishing every creature, and she penetrated the abyss. She is like a good overseer who lets nothing perish that has been assigned to her. But wisdom is also the eye of God, through whom he foresees and governs all things, standing before him as his most beloved friend in loving embrace and with whom he considers and weighs all things. Through wisdom man also is named the height of the heavens, because he surpasses and dominates all creatures through knowledge, which is the eye of wisdom.[82]

In the *Liber divinorum operum* Hildegard goes on to recount a further vision of this wisdom figure who is also simultaneously love and power:

And I saw as amid the airs of the south in the mystery of God a beautiful and marvellous image in human form; her face was of such beauty and light that I could more easily have stared at the sun. [...] The figure spoke: 'I am the supreme fire and energy. I have kindled all the sparks of the living, and I have breathed out nothing deadly, for I judge them for what they are. I have ordained things rightly, circling about the circling circuit with my upper wings, that is with wisdom. I am the fiery life of the substance of divinity, I burn above the beauty of the fields, I shine in the waters, I blaze in sun, moon, and stars.'[83]

Wisdom in Hildegard is the divine presence deep within the creation, what Gerard Manley Hopkins called 'the dearest freshness deep down things' and Thomas Merton the 'invisible fecundity' within in all visible things.[84] It is a vision of the coinherence of God and the world: God in the world and the world in God. Hildegard does not insist on or even particularly emphasize the connection between this cosmic wisdom and Christ.[85] Indeed, wisdom seems to stand primarily for the divine immanence and activity within the creation bringing the creation back into union with God. The feminine dimension of wisdom allows Hildegard to emphasize the gloriously responsive receptivity of the cosmos as it returns lovingly to its source.[86]

---

[82] *Liber vitae meritorum* 1.34 (CCCM 90 26–7).

[83] *Liber divinorum operum* 1.1.1–2 (CCCM 92 46–48).

[84] Hopkins, 'God's Grandeur' (1877) and Thomas Merton, 'Hagia Sophia' (1961). Merton's poem names the divine presence specifically as wisdom: 'There is in all visible things an invisible fecundity, a dimmed light, a meek namelessness, a hidden wholeness. This mysterious Unity and Integrity is Wisdom, the Mother of all, *Natura naturans*.'

[85] Barbara Newman expresses this well: 'Sapientia eludes all precise definition, for the obvious reason that her gender makes it impossible to identify her with any fixed point of dogma. Yet neither does she exclude or supplant these fixed points. She is, rather, a unique perspective on them—a whole realm of associations, images, and spiritual perceptions that may bear on aspects of Christ, or Mary, or the Trinity, but cannot finally be reduced to these.' *Sister of Wisdom*, 66.

[86] Cf. ibid., 'she shared her contemporaries' view of the female as essentially receptive, submissive, and obedient. For this reason the cosmos must naturally be "feminine" vis-à-vis the Creator.'

Hildegard is unique in the surviving literature of the Middle Ages in the extent to which she revels and delights in the specifically feminine dimensions of the Old Testament figure of wisdom. There is nothing like it in either East or West. And, unlike virtually all her contemporaries, she is willing to consider the figure and theme of wisdom without a more or less exclusive focus on Trinitarian theology and Christology. Indeed wisdom is something of a free-floating category in her work that is never tied down to familiar dogmatic categories such as substance and person. Wisdom in Hildegard becomes a distinctly feminine personification of the divine presence in creation urging and bringing that creation back into union with the Creator. Her most obvious epigones are found in later German mystics such as Johannes Tauler and Jakob Boehme. She is thus a powerful but indirect contributor to modern Russian Sophiology. While her orthodoxy was officially affirmed by papal command in her own time (and indeed more recently with her recognition as a doctor of the Roman Catholic Church in 2012), Hildegard's stunning revelations had only limited direct impact on later medieval reflection on the figure of wisdom, perhaps precisely because of their sheer overpowering originality, complexity, and indeterminateness.[87]

6.2.3 Bernard of Clairvaux and Peter Abelard

But medieval men, while never quite as expansive as Hildegard, were not restricted to the rather spare and sober treatment of wisdom found in Anselm. Bernard of Clairvaux (1090–1153), a correspondent and supporter of Hildegard, developed a mystical vision of unusual intensity centred on the Song of Songs. His *Sermons on the Song of Songs* remain one of the great classics of Western spirituality—a magnificent hymn to the awesome power of God's love that has few peers. The founder of the great Cistercian house of Clairvaux, Bernard represents a monastic tradition of great austerity, reach, and reforming zeal. Convinced of his own possession of heavenly wisdom, he was unafraid of controversy and only too willing to lecture fellow abbots, bishops, and even popes on their responsibilities. While not opposed to scholasticism *per se*, Bernard was deeply suspicious of any attempt to investigate the mysteries through reason alone, a tendency he clearly associated with the new universities established in Paris and elsewhere. Bernard's suspicion of certain tendencies within scholasticism is borne out in his mystical theology in which he associates wisdom with love and distinguishes these from more intellective forms of knowledge. There is thus an emerging affective-

---

[87] For a useful survey of Hildegard's legacy see Michael Embach, 'Hildegard of Bingen (1098–1179): A History of Reception'.

intellective (or heart-head) bifurcation in his work which was only to widen in subsequent generations.[88]

The *Sermons on the Song of Songs* are presented as wisdom for the spiritually mature, for those who have already separated themselves from evil through practical application to the keeping of the commandments which is 'consummate wisdom' (S1).[89] Indeed the overall tone, in keeping with the spirit of the Cistercian order, is profoundly practical and ascetic. As in many monastic texts, there is a good deal of emphasis on the absolute disparity between fleshly or earthly wisdom (S0) and the wisdom that comes from God (S2). God is spoken of as wisdom and as possessing a wisdom that knows no bounds or measure (S3).[90] As God, the Holy Spirit is also wisdom.[91] But for the most part wisdom is associated with Christ as 'the incarnate wisdom of God'.[92] He is the eternal wisdom of God who, as Paul put it (I Cor. 1:30), 'became wisdom from God for us'.[93] In marked contrast to Hildegard, Bernard does not dwell on the specifically feminine dimensions of the Old Testament figure of wisdom. Bernard also writes at some length on the rôle of the angels in the vision and transmission of divine wisdom but without obvious indebtedness to Dionysius—his source here is more obviously Pope Gregory.[94]

The gift of wisdom to humans is, again as in Gregory, a kind of lived or tasted knowledge, a savouring of what the mind apprehends.[95] Instruction can bring us learning but experience is what turns that knowledge into wisdom.[96] There is, it may be noted, no opposition between wisdom and knowledge in Bernard.[97] Wisdom is, rather, to be understood as the consummation of knowledge. The wisdom gifted to human beings dwells in the heart.[98] It must never be treated as possession.[99] Wisdom sets up in human beings a burning desire and intense thirst for God. Those propelled in this way can look forward to an authentic if

---

[88] Bernard distinguishes between intellectual and affective forms of contemplation, cf. *Sermons* 49.4 (SC 452 334): 'there are two kinds of transport in blessed contemplation: one in the intellect, the other in the affective faculty. The one comes about in light, the other in warmth; the one consists in knowledge, the other in devotion.'

[89] *Sermons* 1.2 (SC 414 62).

[90] *Sermons* 4.4 (quoting Ps. 146(7):5), 19.7, 78.2 (SC 414 118; 431 122; 511 244).

[91] *Sermons* 8.6 (SC 414 184): 'He is in truth "the Spirit of wisdom and insight" (Is. 11:2), who, like the bee carrying wax and honey, has the power both to shine with the light of knowledge and to infuse the taste of grace.'

[92] *Sermons* 6.7 (SC 414 148). Cf also *Sermons* 48.5, 51.7, 53.5 (SC 452 320; 472 50-2, 86).

[93] *Sermons* 22.5 (SC 431 178-80).   [94] *Sermons* 19.2 (SC 431 108-10).

[95] *Sermons* 9.3 (SC 414 200).   [96] *Sermons* 23.14 (SC 431 228-30).

[97] There is also no opposition between love and knowledge such as we find in the later Latin tradition. See *Sermons* 19.7 (SC 431 122): 'The crafty enemy has no more effective artifice for emptying the heart of love than inducing us to love imprudently and unreasonably'.

[98] *Sermons* 28.8 (SC 431 360).

[99] In *Sermons* 74.10 (SC 511 174). Bernard specifies that the loss of wisdom is the fruit of pride, the product of treating wisdom as a possession rather than a gift. Satan and many human souls have lost wisdom on this account with terrible consequences: 'what is an angel or a soul without wisdom but rough and deformed matter?'

necessarily fleeting mystical encounter with God even in this life, being 'clasped in the arms of wisdom' and 'inundated with the sweetness of divine love'.[100] Through the indwelling of wisdom the soul can become the 'seat of wisdom', shining brightly as it imparts wisdom to others.[101] Paul and John are such luminaries of wisdom, Paul passing into the third heaven to experience divine wisdom and John as if 'immersed in the very innermost parts of the Word and from the hidden depth of his breast drawing forth the holiest marrow of hidden wisdom'.[102]

Bernard's commentary on the Song of Songs ends with a resounding sequence of wisdom references. Wisdom, he opines, is characterized by peace of mind and spiritual sweetness.[103] He goes on to say that it demands great exertion but this is not toilsome, rather 'the more leisure wisdom has, the more it works in its own fashion'. This is true *schola* (from σχολή)—the leisure that makes true learning possible.[104] Indeed far from being grinding toil, wisdom is more akin to taste:

> If anyone defines wisdom as the effort of love, I do not think they are far from the truth. For where there is love there is not labour but taste. Perhaps *sapientia*, comes from *sapor*, or taste, because, when it is added to effort, like some seasoning, it adds taste to something which by itself is tasteless and bitter. I think it would be permissible to define wisdom as a taste for goodness. We lost this taste almost from the creation of our race.[105]

But the corruption of the human palate that crept in swiftly with Eve is overturned by Mary in a veritable reformation of wisdom:

> See that wisdom has filled the heart and body of a woman so that we who were deformed into folly through a woman might be reformed to wisdom by a woman. Now wisdom 'always triumphs over evil' (Wisdom 7:30) in the mind which it has entered, driving out the taste for evil which the other has brought into it, by introducing something better. When wisdom enters, it makes the carnal sense insipid and purifies the mind, cleansing and healing the palate of the heart. The restored palate tastes the good, tastes wisdom itself – the best of all good things.[106]

---

[100] *Sermons* 32.2 (SC 431 450).

[101] *Sermons* 25.6 (SC 431 268). The example discussed is Paul, though Bernard certainly sees himself as one able to impart wisdom to others.

[102] *Sermons* 62.3 (SC 472 266). Of Paul he writes: 'What about he who spoke "wisdom among the perfect"? (I Cor. 2:6) [. . .] Passing through the first and second heavens by his acute but pious curiosity, did the devout explorer not gain at last this wisdom from the third?' Note the accent on Paul's mystical experience—something Bernard shares with the Byzantine tradition (perhaps mediated to him via Pope Gregory).

[103] *Sermons* 85.7 (SC 511 384).   [104] *Sermons* 85.8 (cf. Ecclus. 38:25) (SC 511 386).

[105] Ibid.   [106] *Sermons* 85.8 (SC 511 388).

Bernard saw in contemporary scholastics such as Peter Abelard (1079–1142) a dangerous tendency to think of wisdom in considerably less experiential and affective terms. In the prologue to his monumental *Sic et non*, Abelard argues that doubt is the beginning of wisdom in that doubt leads to enquiry and enquiry to truth.[107] Wisdom here is an intellectual activity of questioning and striving: the mind's struggle to make sense of the obscurities and apparent contradictions of scriptural and patristic tradition. In Abelard, theology is construed principally as an intellectual discipline rather than as the pursuit and articulation of the vision of God. This is a radical departure from the patristic tradition of both East and West. Abelard also gave substantial credence to the wisdom of the pagan philosophers of old. All this was profoundly unsettling for Bernard and his monastic confrères. Abelard's willingness to use logic and dialectic to probe and analyse the mysteries of God brought him to the conclusion that the Father is power, the Son wisdom, and the Holy Spirit goodness.[108] Bernard and his supporters found Abelard's approach destructive of the unity of the Trinity and contrived to have aspects of his teaching condemned at the Council of Sens in 1140.

In the encounter between Bernard and Abelard we see two distinct visions of wisdom: Bernard's distinctly monastic and experiential vision and Abelard's rather more intellectual and rational construal. Abelard conceived wisdom and hence theology in a fundamentally different way than did Bernard. Abelard stands for a tendency within scholasticism to treat theology as an intellectual activity principally concerned with the sifting of authorities and application of reason in a way that Bernard and many contemporaries found both outrageous and unprecedented. Bernard's own approach to theology was far more embedded in scriptural and patristic tradition and noticeably conditioned by mystical experience. Of course, this contrast should not be pushed too hard and certainly not be allowed to fan out into an absolute dichotomy between mysticism/monasticism on the one hand and rationalism/scholasticism on the other. Bernard was no obscurantist, had many friendly contacts with the schoolmen, and made extensive use of human reason, while Abelard was well-versed in scriptural and patristic tradition and spent much of his life as a monk (albeit not a conspicuously successful one). That said, the pair do serve as witnesses to a widening contrast between a more mystical-affective and a more rational-intellectual construct of wisdom within the medieval West.

---

[107] See Beryl Smalley, '*Prima Clavis Sapientiae*: Augustine and Abelard'. Smalley demonstrates the hinterland to Abelard's proposition (especially in Aristotle and Augustine) while also showing its considerable novelty.

[108] See John Marenbon, *The Philosophy of Peter Abelard*, 55–61. Cf. *Commentary on Romans* 1.20 (CCCM 11 68): 'I believe that the entire distinction of the Trinity consists in these three things.' This amounts to a rather extreme version of the exclusive association of wisdom with the Son that the Sophiologists were so keen to avert.

6.2.4 *Sapientia* and *Scientia*

Bernard had distinguished between intellective and affective forms of contemplation without, however, quite disassociating wisdom from knowledge—*sapientia*
from *scientia*. Some later Latin theologians were to go further and drive a wedge
between the two with wisdom standing for mystical-affective apprehension and
knowledge for cognitive-intellective apprehension. One can see this bifurcation
sharply in figures or works such as the *Summa fratris Alexandri*, Thomas Gallus
(*c.* 1200–1246),[109] and Bonaventure (1221–1274),[110] all of whom tend to privilege
the affective over the intellective in their accounts of theology and mystical union.
This position is perhaps most starkly articulated by the Augustinian theologian
Giles of Rome (*c.* 1243/7–1316):

> Because love is simply speaking the goal of theology [...] it should be named
> from it, and because love is in the affect and not the intellect [...] theology should
> properly speaking be called neither theoretical nor practical but affective, because
> it principally induces to affection. For this reason it is well said that it is more
> wisdom [than science] from the fact that it induces to the taste of divine things.[111]

This bifurcation—which never took hold in the Greek East—between wisdom and
knowledge, between affective-experiential and intellective-cognitive apprehension, has strongly marked the Latin theological tradition ever since. Somewhat
ironically, and directly contrary to the original intentions of its framers (who
intended it rather to exalt wisdom and mystical experience), this bifurcation has
contributed to a functional marginalization of mysticism and encouraged the
emergence of a merely academic form of theology cut off from the wellsprings
of living tradition. But scholastic theology was never to fall wholly into this
paradigm of bifurcation. There have always been those within that tradition
who were unwilling to give up on a more expansive vision of wisdom, unwilling
to detach *sapientia* from *scientia*. Of these, the greatest is surely Thomas Aquinas.

6.2.5 Thomas Aquinas

Heir to the long tradition of Western wisdom speculation detailed above, as indeed
to much Greek patristic thought on the topic, Thomas Aquinas's work is

---

[109] See further, Boyd Coolman, *Knowledge, Love, and Ecstasy in the Theology of Thomas Gallus.*
Coolman makes a persuasive case that the relationship between the affective and the intellective is a
subtle and intertwined one.

[110] Cf. Bonaventure's assertion that affective wisdom passes beyond cognition in III *Sent.*, d.35, a.1,
q.3, ad 5 (cited in Blankenhorn, *The Mystery of Union with God*, 437).

[111] See Richard Cross, 'Theology', 44. Note the extent to which Bernard's folk etymology of *sapientia*
had become established as utterly normative by Giles' time.

thoroughly sapiential and sophiological from the outset. But Aquinas, with the Western tradition as a whole, receives little credit for this from the Sophiologists.[112] Bulgakov, in particular, launched what amounts to an all-out assault on virtually every aspect of Thomas' achievement. Even Thomas' one possible saving grace—his acceptance of some form of the doctrine of the divine ideas for creation—comes up short in Bulgakov's estimation. Bulgakov finds (in *ST* I[a] qq. 15, 44, and 46) that Aquinas does have some notion of the divine wisdom as the ultimate source of the ideas and archetypes of all that is but that he fails to connect this doctrine with the doctrine of the Holy Trinity, addressing it only under the general (and overly philosophical) heading of the one God. It is thus a 'sophiologically unfinished' project. Here he makes the important point that, 'Sophiology is not only a doctrine of ideas as the prototypes of things but primarily a doctrine of the self-revelation of the Trinity.' Thomas' work in general constitutes 'a Platonism supplemented by Aristotelianism that is not organically but mechanistically introduced into Christian theology.[113] Given this estimation of Thomas as an unreconstructed amalgam of Plato and Aristotle, it is no surprise to find Bulgakov treating him as the capstone of a barren and dead-end tradition. But is this estimation entirely just?

It is no exaggeration to claim that Aquinas' whole life's work is structured around the theme of wisdom on levels S1–S3.[114] His three major works each open with the theme of wisdom. The *Commentary on the Sentences* presents wisdom as the key to understanding the Lombard's work and, indeed, Christian theology in general. Thomas' prologue opens with Ecclesiasticus 24:40–2: 'I, wisdom, have poured out rivers. I, like a brook out of a river of mighty water: I, like a channel of a river, and like an aqueduct, came out of paradise. I said: "I will water my garden of plants and I will water abundantly the fruits of my meadow."'[115] He goes on to specify that while wisdom pertains to the divine essence it is fittingly associated especially with the Son as the supreme manifestation of the divine wisdom, as maker and exemplar of the creation, and as the one who restores and perfects that creation. Aquinas devotes much discussion to the precise character of theology (specifically as wisdom, science, and understanding), basing his terminology in the first instance on Aristotle. His overall conclusion is that, in its orientation towards the one who is wisdom, Christ, theology (*sacra doctrina*) is not only a form of knowledge or science (both practical and theoretical since it perfects both action and contemplation) but also wisdom in its most proper sense, in that it proceeds directly from the highest cause through revelation and the direct inspiration of

---

[112] The Sophiologists' reception of Aquinas is detailed in my *Orthodox Readings of Aquinas*, 182–4 and 188–93.

[113] *The Bride of the Lamb*, 29–34 [ET 24–28]. Here, 26 [ET 32].

[114] Dante gives full poetic vindication to this interpretation in making Thomas the central figure among the spirits of wisdom (*spiriti sapienti*) that dwell in the heaven of the Sun: *Paradiso* 10–11.

[115] Thomas makes very extensive use of Biblical wisdom literature. This is a recurring feature of the *Commentary on the Sentences* and of both *Summae*.

divine light.[116] The prologue represents a kind of sapiential and sophiological manifesto for Thomas' entire theological project. Even where educational, polemical, and other needs dictate a rather dry, forensic, and even tedious approach, Thomas' whole work aches and aspires to be watered by the rivers of wisdom and bathed in the divine light.

The *Summa contra gentiles* presents itself similarly as an exercise in Christian wisdom, opening with Proverbs 8:7, 'My mouth shall meditate truth, and my lips shall hate impiety' (*SG* 1.1.1). Wisdom, after Aristotle, is especially associated with the principle of order. Christian wisdom is ordered Christ, the one who is wisdom. The wise man or woman is called to meditate upon the divine wisdom which is Christ and to proclaim that wisdom, correcting error wherever necessary— however painstaking that process of correction might be. He goes on to express his own purpose in writing the work as follows:

> Among all human studies the study of wisdom is more perfect, more sublime, more useful, and more full of joy. It is more perfect because, in so far as a man gives himself to the study of wisdom, so far does he even now have some share in true beatitude, as a wise man has said: 'Blessed is the man who shall continue in wisdom' (Ecclus. 14:22). It is more sublime because through this study man especially approaches to a likeness to God who 'made all things in wisdom' (Ps. 103:24). And since likeness is the cause of love, the study of wisdom especially joins man to God in friendship. That is why it is said of wisdom that 'she is an infinite treasure to men which they that acquire become the friends of God' (Wisdom 7:14). It is more useful because through wisdom we arrive at the kingdom of immortality. For 'the desire of wisdom leads to the everlasting kingdom' (Wisdom 6:20). It is more full of joy because 'her conversation has no bitterness and to live with her has no tediousness but mirth and joy.' (Wisdom 8:16).   (*SG* 1.1.2)

One could hardly hope for a more perfect paean to wisdom. Wisdom in its highest sense is a form of participatory and, indeed, deifying knowledge that incorporates human beings into the divine life. It is the gift of immediate and intuitive knowledge that does not rely on book learning or rational argumentation: 'then there is the inspiration given to human minds, so that simple and unlettered persons, filled with the gift of the Holy Spirit, come to obtain in an instant the highest wisdom and eloquence' (*SG* 1.6.1).[117]

---

[116] 'Hence it is necessary that the things which are for the sake of the end be proportioned to the end, since a man while on the way is led by the hand to that contemplation, not through knowledge drawn from creatures, but rather as immediately inspired by the divine light (*sed immediate ex divino lumine inspiratam*) and this is the doctrine of theology.' (*Commentary on the Sentences*, q.1 a.1 co.).

[117] A similar sentiment is found in his exposition of the Apostles' Creed in which he opines that 'none of the philosophers before the coming of Christ was able to know as much about God, and about

Thomas returns to the theme of wisdom frequently in the *Summa contra gentiles*. God is wise by nature 'not only in so far as he effects wisdom, but also because, in so far as we are wise, we imitate to some extent the power by which he makes us wise' (*SG* 1.31.2). Alongside somewhat drier affirmations of God's simplicity and self-identity with his wisdom (and the self-identity of the divine wisdom with the other divine attributes), Aquinas also draws on biblical wisdom literature to defend and illustrate the love, joy, and delight that is in God (*SG* 1.91.13, citing Proverbs 8:30). Aquinas fully appreciates the cosmic dimension of wisdom, seeing the creation as a vast revelation of divine wisdom through contemplation of which human beings may be raised to a certain likeness with the divine wisdom (*SG* 2.2.2, 5). Such contemplation is the ultimate felicity of humankind (*SG* 3.37.8).[118] Wisdom is, on scriptural grounds, associated especially with the Son and this pertains both to his uncreated and created natures.[119] Aquinas devotes a good deal of attention to the ways in which scriptural references to wisdom may be safely navigated without lapsing into Arianism.[120]

Aquinas was also very much concerned to maintain the connection between wisdom and knowledge, between *sapientia* and *scientia*.[121] He begins his other great *summa*, the *Summa theologiae*, precisely with this question.[122] While reason and philosophy certainly have their place, his opening position is that theology (sacred doctrine) depends not on reason but on revelation. This does not mean that it is not a form of science or knowledge because it proceeds from the knowledge or science of God and of the blessed (*ST* I^a q.1 a.2).[123] It is, in fact, the highest and most unitive form of knowledge, subordinate to no other, and indeed uniquely equipped to judge other forms of knowledge or science (*ST* I^a q.1 a.6 ad 2). Theology is, moreover, to be understood as the highest and most absolute wisdom because it deals with the highest cause, not only in so far as he

what is necessary for life, as one old woman knows by faith after Christ's coming': *The Sermon-Conferences of St. Thomas Aquinas on the Apostles' Creed*, I. See further Bruce Marshall, '*Quod scit una uetula*: Aquinas on the Nature of Theology'.

[118] Aquinas draws on and transcends the Aristotelian understanding of wisdom as the ultimate happiness of humankind. Cf. his *Super Boetium de Trinitate* III q.6 a.4 arg. 3.

[119] For more on Aquinas' wisdom Christology, see Joseph Wawrykow, 'Wisdom in the Christology of Thomas Aquinas'. Wawrykow emphasizes the impact of Thomas' discovery of Greek patristic and conciliar material on his elaboration of a wisdom Christology.

[120] e.g. *SG* 4.8.16 and 4.12: 'How the Son of God may be called the wisdom of God'.

[121] The question of the nature and subject-matter of theology was a fraught question at the time. See further Gregory LaNave, '"A Particularly Agitated Topic": Aquinas and the Franciscans on the Subject of Theology in the Mid-Thirteenth Century' and Boyd Taylor Coolman 'On the Subject-Matter of Theology in the *Summa Halensis* and St. Thomas Aquinas'. Both nuance the distinction between Franciscans and Dominicans on this question.

[122] Note that the theme of wisdom is also highlighted in the beginning of several of Thomas' other works, perhaps most notably in the dedicatory letter prefacing the *Catena aurea* on Matthew in which he speaks of the Son as the 'fount of the wisdom of God' through whom the Father 'wisely and sweetly' orders the universe implanting tokens of that same wisdom throughout creation. Thanks to Fr Andrew Hofer for drawing my attention to this letter.

[123] Note again the broadly Aristotelian frame of philosophical reference.

is known through the creation (as the philosophers of old knew him), 'but also as far as he is known to himself alone and revealed to others' (*ST* Iᵃ q.1 a.6 co.). Wisdom may be a higher and more intimate form of knowledge or science, but this is essentially a difference in degree and not of kind. The essential point is that knowledge and wisdom, *scientia* and *sapientia* form a continuum in Aquinas.

Early in the *Summa theologiae* (Iᵃ q.3), Thomas expands on his doctrine of divine simplicity, categorically asserting that God is identical with his essence, which is identical with his existence, which is identical with all other divine attributes. Terms such as wisdom are definitely not to be understood univocally of humans and God: God is wise by essence whereas human beings possess wisdom as a quality (*ST* Iᵃ q.3 a.4). Thomas goes on to emphasize in the question on divine names that attributes such as wisdom and goodness are predicated substantially of God (*ST* Iᵃ q.13 a.2). While identical with one another according to the simplicity of the divine essence, different terms are used by humans to reflect (very imperfectly) one or other aspect of the perfectly simple divinity (*ST* Iᵃ q.13 a.4). When we say that God is wise we mean not only that he is the source of such wisdom as we possess but also that the quality of wisdom in us exists in him in a higher, more excellent, and ultimately incomprehensible way. The same is true of all the perfections that flow from him (*ST* Iᵃ q.13 a.5–6). While many aspects of Thomas' account were to come heavy pressure in subsequent scholastic theology, notably from Duns Scotus, his account has retained enormous weight in both Protestant and Catholic construals of divine simplicity.[124]

The pursuit of wisdom is, for Thomas, necessarily a lived pursuit. It has been said that the whole of the *Summa theologiae* was written for the sake of the Second Part, with Thomas sandwiching the treatise on ethics very deliberately between the broadly Trinitarian and Christological First and Third Parts.[125] Be that as it may, it is certainly true that Thomas' consideration of the virtuous life is intimately bound up with his foregrounding of wisdom as the orienting and ordering principle of human life. This is particularly evident in Question 45 of the *Secunda secundae* (*On the Gift of Wisdom*). Thomas opens the Question with a re-iteration of his understanding of wisdom as the principle of order par excellence:

---

[124] On Duns Scotus, see further Richard Cross, 'Duns Scotus on God's Essence and Attributes: Metaphysics, Semantics, and the Greek Patristic Tradition'. Cross finds in Scotus an extra-mental distinction between God's essence and attributes that draws on the Greek patristic tradition, notably John of Damascus. The Damascene himself transmits the Cappadocian conception of wisdom and other attributes as signifying that which is 'around the essence' rather than the essence itself—thus precisely the 'gap' for Sophiology that we have traced in the Greek East. Some Orthodox theologians, notably George-Gennadios Scholarios, have detected a deep affinity between the Palamite and Scotist distinctions between God and his attributes, but the further leap from Scotus to Sophiology is not one that Bulgakov or anyone else has been prepared to make.

[125] Mark Jordan, *Ordering Wisdom: The Hierarchy of Philosophical Discourses in Aquinas*, 147 (cf. Fergus Kerr, *After Aquinas*, 117).

According to the philosopher [Aristotle] in the beginning of the *Metaphysics*, it pertains to wisdom to consider the highest cause through which we can form judgments that are most certain about other causes, and according to which all things should be set in order   (*ST* II^{a}II^{ae} q.45 a.1 co.)

Aquinas goes on to make it clear that, while study and effort enables one to acquire wisdom as an intellectual virtue (S1), wisdom in its fullest form is a gift of the Holy Spirit (S2):

Thus it belongs to wisdom as an intellectual virtue to pronounce correct judgment about divine things after rational inquiry, but it belongs to wisdom as a gift of the Holy Spirit to judge correctly concerning them on the basis of connaturality with them, as Dionysius says in Chapter 2 of the *Divine Names* that 'Hierotheus is perfect in divine things, not only learning but experiencing (*patiens*) divine things'.[126]   (*ST* II^{a}II^{ae} q.45 a.2 co.)[127]

This connaturality is, Thomas explains, founded on love. It is love that unites divinity to humanity and enables the human to experience divine things. This experiential conception of wisdom corresponds to the sense of wisdom as tasted or lived knowledge seen in many of Thomas' spiritual and intellectual forebears and which Thomas explicitly takes up, albeit with the typically perspicuous acknowledgement that the felicitous connection between *sapor* and *sapientia* does not apply in the Greek (*ST* II^{a}II^{ae} q.45 a.2 ad 2).[128]

The wise life is very much the virtuous life. Wisdom is necessarily not only speculative but also practical: 'to wisdom belongs first of all contemplation of divine things which is the vision of the beginning, and subsequently the direction of human acts according to divine rules' (*ST* II^{a}II^{ae} q.45 a.3 ad 3). Wisdom may in its fullest and highest form be a gift but human beings can prepare themselves for the reception of that gift through intellectual effort and practical action. As a gift conveying a certain union with divine things, wisdom is given in different degrees and with different purposes but it is assuredly present in all who have love and are without mortal sin and even, he notes, in those who lack the mental capacity to live out the gift of wisdom in action because of some form of disability (*ST* II^{a}II^{ae} q.45 a.5 ad 3). Thomas concludes the *quaestio* with a striking treatment of the seventh beatitude (Mt. 5:9): 'Blessed are the peacemakers, for they shall be called

---

[126] This appeal to the hierarch Hierotheos is also found in *ST* I^a q.1 a.6 ad 3. See further Bernhard Blankenhorn, *The Mystery of Union with God*, 411–37.

[127] Cf. also *ST* II^{a}II^{ae} q.45 a.1 ad 2: 'The wisdom which is called a gift of the Holy Spirit, differs from that which is an acquired intellectual virtue, for the latter is attained by human effort, whereas the former is "descending from above"' (Jas. 3:15). *Quaestio* 45 makes extensive use of descriptions of wisdom given in the Epistle of James, especially the distinction between heavenly and devilish wisdom.

[128] Cf. *ST* I^a q.43 a.5 ad 2: 'Et haec proprie dicitur sapientia, quasi sapida scientia.' Cf. also *ST* II^{a}II^{ae} q.46 a.1 co., in which he cites the *Etymologiae* of Isidore of Seville as the source of this etymology.

the children of God'. This beatitude, he avers, is certainly to be understood in terms of wisdom. A life oriented on wisdom brings peace both to oneself and to others and thus is rightly spoken of in terms of peacemaking. This bringing of peace is in turn a means of being conformed to the Son who is begotten wisdom (S3): 'Hence, by participating in the gift of wisdom, the human being attains to the sonship of God' (*ST* II^{a}II^{ae} q.45 a.6 co.).

Unlike many of his Western contemporaries, Thomas refuses to detach the intellective from the affective or to construe wisdom in affective terms as superior to merely intellective cognition. We have already seen the prominent place he assigns to love in his construal of wisdom. He fully appreciates the affective dimension of wisdom without this leading to any sort of downgrading of the intellective. This approach doubtless has much to do with his holistic account of the human person as an integral unity of body and soul. Wisdom is, rather, to be understood as experiential and integral knowledge, a form of knowledge that unites us to God in love.[129]

Thomas' is perhaps the most complete and nuanced theology of wisdom to come out of the Latin Middle Ages. His is a thoroughly scriptural vision of wisdom, profoundly Christocentric and Trinitarian. Wisdom pertains to God as essence (with which it is identical) and represents the pattern and exemplar of the creation. It is through contemplation of this created wisdom implanted in the creation that human beings attain a certain likeness with the uncreated wisdom. Wisdom is also to be associated particularly with the Son who is both uncreated wisdom (in essence) and, as incarnate, created wisdom. Human beings are called to acquire wisdom as an intellectual virtue so as to be able to articulate and defend the faith. They are also called to live wisely in accordance with the dictates of that faith. Through such action and contemplation (S1) they ready themselves and are readied for the gift of the truest and highest wisdom which comes from the Holy Spirit (S2). It is in and through this wisdom that human beings are incorporated into the life of the one who is wisdom (S3). Given such riches of wisdom teaching, it is hard to see how Bulgakov could be justified in writing off Aquinas and the whole tradition in which he stands as inherently unsophiological.

6.3 *Coda* to the Latin West

This survey, while far from entirely comprehensive, should suffice to demonstrate the depth and richness of the Latin tradition of wisdom reflection down to the

---

[129] See further, Étienne Gilson, *Wisdom and Love in Saint Thomas Aquinas*. Also, Reginald Garrigou-Lagrange, 'L'habitation de la Sainte Trinité et l'expérience mystique', 458. Bernhard Blankenhorn warns us, however, against making too much of experiential language in Thomas: *The Mystery of Union with God*, 429.

High Middle Ages. Perhaps the most obvious feature of this tradition is its indebtedness to Augustine, not only in general terms of heartfelt devotion to wisdom but also in very specific terms of the construal of divine wisdom in terms of divine simplicity. This construal means that there is nothing like the Cappadocian glories, the Dionysian processions, the Maximian doctrine of the *logoi*, or the Palamite energies in which to fit an idea of wisdom as divine but not reducible to categories of substance/essence and person/hypostasis. Even the formal distinction between God and his wisdom later proposed by Duns Scotus is scarcely a sufficient framework for the kind of freight that Bulgakov intends the figure of wisdom to bear.

As a consequence, there is some basis to Bulgakov's claim that the West offers no satisfactory resolution regarding the base sophiological problematic of relating created and uncreated natures—nothing, that is, to stand 'in between' God and the world. The only partial exceptions here would be Eriugena, who seems to hold some form of ontological continuity between the two, and Hildegard, whose theology of wisdom is notoriously difficult to pin down.

The Latin tradition is also home to an emerging disjunct between wisdom (*sapientia*) and knowledge (*scientia*), building on an existing distinction between intellective and affective forms of mysticism. Notwithstanding some resistance (in Aquinas and others), this process was to allow for a bifurcation in which mystical experience was increasingly marginalized and distanced from the 'proper' theology of the schools and universities. Again, this stands in sharp contrast with the Greek East in which mystical theology, communicated in a monastic and ascetic framework, remained normative for the elaboration of dogmatic theology, as was most spectacularly the case with Palamas, Bulgakov's chief patristic resource and authority.

But Bulgakov and his fellow Sophiologists have surely missed a trick in not making more of the Latin wisdom tradition not only to support key aspects of Sophiology but also to rectify some of its glaring deficiencies. To begin with the potential supports, the Latin tradition is consistent in associating divine wisdom in the first instance with the divine essence and only secondarily with the persons (with the Son as the begotten wisdom of the Father and the Spirit as the dispenser of wisdom to the creation). This association of wisdom with the divine essence is a central plank of Sophiology. The Latin tradition makes somewhat more of the feminine dimension of wisdom than does the Greek East (especially Boethius, Bede, and Hildegard) and makes some intriguing connections between wisdom and the Church (Bede and Gregory). The Latin tradition furnishes some compelling accounts of divine wisdom as corresponding to the divine ideas for the creation and as manifest in that creation: 'God in the world and the world in God' (Eriugena, Aquinas). We also see some sophisticated instances of wisdom Christology with Christ treated in terms of the union of uncreated and created wisdom (Gregory, Aquinas). These are all classic themes of Sophiology. And while the widespread Latin aspiration to participate in uncreated wisdom is doubtless insufficiently metaphysically grounded for the likes of Bulgakov, amounting to no more than a distant analogical relation, it would be mistaken to write it off as merely *ersatz* deification in comparison with the more robust models of the Greek East.

But the Latin tradition is perhaps especially valuable for what it can offer to remedy some of the deficiencies and *lacunae* of Sophiology. First and foremost, it maintains a consistent emphasis on themes of human *paideia* and virtuous living (S1) rooted in throughgoing engagement with biblical wisdom literature. This is an aspect of Christian wisdom reflection that tended to recede in the Greek East and which is dramatically underdeveloped in Sophiology. The whole idea of wisdom as lived and 'tasted' knowledge, for example, is something that might significantly enhance a re-envisioned sophiology. The Latin tradition, moreover, in line with the Greek East, consistently emphasizes wisdom as a divine gift (S2)—again a dimension lacking sufficient attention within Sophiology with its focus on the mystical and metaphysical aspects of the wisdom question (S3). Both the supports and the remedies will, of course, find their way into the proposed re-orientation of sophiology in Chapter 7.2. But before that, we need to turn to the long-promised resolution of the base question of patristic rootedness.

7

Sophiology Revisited

7.1 The Patristic Roots of Modern Russian Sophiology

The foregoing survey chapters have borne witness to the dazzling scope of Christian wisdom reflection stretching from scripture down to Palamas in the Greek East and Aquinas in the Latin West. While doubtless missing much, this survey is perhaps the most comprehensive and sustained account of *Wisdom in Christian Tradition* attempted to date. The sheer breadth and depth of Christian wisdom reflection is, however, only rather dimly and partially reflected in modern Russian Sophiology, whose interest in the preceding tradition emerges as rather narrow and confined to a limited set of largely S3 considerations. Sophiology misses out vast swathes and important dimensions of patristic wisdom teachings, notably on levels S1–S2, and dismisses the whole Latin tradition after Augustine as functionally irrelevant. But these lacunae notwithstanding, this survey has lighted upon some important aspects of Sophiology that can indeed be solidly grounded in the patristic tradition, together with much that cannot. This section aims to gather up those various threads and bring the whole question of patristic rootedness to a conclusion.

The origins of Sophiology may lie, as we have argued, outside the patristic tradition, but there is no doubt that the unmodern turn of Sophiology intimated in Soloviev and pursued by Florensky and, above all, Bulgakov, has hit upon a rich lode of patristic wisdom reflection that requires considerably greater attention than it has yet received by Sophiologists and anti-Sophiologists alike. This lode embraces not only controverted or lesser-known patristic writings but universally recognized authorities within Orthodox theology such as Irenaeus, Athanasius, the Cappadocian Fathers, Dionysius, Maximus, and Palamas.

This section on patristic roots is divided into three parts, beginning with a discussion of the nature of tradition and the question of patristic fidelity, moving on to a general assessment of patristic rootedness, and then homing in on Athanasius and Palamas—the pre-eminent patristic authorities adduced by Florensky and Bulgakov, respectively.

7.1.1 Patristic Fidelity and the Nature of Tradition

The Sophiologists would never have claimed that their theology was simply a reiteration or repetition of patristic insights and teachings. Soloviev had instilled a

Wisdom in Christian Tradition: The Patristic Roots of Modern Russian Sophiology. Marcus Plested, Oxford University Press. © Marcus Plested 2022. DOI: 10.1093/oso/9780192863225.003.0008

sense of tradition as necessarily creative and living that continued to mark Russian Orthodox theology of all stripes long after his death. This sense of living tradition is very much evident even in Florovksy who, while calling for a return to the Fathers, castigated a 'theology of repetition' as highly undesirable and certainly not properly faithful to the tradition.[1] Soloviev, as we have noted, felt positively propelled to exceed all that had gone before and showed little interest in burnishing the patristic credentials of Sophia. But Florensky and Bulgakov, while fully embracing a dynamic understanding of tradition, evince a greater deference to the patristic witness and devote correspondingly greater effort to the demonstration of the continuity of Sophiology with patristic tradition.[2]

As we saw in Chapter 1.5, in the Sophia controversy of the 1930s both sides affirmed the need for a dynamic and living sense of patristic tradition and for modern Orthodox theology to serve as a creative reaffirmation of that tradition in order to meet contemporary needs and answer contemporary questions. The big question was just how creative that reaffirmation might be—in what sense might one go beyond the Fathers while remaining true to their legacy?

Bulgakov set forth his own take on the question in his essay 'Dogma and Dogmatics', distinguishing between a fixed and rather limited core of dogma and the rather more open sphere of dogmatics or dogmatic theology.[3] The fixed core is presented as inviolable and immovable, albeit always susceptible of further explication and elaboration.[4] But in the more open sphere of dogmatic theology, much more is possible and indeed demanded of the theologian. In this sphere the Fathers are especially precious and authoritative, but not infallible guides.[5] Bulgakov cedes little to Florovsky (or indeed Lossky) in his acknowledgement that, 'It is widely accepted that dogmatic theology has to proceed *according to the Fathers* and to agree with patristic tradition'.[6] But Bulgakov wants to probe what this really means and has a rather more limited sense than Florovsky or Lossky of the extent and scope of the patristic tradition to which conformity is enjoined, amounting in practice to a rather limited sphere of dogma. Beyond that limited sphere, considerable latitude is allowed, albeit always with the professed intent of fidelity to the patristic tradition, broadly conceived. This distinction helps explain the frankness with which he confronts the perceived weaknesses, historical

---

[1] Florovsky, 'St Gregory Palamas and the Tradition of the Fathers', 110–11.

[2] I want to thank Jennifer Newsome Martin for her constructive and suggestive response to my paper on patristic reception in Sophiology at the Boston College Historical Colloquy (2018).

[3] His approach is analogous to that of Origen, who opened his treatise *On First Principles* with the observation that beyond certain necessary points clearly established in the apostolic tradition there was a great deal of scope for lovers of wisdom to explore and expound that tradition further, under the guidance of the Holy Spirit, and so become 'fit and worthy recipients of wisdom' (*DP*, preface 3). Florovsky, for his part, saw Bulgakov as a new Origen and veiled much of his critique of his sometime patron behind an empassioned and sustained antipathy to Origen and Origenism.

[4] 'Dogma and Dogmatics', 8–9 [ET 67–8] and *passim*. Cf. Andrew Louth, 'Is Development of Doctrine a Valid Category for Orthodox Theology?'.

[5] 'Dogma and Dogmatics', 12–17 [ET 70–3].   [6] 'Dogma and Dogmatics', 12 [ET 70].

limitations, plurivocity, and incompleteness of patristic theology, as well as his willingness to expand upon patristic testimony with his own intellectual contributions. Bulgakov was rightly convinced that the scope of revelation (and indeed the patristic age itself) was not yet closed, that the Holy Spirit has much yet to teach us (cf. John 14:26). He was also consistent in acknowledging the provisional and speculative nature of his Sophiology. As he put it to Metropolitan Evlogy in the midst of the Sophia controversy: 'I profess all the true dogmas of Orthodoxy. My sophiology has nothing to do with the actual content of those dogmas, but merely with their theological interpretation'.[7] Where he came unstuck was, of course, precisely on this question of interpretation—on quite how creative one could be in retrieving the Fathers.

In practice there is little to separate Bulgakov or indeed Florensky from their neo-patristic epigones in terms of the vision of Orthodox theology as a dynamic and creative reaffirmation of patristic tradition. Where Bulgakov, in particular, differs from his detractors lies not so much in his readiness to explore, expound, and interpret the patristic tradition—everyone was doing that—but in his overt willingness to 'complete' that tradition in some core respects. His detractors tended to stay within what Florensky had called 'the bounds of Church ideas'— interpreting the Fathers, certainly, but refraining from overt criticism or from positing conclusions that could not be readily grounded in the patristic tradition. The difference here is not between two divergent theological systems: one patristic and traditional and the other philosophical and innovative.[8] The difference is rather one of degree within a Russian theological community that shared many of the same basic assumptions.

Bulgakov did much to inspire the return to the Fathers that has marked so much of Orthodox theology in the twentieth century. In pursuing Sophiology's unmodern turn, his own theology became profoundly patristic in its grounding, inspiration, and shape. His mature theology is in no way 'post-patristic', nor does it espouse a notion of development of doctrine that would in any way supplement or add to the given fullness of the faith of the Church. Like his detractors, he regards the patristic witness as essentially *normative*: the Church Fathers are seen to provide a paradigm of theology and practice which we are called on to faithfully and creatively 'translate' to our own specific contexts—preferably within the context of a living tradition, a continuum of faith.[9] But while sharing an aspiration

---

[7] Cited in Nikolai Lossky, *History of Russian Philosophy*, 232.

[8] There is a growing recognition in modern Orthodox theology of the substantial commonalities between the neo-patristic and Russian Religious 'schools'. See especially the work of Paul Gavrilyuk (e.g. *Georges Florovsky and the Russian Religious Renaissance* (esp. Chapters 8 and 15)) and Brandon Gallaher (e.g. 'The "Sophiological" Origins of Vladimir Lossky's Apophaticism'). Some of my own thoughts on the topic were adumbrated in a review of Paul Vallière's *Modern Russian Theology* which works very much with a sense of eternal opposition between the two 'schools'.

[9] Cf. the seven models of patristic reception and re-appropriation in my 'Reflection on the Reception of the Church Fathers in the Contemporary Context', 12–13.

to creative fidelity with his detractors, Bulgakov differs from them in his willingness to boldly go beyond the Fathers and to 'complete' their work. This is not
something his detractors could countenance, at least not openly.

The tragedy here is that, for all the basic similarities of approach, the success
and effectiveness of the anti-Sophiological reaction to certain aspects of
Bulgakov's patristic *transcensus* has tended to militate against any very serious
constructive engagement with Sophiology in modern Orthodox thought of a
broadly neo-patristic or neo-Palamite persuasion. To identify or even sympathize
with Sophiology is still a perilous exercise for an Orthodox theologian interested
in maintaining his or her reputation as a faithful Orthodox. More to the point, the
anti-Sophiological reaction has seriously obscured the very real degree to which
Sophiology (at least as pursued by Florensky and, especially, Bulgakov) has indeed
tapped into a rich vein of patristic sophiology and sapiential theology. While
starting life well outside the Orthodox mainstream, Sophiology's unmodern turn
found far more grounding in patristic tradition than its detractors were ever able
to allow.

7.1.2 General Assessment

While a general assessment of the patristic rootedness of Sophiology must contend
not only with the sheer vastness of the patristic tradition but also with the
multifarious plurivocity of Sophiology, it is nonetheless possible to distinguish
some areas in which Sophiology across its various manifestations was able to find
purchase. Throughout the survey chapters we have noted a clear and consistent
sense of wisdom as a primary, if not *the* primary, designation of God, both
according to essence and according to hypostasis. On the hypostatic level, the
standard association of wisdom with the person of the Son (going back to Justin
and Origen) has obvious scriptural and exegetical grounds but is complemented
by a recurrent association of wisdom with the Spirit (Irenaeus, Hippolytus,
Theophilus, Evagrius) and with the work of the Spirit (Maximus, Palamas).
Moreover, the association of wisdom principally with the essence or substance
of God is crystal clear in the Cappadocians, Augustine, Dionysius, Maximus, and
Palamas—and indeed the entire Latin tradition. Thus Sophiology's consistent
contention that the category of wisdom cannot simply be reduced to the person
of the Son has some very heavyweight support.

God's self-revelation in the creation is also routinely described in terms of
wisdom in patristic tradition. Wisdom is an indispensable category of patristic
cosmology and amounts to a perfectly sophianic vision of the cosmos—a world
alive and aflame with the wisdom of God. The Church Fathers furnish numerous
examples of a non-dualist and even perichoretic account of the relationship
between God and the world that fully respects their ontological discontinuity.

There are, in other words, ample grounds in patristic tradition for asserting a robust vision of 'God in the world and the world in God'. One of the chief supports for this sophianic vision is, as we have seen, the idea of the eternal pre-existence of the ideas of the creation within God. This broadly Platonic theme is absolutely commonplace in patristic tradition, albeit with some considerable variation in the understanding of their mutual interrelation and ontological character. Broadly speaking, we may suggest that the Greek tradition (Clement of Alexandria, Athanasius, the Cappadocians, Dionysius, Maximus, and Palamas) tends to regard the divine ideas for the creation as eternal and therefore uncreated while the Latin tradition (Tertullian and Augustine, followed later by Aquinas) tends to regard them as sourced in God but themselves temporal (or perhaps pan-temporal) and created. The two traditions thus focus respectively on the divine and created aspects of wisdom while attempting, in their rather different ways, to relate the one to the other.

In the Greek tradition, it becomes possible to distinguish divine wisdom from categories of essence and hypostasis and so speak of wisdom variously in terms of the glories, processions, predeterminations, *logoi*, or energies pertaining to the essence and made manifest in and through the divine persons. This construal of wisdom as distinct but inseparable from both essence and hypostasis allows for radical divine immanence and for the real participation of the creature in God without compromising either divine simplicity or divine transcendence. The dominant Latin model of divine simplicity in terms of the identity of God and his attributes precludes acceptance of such a construal. The Latin tradition, of course, has its own particular ways of relating the creature to its uncreated origin, whether by way of analogy or by way of created grace, enabling the creature to rise up and to meet its God. Neither Greek nor Latin tradition, however, quite comes up to scratch as far as Bulgakov is concerned, whether through alleged failure to connect divine wisdom with the divine persons or through insufficient thinking-through of the implications of the doctrine in terms of the relation between the created and uncreated aspects of wisdom as reflecting two aspects of the same reality. That said, Bulgakov rightly saw greater potential in the Greek East and was certainly correct to latch onto this Greek tradition as proffering a space or gap for Sophiology that was lacking in to the Latin West.

For many Fathers (Athanasius, Augustine, the Cappadocians, and Gregory the Great, and also figures such as Origen and Aquinas), created and uncreated wisdom are seen to be united in the person of Christ—a mystery of unconfused union that found its least imperfect expression in the Definition of Chalcedon. Bulgakov made ever more use of this Christological dimension of wisdom in his works of exile, above all *The Lamb of God*, which signals a move from the antinomical 'neither-nor' model of his pre-exilic works to the more dogmatically secure 'both-and' model of his later works—wisdom, that is, as both uncreated and created. While Bulgakov continued to resist any very exclusive association of wisdom with the Son, he was certainly onto something of cardinal importance in returning to and renewing patristic wisdom Christology in this way.

Bulgakov's increasing Christological emphasis tapped into a broader stream of patristic wisdom reflection in which wisdom is inescapably bound up with soteriology—with God's providential and salvific ordering of the creation *in via*. While it is open to considerable doubt whether Bulgakov or indeed any of the Sophiologists fully centre their world view on the apparent folly of the Cross, Bulgakov's musings on, for example, divine *kenosis* and the eternity of Golgotha within the divine being are of perennial fascination and immense value.[10]

Sophiology has surely also filled something of a lacuna in the patristic wisdom tradition in attempting to give real meaning and import to the specifically feminine character of wisdom as presented in the Old Testament. This is an aspect of the biblical wisdom tradition that is regrettably muted in patristic and indeed medieval treatments of wisdom—with some splendid exceptions. The related connection between wisdom and the pre-existent Church (also typically understood as a feminine) does, on the other hand, have definite purchase in the tradition.[11] Connections between Mary, the Mother of God, and wisdom are perhaps more evident in liturgical sources rather than patristic texts while connections made between wisdom and the saints and angels have ample if rather general grounding in the tradition. Sophiology has done a great service in emphasizing the sheer breadth and depth of wisdom's multi-faceted manifestations even as it struggled mightily to maintain some hold on that elusive plurivocity.

But there is much in modern Russian Sophiology that has no ready grounding in patristic tradition: above all the idea of wisdom as God's primal self-revelation to himself constituting a divine 'other', a liminal principle of divine humanity (as in Soloviev and Florensky) or, more specifically (as in Bulgakov), a principle of divine humanity capable of hypostasization in multiple uncreated and created forms. The patristic tradition does not warrant any idea of God's self-revelation to himself except in relation to the Trinitarian persons and certainly not as constituting some sort of underlying pre-principle manifest in those divine persons, in Christ, in Mary, in the world, in the angels and the saints, etc. Any hint of a ground or fount of divinity distinct from the Trinity must be reckoned as decidedly foreign to patristic thinking. Similarly, the absolute-relative axis so regularly employed within Sophiology emphatically does not map onto patristic treatments of divine transcendence and immanence, hiddenness and revelation,

---

[10] See further on this theme Nadejda Gorodetzky, *The Humiliated Christ in Modern Russian Thought* and Piero Coda, *L'altro di Dio: rivelazione e kenosi in Sergej Bulgakov*.

[11] The connection between wisdom and the Church is most explicit in Hermas, Gregory the Great, and Bede. Hermas (but not Gregory or Bede) is made much of by both Florensky and Bulgakov. The connection between wisdom and Mary, while long established in the liturgical tradition (including the early Byzantine *Akathist Hymn*), seems to be more obviously a feature of the later Latin theological tradition—as seen especially in Hildegard and Bernard.

and so forth. All of these elements—which amount to a considerable part of what Sophiology is—issue from sources extrinsic to the patristic tradition and, indeed, Orthodox tradition more generally.

Sophiology, moreover, misses a great deal from the tradition—not least from the Bible. Soloviev's Sophia has only distant connections to the wisdom figure of the Old Testament, while Florensky and Bulgakov tend to focus on that rather ambiguous figure somewhat at the expense of the rather more concrete wisdom figure of the New Testament—Christ. Even when it comes to the New Testament, there is more attention paid to the mysterious and enigmatic images of Revelation than the more down-to-earth picture of incarnate wisdom presented in the Gospels. There is, moreover, little remaining in Sophiology of the specifically sapiential and pedagogical dimension of biblical and classical wisdom traditions that so permeates patristic and later Latin treatments of the theme. We also have little in Sophiology on the potential usefulness or otherwise of merely human knowledge (S0–S1). Sophiology, furthermore, provides scant guidance on basic issues of ethics and virtuous living—on life and how to live it. It does not draw deeply on biblical and later Christian wisdom literature or, indeed, of the vast store of the lived wisdom of the great ascetics and monastics, beyond the rather general inspiration adduced in particular by Florensky. Similarly, the prominent patristic theme of participatory and gifted knowledge (S2) is rather subsumed in Sophiology behind considerations of a more mystical and metaphysical character (S3).

In sum, Sophiology, especially as articulated by Bulgakov, is indeed firmly rooted in patristic tradition in some of its base affirmations, notably in its apperception of the coinherence of God and the world, its insistence that divine wisdom is not reducible to the person of the Son, its intuition of the potential utility of the essence-energies distinction, and its renewal of a wisdom Christology. In all of these respects it can find considerable grounding and support. Sophiology has also rightly retrieved some understated aspects of Christian wisdom reflection, notably the feminine dimension of wisdom and the connection between wisdom, the Church, and the Mother of God. But quite apart from its missing so much on levels S1–S2, there is a glaring problem in that some of the key intuitions of Sophiology are blatantly incompatible with patristic tradition—above all the idea of wisdom as a primal other, a pre-principle of divine humanity irreducible to categories of essence and hypostasis. Sophiology is clearly rooted in patristic tradition, but only up to a point.

To put all this in iconic terms is not easy. Sophia is something of a shape-shifter, varying considerably both within and between the works of her chief advocates. There are fleeting glimpses of recognizable continuity with the image of wisdom depicted in the patristic tradition but also some curious omissions and some highly problematic additions. Even in Bulgakov's mature work, in which Sophia is most expressly and intentionally conformed to patristic tradition, she remains somewhat fuzzy: not unambiguously the 'Sophia of the Church' but, then again, not entirely the 'other Sophia' of Florovsky's schema—the Sophia of Philo and the Gnostics, of Boehme and the Kabbalah.[12] To go deeper in our exploration of patristic rootedness, we need a fixed point of reference in figures whom the Sophiologists themselves invite us to focus on as pre-eminent instances of patristic authority.

7.1.3 Specific Fathers: Athanasius and Palamas

Discussion of patristic rootedness in general terms clearly gets us only so far. It would be very easy to get bogged down in discussions of the possibility of doctrinal development within Orthodox theology, or of Sophiology's fidelity to this or that patristic or conciliar teaching, or of permissible degrees of creativity in the retrieval of tradition. As we have demonstrated, there is plainly much in Sophiology that finds deep roots in Orthodox tradition and much that is clearly and avowedly new and unprecedented in relation to that tradition. The Sophiologists themselves make no bones about this. But where we can make a very exact judgement concerning continuity or otherwise with patristic tradition is precisely in respect of the figures they invite us to concentrate on—St Athanasius in Florensky's case and St Gregory Palamas for Bulgakov. Many Church Fathers are mentioned and appealed to in the course of Sophiology's unmodern turn but these two alone stand out as peerless authorities. While Soloviev had adduced no prime patristic authority, Florensky declares that *The Pillar and Ground of Truth* comes out of the ideas of Athanasius, and Bulgakov goes even further in claiming that, in accepting Palamite theology, the Orthodox Church has 'definitively entered onto the path of accepting the sophiological dogma'.[13] For all its perceived incompleteness and deficiencies, most notably in respect of Trinitarian theology, Bulgakov sees a direct continuity and conformity between his theology and that of St Gregory Palamas 'in its inner sense'.[14] This typically pugnacious claim with sweeping ramifications merits particularly close analysis. But first, and somewhat more briefly, let us turn to Florensky.

Florensky, as we have noted, asserts that the central features of Sophiology are 'scattered in abundance' in scripture and patristic tradition. By this he meant above all the pre-existence of Sophia as the eternal archetype of creation, as the 'hypostatic system of the world-creating thoughts of God, and the true pole and incorruptible aspect of created being'.[15] There is no doubt that Florensky is justified in appealing to Athanasius as a key patristic witness for the idea of creaturely wisdom as the imprint and image of the hypostatic wisdom in whom

---

[12] Cf. above, pp.68–9.   [13] *The Bride of the Lamb*, 24 [ET 19].
[14] *The Burning Bush*, 287 [ET 156].   [15] *The Pillar and Ground of Truth*, 332 [ET 241].

the whole creation is eternally pre-figured.[16] Florensky values Athanasius as someone who could never be accused of pantheism despite affirming the 'divine side' of creation: '[Athanasius] devoted his entire life to the definitive condemnation of heretics who were attempting to erase the boundary between Creator and creation. That is why Athanasius' testimony is of incomparable importance to us.'[17] Florensky is of course only too aware of the charges of pantheism that have perennially accompanied modern Russian Sophiology.[18] He sums up his overall debt to Athanasius in the most far-reaching of terms:

> The dogma of the consubstantiality of the Trinity, the idea of the deification of the flesh, the demands of asceticism, the longing for the Spirit, the Comforter, and the recognition that the creation has an incorruptible, pre-mundane significance – these are the leitmotifs of Athanasius' dogmatic system. These leitmotifs are so closely intertwined that one cannot hear one without discovering it in all the others. This entire book is built on these leitmotifs so that one can truly say that it comes out of the ideas of St Athanasius the Great.[19]

While deeply revealing on the overall motivations of Florensky's project, it has to be said that Florensky has built rather more on this foundation than is immediately warranted by Athanasius himself. For example, he breaks the unshakeable connection that Athanasius established between wisdom (both created and uncreated) and the incarnate Word of God, preferring instead to emphasize the Trinitarian dimension of wisdom as God's self-revelation in the form of an eternal creation. When Florensky claims that Athanasius professes wisdom as 'a pre-cosmic hypostatic collection of divine prototypes of that which exists' the referent of the term 'hypostatic' is quite different from anything found in Athanasius, in whom the term points unambiguously to the Son.[20] And while it is not in itself problematic to emphasize the Trinitarian as opposed to logocentric dimension of wisdom—many of the Fathers did that—what is far more problematic is Florensky's making of wisdom a quasi-divine hypostasis (not God but also not not God) who inhabits something of a liminal zone in-between creation and the Creator: created but supra-mundane and somehow eternal.[21] As a free-floating, quasi-divine creature present both in the creation and in God, Florensky's Sophia occupies a rather anomalous position in terms of patristic theology. There is also scant patristic warrant—in Athanasius or anyone else—for the personalization of

---

[16] Cf. Chapter 1.3. [17] *The Pillar and Ground of Truth*, 348 [ET 252].

[18] Cf. also Florensky's criticism of the pantheism of Count Speransky: *The Pillar and Ground of Truth*, 331–2 [ET 241].

[19] *The Pillar and Ground of Truth*, 348–9 [ET 252].

[20] *The Pillar and Ground of Truth*, 348 [ET 251–52].

[21] One might almost say, with Arius, 'a creature, but not as one of the creatures'. Athanasius was, of course, precisely concerned to eliminate any such liminal zone.

divine Sophia except by reference back to the persons of the Trinity. All in all, while there are certainly plentiful connections to be drawn between Florensky's Sophiology and patristic tradition more generally, the specific instance of Athanasius allows us to make a more definite and precise judgement. In a nutshell, Florensky's appeal to Athanasius, and indeed patristic tradition more generally, must be regarded more as fidelity by intent than in actual execution. In practice, he has indeed gone far beyond his ostensible self-restriction within the 'bounds of Church ideas'.

Turning now to our other dyad of Bulgakov and Palamas, it is worth under-lining once again quite how pioneering Fr Sergius' work was: he was ahead of most of his compatriots in devoting so much attention to Palamas, and even in the Greek world serious studies were few and far between.[22] The whole Palamite retrieval in twentieth century Orthodox theology owes a great deal to Bulgakov, even if it was largely dedicated to proving him wrong. But Bulgakov's treatment of Palamas remains rather sparing and necessarily limited in its access to and use of primary sources. He offers no very sustained exploration of Palamas' theology tending rather to assert repeatedly its consistency with Sophiological teaching. He also regularly kicks the question of the relation between the persons of the Trinity and the energies into the long grass. But it is nonetheless clear that Bulgakov is in many respects a reliable guide to St Gregory's theology. For instance, he sees clearly that the essence-energies distinction is not a derogation of divine simplicity and that it does not introduce some sort of sealed-off and forbidden dimension in God to which we have no access since the *energeia* of God is precisely the *ousia* revealed.[23] As Bulgakov rightly observes: 'energy proves to be the means of communicating οὐσία'.[24] Because the essence of God is simple and indivisible, the multiform and 'myriohypostatic' energies communicate the whole God.[25] As Palamas himself puts it: 'the imparticipability of the essence does not in any way prevent participation in or knowledge of the whole God through each of the energies'.[26]

But Bulgakov is also prone to some serious misunderstandings of Palamas, notably his mapping of the essence-energies distinction onto the boundaries between cataphatic and apophatic theology and the related assumption that the

[22] Grigorios Papamichail is an exception. See his 1911 publication, Ὁ ἅγιος Γρηγόριος Παλαμᾶς ἀρχιεπίσκοπος Θεσσαλονίκης.
[23] See further my 'St Gregory Palamas on the Divine Simplicity', 509.
[24] *Unfading Light*, 126 [ET 133].
[25] Bulgakov (ibid.) cites 'PG 151 941' here (= *Theophanes* 20; Chrestou II 245–6). In this passage, Gregory is making the point that while the energy of God is the common action of the trihypostatic divinity, this single energy is communicated in myriad ways. Note that Gregory himself (as 'Theophanes') does not describe the energies precisely as 'myriohyposatic'. The term comes from Theophanes' ostensible interlocutor Theotimos, who fears that such talk might lead to a multiplication of the persons of the divinity (PG 151 941A; Chrestou II 245)). Bulgakov has slightly mispresented or misread the source here, but not the overall sense.
[26] *Theophanes* 16 (PG 151 936B; Chrestou II 240). Cited from PG in *Unfading Light*, 126 [ET 133].

energies are to be understood solely as an operation of God *ad extra*. As Bulgakov puts it: 'the distinction between οὐσία and ἐνέργεια coincides with the boundaries between negative and positive theology: οὐσία corresponds to the transcendent essence of God, ἐνέργεια is his manifestation in the world'.[27] Some energies, in Palamas' account, do indeed relate to the world (such as the energy of creation or of deification), but others (such as wisdom, goodness, and power) clearly relate to the eternal being and character of God.[28] God, moreover, always remains unknowable even as he communicates something of himself in his energies.

There are other oddities in Bulgakov's presentation of Palamas, including his strange conflation of *ousia* and Sophia as the source of the energies and thus generative of wisdom in her creaturely aspect.[29] Similarly problematic is his presentation of Palamite theology as a species of antinomy corresponding to the Absolute-Relative dialectic of German Idealism.[30] Bulgakov reads Palamas' teaching on the divine energies not only as 'myriohypostatic' but also as 'God's self-realization as God'.[31] This framing of Palamas's teaching as God's self-realization in multiple hypostatic forms prepares the ground for much of what Bulgakov goes on to say on the subject of Sophia. But such talk of God's self-realization as God is certainly not readily attested in Palamas.

Some of Bulgakov's misapprehensions are shared by Vladimir Lossky who similarly reads the essence-energies distinction along apophatic-cataphatic lines and claims that the attributes or energies are 'subsequent to the essence and are its natural manifestations but are external to the very being of the Trinity'.[32] Lossky is here attacking Bulgakov's peculiar conflation of *ousia* and Sophia as the principle of the godhead and thus emphasizing the exteriority and even inferiority of the energies. Lossky also mirrors Bulgakov in treating the essence-energies distinction as a species of antinomy rather than as the carefully worked-out and rationally coherent doctrine it is in Palamas' own works.[33] Both Bulgakov and Lossky run a serious risk of presenting Palamas as a functional neo-Platonist with the energies 'streaming' or 'radiating' from the hidden oneness of God without apparent reference to the Trinitarian persons.

John Meyendorff has done much to correct some of the misapprehensions of both Lossky and Bulgakov on the basis of a deep plunge into the whole Palamite corpus founded on some magnificent manuscript work. Meyendorff plays down the notion of antinomy and noticeably avoids reducing the essence-energies distinction to a simple apophatic–cataphatic axis. Furthermore, he refuses to

---

[27] *Unfading Light*, 125 [ET] 133.
[28] Cf. Maximus on the eternal *logoi* and *logoi* of created things above, p.176.
[29] *The Bride of the Lamb*, 72 [ET 63].   [30] *Lamb of God*, 143n [ET 122n].
[31] *Unfading Light*, 124–6 [ET 132–33] (referring to *Theophanes* 20 in PG 941 A-D (= Chrestou II 245–46)).
[32] *Mystical Theology*, 80–1.
[33] See further, Norman Russell, *Gregory Palamas and the Making of Palamism in the Modern Age*, 3, 64–5.

limit his understanding of the energies to the relation between God and the world, rightly recognizing the energies to pertain to God both *ad intra* and *ad extra*. Against Bulgakov, Meyendorff flatly denies that God contemplates, loves, or realizes himself in the energies. There is no passivity in the action of God which is properly pure act: 'the energies are not an object and neither do they constitute a Platonic ideal world or a Bulgakovian Sophia which, while identifying itself with the essence of God, is an object of love for him'.[34] Most crucially, Meyendorff upholds the clear connection Palamas makes between Trinitarian theology and the essence-energies distinction—a connection neither Bulgakov nor Lossky fully appreciated.

Meyendorff's retrieval of Palamas is expressly anti-Bulgakovian: he is certainly not prepared to allow that Bulgakov's teaching is a natural outworking of Palamite theology. But in correcting some of Bulgakov's (and, less explicitly, Lossky's) misapprehensions, Meyendorff offers some important pointers towards a possible reconfiguration of sophiology in line with Palamite teaching. Such a reconfiguration requires in particular a concerted reconsideration of the Trinitarian dimension of that teaching.

There is a basic weakness in Bulgakov's attempted appropriation of Palamas in that he fails to appreciate the connection Palamas establishes between the energies and the divine persons. In particular, Bulgakov misses the appeal to the principles of the Sixth Ecumenical Council (Constantinople III) that was so central to both Palamas and his supporters.[35] The sixth council established a basically Aristotelian parallelism between nature and energy: where there is a nature, there is an energy. Thus while the divine energies are multiple in character, they are to be understood as manifestations of the single undifferentiated energy of the divine nature. The sixth council, however, also established that energy is operative on the level of the person or hypostasis. In Christ there are two natures, thus two energies (and wills) but only one active subject—one person, one actor, one willer. By extension, the energy or operation of God is only ever a Trinitarian operation. The energies are not impersonal but come from the Father, through the Son, and in the Spirit. This dynamic, both eternal and temporal, is evident even in his early *Apodictic Treatises*: 'The Spirit eternally flows forth from the Father into the Son and becomes manifest in the saints from the Father through the Son.'[36] This dynamic is also apparent in Palamas' brief but exact *Confession* produced at the Council of Constantinople in 1351.[37] Having evoked the eternal divine *perichoresis* in which the Spirit proceeds from the Father and rests eternally in the Son, Palamas goes on to speak of the manifestation of the Spirit in the creation from the Father through

---

[34] *Introduction à l'étude de saint Grégoire Palamas*, 309.
[35] See further my 'Divine simplicity in St Gregory Palamas', 511.
[36] *Apodictic Treatise* 2.58 (Chrestou I 131).
[37] *Confession of 1351* (PG 151 763D–768C [ET 339]).

the Son. But this mission of the Spirit, this manifestation of God in the world, is a common task. As Palamas goes on to explain:

> [The Spirit] is not made known according to essence – for no one has ever seen or revealed God's nature – but according to grace, power, operation, which is common to the Father, and the Son, and the Spirit. The distinguishing feature of each is the hypostasis and whatever refers to it. They not only possess mutually the superessential essence which is entirely unnameable, unrevealed, and incommunicable (for it is above every name, manifestation and participation), but the grace, the power, the operation, the brightness, the kingdom, the incorruption, and to put it simply, all the means by which God communicates, and by which, according to grace, he is united with the holy angels and humans; without being deprived of his simplicity either as a result of the divisibility and distinction of the hypostases or as a result of the divisibility and multiplicity of the powers and operations.

The divine energies are, in short, inescapably Trinitarian in character. Although themselves non-hypostatic, they are the common operations or attributes of the three persons or hypostases of the Trinity. While it is frequently the Spirit who is invoked as the source of sanctification and deification, as the one who incorporates humans into the divine life, this is always to be understood as a Trinitarian operation.[38] In his most mature work, Palamas expresses the reciprocal relation between Trinitarian theology and the divine energies in the most exquisitely precise of terms:

> The names particular to the divine hypostases are common with regard to the energies whereas the names common to the hypostases are particular with regard to the divine energies. For life is the common name of the Father, Son, and Spirit but foreknowledge is not called life, nor simplicity, nor immutability, nor any other such thing. Thus each of the things which we have enumerated is the common name of the Father, Son, and Spirit, of one energy but not of all, for each bears but one meaning. But the particular name of one of the hypostases, the 'Father', encompasses all of these for he is not only life but also immutability and mercy and divine simplicity and all such things. Similarly with the names 'Son' and 'Holy Spirit', for 'all mine are thine and thine are mine' (Jn. 17:10), as the divine Word says to his own Father. And in turn, all that is of the Father and of [the Son] is to be attributed in common and unitedly to the divine Spirit. Thus God is divided according to the hypostases, while remaining united according to the energies, for these are the energies of the Father, the Son, and the Holy Spirit.[39]

---

[38] See, for example, *Triads* 3.1.33.

[39] *Against Akindynos* 5.27.113 (Chrestou III 373–4). Palamas goes on to draw out the implications of all this for human deification: the whole God is present in each of the persons and in each of the energies thus participation in one of the energies is participation in the whole of God, in the Father, the Son, and the Holy Spirit. As noted above (p.42) this is not a work that was accessible to Bulgakov.

Passages such as these, which could be multiplied further, should suffice to show the baselessness of the charge put by Bulgakov and other modern critics that Palamas has not sufficiently thought through the connection between his teaching on the divine energies and Trinitarian dogma.[40] Far from being impersonal rays streaming out antinomically from some unfathomable and inaccessible *Urgrund* of divinity, the energies are inescapably the operations and attributes of the Father, the Son, and the Holy Spirit.

The fact that the energies are irrefragably tied to the Holy Trinity in this way means, of course, that there is no space for uncreated wisdom in the Palamite schema except in relation to the categories of essence, hypostasis, and energy: God is wisdom, Father, Son, and Spirit are wisdom, and wisdom is an eternal operation or attribute of God. The Son is to be understood and confessed specifically as wisdom incarnate. We may also, according to Palamas, speak of a wisdom implanted in the natural creation—of created wisdom.[41] But there is no scope for wisdom as principle capable of hypostasization that is not itself a hypostasis, as somehow hovering between created and uncreated modes of being, or as the source (as 'ousia-sophia') of the radiating energies.[42] While Palamas might certainly have made more of the specifically Christological and indeed the feminine dimension of wisdom so stressed by Bulgakov, it has to be acknowledged that there is nothing glaringly incomplete about his conceptualization of wisdom. By the same token, acceptance of Palamite doctrine can scarcely be said to set one irrevocably on the road to accepting Bulgakovian Sophiology.

Ultimately, as with Florensky's appeal to Athanasius, Bulgakov has built rather more on Palamas than is immediately warranted, producing a very different image of Sophia. Bulgakov's portrayal of Palamas is distinctly awry, above all in his construal of the essence-energies distinction and his failure to appreciate the relation between the energies and the Trinity. This leads one to wonder, given the extraordinary premium he places on Palamas, what sophiology might look like were it to be more fully and accurately grounded in Palamas.

Bulgakov's failure to perceive the rather precise way in which Palamas ties the energies to Trinitarian theology reflects something of a general weakness in his own thinking. In his schema, Sophia hovers between the traditional Orthodox dogmatic categories of essence, hypostasis, and energy—and indeed between Creator and creation. Bulgakov evidently feels the need for a 'missing link' to tie these categories together within God and in turn to bind God to the world in an eternal embrace. But is such a 'missing link' really necessary? Is it not possible that a 'correct sophiology' conformed to patristic and specifically Palamite theology, along the lines suggested by Evdokimov, might fulfil virtually all that Bulgakov

---

[40] For modern critics of Palamas' Trinitarian theology (LaCugna, Jenson, Wendebourg, etc.) see my *Orthodox Readings of Aquinas*, 32–4.
[41] For Palamas on created wisdom, cf. above, p.183.   [42] Cf. above, p.57.

aspires to achieve without recourse to a theologically indeterminate and inherently problematic notion of Sophia? It is my contention that such a 'correct sophiology', grounded on firm scriptural and patristic foundations (including what Florovsky called the 'Sophia of the Church'), can convey and underpin all the essentials of Bulgakov's Sophiology: a vision of the coinherence of God and the world ('God in the world and the world in God'); a unified account of God (as essence, hypostasis, and energy) eternally united to the creation in a mystery of union without confusion; a pattern and paradigm for human salvation and deification; a revitalization of Orthodox systematic theology; a theologically grounded epistemology and philosophy of history; a theology that is profoundly traditional but also creative—in short, an unmodern theology ready and equipped to engage the modern world.

7.2 A Re-Oriented Sophiology

In proposing a re-oriented sophiology I do not suppose myself to be vying with Bulgakov's astonishing theological genius: this is very much dwarves on the shoulders of giants territory. What I am trying to do is to complete, or at least point to the completion of, Sophiology's unmodern turn. This constructive proposal, in other words, seeks to bring to fruition the turn to the patristic and specifically Palamite tradition marked out within Sophiology itself, above all in the work of Bulgakov.

Sophiology's unmodern turn, hinted at in Soloviev, taken up by Florensky, and coming closest to realization in Bulgakov, represents something of a reverse flip in a theological movement that began as a species of anti-modernism with numerous non-o/Orthodox sources and inspirations but which ended up rediscovering something of immense importance and enduring value within the Orthodox Christian tradition.

As noted in the introduction, this constructive proposal may be considered as a process of 'orientation and descent'. To pursue and complete the unmodern turn of Sophiology requires a re-alignment with patristic and specifically Palamite tradition accompanied by a deep plunge into the wisdom reflection of both East and West. There is, of course, nothing new to the suggestion that Sophiology might stand in need of some correction. In addition to Evdokimov's call for a 'correct' (i.e. Palamite) sophiology, Olivier Clément—another great modern advocate of Sophiology—wrote of the need for it to be 'purified'.[43] The eminent Catholic theologian Louis Bouyer was quite convinced that Bulgakov's

---

[43] Letter to Demetrios Koutroubis dated 6 October 1970 and characterizing Evdokimov's own work as a 'synthèse de la tradition patristique et Palamite et de la philosophie religieuse russe'. Koutroubis archive (Athens), courtesy of Demetrios Mavropoulos.

Sophiology, apart from some regrettable Gnostic elements, stood firmly in the tradition of St Gregory Palamas.[44] Others have written of the need for a 'Christological' or 'stavrological' corrective.[45] But perhaps the most spectacular example of 'correction' is provided in St Sophrony of Essex (1896–1993) in his thoroughgoing but critical appropriation of Bulgakov. St Sophrony, one of the great theologians and *startsi* of the modern age, draws deeply on Bulgakov, notably in his guiding concept of the hypostatic principle, while eschewing Sophiology's more problematic elements—even down to the figure of Sophia herself.[46] Not unlike St Irenaeus of Lyons and the Gnostics, Sophrony is able to wrest some of the key intuitions of Sophiology away from dubious and inessential accretions.[47]

The idea of sophiology without Sophia is perhaps not as absurd as it might at first seem.[48] The figure of Sophia is, ironically, modern Russian Sophiology's weak link: shifting, imprecise, indefinable, ungraspable, elusive. All of the Sophiologists struggled to pin her down and express her in any sort of remotely coherent fashion—hence the radical plurivocity evident in their various and varying presentations of this divine creature. To some, attempting to tie Sophia down to patristic and Palamite theology might seem like a typically masculine enterprise. The Sophiologists themselves positively revelled in the specifically feminine character of Sophia and decried the 'crude and hateful pincers and scalpels' necessary in order to present her ever-burgeoning beauty and sheer poetic glory in the wooden prose of dogmatic theology.[49] But the Sophiologists dealt in gender categories that most today would regard as outdated, lauding 'woman' and the feminine as intuitive rather than rational and as all-encompassing rather than strictly focussed. There is, it seems to me, nothing inherently feminine about vagueness or inherently masculine about precision.

If we are to come to a more precise and grounded sophiology, then Fr Georges Florovsky's notion of the 'Sophia of the Church' may prove crucial. This suggestion stands as a useful, if only partial, recognition by Florovsky of the depth and extent of patristic sophiology. Florovsky saw much that was solid in Bulgakov's Sophiology, drawing attention in this respect to Athanasius, the Cappadocians, Augustine, and Palamas, all of whom speak of the 'Sophia of the Church'. But he also found all too much in Bulgakov of the esoteric 'other Sophia' of the Gnostics,

---

[44] *Mémoires*, 74–5.

[45] For example, Brandon Gallaher, 'Graced Creatureliness: Ontological Tension in the Uncreated/ Created Distinction in the Sophiologies of Solov'ev, Bulgakov and Milbank'. Cf. also my 'The Aesthetics of Sophiology' with its suggestion of a 'stavrological corrective'.

[46] See Nikolai Sakharov, *I Love, Therefore I Am: The Theological Legacy of Archimandrite Sophrony*, 69–92 and *passim*.

[47] For Irenaeus, see above, p.116.

[48] Natalia Vaganova plays with this notion in her 'С.Н. Булгаков: софиология без Софии' but in a rather different context: Bulgakov's Crimean period (1918–22) when, she argues, he was ready to give up the whole idea of Sophia in a period of 'Catholic temptation'.

[49] *The Pillar and Ground of Truth*, 324 [ET 236].

Boehme, and the Kabbalah. What Florovsky especially objected to in Bulgakov was the idea of Sophia as a world of ideas or world-soul, the quasi-divine but created substrate of creation. For Florovsky, the Sophia of the Church is principally to be understood as relating either to the hypostasis of the Son or to the 'thrice-radiant glory' of God—the uncreated energy or activity of the triune God in respect of the creation.[50]

Florovsky, along with Lossky and Meyendorff, offer some vital and salutary counterblasts to Bulgakov, calling out the enduring esoteric dimensions of his thought, questioning his appeal to certain rather late iconographic and liturgical forms, and reining in many of his more speculative flights. But the anti-Sophiological reaction scarcely does justice to the full range and richness of patristic sophiology. Perhaps for sophiology to truly flourish it needs to dispense with its mother to discover its true mother: to expunge the 'other Sophia' in order to unlock and reveal the manifold riches of the 'Sophia of the Church'.

Bulgakov, as I have indicated, consistently struggled to express the poetry and power of his profoundly personal, liturgical, and mystical vision of Sophia in terms of the traditional dogmatic categories of essence, hypostasis, and energy. Indeed, while he was convinced of the fundamental congruity of his Sophiology with the preceding tradition of the Church (patristic, conciliar, liturgical, and iconographic), he was equally convinced that more was required of and possible for the Church if it were truly to do justice to all the multi-facetted glory of God's self-revelation as wisdom (in both created and uncreated forms). As far as Bulgakov was concerned, patristic sophiology, even in Palamas, was incomplete. Bulgakov's attempts to remedy this deficiency produced some astounding insights and amount to a truly breath-taking theological achievement. Where Bulgakov comes unstuck, and his work more like *papier mâché* than solid rock, is where he attempts to go beyond anything that can be readily grounded in that tradition—for instance in his ruminations on God's self-revelation to himself as wisdom, on Sophia as a divine realm of ideas somehow distinct from the Trinitarian persons, and especially on Sophia as a principle subsisting in multiple created and uncreated forms but reducible to neither. Here we see Sophia occupying something of a free-floating category—neither essence, nor hypostasis, nor energy. While Bulgakov himself made strenuous efforts in the course of his life to align his teaching more closely with Church tradition, rowing back on the incautious 'fourth hypostasis' language of *Unfading Light* and insisting ever more closely on the normative character of the Chalcedonian Definition, a fatal ambiguity remains. Sophia is neither fish nor fowl, neither one thing nor t'other, neither created nor uncreated. She remains somehow 'in-between', a denizen of the liminal, a bordering presence.

---

[50] See Pentkovskii, 'Письма Г. Флоровского С. Булгакову и С.Тышкевичу', 202–7.

In a re-oriented sophiology, there can be no 'in-between' that is not expressible in terms of essence, hypostasis, and energy. God is wisdom as essence, hypostasis, and energy—but not otherwise. The category of energy articulated in the Greek East allows for a construal of wisdom as divine but distinct from categories of essence and hypostasis. In focussing the question in this way I am very consciously following Evdokimov's suggestion that the path to a 'correct sophiology' lies in its re-alignment with the theology of Palamas, itself an expression of long-standing patristic tradition. And this is no arbitrary or random correction of Bulgakov, no imposition of an alien grid or frame of reference. It is axiomatic that Bulgakov must be understood and appraised principally within the tradition within which he stands and in which he firmly and unambiguously planted himself. Bulgakov, as I have laboured to show, consistently laid claim to the patristic tradition in general and to Palamite theology in particular. In insisting that Sophiology is a natural outworking of this tradition and that, furthermore, the Orthodox Church has set itself on a Sophiological path in accepting Palamite doctrine, Bulgakov has invited precisely such a correction. In that vein, I offer the following framework for a re-oriented sophiology:

God is wisdom according to essence, hypostasis, and energy. God is wisdom in his unknowable and transcendent essence; the Father, the Son, and the Holy Spirit are essential wisdom—one wisdom. The Son is incarnate wisdom in whom created and uncreated wisdom are united. He is the one mediator (μεσίτης) between God and man (cf. I Tim. 2:5); in him alone is eternal divine humanity.

God reveals his essential wisdom in the eternal energetic relation of the Trinitarian persons coming forth from the Father, resting in the Son, and shining-forth from the Holy Spirit. Wisdom in this sense is one of the eternal 'glories pertaining to the essence' spoken of by the Cappadocians.

The creation as a whole is a manifestation of the divine wisdom, the eternal ideas for the creation corresponding to the uncreated divine energies sustaining and underpinning the creation. As Palamas puts it: 'God is in all things and all things are in God.'[51] In his energies, God makes himself the link-piece of the universe, the in-between (μεταξύ): who or what else could ever perform such a function?

God thus creates, indwells, and draws all creation back to himself as wisdom according to energy or operation while remaining perfectly simple. This deifying operation is a single operation corresponding to the one nature but opening into multiplicity as God extends himself into the creation. The deifying energies extend to the creation from the Father, through the Son, and in the Spirit, embracing angels and humans within the eternal and coinherent Trinitarian dynamic of love.

---

[51] Palamas, *Capita* 104.

In the energies, God expresses himself not only in masculine but also in feminine terms. The feminine figure of wisdom in the Old Testament can be understood not only in terms of the Son or the Holy Spirit but, as Philotheos Kokkinos suggests, as an icon of the uncreated energy of wisdom ever-active within the creation.[52]

In all holy men and women, God is made manifest in the energy of wisdom. The Mother of God, above all, becomes, as Palamas puts it, the very boundary (μεθόριον) between created and uncreated nature—the one in and through whom God was able to unite himself to human nature and thus open to all human beings the promise of participation in the deifying energies of God.[53] *As vessel and house of wisdom, the Mother of God is also to be identified with the Church as the body of wisdom incarnate and the pre-eminent means by which humans are incorporated into the divine life.*

Human life gains meaning and purpose in so far as it is oriented on perception of and participation in the 'thrice-radiant glory' of the energy of the wisdom of God. All human beings are called to conform to their creation in wisdom, to become, in Macarius' words, 'all wisdom'.[54] *All human knowledge, learning, and skill, all human wisdom, finds its source and fulfilment in receptivity to the divine* paideia *that is, ultimately, God's primal act of self-giving wisdom. Human history, similarly, makes sense only in relation to the unfathomable workings of the wisdom of God among beings able to love, reject, or ignore him, even as he sustains and redeems their world.*

This framework addresses Russian Sophiology's fatal doctrinal ambiguity while also providing a basis and buttress for many of its most significant theological insights and contributions. A sophiology conceived along these lines does away with the ambiguous and shape-shifting 'other Sophia' while opening the way to the full revelation of the 'Sophia of the Church'. I suggest that the dismantling of the 'other Sophia' clears away much of what has hitherto hindered full appreciation and appropriation of Sophiology—and its true mother—within modern Orthodox theology.

While based in the first instance on Palamas, the proposed framework is presented as a distillation of the patristic and medieval wisdom reflection surveyed in this book, including elements both highlighted and overlooked by the Sophiologists. The framework is, of course, just the beginning. Much more remains to be built onto it, particularly in terms of the Christological, feminine, and sapiential dimensions of the wisdom question.

In terms of Christology, a re-oriented sophiology entails an insistence that absolutely the only foundation of union between created and uncreated wisdom

---

[52] Philotheos Kokkinos, Logos 3.15 on Proverbs 9:1 (Pseftonkas 89–90).
[53] Palamas, *Homilies* 14.15 (*On the Annunciation*) (Chrestou VI 172).   [54] Macarius, I 15.1.5.

is in the hypostasis of Christ. He is the one in whom 'all things hold together' (Col. 1:17), the one in whom divinity and humanity are eternally united in a primordial mystery of union without confusion. That deifying union in Christ is extended to humans through the Trinitarian activity or energy of self-giving love. Concomitant with this Christological focus there must also surely be a far greater focus on the apparent absurd folly of the Cross—the death of wisdom incarnate. The determination to know only Christ 'and him crucified' (I Cor. 2:2) has never been an obvious feature of Sophiology.

A re-oriented sophiology will require a reassertion of the feminine dimension of wisdom so evident in scripture but fully appreciated by relatively few in subsequent Christian tradition. Here, more work is needed not only on the divine side of the equation (especially regarding the energies) but also on connections between wisdom, the Church, and the Mother of God.

A re-oriented sophiology will also require an ongoing descent or plunge into the whole history of sapiential theology so amply in evidence in Chapters 2–6. This will involve a renewed engagement with biblical wisdom literature and an intense focus on the liturgical and ascetic dimension of the pursuit of wisdom emphasized in both East and West. It may even involve production of new forms of wisdom literature to inculcate the taste and experience of lived wisdom in our own time. A recovery of this sapiential tradition of both East and West would do much to hold together the various dimensions of wisdom in a single continuum— from the nitty-gritty to the sublime and more-than-sublime. This is where human *paideia* meets the divine *paideia*.

As Evdokimov rightly observed, modern Russian Sophiology is indeed the 'glory of modern Orthodox theology'.[55] It is a startling and beautiful vision, however flawed. It reminds us that the scope of revelation is not yet closed and offers a compelling vision of a comprehensive theology that connects all aspects of human life and experience to one another and to their divine source and origin. But, for its message to ring clear, it stands in need of a corrective or, better, completion—as recognized even by some of its most ardent defenders. I have attempted to sketch the framework of a richer and more theologically grounded sophiology in this closing section and do so in the spirit of creative reaffirmation that must mark any attempt at constructive fidelity to the living tradition of the Church Fathers.

This long journey through *Wisdom in Christian Tradition*, finally, reveals a great deal about the nature of Orthodox theology itself. Orthodox theology is a communal and living enterprise conducted across the centuries—or it is nothing. Orthodox theology can never be the preserve of the solitary practitioner, however gifted, but rests rather on the accrued wisdom of the ages. The wisdom to be found in scripture and tradition, in nature and art, in history and culture all points

---

[55] *L'Orthodoxie*, 87 [ET 93].

beyond the individual to the one who is wisdom. Orthodox theology is distinct-ively unmodern, offering answers to the problems of modernity from a tradition embedded in history but not conditioned by any particular time-bound historical or cultural construct. The process of orientation and descent undertaken in this book is intended as an illustration of just such an approach: a vision of Orthodox theology founded on a disciplined and non-eclectic reading of scripture and tradition; a vision of Orthodox theology willing to embrace the good and true wherever found, including the later Latin tradition; in short, a vision of Orthodox theology as offering real answers to real problems, bringing light, hope, and meaning to a beautiful but fractured world.

Τέλος καὶ τῷ Θεῷ δόξα.

Bibliography

Primary Sources

Alcuin of York

Deshusses, J., *Le Sacramentaire grégorien: Ses principales formes d'après les plus anciens manuscrits*, vol. II (Spicilegium Friburgense 24; Fribourg, 1988).

Dümmler, E. et al., *Monumenta Germaniae historica* I: *Poetae latini aevi Carolini* I (Berlin 1881).

Godman, P., *The Bishops, Kings and Saints of York* (Oxford Medieval Texts; Oxford 1982).

Knibbs, E. and E. Matter, *De fide Sanctae Trinitatis et de incarnatione Christi. Quaestiones de Sancta Trinitate* (CCCM 249; Turnhout 2012).

—— *Disputatio de vera philosophia* (PL 101 849–54). [= *Disputatio*]

Alexander of Alexandria

Encyclical Letter to All Bishops (Ἑνὸς σώματος), in H.-G. Opitz, *Athanasius Werke*, III/1: *Urkunden zur Geschichte des arianischen Streites* (Berlin 1934), 318–28.

Anselm

Schmitt, F., *Anselmi Opera Omnia* (6 vols.) (Edinburgh/Rome 1938–68). [= *Proslogion, Monologion, Cur Deus homo?*]

Aristides

Robinson, J., *Texts and Studies: Contributions to Biblical and Patristic Literature* (vol. 1) (Cambridge 1891), 35–51.

Apophthegmata Patrum

Alphabetical Collection in PG 65 72–440 [ET B. Ward, *The Sayings of the Desert Fathers* (Oxford/Kalamazoo 1975)]. [= *AP (Alph.)*]

Systematic Collection in PL 73 89–988. [= *AP (Syst.)*]

Aristotle

Bywater, I., *Ethica Nicomachea* (OCT; Oxford 1920). [= *Nicomachean Ethics*]

Jaeger, W., *Metaphysica* (OCT; Oxford 1957). [= *Metaphysics*]

Ross, D., *De Anima* (OCT; Oxford 1956).

Athanasius of Alexandria

Series: H.-G. Opitz et al., *Athanasius Werke* (Berlin 1934–). [= *AW*]

Bartelink, G., *Vie d'Antoine* (SC 400; Paris 1994). [= *VA*]

Metzler, K. and K. Savvidis, *Orationes contra Arianos I–III*, in *AW* I/1 (1998–2000), 109–381. [= *CA*]

Opitz, H.-G., *De decretis Nicaenae synodi*, in *AW* II/1 (1940), 1–45. [= *De decretis*]

Opitz, H.-G., *De synodis Arimini et Seleuciae*, in *AW* II/1 (1935), 231–78. [= *De synodis*]

Thomson, R., *Athanasius: Contra Gentes and De Incarnatione* (OECT; Oxford 1971). [= *Against the Heathen* and *On the Incarnation*]
—— *Epistolae Heortasticae* in PG 26 1360–1432. [= *Ep.*]

Athenagoras

Schoedel, W., *Athenagoras: Legatio and De Resurrectione* (OECT; Oxford 1972). [= *Plea for the Christians* and *On the Resurrection*]

Augustine

Daur, K. and J. Martin, *De doctrina christiana, De vera religione* (CCSL 32; Turnhout 1962).
Dombart, B. and A. Kalb, *De civitate dei* (2 vols.) (CCSL 47–8; Turnhout 1955). [= *City of God*]
Green, W. and K. Daur, *Contra academicos, De beata vita, De ordine, De magistro, De libero arbitrio* (CCSL 29; Turnhout 1970).
Hörmann, H., *Soliloquiorum libri duo* (CSEL 89; Vienna 1986). [= *Sol.*]
Mountain, W. and F. Glorie, *De trinitate libri XV* (CCSL 50-50A; Turnhout 1968).
Mutzenbecher, A., *De sermone domini in monte* (CCSL 35; Turnhout 1967). [= *On the Sermon of the Mount*]
Verheijen, L., *Confessionum libri XIII* (CCSL 27; Turnhout 1981) [ET A. C. Outler, *Augustine: Confessions and Enchiridion* (Philadelphia 1955)]. [= *Conf.*]

Barnabas

Prigent, P. and R. Kraft, *Épître de Barnabé* (SC 172; Paris 1971).

Basil of Caesarea

Courtonne, Y., *Saint Basile: Lettres* (3 vols.) (Paris 1957–66) [Text (with ET) also in R. Deferrari, *Letters* (4 vols.) (LCL 190, 215, 243, 270; Cambridge, MA 1926–34)]. [= *Letters*]
Giet, S., *Homélies sur l'Hexaéméron* (SC 26; Paris 1968). [= *Hex.*]
Pruche, R., *Sur le Saint-Esprit* (SC 17 bis; Paris 1968). [= *HS*]
Contra Eunomium (PG 29 497–768). [= *Eun.*]
Homilia in Principium Proverbiorum (PG 31 385–424). [= *Prov.*]
De Fide (PG 31 464–72). [= *On Faith*]
De legendis gentilium libris (PG 31 563–90). [*Address to Young Men*]
Regulae fusius tractatae (PG 31 889–1052). [= *Longer Rules*]

Bede

Crépin, A. et al., *Histoire ecclésiastique du peuple anglaise* (3 vols.) (SC 489, 490, 491; Paris 2005). [= *Ecclesiastical History of the English People*]
Hurst, D., *Opera exegetica* 2A (CCSL 119A; Turnhout 1969). [= *De Templo Salomonis*]
Hurst, D. and J. Hudson, *Opera exegetica* 2B (CCSL 119B; Turnhout 1983) [= *In Proverbia Salomonis* and *In Cantica canticorum*]
Holder, A. (ET), *The Venerable Bede: On the Song of Songs and Selected Writings* (New York/Mahwah 2011).

Bernard of Clairvaux

Verdeyen, P., R. Fassetta, et al., *Sermons sur le Cantique* (SC 414, 431, 452, 472, 511; Paris 1996, 1998, 2000, 2003, 2007). [= *Sermons*]

Boethius

Bieler, L., *Philosophiae consolatio* (CCSL 94; Turnhout 1957, 1984). [= *Consolation*]
Brandt, S., *In Isagogen Porphyrii Commenta* (Vienna/Leipzig 1906 (CSEL 38). [= *In Isagoge*]

Cassiodorus

Adriaen, M., *Expositio Psalmorum* (2 vols.) (CCSL 97–8; Turnhout 1958). [ET P. Walsh, *Explanation of the Psalms* (3 vols.) (Ancient Christian Writers 51–3; New York/Mahwah 1990)]
Mynors, R., *Cassiodori Senatoris Institutiones* (Oxford 1961²). [= *Institutes*]

Cicero

Winterbottom, M., *De Officiis* (OCT; Oxford 1994). [ET M. T. Griffin and E. M. Atkins, *On Duties* (Cambridge 1991)]

Clement of Alexandria

Marrou, H.-I., C. Mondésert, et al., *Clément d'Alexandrie: Le Pédagogue, I–III* (SC 70, 108, 158; Paris 1960, 1965, 1970). [=*Paid.*]
Mondésert, C. and A. Plassart, *Clément d'Alexandrie: Le Protreptique* (SC 2; Paris 1941, 1949). [=*Prot.*]
Stählin, O., L. Früchtel, and U. Treu, *Clemens Alexandrinus II, Stromata Buch I–VI* (GCS 52; Berlin 1985). [=*Strom.*]
—— *Clemens Alexandrinus III, Stromata Buch VII–VIII, Excerpta ex Theodoto, Eclogae Propheticae, Quis dives salvetur, Fragmente* (GCS 17; Berlin1970). [=*Strom.*]

Clement of Rome

Jaubert, A., *Clément de Rome. Épître aux Corinthiens* (SC 167; Paris 1971).

(Pseudo-) Clement of Rome

Rehm, B. and I. Irmscher, *Die Pseudoklementinen I: Homilien* (GCS 42; Berlin 1953). [= *Homilies*]

Councils of Valence (855) and Langres (859)

Mansi, J., *Sacrorum conciliorum nova et amplissima ollection*, vol. XVI (Venice 1770).

Didache

Audet, J.-P., *La Didachè, Instructions des Apôtres* (Études Bibliques; Paris 1958).

Didascalia Apostolorum

Vööbus, A., *The Didascalia Apostolorum in Syriac* (CSCO 179; Louvain 1979).

Diogenes Laertius

Hicks, R. D., *Lives of Eminent Philosophers* (2 vols.) (LCL 184–5; Cambridge, MA 1950).

Dionysius the Areopagite

Suchla, B. et al., *Corpus Dionysiacum* (2 vols.) (PTS 33, 36; Berlin 1990–1) [ET C. Luibheid, *Pseudo-Dionysius: The Complete Works* (New York/Mahwah 1987)]. [= *DN (Divine Names), MT (Mystical Theology), EH (Ecclesiastical Hierarchy), CH (Celestial Hierarchy), Ep.(Epistles)*]

Epicurus

Arrighetti, G., *Epicuro, Opere* (Turin 1960).

Epistle to Diognetus

Marrou, H.-I., *À Diognète* (SC 33; Paris 1952).

Eunomius

Vaggione, R., *Eunomius: The Extant Works* (OECT; Oxford 1987).

Eusebius of Caesarea

Bardy, G., *Histoire Ecclésiastique* (4 vols.) (SC 31, 41, 55, 73; Paris 1952–58). [= *HE*]

Evagrius of Pontus

Scholia on Psalms in PG 12 and J. Pitra, *Analecta sacra spicilegio Solesmensi parata* II, 444–83 and III, 1–364 (Venice 1883, 1884) [Ascribed to Origen. For a key to attribution see M. Rondeau, 'Le commentaire sur les Psaumes d'Évagre le Pontique', *Orientalia christiana periodica* 26 (1960), 307–48].

Fogielman, C.-A., *À Euloge, Les vices opposés aux vertus* (SC 591; Paris 2017). [= *To Eulogius* and *On the Vices*]

Frankenberg, W., *Evagrius Ponticus* (Berlin 1912), 613–19. [= *Great Letter*]

Géhin, P., *Chapitres sur la prière* (SC 589; Paris 2017). [= *OP*]

—— *Scholies aux Proverbes* (SC 340; Paris 1987). [= *Scholia on Proverbs*]

—— *Scholies à l'Ecclésiaste* (SC 397; Paris 1993). [*Scholia on Ecclesiastes*]

Greßmann, H., *Nonnenspiegel und Mönchsspiegel des Evagrios Pontikos* (TU 39.4; Leipzig 1913). [= *Ad Monachos*]

Guillaumont, A., *Les Six Centuries des 'Kephalaia Gnostica' d'Évagre le Pontique* (PO 28; Paris 1958). [= *KG*]

Guillaumont, A. and C. Guillaumont, *Traité pratique ou le moine* (2 vols.) (SC 170–1; Paris 1971). [= *Praktikos*]

Gregory of Nyssa

Series: W. Jaeger, *Gregorii Nysseni Opera* (Leiden 1952–). [= GNO]

Callahan, J., *De Orationio Dominica, De Beatitudinibus* (GNO VII/2; 1992). [= *On the Beatitudes*]

Cavarnos, J., *De virginitate*, in *Opera Ascetica* (GNO VIII/1; 1952), 215–343. [= *Virg.*]

Jaeger, W., *Contra Eunomium Libri I-III* (GNO I-II; 1960). [= *Against Eunomius*]

—— *Refutatio confessionis Eunomii* (GNO II; 1960). [= *Refutation of the Confession of Eunomius*]

Mueller, F., *Ad Ablabium, Quod non sint tres dei*, in *Opera Dogmatica Minora I* (GNO III/1; 1958), 25–57. [= *To Ablabius*]

Mühlenberg, E., *Oratio Catechetica* (GNO III/4; 1996). [= *Or. Cat.*]

Staats, R., *Makarios-Symeon: Epistola Magna* (Göttingen 1984) [= *De instituto christiano*]

In Hexæmeron liber (PG 44 62A–124C).

Gregory Palamas

Series: P. Chrestou, Γρηγορίου τοῦ Παλαμᾶ συγγράμματα (6 vols.) (Thessalonica 1962–2015). [= Chrestou]

Bobrinskoy, B., Λόγοι ἀποδεικτικοὶ δύο περὶ τῆς ἐκπορεύσεως τοῦ Ἁγίου Πνεύματος in Chrestou I (1962), 23–153. [= Apodictic Treatises]

Chrestou, P., Διάλεξις μετὰ Γρηγορᾶ in Chrestou IV (1988), 191–230. [= Dialogue with Gregoras]

—— Πρὸς Ἰωάννην καὶ Θεόδωρον Τοὺς Φιλοσόφους in Chrestou V (1992) 231–46. [= To John and Theodore]

Kontogiannes, L. and B. Phanourgakes, Ἀντιρρητικοὶ πρὸς Ἀκίνδυνον in Chrestou III (1970), 39–506. [= Against Akindynos]

Mantzarides, G., Περὶ θείας ἑνώσεως καὶ Διακρίσις in Chrestou II (1966), 69–95. [= On Union and Distinction]

Mantzarides, G., Ἀπολογία (vel Περὶ θείων ἐνεργειῶν) in Chrestou II (1966), 96–136. [= Apology]

—— Θεοφάνης in Chrestou II (1966), 219–62. [= Theophanes]

Matsoukas, N., Ἐπιστολαί in Chrestou II (1966), 315–547. [= Epistles]

Meyendorff, J., Ἐπιστολὴ Α΄ πρὸς Βαρλαάμ in Chrestou I (1962), 225–59. [= First Letter to Barlaam]

—— Grégoire Palamas. Défense des saints hésychastes (Spicilegium Sacrum Lovaniense. Études et documents 30; Louvain 1973²). [= Triads]

Pseftonkas, B., Ὁμιλίαι in Chrestou VI (2015), 39–683. [= Homilies]

Sinkewicz, R., Saint Gregory Palamas, The One Hundred and Fifty Chapters (Studies and Texts 83; Toronto 1988). [= Capita]

Confession of 1351 in PG 151 763D–768C [ET in A. Papadakis, 'Gregory Palamas at the Council of Blachernae, 1351', Greek, Roman and Byzantine Studies 10 (1969), 333–42].

Gregory the Great

Adriaen, M., Moralia in Iob (3 vols.) (CCSL 143, 143A, 143B; Turnhout 1979–85) [ET J. H. Parker and J. Rivington (eds.), J. Bliss, Morals on the Book of Job: In Three Volumes (Oxford 1844–50)]. [= Moralia]

Gregory the Theologian

Orationes 13–19 (PG 35). [= Orations]

Bernardi, J. et al., Discours 1–12, 20–43 (SC 247 (1–3), 309 (4–5), 405 (6–12), 270 (20–3), 284 (24–6), 250 (27–31), 318 (32–7), 358 (38–41), 384 (42–3); Paris 1978–95). [= Orations]

Henry Suso

Das Büchlein der ewigen Weisheit, in K. Bihlmeyer (ed.), Heinrich Seuse: Deutsche Schriften, 1907. [= The Little Book of Eternal Wisdom]

Horologium Sapientiae, in P. Künzle (ed.), Heinrich Seuses Horologium sapientiae (Freiburg 1977). [= Clock of Wisdom]

Hermas

Joly, R., Hermas: Le Pasteur (SC 53; Paris 1958).

Hildegard of Bingen

Carlevaris, A., Liber vitae meritorum (CCCM 90; Turnhout 1995).

Derolez, A. and P. Dronke, Liber divinorum operum (CCCM 92; Turnhout 1996) [ET (partial) M. Atherton, Selected Writings: Hildegard of Bingen (London 2001)].

Führkötter, A. and A. Carlevaris, *Scivias* (2 vols.) (CCCM 43–43A; Turnhout 1978). [ET C. Hart and J. Bishop, *Hildegard of Bingen: Scivias* (New York/Mahwah 1990)]

Klaes, M., *Vita sanctae Hildegardis* (CCCM 126; Turnhout 1993). [= *Life of Hildegard*]

Hippolytus

Achelis, H., *Kleinere exegetische und homiletische Schriften* (GCS 1.2; Leipzig 1897) [= *On the Antichrist, Commentary on Proverbs*]

Brière, M. et al., *Hippolyte de Rome: Sur les bénédictions d'Isaac, de Jacob et de Moïse* (PO 27; Paris 1954). [= *On the Blessing of Isaac and Jacob*]

Butterworth, R., *Hippolytus of Rome: Contra Noetum* (London 1977). [= *Against the Heresy of Noetus*]

Richard, M., 'Les fragments du Commentaire de S. Hippolyte sur les Proverbes de Salomon', in E. Dekkers et al., *Opera minora* I (Turnhout 1976), 339–444. [= *Fragments in Proverbs*]

Ignatius of Antioch

Camelot, P.-T., *Ignace d'Antioche, Polycarpe de Smyrne. Lettres, Martyre de Polycarpe* (SC 10; Paris 1951).

Irenaeus of Lyons

Rousseau, A., *Démonstration de la prédication apostolique* (SC 406; Paris 1995) [ET J. Behr, *On the Apostolic Preaching* (Crestwood, NY 1998)]. [= *Demonstration*]

Rousseau, A. et al., *Contre les hérésies* I–V (SC 263–4 (I), SC 293–4 (II), SC 210–11 (III), SC 100 (IV), SC 152–3 (V); Paris 1965–79). [= *AH*]

John Scotus Eriugena

Barbet, J., *Expositiones in hierarchiam coelestem* (CCCM 31; Turnhout 1975). [= *Commentary on the Celestial Hierarchy*]

Jeauneau, E., *Periphyseon* (5 vols.) (CCCM 161–5; Turnhout 1996–2003) [ET (of text in Dublin edition (ed. I. P. Sheldon-Williams; Dublin 1968–81) (I–III) and PL 122 (IV–V)) I. P. Sheldon-Williams and J. O'Meara, *Eriugena: Periphyseon (The Division of Nature)* (Montreal/Washington, DC 1987)]. [= *Periphyseon*]

Jeauneau, E., *Homilia et commentarius in evangelium Iohannis* (CCCM 166; Turnhout 2008). [*Homily on the Prologue of John*]

Lutz, C., *Annotationes in Marcianum* (Cambridge, MA 1939). [= *Annotations on Martianus*]

Madec, C. *Iohannis Scotti de divina praedestinatione* (CCCM 50; Turnhout 1978). [*On Divine Predestination*]

Justin Martyr

Goodspeed, E. J., *Justinus Martyr, Dialogus*, in idem, *Die ältesten apologeten* (Göttingen 1914), 90–265. [= *Dial.*]

Minns, D. and P. Parvis, *Justin, Philosopher and Martyr: Apologies* (OECT; Oxford 2009). [= *Apol.*]

Macarius (Macarius-Symeon)

Berthold, H., *Makarios/Symeon, Reden und Briefe. Die Sammlung I des Vaticanus Graecus 694 (B)* (2 vols.) (GCS 55–6; Berlin 1973). [= I]

Desprez, V., *Pseudo-Macaire: Oeuvres spirituelles I: Homélies propres à la Collection III* (SC 275; Paris 1980). [= III]

Dörries, H., E. Klostermann, and M. Kroeger, *Die 50 Geistlichen Homilien des Makarios* (PTS 4; Berlin 1964). [= II]

Marcus Aurelius

Farquharson, A. (ed.), *The Meditations of the Emperor Marcus Antoninus* (Oxford 1944). [= *Meditations*]

Maximus the Confessor

Ceresa-Gastaldo, A., *Capitoli sulla carità* (Verba seniorum 3; Rome 1963). [= CC]

Janssens, B., *Ambigua ad Thomam una cum Epistula secunda ad eundem* (CCSG 48; Turnhout 2002). [= *Ambigua ad Thomam*]

Laga, C., and Steel, C., *Quaestiones ad Thalassium* (CCSG 7, 22; Turnhout 1980, 1990). [= QT]

Ambigua (PG 91 1031–1418). [= *Amb.*]

Capita theologiae et oeconomiae (PG 90 1033–1176). [= CT]

Epistulae (PG 91 362–650). [= *Ep.*]

Mystagogia (PG 91 658–718). [= *Mystagogy*]

Louth, A., *Maximus the Confessor* (London 1996). [ET of *Ep.* 2; *Amb.* 1, 5, 10, 41, 71; *Opuscula theologica et polemica* 3, 7]

Palmer, G., P. Sherrard, and K. T. Ware, *The Philokalia*, vol. 2 (London 1981). [ET of CC, CT]

Mechthild of Magdeburg

Neumann, H. *Das fließende Licht der Gottheit* (Munich 1990). [ET F. Tobin, *The Flowing Light of the Godhead* (New York/Mahwah 1998)]

Melito of Sardis

Perler, O., *Méliton de Sardes: Sur la Pâque* (SC 123; Paris 1966).

Odes of Solomon

Charlesworth, J. H., *The Odes of Solomon: The Syriac Texts* (Oxford 1973).

Origen of Alexandria

Series: P. Koetschau et al., *Origenes Werke* in GCS (Berlin 1899–).

Baehrens, W., Homilien zum Hexateuch (GCS 29–30; Berlin 1920–21). [= *On Genesis, On Joshua*]

Borret, M., *Homélies sur l'Exode* (SC 321 85). [= *On Exodus*]

Brésard, L., H. Crouzel, and M. Borret, *Commentaire sur le Cantique des Cantiques*, I–II (SC 375–6; Paris 1991–2). [= *Commentary on the Song of Songs*]

Crouzel, H., *Remerciement à Origène suivi de la Lettre d'Origène à Grégoire* (SC 148; Paris 1969). [= *To Gregory*]

Harl, M., *Origène, Philocalie 1–20* (SC 302; Paris (1983). [= *Philocalia*]

Klostermann E. and E. Benz, *Commentarius in Matthaeum I* (GCS 40; Berlin 1935). [= *On Matthew*]

Klostermann, E. and P. Nautin, *Homiliae in Ieremiam, Fragmenta in Lamentationes* (GCS 6; Berlin 1901, 1983). [= *On Jeremiah, On Lamentations*]

Koetschau, P., *Contra Celsum I–IV* (GCS 2; Berlin 1899). [= CC]]

—— *Contra Celsum V–VIII, De oratione* (GCS 3; Berlin 1899). [= CC]

Koetschau, P., *De principiis* (GCS 22; Berlin 1913) [ET H. Butterworth, *Origen: On First Principles* (New York 1966)]. [= *DP*]
Preuschen, E., *Commentarius in Iohannem* (GCS 10; Berlin 1903). [= *On John*]

Peter Abelard
Commentaria in Epistolam Pauli ad Romanos, in E. M. Buytaert, *Opera theologica I* (CCCM 11; Turnhout1969). [= *Commentary on Romans*]
Boyer, B. and R. McKeon, *Peter Abailard, Sic et Non: A Critical Edition* (Chicago 1977). [= *Sic et Non*]

Philo of Alexandria
Series: L. Cohn and P. Wendland, *Philonis Alexandrini opera quae supersunt, editio maior* (Berlin 1896-1963). [ET C. D. Yonge, *The Works of Philo Judaeus, the Contemporary of Josephus* (London 1854-5); reprinted as *The Works of Philo: Complete and Unabridged* (Peabody, MA 1993)]
Cohn, L., *De opificio mundi*, in vol. I (Berlin 1963), 1-60. [= *Opif.*]
—— *Legum allegoriarum (I-III)*, in vol. I (Berlin 1963), 61-169. [= *Leg.*]
—— *De specialibus legibus (I-IV)*, in vol. V (Berlin 1963), 1-265. [= *Spec.*]
—— *De vita Mosis (I-II)*, in vol. IV (Berlin 1963), 119-268. [= *Mos.*]
Wendland, P., *De congressu eruditionis gratia*, in vol. III (Berlin 1963), 72-109. [= *De congressu*]
—— *De fuga et inventione*, in vol. III (Berlin 1963), 110-55. [=*De fuga*]
—— *De posteritate Caini*, in vol. II (Berlin 1963), 1-41. [= *Poster.*]
—— *De somniis (I-II)*, in vol. III (Berlin 1963), 204-306. [= *Somn.*]
—— *Quis rerum divinarum heres sit*, in vol. III (Berlin 1963), 1-71. [= *Heres*]
—— *Quod deus sit immutabilis*, in vol. II (Berlin 1963), 56-94. [= *Deus*]

Philotheos Kokkinos
Pseftonkas, B., *Φιλοθέου Κοκκίνου λόγοι καὶ ὁμιλίαι* (Thessalonian Byzantine Writers 2; Thessalonica 1981).

Pistis Sophia
Schmidt, C. and V. MacDermot, *Pistis Sophia* (Leiden 1978).

Plato
Series: E. Duke et al., *Platonis Opera* (OCT; Oxford 1901-).

Plotinus
Enneades, in P. Henry and H.-R. Schwyzer, *Plotini Opera, editio minor* (3 vols.) (OCT; Oxford 1964-83) [ET S. Mckenna, *Plotinus: The Enneads* (5 vols.) (London 1921-30)]. [= *Enneads*]

Pre-Socratics
Diels, H, *Die Fragmente der Vorsokratiker, griechisch und deutsch* (Zürich 1951⁶) [ET (selections) G. S. Kirk, J. E. Raven, and M. Schofield (eds.), *The Presocratic Philosophers: A Critical History with a Selection of Texts* (Cambridge 1983)].

Russian Primary Chronicle
Cross, S. and O. Sherbowitz-Wetzor, *The Russian Primary Chronicle: Laurentian Text* (Cambridge, MA 1953).

Seneca

Reynolds, L., *Ad Lucilium Epistulae Morales* (2 vols.) (OCT; Oxford 1965).

Septuagint

Brenton, L., *The Septuagint Version of the Old Testament and Apocrypha: With an English Translation and with Various Readings and Critical Notes* (London 1870).
Rahlfs, A., Septuaginta (Stuttgart 1935, 1979).

Sextus

Chadwick, H., *The Sentences of Sextus: A Contribution to the History of Early Christian Ethics* (Cambridge 1959).

Sextus Empiricus

Bury, R., *Sextus Empiricus* II (LCL 291; Cambridge, MA 1935). [= *Against the Logicians*]

Silvanus

Janssens, Y., *Les Leçons de Silvanos* (Bibliothèque copte de Nag Hammadi VII, 4; Québec 1983). [ET J. M. Robinson, *The Nag Hammadi Library in English* (New York 1977)]. [= *Teachings of Silvanus*]

Tatian

Goodspeed, E. J., *Tatianus, Oratio ad Graecos*, in idem *Die ältesten apologeten* (Göttingen 1914), 268–305. [= *Oration to the Greeks*]

Tertullian

Series: E. Dekkers et al., *Opera* (2 vols.) (CCSL 1–2; Turnhout 1954).
Borleffs, J., *Ad Nationes* (CCSL 1 11–75). [= *To the Nations*]
Dekkers, E., *Apologeticum* (CCSL 1 85–171). [= *Apology*]
Kroymann, E., *Adversus Hermogenem* (CCSL 1 397–435). [= *Against Hermogenes*]
—— *Adversus Marcionem* (CCSL 1 441–726). [= *Against Marcion*]
—— *De Carne Christi* (CCSL 2 873–917). [= *On the Flesh of Christ*]
—— *De Corona* (CCSL 2 1037–65). [= *On the Crown*]
Kroymann, E. and E. Evans, *Adversus Praxean* (CCSL 2 1159–205). [= *Against Praxeas*]
Refoulé, R., *De Praescriptione Haereticorum* (CCSL 1 187–224). [= *On the Prescription of Heretics*]
Reifferschied, A. and G. Wissowa, *Scorpiace* (CCSL 2 1069–97).
Waszink, J., *De Anima* (CCSL 2 779–869). [= *On the Soul*]

Theophilus of Antioch

Grant, R. M., *Theophilus of Antioch: Ad Autolycum* (OECT; Oxford 1970).

Thomas Aquinas

Ayo, N., *Sermon-Conferences of St. Thomas Aquinas on the Apostles' Creed* (Notre Dame, IN 1988) [based on *Collationes Credo in Deum* (*Editio Leonina* 44, forthcoming)].
Busa, R., *Summa theologiae* (*Editio Leonina* 4–12) (Rome 1888–1906). [= *ST*]
Gils, P.-M., *Super Boetium De Trinitate* (*Editio Leonina* 50) (Rome/Paris 1992).
Madonnet, P. and F. Moos, *Scriptum super libros Sententiarum Petri Lombardi* (Paris 1927–56). [= *Commentary on the Sentences*]

Ucelli, P. et al., *Summa contra gentiles* (*Editio Leonina*) 13–15 (Rome 1918–30, 1961). [= *SG*]

Treatise on the Two Spirits
Metso, S., *The Community Rule: A Critical Edition with Translation* (Atlanta 2019), 20–5.

Secondary and Modern Sources

Adams, S., and M. Goff (eds.), *The Wiley Blackwell Companion to Wisdom Literature* (Chichester/Hoboken, NJ 2020).

Alberi, M., 'The "Mystery of the Incarnation" and Wisdom's House (Prov. 9:1) in Alcuin's *Disputatio de vera philosophia*', *JTS* 48 (1997), 505–16.

Alberi, M., '"The Better Paths of Wisdom": Alcuin's Monastic "True Philosophy" and the Worldly Court', *Speculum* 76 (2001), 896–910.

Aletti, J.-N., 'Sagesse III: Nouveau Testament', in *DS* 14 (Paris 1990), 91–6.

Anastos, M., 'Pletho's Calendar and Liturgy', *Dumbarton Oaks Papers* 4 (1948), 183–305.

Anatolios, K., *Retrieving Nicaea: The Development and Meaning of Trinitarian Doctrine* (Grand Rapids, MI 2011).

Angelov, A., P. Pavlov, and S. Tanev, 'The Sophiological Controversy as a Clash of Different Patristic Interpretations', in Hainthaler et al. (eds.), *Sophia: The Wisdom of God* (q.v.), 55–81.

Arjakovsky, A., *Essai sur le père Serge Boulgakov (1871–1944): Philosophe et théologien chrétien* (Paris 2006).

Arndt, J., *Wahres Christentum* (Frankfurt/Magdeburg 1605–10).

Ashton, J., 'The Transformation of Wisdom: A Study of John's Prologue', *New Testament Studies* 32 (1986), 161–86.

Avernitsev, S., 'Премудрость Божия построила «Дом» (Книга Притчей Соломоновых 9:1) для пребывания Божия с нами: понятие Софии и смысл иконы' ('The Wisdom of God has built a "house" (Book of the Proverbs of Solomon 9:1) for the dwelling of God with us: the idea of Sophia and the meaning of the icon') in София Премудрость Божия. Выставка русской иконописи XIII–XIX веков из собраний музеев России (q.v.), 4–8.

Ayres, L., *Nicaea and its Legacy: An Approach to Fourth-Century Trinitarian Theology* (Oxford 2004).

—— *Augustine and the Trinity* (Cambridge 2010).

Baehr, J., 'Sophia: Theoretical Wisdom and Contemporary Epistemology' in K. Timpe and C. Boyd (eds.), *Virtues and their Vices* (Oxford 2014).

Balčarek, P., 'The Image of Sophia in Medieval Russian Iconography and Its Sources', *Byzantinoslavica* 60.2 (Prague 1999), 593–610.

Barker, M., *The Revelation of Jesus Christ: Which God Gave to Him to Show to His Servants What Must Soon Take Place (Revelation 1.1)* (Edinburgh 2000).

Barnes, M. R., '*De Trinitate* VI and VII: Augustine and the Limits of Nicene Orthodoxy', *Augustinian Studies* 38 (2007), 189–202.

Barton, S. (ed.), *Where Shall Wisdom Be Found?: Wisdom in the Bible, the Church and the Contemporary World* (Edinburgh 1999).

—— 'Gospel Wisdom', in idem (ed.), *Where Shall Wisdom Be Found?* (q.v.), 93–110.

Bauckham, R., *James: Wisdom of James, Disciple of Jesus the Sage* (London 1999).

Benz, E., *Die protestantische Thebais: zur Nachwirkung Makarius des Ägypters in Protestantismus des 17. und 18. Jahrhunderts in Europa und Amerika* (Mainz 1963).

Berdiaev, N., 'Изъ этюдовъ о Я. Бемѣ. Этюдъ I. Ученіе объ Ungrund'ѣ и свободъ', *Путь (The Way)* 20 (1930), 47–79. [= 'Studies Concerning Jacob Boehme: Étude I. The Teaching about the Ungrund and Freedom']

Blankenhorn, B., *The Mystery of Union with God: Dionysian Mysticism in Albert The Great and Thomas Aquinas* (Washington, DC 2015).

Blenkinsopp, J., *Wisdom and Law in the Old Testament: The Ordering of Life in Israel and Early Judaism* (Oxford 1995).

Blowers, P. M., *Maximus the Confessor: Jesus Christ and the Transfiguration of the World* (Oxford 2016).

Bobrinskoy, B., *La compassion du Père* (Paris 2000).

Boehme, J., *Sämtliche Schriften*² (A. Faust and W.-E. Peuckert, eds.) (11 vols.) (Stuttgart 1955–1961). [= SS]

—— *Theosophical Epistles* (1618–24) in *SS* IX.XXI (Stuttgart 1956), 1–262.

—— *Three Principles* (1619) in *SS* II.II (Stuttgart 1960), 1–482.

—— *Six Theosophical Points* (1620) in *SS* IV.VI (Stuttgart 1957), 1–96.

—— *Second Apology to Balthasar Tilken* (1621) in *SS* V.X (Stuttgart 1960), 101–64.

Bouyer, L., 'An Introduction to the Theme of Wisdom and Creation in the Tradition', *Le Messager Orthodoxe* 98 (1985), 149–61.

Bouyer, L., *Mémoires* (ed. J. Duchesne) (Paris 2014).

Brent, A., *A Political History of Early Christianity* (London 2009).

Brouwer, R., *The Stoic Sage: The Early Stoics on Wisdom, Sagehood and Socrates* (New York 2014).

Brzozowska, Z., 'The Church of Divine Wisdom or of Christ – the Incarnate *Logos*? Dedication of *Hagia Sophia* in Constantinople in the Light of Byzantine Sources from 5th to 14th Century', *Studia Ceranea* 2 (2012), 85–96.

Buda, D., 'Sophia in Theophilus of Antioch', in T. Hainthaler et al. (eds.), *Sophia: The Wisdom of God* (q.v.), 85–102.

Bulgakov, S., Философия хозяйства (Moscow 1912) [ET C. Evtuhov (New Haven, CT 2000]. [= *Philosophy of Economy*]

—— 'Афонское дело', *Русская мысль* [*Russian Thought*] (1913), 37–46. [= 'The Athos Affair']

—— Свѣтъ Невечерний (созерцания и умозрѣния) (Moscow 1917) [ET T.A. Smith (Grand Rapids, MI 2012). [= *Unfading Light*]

—— Ипостась и ипостасность (Scholia к «Свету Невечернему») in Festschrift Peter Struve (Prague 1925), 353–57 [ET A. F. Dobbie Bateman, B. Gallaher, and I. Kukota, *SVTQ*, 49 (2005), 5–46]. [= 'Hypostasis and Hypostaseity']

—— *Die Tragödie der Philosophie* (Darmstadt 1927) [ET S. Churchyard (New York 2020)]. [= *The Tragedy of Philosophy*]

—— Купина неопалимая (Paris 1927) [ET T. A. Smith (Grand Rapids, MI 2009)]. [= *The Burning Bush*]

—— Другъ Жениха (Paris 1927) [ET (abridged) B. Jakim (Grand Rapids, MI 2003)]. [= *The Friend of the Bridegroom*]

—— Лѣствица Иаковля (Paris 1929) [ET T. A. Smith (Grand Rapids, MI 2010]. [= *Jacob's Ladder*]

—— 'Евхаристическій догматъ', *Путь (The Way)* 20 (1930), 3–46; 21 (1930), 3–33. [= 'The Eucharistic Dogma']

—— Икона и иконопочитаніе (Paris 1931). [= *Icons and Icon-Veneration*]

Bulgakov, S., 'Святый Грааль', *Путь* (*The Way*) 32 (1932), 3–42. [= 'The Holy Grail']

—— Агнецъ Божій (Paris 1933) [ET (abridged) B. Jakim (Grand Rapids, MI 2008)]. [= *The Lamb of God*]

—— *The Orthodox Church* (London 1935). [= First Publication of Complete Text]

—— *Sophia: The Wisdom of God. An Outline of Sophiology* (tr. C. Bamford) (Hudson, NY 1993) [= revised version of *The Wisdom of God: A Brief Summary of Sophiology* (tr. P. Thompson et al.) (London 1937)]. [= *The Wisdom of God*].

—— О Софіи, Премудрости Божіей. Указь Московской патріархіи и докладные записки проф. прот. С. Булгакова митрополиту Евлогию (*Sophia, The Wisdom of God. Decree of the Moscow Patriarchate and Memoranda of Prof. Prot. S. Bulgakov to Metropolitan Evlogy*) (Paris 1935).

—— Утѣшитель (Paris 1936) [ET (abridged) B. Jakim (Grand Rapids, MI 2008)]. [= *The Comforter*]

—— Догмать и догматика, in *Живое преданіе* (*Living Tradition*) (Paris 1937), 8–25 [ET P. Bouteneff in M. Plekon (ed.), *Tradition Alive: On the Church and the Christian Life in Our Time* Bulgakov, S., *Readings from the Eastern Church* (Lanham, MD 2003), 67–80. [= 'Dogma and Dogmatics']

—— 'Thesen über die Kirche', in H. Alivisatos (ed.), *Procès-Verbaux du premier Congrès de Théologie Orthodoxe à Athènes* (Athens 1939), 127–34.

—— Невѣста Агнца (Paris 1945). [ET (abridged) B. Yakim (Grand Rapids, MI 2002). Excursus ('Augustinianism and Predestination') in R. De La Noval, *Journal of Orthodox Christian Studies* 2 (2019), 65–99]. [= *Bride of the Lamb*]

—— Автобіографичёеские замѣтки (ed. L. Zander) (Paris 1947). [= *Autobiographical Notes*]

—— Апокалипсис Иоанна (Опыт догматического истолкования) (Paris 1948) [ET M. Whitton (Münster 2019)]. [= *Apocalypse of John*]

—— 'Богословие Евангелия Иоанна Богослова', *Вестник* (*Messenger*) 131 (1980), 134, (1981 59–81), 135 (1981), 26–38, 136 (1982), 137 (1982) 92–107. [= 'The Theology of the Gospel of John']

Bullough, D., *Alcuin: Achievement and Reputation* (Leiden 2004).

Byron, R., *The Byzantine Achievement* (London 1929).

Carabine, D., *John Scottus Eriugena* (Oxford 2000).

Cazeaux, J., 'Sagesse II: La sagesse selon Philon d'Alexandrie', in *DS* 14 (Paris 1990), 81–91.

Cerbelaud, D., *Sophie: la figure biblique de la Sagesse et ses interprétations* (Paris 2016).

Chadwick, H., *Early Christian Thought and the Classical Tradition* (Oxford 1966).

—— 'Some Reflections on the Character and Theology of the *Odes of Solomon*', in P. Granfield and J. Jungmann (eds.), *Kyriakon: Festschrift Johannes Quasten* (Münster 1970), 266–70.

Charry, E., *By the Renewing of Your Minds* (Oxford 1997).

Clément, O., *Orient-Occident: Deux passeurs: Vladimir Lossky et Paul Evdokimov* (Geneva 1985).

Coakley, S., 'Why Three? Some Further Reflections on the Origins of the Doctrine of the Trinity', in eadem and D. A. Pailin (eds.), *The Making and Remaking of Christian Doctrine: Essays in Honour of Maurice Wiles* (Oxford 1993), 29–56.

—— *God, Sexuality, and the Self: An Essay 'On the Trinity'* (Cambridge 2013).

Coates, R., *Deification in Russian Religious Thought: Between the Revolutions, 1905–1917* (Oxford 2019).

Coda, P., *L'altro di Dio: rivelazione e kenosi in Sergej Bulgakov* (Rome 1998).

—— *Sergej Bulgakov* (Brescia 2003).

Collins, J., *Jewish Wisdom in the Hellenistic Age* (Louisville 1997).

Constas, M., 'The Reception of Paul and of Pauline Theology in the Byzantine Period', in D. Krueger and R. Nelson (eds.), *The New Testament in Byzantium* (Washington, DC 2016), 147–76.

Conway, D., *The Rediscovery of Wisdom: From Here to Antiquity in Quest of Sophia* (London 2000).

Coolman, B. T., 'On the Subject-Matter of Theology in the *Summa Halensis* and St. Thomas Aquinas', *The Thomist* 79 (2015), 439–66.

—— *Knowledge, Love, and Ecstasy in the Theology of Thomas Gallus* (Oxford 2017).

Crenshaw, J., *Old Testament Wisdom: An Introduction* (Louisville 2010).

Cross, R., 'Duns Scotus on God's Essence and Attributes: Metaphysics, Semantics, and the Greek Patristic Tradition', *Recherches de Théologie et Philosophie Médiévales* 83 (2016), 353–83.

—— 'Theology', in C. Briggs and P. Eardley (eds.), *A Companion to Giles of Rome* (Leiden 2016), 34–72.

Crouzel, H., *Origène et la 'connaissance mystique'* (Paris 1961).

—— *Origène et la philosophie* (Paris 1962).

Dales, D., *Alcuin: His Life and Legacy* (Cambridge 2012).

Daley, B., 'Boethius' Theological Tracts and Early Byzantine Scholasticism', *Mediaeval Studies* 46 (1984), 158–91.

David, Z., 'The Influence of Jacob Boehme on Russian Religious Thought', *Slavic Review* 21 (1962), 43–64.

Deane-Drummond, C., *Creation through Wisdom: Theology and the New Biology* (Edinburgh 2000).

—— *Theological Ethics Through a Multispecies Lens: The Evolution of Wisdom Volume I* (Oxford 2019).

—— *Shadow Sophia: The Evolution of Wisdom Volume II* (Oxford 2021).

Dell, K., *'Get Wisdom, Get Insight': An Introduction to Israel's Wisdom Literature* (London 2000).

Dell, K. and M. Barker (eds.), *Wisdom: The Collected Articles of Norman Whybray* (Aldershot 2005).

Djuth, M., 'Augustine, Monica, and the Love of Wisdom', *Augustinian Studies* 40 (2010), 217–32.

Dobbie-Bateman, A. F., 'Footnotes IX in quos fines saeculorum', *Sobornost* 3 (1935), 23–6.

Dunn, J., 'Jesus: Teacher of Wisdom or Wisdom Incarnate', in S. Barton (ed.), *Where Shall Wisdom Be Found?* (q.v.), 75–92.

Edwards, M., 'Justin's Logos and the Word of God', *JECS* 3 (1995), 261–80.

—— *Origen against Plato* (Aldershot 2002).

Eliot, T. S., *Choruses from 'The Rock'* (London 1934).

Ellard, G., 'Alcuin and Some Favored Votive Masses', *Theological Studies* 1 (1940), 37–61.

Embach, M., 'Hildegard of Bingen (1098–1179): A History of Reception', in D. Stoudt et al. (eds.), *A Companion to Hildegard of Bingen* (Leiden 2014), 273–304.

Erb, H., 'The Varieties of Wisdom and the Consolation of Philosophy', *Logos: A Journal of Catholic Thought and Culture* 15 (2012), 161–89.

Evdokimov, P., *L'Orthodoxie* (Paris 1965) [ET J. Hummerstone, *Orthodoxy* (Hyde Park, NY 2011)].

Evdokimov, P., *L'Art de l'icône. La théologie de la beauté* (Paris 1970).

—— *L'Amour fou de Dieu* (Paris 1973).

—— *La femme et le salut du monde* (Paris 1978).

Evtuhov, C., *The Cross and the Sickle: Sergei Bulgakov and the Fate of Russian Religious Philosophy* (Ithaca, NY 1997).

Felmy, K. C. and E. Haustein-Bartsch (eds.), *Die Weisheit baute ihr Haus: Untersuchungen zu Hymnischen und Didaktischen Ikonen* (Munich 1999).

Feuillet, A., *Le Christ, sagesse de Dieu, d'après les épîtres pauliniennes* (Paris 1966).

Fiddes, P., *Seeing the World and Knowing God: Hebrew Wisdom and Christian Doctrine in a Late-Modern Context* (Oxford 2013).

Fiene, D., 'What Is the Appearance of Divine Sophia?', *Slavic Review* 48 (1989), 449–76.

Fiorenza, E. S, 'Wisdom Mythology and the Christological Hymns of the New Testament', in R. Wilken (ed.), *Aspects of Wisdom in Judaism and Early Christianity* (Notre Dame, IN 1975), 17–41.

Florensky, P., Столпъ и утверждение истины (Moscow 1914) [ET B. Jakim (Princeton 1997)]. [= *The Pillar and Ground of Truth*]

Florovsky, G., *The Collected Works of Georges Florovsky* (14 vols.) (ed. R. Haugh) (Belmont, MA 1972–1979 [vols. 1–5] and Vaduz 1987–1989 [vols. 6–14]). [= *Collected Works*]

—— 'О почитании Софии, Премудрости Божией, в Византии и на Руси' ('On the Veneration of Sophia, the Wisdom of God, in Byzantium and in Russia' in Труды V съезда русских академических организаций за границей (*Proceedings of the V Congress of Russian Academic Organisations Abroad*) (Sofia 1932), 485–500.

—— 'The Lamb of God', *Scottish Journal of Theology* 4 (1951), 13–28.

—— 'Saint Gregory Palamas and the Tradition of the Fathers', in *Collected Works* I, 105–20 [original in *Sobornost* 4.1 (1961), 165–76]

—— 'Creation and Creaturehood', in *Collected Works* III, 43–78.

—— 'The Ever-Virgin Mother of God', in *Collected Works* III, 171–88. [original in E. L. Mascall (ed.), *The Mother of God* (London 1949), 51–63]

—— 'St. Athanasius' Concept of Creation', in *Collected Works* IV, 45–72.

—— 'The Hagia Sophia Churches', in *Collected Works* IV, 131–35. [= unfootnoted résumé of 'Christ, the Wisdom of God, in Byzantine Theology', in *Résumés des Rapports et Communications, Sixième Congrès International d'Etudes Byzantines* (Paris 1940), 255–60]

—— *Ways of Russian Theology* (2 vols.) (Belmont, MA 1979; Vaduz 1987). [= *Collected Works* V and VI]

Fokin, A., 'The Wisdom of God as *Ars Dei* in St Augustine: Between Neo-Platonism and Christianity', in T. Hainthaler et al. (eds.), *Sophia: The Wisdom of God* (q.v.), 259–68.

Ford, D. F., *Christian Wisdom* (Cambridge 2007).

Fowden, G., *The Egyptian Hermes: A Historical Approach to the Late Pagan Mind* (Princeton 1993).

Frank, S. L. (ed.), *A Solovyov Anthology* (New York 1950).

Gallaher, B., 'Graced Creatureliness: Ontological Tension in the Uncreated/Created Distinction in the Sophiologies of Solov'ev, Bulgakov and Milbank', *Logos: A Journal of Eastern Christian Studies* 47 (2006), 163–90.

—— 'The Christological Focus of Vladimir Solov'ev's Sophiology', *Modern Theology* 25 (2009), 617–46.

—— 'The "Sophiological" Origins of Vladimir Lossky's Apophaticism', *Scottish Journal of Theology* 66 (2013), 278–98.

—— *Freedom and Necessity in Modern Trinitarian Theology* (Oxford 2016).

Garrigou-Lagrange, R., 'L'habitation de la Sainte Trinité et l'expérience mystique', *Revue Thomiste* 33 (1928), 449–74.

Gavrilyuk, P., *Georges Florovsky and the Russian Religious Renaissance* (Oxford 2014).
—— *On Christian Leadership: The Letters of Alexander Schmemann and Georges Florovsky (1947–1955)* (Crestwood, NY 2020).
Gershenzon, M. (ed.), Вѣхи: Сборникъ статей о русской интеллигенціи (*Signposts: Collected articles on the Russian intelligentsia*) (Moscow 1909).
Gilson, E., *Wisdom and Love in Saint Thomas Aquinas: Under the Auspices of the Aristotelian Society of Marquette University* (Milwaukee 1951).
Golitzin, A., 'Hierarchy versus Anarchy? Dionysus Areopagita, Symeon the New Theologian, Nicetas Stethatos, and their Common Roots in Ascetical Tradition', *SVTQ* 38 (1994), 131–79.
—— *Mystagogy: A Monastic Reading of Dionysius Areopagita* (Collegeville, MN 2013).
Goodrick-Clarke, N., *The Western Esoteric Traditions: A Historical Introduction* (Oxford 2010).
Gorodetzky, N., *The Humiliated Christ in Modern Russian Thought* (London 1938).
Grant, R. M., *Gnosticism and Early Christianity* (New York 1966).
—— *Irenaeus of Lyons* (New York 1977).
Gustafson, R., 'Soloviev's Doctrine of Salvation', in J. Kornblatt and idem (eds.), *Russian Religious Thought* (Madison, WI 1996), 31–48.
Hainthaler, T. et al. (eds.), *Sophia: The Wisdom of God—Die Weisheit Gottes: Forscher aus dem Osten und Westen Europas an den Quellen des gemeinsamen Glaubens* (Vienna 2017).
Hallensleben, B. and R. Zwahlen (eds.), *Sergij Bulgakov, Bibliographie: Werke, Briefwechsel und Übersetzungen: Mit ausgewählter Sekundärliteratur und einem tabellarischen Lebenslauf* (Münster 2017).
Hays, R., 'Wisdom According to Paul', in S. Barton (ed.), *Where Shall Wisdom Be Found?* (q.v), 111–23.
Hayward, C. T. R., 'Sirach and Wisdom's Dwelling Place', in S. Barton (ed.), *Where Shall Wisdom Be Found?* (q.v.), 31–46.
Hegel, G. W. F., *Lectures on the History of Philosophy* (3 vols.) [ET E. Haldane and F. Simson] (London 1892).
Hladký, V., *The Philosophy of Gemistos Plethon: Platonism in Late Byzantium, between Hellenism and Orthodoxy* (Farnham 2014).
Hopkins, G. M., 'God's Grandeur' (1877), in R. Bridges (ed.), *Poems of Gerard Manley Hopkins* (London 1918).
Ivanov, A., 'The Impact of Protestant Spirituality in Catherinian Russia: The Works of St. Tikhon of Zadonsk', Вивлиоѳика 5 (2017), 40–72.
Jaeger, H., 'The Patristic Conception of Wisdom in the Light of Biblical and Rabbinical Research', in *Studia Patristica* 4 (Berlin 1961), 90–106.
Jaeger, W., *Early Christianity and Greek Paideia* (Cambridge, MA 1961).
John (Maximovitch), Saint, *The Orthodox Veneration of the Mother of God* (ET Platina, CA 2012).
Jordan, M., *Ordering Wisdom: The Hierarchy of Philosophical Discourses in Aquinas* (Notre Dame, IN 1986).
Jugie, M., 'Palamite (Controverse)', in *DTC* 11/2 (Paris 1932), 1777–1818.
Karfíková, L., '*Sapientiae amor*: Die Weisheit in Augustins Gespächen aus Cassiciacum', in T. Hainthaler et al. (eds.), *Sophia: The Wisdom of God* (q.v.), 235–58.
Kerr, F., *After Aquinas: Versions of Thomism* (Oxford 2002).
Kireevsky, I., Полное собраніе сочиненій (2 vols.) (ed. M. Gershenzon) (Moscow 1911). [= *Complete Works*]

Klimoff, A., 'Georges Florovsky and the Sophiological Controversy', *SVTQ* 49 (2005), 67–100.

Kornblatt, J. (ed.), *Divine Sophia: The Wisdom Writings of Vladimir Solovyov* (Ithaca, NY 2009).

Kriza, Á., 'The Russian Gnadenstuhl', *Journal of the Warburg and Courtauld Institutes* 79 (2016), 79–130.

—— 'Depicting Orthodoxy: The Novgorod Sophia Icon Reconsidered' (Diss. University of Cambridge 2018).

Kynes, W., *An Obituary for 'Wisdom Literature': The Birth, Death, and Intertextual Reintegration of a Biblical Corpus* (Oxford 2019).

Lake, S., *Wisdom and Wonder* (New York 2011).

—— *Wisdom Songs* (New York 2011).

—— *Wisdom, Prophecy and Prayer* (New York 2014).

—— *Wisdom, Glory and the Name* (New York 2017).

LaNave, G., '"A Particularly Agitated Topic": Aquinas and the Franciscans on the Subject of Theology in the Mid-Thirteenth Century', *The Thomist* 79 (2015), 467–91.

Laporte, J., 'Philo in the Tradition of Biblical Wisdom Literature', in R. Wilken (ed.), *Aspects of Wisdom in Judaism and Early Christianity* (q.v.), 103–41.

Leclercq, J., *The Love of Learning and the Desire for God: A Study of Monastic Culture* (New York 1982).

Legaspi, M., *Wisdom in Classical and Biblical Tradition* (Oxford 2018).

Lévy, A., *Le créé et l'incréé: Maxime le Confesseur et Thomas d'Aquin* (Paris 2006).

Lewis, C. S., *Surprised by Joy* (London 1955).

Lilienfeld, F. von, '"Frau Weisheit" in byzantinischen und karolingischen Quellen des 9. Jahrhunderts. Allegorische Personifikation, Hypostase oder Typos?', in M. Schmidt and C.-F. Geyer (eds.), *Typus, Symbol, Allegorie bei den östlichen Vätern und ihre Parallelen im Mittelalter* (Regensburg 1983), 146–86.

—— 'Sophia: die Weisheit Gottes: über die Visionen des Wladimir Solowjew als Grundlage seiner "Sophiologie"', *Una sancta* 39 (1984), 113–29.

—— 'Die Weisheit Gottes – Die Schau der Sophia bei Wladimir Solowjew', in V. Wodtke (ed.), *Auf den Spuren der Weisheit* (Freiburg im Breisgau 1991), 118–37.

—— 'Das Patrocinium der "Heiligen Sophia" in Europa und besonders in Rußland', in G. von Hermann (ed.), *Tausend Jahre Taufe Rußlands—Rußland in Europa* (Berlin 1993), 469–76.

Logan, A., *Gnostic Truth and Christian Heresy: A Study in the History of Gnosticism* (Edinburgh 1996).

Losev, A., Владимир Соловьев (Vladimir Soloviev) (Moscow 1983).

—— Владимир Соловьев и его время (Vladimir Soloviev and his Time) (Moscow 2000).

Lossky, N., *History of Russian Philosophy* (London 1952).

Lossky, V., Споръ о Софіи: 'Докладная записка' прот. С. Булгакова и смыслъ Указа Московской патриархіи (Paris 1936) [= *The Sophia Controversy*].

—— *Essai sur la théologie mystique de l'Église d'Orient* (Paris 1944). [ET *The Mystical Theology of the Eastern Church* (London 1957)]. [= *Mystical Theology*]

—— *Orthodox Theology: An Introduction* (Crestwood, NY 1978).

Loudovikos, N., 'Being and Essence Revisited: Reciprocal Logoi and Energies in Maximus the Confessor and Thomas Aquinas, and the Genesis of the Self-referring Subject', *Revista Portuguesa de Filosofia* 72 (2016), 117–46.

Louth, A., *Denys the Areopagite* (London 1989).

Louth, A., 'Is Development of Doctrine a Valid Category for Orthodox Theology?', in V. Hotchkiss and P. Henry (eds.), *Orthodoxy & Western Culture: A Collection of Essays Honoring Jaroslav Pelikan on his Eightieth Birthday* (Crestwood, NY 2005), 45–63.

—— 'The Eucharist in the Theology of Fr Sergii Bulgakov' *Sobornost/ECR* 27.2 (2005), 36–56.

—— 'Sergii Bulgakov and the Task of Theology', *Irish Theological Quarterly* 74.3 (2009), 243–57.

—— 'Sophia, the Wisdom of God, in St Maximos the Confessor', in T. Hainthaler et al. (eds.), *Sophia: The Wisdom of God* (q.v.), 349–58.

MacRae, G. W., 'The Jewish Background of the Gnostic Sophia Myth', *Novum Testamentum* 12 (1970), 86–101.

Marenbon, J., *The Philosophy of Peter Abelard* (Cambridge 1997).

Markus, R., *Gregory the Great and His World* (Cambridge 1997).

Marshall, B., '*Quod scit una uetula*: Aquinas on the Nature of Theology', in R. van Nieuwenhove and J. Wawrykow (eds.), *The Theology of Thomas Aquinas* (Notre Dame, IN 2005), 1–35.

Marshall, R. and T. Bird (eds.), *Hryhorij Savyč Skovoroda: An Anthology of Critical Articles* (Edmonton/Toronto 1994).

Mary, Mother and Archimandrite Kallistos Ware, *The Lenten Triodion* (London: 1978).

McGinn, B., *The Mystical Thought of Meister Eckhart: The Man from Whom God Hid Nothing* (New York 2001).

McGinn, B. and W. Otten (eds.), *Eriugena: East and West* (Notre Dame 1994).

McInerny, R., *Boethius and Aquinas* (Washington, DC 2012).

McNally, R. and R. Tempest (eds.), *Philosophical Works by Peter Chaadaev*, 18–31. [ET of French original]

Merton, T., 'Hagia Sophia' in idem, *Emblems of a Season of Fury* (New York 1963).

Meyendorff, J., *Introduction à l'étude de Grégoire Palamas* (Paris 1959).

—— 'L'iconographie de la Sagesse Divine dans la tradition Byzantine', *Cahiers Archéologiques* 10 (1959), 259–77.

—— 'Creation in the History of Orthodox Theology', *SVTQ* 27 (1983), 27–37.

—— 'The Mediterranean World in the Thirteenth Century, Theology: East and West', *The 17th International Byzantine Congress: Major Papers* (New York 1986), 669–82. [Revised versions in J. Chrysostomides (ed.) *Kathēgētria* (Festschrift Joan Hussey) (Camberley 1988) and the collected volume *Rome, Constantinople, Moscow: Historical and theological studies* (New York 1996)]

—— 'Wisdom-Sophia: Contrasting Approaches to a Complex Theme', *Dumbarton Oaks Papers* 41 (1987), 391–401.

Midgely, M., *Wisdom, Information, and Wonder. What is Knowledge For?* (London 1991).

Mikhaylov, P., 'Sophia, the Wisdom of God, in the *Hexaemeron* of St Basil', in T. Hainthaler et al. (eds.), *Sophia: The Wisdom of God* (q.v.), 173–80.

Milbank, J, 'Sophiology and Theurgy: The New Theological Horizon', in A. Pabst and C. Schneider (eds.), *Encounter Between Eastern Orthodoxy and Radical Orthodoxy: Transfiguring the World Through the Word* (Farnham 2008), 45–85.

Moberly, R. W., 'Solomon and Job: Divine Wisdom in Human Life', in S. Barton (ed.), *Where Shall Wisdom Be Found?* (q.v.), 3–17.

Moran, D., *The Philosophy of John Scottus Eriugena: A Study of Idealism in the Middle Ages* (Cambridge 1989).

Morris, R., 'Alcuin, York and the *Alma Sophia*', in L. Butler and R. Morris (eds.), *The Anglo-Saxon Church: Papers on History, Architecture, and Archaeology in Honour of Dr H M Taylor* (London 1986), 80–9.

Murphy, R., *The Tree of Life: An Exploration of Biblical Wisdom Literature* (Grand Rapids, MI 2002).

Newman, B., *Sister of Wisdom: St. Hildegard's Theology of the Feminine* (Berkeley, CA 1989).

Nichols, A., *Wisdom from Above: A Primer in the Theology of Father Sergei Bulgakov* (Leominster 2005).

O'Meara, J., *Eriugena* (Oxford 1988).

O'Regan, C., *Gnostic Apocalypse: Jacob Boehme's Haunted Narrative* (Albany, NY 2002).

Osborn, E., *Justin Martyr* (Tübingen 1973).

Osborn, E., *Tertullian, First Theologian of the West* (Cambridge 1997).

Ouspensky, L., *Theology of the Icon* (Crestwood, NY 1992).

Pain, J. and N. Zernov (eds.), *A Bulgakov Anthology* (London 1976).

Papamichail, G., Ὁ ἅγιος Γρηγόριος Παλαμᾶς ἀρχιεπίσκοπος Θεσσαλονίκης (*St Gregory Palamas Archbishop of Thessalonica*) (St Petersburg/Alexandria 1911).

Pearson, B., 'Hellenistic-Jewish Wisdom Speculation and Paul', in R. Wilken (ed.), *Aspects of Wisdom in Judaism and Early Christianity* (q.v.), 43–66.

Pentkovskii, A., 'Письма Г. Флоровского С. Булгакову и С.Тышкевичу' ('Letters of G. Florovsky to S. Bulgakov and S. Tyshkevich', *Символ* (*Symbol*) 29 (1993), 199–216.

Perišić, V., 'The Ontological Status of Wisdom in Origen', in Hainthaler et al. (eds.), *Sophia: The Wisdom of God* (q.v.), 103–14.

Pétrement, S., *Le Dieu séparé: les origines du gnosticisme* (Paris 1984) [ET C. Harrison, *A Separate God: The Christian Origins of Gnosticism* (San Francisco, CA 1990)].

Pilch, J., *'Breathing the Spirit with Both Lungs': Deification in the Work of Vladimir Solov'ev* (Leuven 2018).

Pino, T., 'An Essence-Energy Distinction in Philo as the Basis for the Language of Deification', *JTS* 68 (2017), 551–71.

Plantinga, A., *Does God Have a Nature?* (Milwaukee, WI 1980).

Plested, M., Review of P. Vallière, *Modern Russian Theology: Bukharev, Soloviev, Bulgakov: Orthodox Theology in a New Key*, Sobornost/ECR 25.2 (2003), 135–38.

—— *The Macarian Legacy: The Place of Macarius-Symeon in the Eastern Christian Tradition* (Oxford 2004).

—— 'Wisdom in St Maximus the Confessor', in *Studia Patristica* 42 (Leuven 2006), 205–9.

—— 'The Aesthetics of Sophiology', in A. Kattan and F. Georgi (eds.), *Thinking Modernity* (Balamand 2010), 155–63.

—— *Orthodox Readings of Aquinas* (Oxford 2012).

—— 'Reflections on the Reception of the Church Fathers in the Contemporary Context', in A. Cole (ed.), *Theology in Service to the Church* (Eugene, OR 2012), 12–17.

—— 'The Ascetic Dimension', in P. Allen and B. Neil (eds.), *The Oxford Handbook of Maximus the Confessor* (Oxford 2015), 164–74.

—— 'St Gregory Palamas on the Divine Simplicity', *Modern Theology* 35 (2019), 508–21.

Podskalsky, G., *Theologische Literatur des Mittelalters in Bulgarien und Serbien 865–1459* (Munich 2000).

Porphyrios (Bairaktaris), Saint, *Wounded by Love: The Life and Wisdom of Elder Porphyrios* (Limni 2005).

Pyman, A., *Pavel Florensky: A Quiet Genius* (London 2010).

Rad, G. von, *Weisheit in Israel* (Neukirchen-Vluyn 1970) [ET J. Martin, *Wisdom in Israel* (Harrisburg 1993)].

Radde-Gallwitz, A., *Basil of Caesarea, Gregory of Nyssa, and the Transformation of Divine Simplicity* (Oxford 2009).

Radice, R., 'Philo's Theology and Theory of Creation', in A. Kamesar (ed.), *The Cambridge Companion to Philo* (Cambridge 2009), 124–45.

Robinson, J., 'Jesus as Sophos and Sophia: Wisdom Tradition and the Gospels', in R. Wilken (ed.), *Aspects of Wisdom in Judaism and Early Christianity* (q.v.), 1–16.

Rossum, J. van, 'Palamisme et Sophiologie', *Contacts* 222 (2008), 133-45.

Rowland, C., '"Sweet Science Reigns": Divine and Human Wisdom in the Apocalyptic Tradition', in S. Barton (ed.), *Where Shall Wisdom Be Found?* (q.v.), 61–74.

Rubenson, S., *The Letters of St Anthony: Origenist Theology, Monastic Tradition and the Making of a Saint* (Lund 1990).

Russell, N., *Gregory Palamas and the Making of Palamism in the Modern Age* (Oxford 2019).

Sakharov, N., *I Love, Therefore I Am: The Theological Legacy of Archimandrite Sophrony* (Crestwood, NY 2002).

Sapronov, P., Русская софиология и софийность (*Russian Sophiology and Sophianicity*) (St Petersburg 2006).

Schelling, F. W. J., *Darstellung des philosophischen Empirismus*, in *Schellings Werke* V (Munich 1928).

—— *Grundlegung der positiven Philosophie*, in *Schellings Werke* V (Munich 1928).

—— *Philosophie der Offenbarung*, in *Schellings Werke* (Supplemental) VI (Munich 1954).

Schmemann, A, 'Trois images', *Le Messager Orthodoxe* 57 (1972), 2–20.

Schnabel, E., *Law and Wisdom from Ben Sira to Paul: A Tradition Historical Enquiry into the Relation of Law, Wisdom, and Ethics* (Tübingen 1985).

Scholem, G., *Kabbalah* (New York 1978).

—— *Origins of the Kabbalah* (Princeton 1987).

Sciurie, H., 'Weisheit: Ikonographisch', in *Lexikon für Theologie und Kirche* 10 (2001).

Sherrard, P., *Orientation and Descent* (Eton 1953).

—— *The Greek East and the Latin West: A Study in the Christian Tradition* (Oxford 1959).

Sikora, J., 'Philosophy and Christian Wisdom According to Saint Justin Martyr', *Franciscan Studies* 23 (1963), 244–56.

Siniossoglou, N., *Radical Platonism in Byzantium: Illumination and Utopia in Gemistos Plethon* (Cambridge 2011).

Slesinski, R., *The Theology of Sergius Bulgakov* (Crestwood, NY 2017).

Smalley, B., '*Prima Clavis Sapientiae*: Augustine and Abelard', in eadem (ed.), *Studies in Medieval Thought and Learning from Abelard to Wyclif* (London 1981).

Smith, O., *Vladimir Soloviev and the Spiritualization of Matter* (Boston 2011).

София Премудрость Божия. Выставка русской иконописи XIII–XIX веков из собраний музеев России (Sophia, the Wisdom of God. Exhibition of C13-C19 Russian Iconography in the Collections of Russian Museums [catalogue, no ed.]) (Moscow 2000).

Solignac, A., 'Sagesse IV. Sagesse antique et sagesse chrétienne', in *DS* 14 (Paris 1990), 96–114.

Soloviev, V., *La Russie et l'Église universelle* (Paris 1889).

—— Письма (3 vols.) (ed. E. Radlov) (St Petersburg 1908–11). [= *Letters*]

—— Собраніе сочиненій² (10 vols.) (eds. S. M. Soloviev and E. Radlov) (St Petersburg 1911–14). [= *Collected Works I–X*]

—— Собрание сочинений (supplementary 2 vols.) (Brussels 1969–70). [= *Collected Works XI–XII*]

—— Полное собрание сочинений и писем (20 vols., projected) (ed. A. Nosov) (Moscow 2000–). [= *Complete Works and Letters*]

Špidlík, T., *La sophiologie de saint Basile* (Rome 1961).

—— 'L'idéal du monachisme basilien', in P. Fedwick (ed.), *Basil of Caesarea, Christian, Humanist, Ascetic* (Toronto 1981), 361–74.

Stead, C., 'The Valentinian Myth of Sophia', *JTS* 20 (1969), 75–104.

Tambrun-Krasker, B., *Pléthon: le retour de Platon* (Paris 2006).

Tataryn, M., *Augustine and Russian Orthodoxy: Russian Orthodox Theologians and Augustine of Hippo, A Twentieth Century Dialogue* (Lanham, MD 2000).

Techert, M., 'La notion de la Sagesse dans les trois premiers siècles de notre ère', *Archiv für Geschichte der Philosophie* 39 (1929), 1–27.

Tibiletti, C., 'Filosofia e cristianesimo in Tertulliano', *Annali della Facoltà di Lettere e di Filosofia dell'Università di Macerata* 3–4 (1970–1), 98–133.

Torrance, T., *Divine Meaning: Studies in Patristic Hermeneutics* (Edinburgh 1995).

Uspensky, P., История Афона (*History of Athos*) (2 vols.) (Kiev 1871).

Vaganova, N., 'С. Н. Булгаков: софиология без Софии. «Католическое искушение» и отход от софиологии в сочинениях крымского периода' (S. N. Bulgakov: Sophiology without Sophia. 'Catholic temptation' and a departure from Sophiology in writings of the Crimean period'), *Вестник ПСТГУ* [*Messenger of St Tikhon's Orthodox University*] I (Theology. Philosophy): 2 (18) (2007), 69–79.

—— Софиология протоиерея Сергия Булгакова (*The Sophiology of Archpriest Sergius Bulgakov*) (Moscow 2011).

Vallière, P., *Modern Russian Theology: Bukharev, Soloviev, Bulgakov: Orthodox Theology in a New Key* (Edinburgh 2000).

Völker, W., 'Die Verwertung der Wesiheits-Literatur bei den christlichen Alexandrinen', *Zeitschrift für Kirchengeschichte* 64 (1953), 1–33.

Wallach, L., 'The Epitaph of Alcuin: A Model of Carolingian Epigraphy', *Speculum* 30.3 (1955), 367–73.

Wawrykow, J., 'Wisdom in the Christology of Thomas Aquinas', in K. Emery and idem (eds.), *Christ among the Medieval Dominicans: Representations of Christ in the Texts and Images of the Order of Preachers* (Notre Dame 1998), 175–96.

Weeks, S., *Early Israelite Wisdom* (Oxford 1994).

Weidmann, C., 'Vorankündigung: Eine unbekannte lateinische Übersetzung der Predigten des Pseudo-Makarios', *Zeitschrift für Antikes Christentum* 24(2) (2020), 449–52.

Wiles, M., *Archetypal Heresy: Arianism through the Centuries* (Oxford 1996).

Wilken, R., *Aspects of Wisdom in Judaism and Early Christianity* (Notre Dame, IN 1975).

—— 'Wisdom and Philosophy in Early Christianity', in idem (ed.), *Aspects of Wisdom in Judaism and Early Christianity* (q.v.), 143–68.

Williams, R., 'The Theology of Vladimir Nikolaievich Lossky: An Exposition and Critique' (Diss. University of Oxford 1975).

—— *Arius: Heresy and Tradition* (London 1987).

—— '*Sapientia* and the Trinity: Reflections on the *De trinitate*', *Augustiniana* 40.1/4 (1990), 317–32.

Williams, R., *Sergii Bulgakov: Towards a Russian Political Theology* (Edinburgh 1999).
—— *On Augustine* (London 2016).
Wilson, J., 'The Allegory of Wisdom in Chrelja's Tower seen through Philotheos Kokkinos' in M. Rossi and A. Sullivan (eds.), *Byzantium in Eastern European Visual Culture in the Late Middle Ages*, (Leiden 2020), 1–27.
Witherington III, B., *Jesus the Sage: The Pilgrimage of Wisdom* (Minneapolis, MN 1994).
Wood, J., *Wisdom Literature: An Introduction* (London 1967).
Woodhouse, C. M., *George Gemistos Plethon: The Last of the Hellenes* (Oxford 1986).
Yeats, W.B., *The Tower* (London 1928).
Young, F., 'The Rhetorical Schools and Their Influence on Patristic Exegesis', in R. Williams (ed.), *The Making of Orthodoxy: Essays in Honour of Henry Chadwick* (Cambridge 1989), 182–99.
—— *Biblical Exegesis and the Formation of Christian Culture* (Cambridge 1997).
Zander, L., Бог и мир (миросозерцание отца Сергия Булгакова) (*God and the World (The world-view of Fr Sergius Bulgakov)*) (2 vols.) (Paris 1948).
—— 'Die Weisheit Gottes im russischen Glauben und Denken', in K. Rahner and K. Lehmann (eds.), *Kerygma und Dogma* (vol. 2) (Göttingen 1959).

Index

For the benefit of digital users, indexed terms that span two pages (e.g., 52–53) may, on occasion, appear on only one of those pages.